FEMINIST CONNECTIONS

FEMINIST CONNECTIONS

Rhetoric and Activism across Time, Space, and Place

EDITED BY KATHERINE FREDLUND, KERRI HAUMAN,
AND JESSICA OUELLETTE

THE UNIVERSITY OF ALABAMA PRESS   TUSCALOOSA

The University of Alabama Press
Tuscaloosa, Alabama 35487-0380
uapress.ua.edu

Inquiries about reproducing material from this work should be
addressed to the University of Alabama Press.

Typeface: Garamond Premiere Pro

Cover image: *Top*, feminists fighting for women's rights (iStockphoto/Rawpixel);
bottom, Harris & Ewing, *Pennsylvania on the Picket Line*, Washington, DC, 1917
(Library of Congress, Prints and Photographs Division)
Cover design: Mary-Frances Burt / Burt&Burt

Cataloging-in-Publication data is available from the Library of Congress.
ISBN: 978-0-8173-2064-5
E-ISBN: 978-0-8173-9322-9

To the feminists who came before us—those who raised, taught, and mentored us. And to the feminists who will come after us—those who will challenge, teach, and sustain us.

Contents

Illustrations

Foreword

Writing against Reactionary Logics

Tarez Samra Graban

Prejudicially by now, Nathaniel Hawthorne's "damned mob of scribbling women" succeeded in littering the 1855 literary marketplace with ephemeral "trash,"[1] while Ambrose Bierce's 1905 working woman—representative of her species's encroachment on commercial, professional, and industrial activities—reflected a "marked demerit of the new order of things," advantageous only to the male employer and thus indicative of a failure of women's superior moral character.[2] In their respective critical contexts, each prejudice raised a dilemma—a lamentation that the study of literature would fast become "the study of something else,"[3] or an intervention into fin de siècle logic that America's workplace required the presence of women in order to compensate for derelict men.[4] Yet, transcribed onto the present context, these prejudicial assumptions about women's compositional practices raise a vital question: At what other critical moments in feminist rhetorical history have such reactionary logics been exercised in our field?

The contents of this anthology may equip contemporary historians to "release hold" on several sacrosanct assumptions: that origin stories are coherent, that analog and digital historical methodologies are discrete, and that the feminist digital moment is a recent rhetorical invention.[5] These feminist connections in rhetoric and composition have quietly but steadily emerged from the engendering forces that give purpose to our efforts to liberate the ways we view the past—from the various "discursive, material, and embodied articulations and performances that create and disturb gendered distinctions, social categories, and asymmetrical power relationships," irrespective of analog or digital form.[6] *The digital*, then, is neither a historic moment nor a deterministic convergence of practices and spaces, but an epistemology that may have preceded and may well transcend what historians do with digital tools.

The organization of this anthology speaks resolutely to that fact. Here, eighteen contributors not only perform cross-historical comparisons between pre-digital and digitally native figures or texts; they also challenge the tendency to ideologically "fit" feminist digital methodologies into an extant analog tradition, offering us ways to understand how digital historical dilemmas have grown from characteristically rhetorical concerns. Questions about whether and how digital platforms can (re)humanize (or highlight the difficulties of [re]humanizing) public rhetorical participation guide the section on *circulatory rhetorics*. Questions about how and when to historically mark ourselves as white, nonwhite, speaking, or listening in our uses of digital technologies guide the section on *response rhetorics*, bringing into relief, as Paige V. Banaji writes, "the problematics of white feminism."[7] And questions about when and why technical hierarchies and political signifiers have aligned with sex-typing and gender differentiation guide the section on *revisionary rhetorics*. This tripartite attitude toward feminist historical scholarship marks, above all things, a move to recognize the interstitial alongside the intersectional in digital spaces.

To differentiate between *intersectional* and *interstitial* here is to consider the spaces between agents and subject positions as critical interventions in themselves. Interstitial study invites historians to recognize what occurs between organizations, their archives, their practices, and their beliefs that cause some figures to come perpetually under erasure due to systemic ways of looking.[8] Interstitial study also relies on historians' ability to consider that the algorithmic,[9] transactional,[10] and theoretical[11] are complementary forces in the same feminist entanglement.

As an intersectional concept, then, interstitiality poses a direct challenge to notions of modernity and modernist thinking that strive to "compose the world as a picture."[12] Approaching feminist historical work interstitially permits us to accept *the digital* as more than a modality for showcasing our histories, and more than a framework for analyzing our historical subjects. In interstitial thinking, *the digital* becomes a set of phenomenological conflicts to embrace: the need to question the motivations and methods undergirding how we do digital description and distribution;[13] the need to reveal how even broad networks and layered ecologies have become historically privileged spaces;[14] and the need to relinquish the intellectual genealogies, information architectures, and taxonomies under which we frequently operate.[15] Indeed, *the digital* becomes an invitation for historians to witness how the material and the cultural can co-occur; to trace their past and present representations through social media applications, in technics and technical relationships, and in places of repository or display;[16] and to use these tracings to dislodge the securities of what have been our disciplinary and archival locations, corpora, and major themes or players, offering something like an "epistemic reconstruction—a putting back together [of historical knowledge] of a more inclusive or productive way of questioning."[17]

Furthermore, working interstitially toward feminist digital recovery may allow for a mining of archival interspaces for historiographic clues about the positioning that occurs between roles and within institutional visibilities, linguistic hybridities, and data practices.[18] In short, the eighteen contributors to this anthology do not stop at questioning the available *means* of feminist rhetorical traditions. Instead, they cause us to question our available *tools* as feminist historiographers, how those tools influence what counts as knowledge, whether and how that knowledge gets transferred, and what reactionary logics might disrupt that transferal. They ask us to consider how historians have understood feminist participation as iterative and in tandem with particular text technologies, and to question how the interspaces themselves have served as compasses for our questioning. At its best, Fredlund, Hauman, and Ouellette's timely anthology demonstrates that historicization occurs across many moments of dissemination, for the collection's nonchronological approach challenges scholars to think about rhetorical practices in a new light.

In response to how this anthology interrogates beginnings, we might task ourselves with interrogating perceptions of how and where this collection began. In what moments or spaces could we retroactively locate the importance of digital and historical scholars working together? I make one interrogation here, not to offer a single origin story but to reconstruct several glimpses into key epistemological conflicts that may or may not have precluded an earlier arrival of this collection or something like it. When Patricia Sullivan published "Women on the Networks" with Gail Hawisher in 1998,[19] it was one of a dozen already well-circulating book chapters and articles to call for a substantive examination of networked identifications informed by feminist rhetorical epistemology, eventually fueling more historical and critical analysis of women in/and digital environments and becoming subsumed under the disciplinary tags of "computers and composition" and "professional and technical writing,"[20] at the time seen as epistemologically distinct from rhetoric and composition writ large.[21] Yet, that essay and others like it would reflect what we now understand as early attempts to move composition research methods into feminist digital spaces if it were not for two factors: the shading of such projects from our field's flagship journals until recently,[22] and an unspoken assumption that feminist historical digital work was roughly equivalent to "making websites,"[23] in turn invoking a more systemic debate about whether prototyping, text encoding, or interface building could in fact constitute serious intellectual work.[24] For myriad reasons, including these, very little of this work prior to 2000 circulated in *College Composition and Communication*, *Rhetoric Review*, *Rhetoric Society Quarterly*, or *College English*, constituting what we might now perceive as an intrinsic scholarly gap.

By 2008, I had joined Sullivan in contending with this gap, writing an article in which we argued for orienting critical feminist practices toward digital historiography, without a clear sense that rhetoric and composition had fully embraced the conversation or adapted a vocabulary to normalize the work. For over a decade prior, Sullivan had been quietly articulating the facets of an approach to digital historiography that had its roots in rhetorical (rather than literary) understandings of text technology evolutions, emphasizing how the material and the critical converge in a series of "production-oriented interactions between history and technology."[25] Over eighteen months, we engaged in three lengthy revise-and-resubmit conversations with two different journals on this article. The conversations were lengthy because early drafts of this article were unwieldy, but several things made these conversations especially surprising. First, there was one reviewer's insistence that a term we had employed was not "going to catch on [for doing historical work] because it is too closely associated with the development and production of multi-media work (webpages, video, *Kairos* type of documents)," nor could it "accurately describe" our concurrent interests in methods/methodology and rhetorical histories. The term we employed was *digital rhetoric*, and in fact, our article made an argument for precisely that point: that what differentiated digital rhetoric from digital history writ large was its emphasis on production, circulation, and deployment. Thinking back to Richard Lanham's 1992 "Digital Rhetoric and the Digital Arts" and Kathleen Welch's 1999 *Electric Rhetoric*,[26] we viewed this term as the most accurate we could avail to describe what we saw occurring through feminist historiographic methods in digital spaces. We understood all historical work in rhetoric and composition as a *techne* (a form of "doing"), yet the reviewer's insistence that the *digitally rhetorical could not be discussed in the same space as the digitally historical* caught us off guard and reflected what seemed to be an error of epistemology.

At the next journal, the following reviewer's comment reinforced the very disparity we had hoped to bridge: "We might be using digital tools to force new questions, rethink new linkages, and create different repositories of archival materials, but [that's] not 'digital rhetoric.'" This disparity has since been bridged in work quite signature to our field, as evidenced by Douglas Eyman's *Digital Rhetoric*,[27] as well as a host of conference papers, presentations, and (now) publications in our flagship journals, attesting to a wide co-optation of digital historical methodologies that double as rhetorical criticism.[28] At the time, however, our reviewer's response indicated that marrying the digital with the historical under rhetoric's umbrella was at best a gratuitous activity, rather than the text-technology evolution for which we tried to argue at the intersection of library and information sciences (LIS), Web 2.0, and rhetorical historiography. We could not proceed past this reactionary logic.

Finally, there were the journal editors' insistence that the term, and the work, was "not enough in the mainstream." For one journal, this critique meant that the term *digital rhetoric* was not yet in vogue, although we had seen the term beginning to circulate, and Sullivan had used the term in earlier work. For another, this meant that the work could not be legitimated without evidence that scholars in "computers and libraries" would corroborate the need for rhetorical historians to become more digitally conscious of how they interacted with their histories and subjects. The latter response was a catch-22 out of which our manuscript never emerged. A perspectival shift we saw already occurring in our graduate seminars and conference papers was deemed unfit for circulation in our own field's journals due to the journals' uncertainty about how readers outside the field (i.e., librarians and computer scientists) might view our work.

Sullivan's introduction of digital historiographic methods into rhetoric seminars a decade prior, her extensive background in libraries, archives, and museums (LAM) scholarship, and her longtime direction of a rhetoric and composition graduate program in good standing were insufficient to demonstrate to these journals that the feminist, the historical, and the digital could and must reside together in the same critical space for rhetoric and composition, and indeed, that they had already done so. At that time, it must have seemed infeasible for rhetorical historiographers to theorize about technics, or for feminist projects to require such theory building, without invoking disciplinary confusion (or, perhaps, intellectual embarrassment). And while ours was a single experience, it was likely not an isolated one. Other scholars and scholarly teams between the early 1990s and the early 2000s may have been similarly discouraged or unable to locate an audience in field for need of reconciling the historical and the digital, in ways not yet normalized to rhetoric and composition, and subsequently kept to the margins of more serious feminist historical work.

I do not recall this experience in order to leverage a complaint against the journals or their editors, or to exonerate our early drafts, but rather to illustrate one of the many ways in which this anthology can be useful: by providing insight into our reactionary logics where technics are concerned. Across all three attitudes informing feminist analysis and recovery throughout this collection (i.e., circulatory, response, and revisionary), readers can gain insight into how historical conversations about the feminist and the digital came to be subsumed under nonfield paradigms. What are the critical possibilities of considering whether our field might be missing a historical moment where women's compositional practices are concerned? In many ways, the collection's thirteen chapters are motivated by the same desire to interrogate feminist rhetorical histories and to question technological determinism as were the two journals with whom we corresponded in 2008. Yet, while these journals could not envisage these conversations occurring in tandem, this collection is founded on the premise that they have always already done so. Indeed, this anthology demonstrates that what occurs (or can occur) at the convergence of the feminist historical with the feminist digital goes well beyond "women making websites."

Notes

1. John T. Frederick, "Hawthorne's 'Scribbling Women,'" *New England Quarterly* 48, no. 2 (1975): 231.

2. Ambrose Bierce, "Emancipated Woman," in *The Shadow on the Dial and Other Essays*, ed. S. O. Howes (San Francisco: A. M. Robertson, 1909), par. 4.

3. Frederick, "Hawthorne's Scribbling Women," 231.

4. Bierce, "Emancipated Woman," par. 2.

5. Jessica Enoch, "Releasing Hold: Feminist Historiography without the Tradition," in *Theorizing Histories of Rhetoric*, ed. Michelle Ballif (Carbondale: Southern Illinois University Press, 2013), 58–73.

6. Enoch, 68.

7. See chapter 12 in this volume.

8. Tarez Samra Graban, "Re/Situating the Digital Archive in John T. McCutcheon's 'Publics,' Then and Now," *Peitho* 17, no. 1 (2014): 73–88.

9. Safiya Umoja Noble, *Algorithms of Oppression: How Search Engines Reinforce Racism* (New York: New York University Press, 2018).

10. Transactional occurrences rely on an element of trust. Composed several years apart, both Elizabeth A. Flynn's *Feminism beyond Modernism* (Carbondale: Southern Illinois University Press, 2002) and Susan Miller's *Trust in Texts: A Different History of Rhetoric* (Carbondale: Southern Illinois University Press, 2007) imply that critical agents are those for whom meaning "does not reside in the text as it does for the New Critics . . . but in the transactional process that is the result of the merging of reader and text" (Flynn, 114). Thus, historical documents become accessible not as material forms that contain historical content, but as evidence of a mobility of trust in what should be the nature of their use, where "trust" is a socially and culturally structured emotional expression, and our ability to persuade and to communicate depends on it. As Flynn and Miller argue, historians only trust discourse because it participates in "infrastructures of trustworthiness we are schooled to recognize, sometimes by lessons and habits we cannot name" (Miller, 1–2).

11. Homi Bhabha, *The Location of Culture* (London: Routledge, 1994).

12. Arturo Escobar, *Encountering Development: The Making and Unmaking of the Third World* (Princeton, NJ: Princeton University Press, 1995), 56.

13. Richard Jean So, "All Models Are Wrong," *PMLA* 132, no. 3 (2017): 668–73; Alexander R. Galloway, "'Everything Is Computation': Franco Moretti's Distant Reading: A Symposium," *Los Angeles Review of Books*, June 27, 2013; Paul Luna, "Books and Bits: Texts and Technology 1970–2000," in *A Companion to the History of the Book*, ed. Simon Eliot and Jonathan Rose (West Sussex, UK: Blackwell, 2009), 381–94.

14. Roopika Risam, "Beyond the Margins: Intersectionality and the Digital Humanities," *Digital Humanities Quarterly* 9, no. 2 (2015), http://www.digitalhumanities.org/dhq; Ramesh Srinivasan et al., "Digital Museums and Diverse Cultural Knowledges: Moving Past the Traditional Catalog," *Information Society* 25, no. 4 (2009): 265–78.

15. Patricia Donahue and Gretchen Flesher Moon, eds., *Local Histories: Reading the Archives of Composition* (Pittsburgh, PA: University of Pittsburgh Press, 2007); Liz Stanley and Sue Wise, *Breaking Out Again: Feminist Ontology and Epistemology*, new ed. (London: Routledge, 1993).

16. Richard Yeo, "Lost Encyclopedias: Before and after the Enlightenment," *Book History* 10 (2007): 47–68.

17. Patricia Sullivan and Tarez Samra Graban, "Digital and Dustfree: A Conversation on the Possibilities of Digital-Only Searching for Third-Wave Historical Recovery," *Peitho* 13, no. 2 (2011): 2.

18. Graban, "Re/Situating"; Tarez Samra Graban, "From Location(s) to Locatability: Mapping Feminist Recovery and Archival Activity through Metadata," *College English* 76, no. 2 (2013): 171–93.

19. Gail E. Hawisher and Patricia A. Sullivan, "Women on the Networks: Searching for E-Spaces of Their Own," in *Feminism and Composition Studies: In Other Words*, ed. Susan C. Jarratt and Lynn Worsham (New York: Modern Language Association, 1998), 172–97.

20. This shared genealogy is notably broad and deep. See Katherine T. Durack, "Gender, Technology, and the History of Technical Communication," *Technical Communication Quarterly* 6, no. 3 (1997): 249–60; Christine Tamblyn, "She Loves It, She Loves It Not: Women and Technology," in *Processed Lives: Gender and Technology in Everyday Life*, ed. Jennifer Terry and Melodie Calvert (New York: Routledge, 1997), 47–50; Kristine Blair and Pamela Takayoshi, "Navigating the Image of Woman Online," *Kairos: A Journal of Rhetoric, Technology, and Pedagogy* 2, no. 2 (1997), http://kairos.technorhetoric.net; Anne Balsamo, *Technologies of the Gendered Body: Reading Cyborg Women* (Durham, NC: Duke University Press, 1996); Keith Grint and Rosalind Gill, eds., *The Gender-Technology Relation: Contemporary Theory and Research* (Bristol, PA: Taylor and Francis, 1995); Ruth Ray and Ellen Barton, "Technology and Authority," in *Evolving Perspectives on Computers and Composition Studies: Questions for the 1990s*, ed. Gail E. Hawisher and Cynthia L. Selfe (Urbana, IL: National Council of Teachers of English, 1991), 279–99; Ruth Perry and Lisa Greber, "Women and Computers: An Introduction," *Signs* 16, no. 1 (1990): 74–101; and finally R. Giordano, "From the Frontier to the Border: Women in Data Processing, 1940–1959," *Proceedings of the Joint Conference of the British Society for the History of Science and the History of Science Society* (Manchester, UK: unpublished, 1988), 357–64.

21. Kristine Blair and Pamela Takayoshi, eds., *Feminist Cyberscapes: Mapping Gendered Academic Spaces* (Stamford, CT: Ablex, 1999).

22. In a 2015 special digital insert of *Peitho: The Journal of the Coalition of Feminist Scholars in the History of Rhetoric and Composition*, Lavinia Hirsu offers a brief historical retrospective of the topic's absences as well as recent presences in other field journals. See Hirsu, "An Overview of Digital Feminist Scholarship (2005–2014): Methods and Methodologies," part of "From Installation to Remediation: CWSHRC Digital New Work Showcase," *Peitho* 18, no. 1 (2015), http://cwshrc.org/newwork2015.

23. No allusions were made to Hawthorne, of course, but my memory of this correspondence is that it reflected a twenty-first-century version of the complaint against "scribbling women."

24. Stephen Ramsay and Geoffrey Rockwell, "Developing Things: Notes toward an Epistemology of Building in the Digital Humanities," in *Debates in the Digital Humanities*, ed. Matthew K. Gold (Minneapolis: University of Minnesota Press, 2012), 75–84.

25. Sullivan and Graban, "Digital and Dustfree," 6.

26. Richard Lanham, "Digital Rhetoric: Theory, Practice, and Property," in *Literacy Online: The Promise (and Peril) of Reading and Writing with Computers*, ed. Myron Tuman (Pittsburgh, PA: University of Pittsburgh Press, 1992), 221–43; Kathleen Welch, *Electric Rhetoric: Classical Rhetoric, Oralism, and a New Literacy* (Cambridge: MIT Press, 1999).

27. Douglas Eyman, *Digital Rhetoric: Theory, Method, Practice* (Ann Arbor: University of Michigan Press, 2015).

28. See, for example, Jim Ridolfo and William Hart-Davidson, *Rhetoric and the Digital Humanities* (Chicago: University of Chicago Press, 2014); Tarez Samra Graban and Shirley K. Rose, eds., "The Critical Place of the Networked Archive," special issue, *Peitho* 17, no. 1 (2014); and the 2015 publishing schedule of the journal *Advances in the History of Rhetoric*, among others.

Acknowledgments

THIS BOOK IS THE PRODUCT of many passionate collaborations, and we deeply thank those who shared their time, insight, and support. First, we thank our contributors for their dedication to this project and their patience with our many requests for revision. We thank the folks at the University of Alabama Press, and especially our editor, Daniel Waterman, for believing in this project and helping to make its production a possibility. We thank the reviewers of our proposal and our manuscript, all of whom encouraged us and provided useful feedback, and we especially thank "Reviewer A" for their very thorough and thoughtful suggestions that pushed us to more clearly articulate our methodology. We thank the people who attended our panel at the 2017 Feminisms and Rhetorics Conference and who offered us conversation and feedback. Finally, we offer a special thanks to our families, friends, and colleagues for supporting us in numerous ways throughout this process and throughout our careers.

FEMINIST CONNECTIONS

Introduction

Exposing Feminist Connections

KATHERINE FREDLUND, KERRI HAUMAN,
AND JESSICA OUELLETTE

CONNECTIONS ARE THE FOUNDATION OF scholarly work. Whether we are seeking connections with other scholars at conferences or recognizing those connections through citational practices, our scholarship connects threads of existing knowledge in order to produce new knowledge. In our attempts to locate connections, we also discover productive disconnections. Yet, despite the foundational role connections and disconnections play in scholarly work, habitual practices of knowledge production in rhetorical studies—namely, focusing on time, content, and media—limit our vision, causing us to overlook potentially fruitful connections and disconnections. In *Feminist Connections: Rhetoric and Activism across Time, Space, and Place*, contributors seek connections through a methodological intervention that departs from these habitual ways of knowing and considers how feminist activists from different eras have utilized similar rhetorical practices across time, content, and media in order to present messages to each other and to publics. In attending to rhetorical connections across time and space, our contributors map evolutions of feminist rhetorical practices while theorizing how factors such as media, identity, and content impact rhetorical practices.[1]

While many scholars have focused on the distinctness of a particular feminism under the larger banner of feminisms, *Feminist Connections* recognizes that the rhetorical strategies feminists repeatedly turn to are numerous and diverse yet interconnected via their reliance on similar rhetorical devices (rather than only the content of their rhetoric).[2] Indeed, as the feminist movement evolves and goals change, the rhetorical practices feminists use remain surprisingly consistent despite the emergence of new forms of media and the evolution of feminist thought. These consistencies, however, have been rendered nearly unrecognizable because feminists have remediated and revised their rhetorical practices

FIGURE I.1. Suffragists stand with "Mr. President" sign in front of the White House in 1917. Harris & Ewing, *Pennsylvania on the Picket Line*, Washington, DC, 1917. Photograph, https://www.loc.gov/item/mnwp000212/.

to respond to ever-changing technologies and media. Thus, the chapters in this collection reach beyond boundaries of time, content, and media and unpack feminist rhetorical practices by tracking the circulation, functions, and effects of feminist rhetoric across a global social movement that began over a century ago.

While studies of feminist rhetoric often limit their focus by time period, content, and genre of delivery, some feminist scholarship has crossed these boundaries. For example, Alison Piepmeier's examination of grrrl zines traces a feminist trajectory from nineteenth-century women's club scrapbooks to second wave feminists' mimeographed manifestos to grrrl zines of the late twentieth and early twenty-first centuries.[3] Many such connections between feminists of different spaces, places, and eras, however, have yet to be considered let alone understood. For instance, in 1917 Alice Paul and other suffragists famously picketed in front of the White House while holding banners with short, pithy sayings such as "Mr. President: How long must women wait for Liberty?" (figure I.1). Looking at this example of feminist rhetorical action now reveals that their juxtaposition of their bodies and this short phrase with the image of the White House (a symbol of liberty and justice) relies on the same rhetorical practices as memes, a genre that contemporary feminists have used to make arguments about reproductive rights, Black Lives Matter, and sex-positivity. By forefronting such rhetorical connections across time periods and then also considering disconnections, the authors in this collection enrich our understanding of rhetorical practices and their relationship to media, gender, and more.

As feminist scholars, we view the goal of seeking connections as all the more necessary, and intersectional feminism demands these connections be ingrained in the fabric of our work. And yet, the forging of connections is not always easy or even possible. In fact, we came to this project because of a perceived disconnection. At the 2016 Conference on College Composition and Communication, held in Houston, Texas, Hauman and Ouellette attended sessions on digital feminist work, while Fredlund primarily attended sessions on feminist historical work. When we came back together one evening, we realized we had spent the day within two largely disconnected subfields of feminist rhetorical studies (FRS): one focused on the digital, the other on the historical. Yet, in coming together, we discovered that we had discussed the same rhetorical practices—albeit their uses in different centuries—and that our own understanding of those practices was complicated and enriched after discussing both their historical and contemporary uses. At that moment, we became keenly aware of the importance of making connections between and among our work and realized that these connections could help us rethink the work we do in our subfields while also allowing for increasingly complex theorization of rhetorical strategies and devices more broadly. Consequently, *Feminist Connections* brings the scholarship of feminist historical rhetorics and that of digital feminist rhetorics into conversation with one another.

RHETORICAL TRANSVERSAL METHODOLOGY

In order to make these connections between digital and historical feminist work explicit, we asked our contributors to use what we are calling a Rhetorical Transversal Methodology (RTM). Such a methodology encourages researchers to consider that which "[lies] or passes across" barriers of time, content, and media—barriers that often hinder researchers' ability to see connections beyond them.[4] While other fields such as architecture and sociology have used transversal methodologies, their use of *transversal* often simply indicates a mixed methods approach to research. Architect Pelin Tan, however, takes transversal methodology further, using it to "[ensure] a trans-local, borderless knowledge production that in a rhizomatic form reaches beyond topics of architecture and design to include citizenship, militant pedagogy, institutionalism, borders, war, being a refugee, documents/documenting, urban segregation, commons and others."[5] Tan further explains that "the transversal method—which by its very nature resists dwelling only on questions of objects or subjectivities—helps us question what we think we know about architectural practice."[6] Thus, Tan's work uses a transversal methodology to extend conversations beyond the limits of traditional architecture and design scholarship. RTM takes a similarly rhizomatic approach—while also resisting the tendency to dwell on objects and subjectivities—in order to help us question what we think we know about rhetorical practices and their emergence and reemergence in different places, spaces, and time periods.

Within geometric understanding, transversals are lines which intersect parallel lines, creating a connection between two lines that would never encounter one another. In this way, RTM homes in on rhetorical strategies and devices as transversals between historical feminist and digital feminist work in rhetorical studies. While we would not say the lines of historical feminist and digital feminist rhetorical work are parallel, in that they would never or have never met, the two subfields have been, as we discussed earlier, on largely separate trajectories that do not often intersect. The employment of RTM encourages authors and readers to look from a transversal and rhizomatic vantage point, cutting across the subfields in order to make new knowledge.

These subfields often lack transversals because time, content, and media have such an immense impact on rhetorical practices that they obfuscate researchers' ability to see connections beyond them. Thus, while we recognize time, content, and media as essential aspects of rhetorical ecologies and of feminist research more generally, RTM encourages researchers to look beyond these cognitive barriers (as much as possible and only for a time), thus allowing researchers to uncover rhetorical practices that are used repeatedly by specific groups with specific goals (across time, space, social identity markers, technology, etc.). Such a repetition indicates the necessity of better understanding these rhetorical practices. Then, once identified, RTM directs researchers to return to the disconnections located in time, content, and media—and all they entail—in order to theorize how rhetorical practices evolve and are remediated by rhetors, technology, and the evolution of ideas.

As feminist researchers and rhetoricians, we recognize that one's identity necessarily shapes any rhetorical practice, affording different rhetors with different means of persuasion. Therefore, in promoting RTM, we do not encourage researchers to pretend identity markers; socialization practices; and systems of power, oppression, and privilege do not exist or do not matter in shaping rhetorical practices. Rather, we posit that shifting our initial focus away from objects and subjectivities to rhetorical practices will enable researchers to consider connections that would have otherwise gone unnoticed, connections that create new possibilities for rhetorical inquiry.[7]

In FRS and rhetorical studies more broadly, the use of the prefix *trans*—and particularly its use in the term *transnational*—has played an important role in reframing the way we theorize rhetoric. In her landmark essay "Global Turns and Cautions in Rhetoric and Composition Studies," Wendy Hesford calls on the field to turn its focus to transnational matters—matters that necessitate "a reexamination of existing protocols and divisions, and the formation of new critical frameworks in light of a changing world."[8] While Hesford's article was published in 2006, much of it remains relevant for our field today. Hesford's deliberate reference to a changing world speaks to the ways in which the intersections between culture, power, politics, and economics are undergoing significant change due to the uneven processes of globalization. Thus, the move to consider the transnational in rhetorical studies, and specifically in FRS, has signified the move to consider how writing and rhetoric are always already involved in the transnational flows of people, ideas, technology, and communication across national boundaries.[9] Like Tan, we see important affinities embedded in the *trans* prefix. Just as the *trans* in *transnationalism* is used to destabilize the nation, and as the *transnational* in *transnational feminism* is used to destabilize a fixed, singular understanding of feminism, RTM intends to destabilize understandings of rhetorical practices that are bound to linear conceptions of time, fixed ideas about space, and a privileging of content and media. This act of destabilizing, exposing, and questioning preconceived and preexisting ideas about rhetorical work drives our use of RTM throughout this collection.

Indeed, this destabilization exposes methodological pathways that pivot away from the normally central aspects of time, content, and media. These exposed pathways then allow for the creation of new knowledge about rhetorical practices. As Jacqueline Jones Royster explains, "While, with each run through a territory, we must inevitably choose a path, we need more than one crossing to see what is really going on. Always, we need sensibilities that acknowledge converging actions, reactions, and realities. The more pathways we create, the more dialectical the analysis, and the more we take in the periphery of our own vision and experiences, the greater the chance we have of accounting more adequately and more sensitively to complex worlds."[10] Thus, with Royster's words in mind, researchers can use RTM to seek additional pathways and crossings after first exploring the destabilizing pathways this methodology exposes.

After a researcher identifies a rhetorical practice of interest, RTM directs the researcher to search for other uses of the practice. For instance, a researcher may be looking at the suffragists in figure I.1 and notice that the women intentionally juxtaposed a phrase and their bodies with an image of the White House. Using RTM, the researcher would then ask themselves how other rhetors have juxtaposed images with concise prose to make a rhetorical point. This question may lead the researcher to consider contemporary activists' use of memes or to study famous civil rights movement photos that capture activists strategically placing their bodies alongside protest signs. After researchers identify multiple uses of a practice, their second, third, and even fourth pathways should then consider aspects of rhetorical ecologies more typically associated with feminist rhetorical research (e.g., content, identity, time period, technology). The goals of this collection led us to direct our contributors to consider media on their second pathway before allowing their own observations and values to direct subsequent pathways. These subsequent pathways allow the researcher to better understand how the rhetorical practice they identified functions across time, in different places, through different media, for different goals, with unique content, and by different rhetors. While the initial pathway allows researchers to identify multiple—if somewhat disparate—uses of a rhetorical practice, these later pathways allow researchers to consider how such practices are impacted by content, technology, and identity. Such a methodology, then, initially sidesteps that which is habitually central to our understanding of rhetoric in order to eventually understand rhetoric more fully. Ultimately, RTM presents an understanding of rhetoric that does not ignore time, content, or media but that simply puts these aspects of rhetorical ecologies aside momentarily (as much as we ever can) in order to later return to them and better capture the ways they remediate, revise, and repurpose rhetorical practices.

While this collection illustrates how RTM is useful for feminist researchers, RTM is not an explicitly feminist methodology. Although it is proposed by three feminist researchers and applied to feminist activism and rhetoric within this collection, RTM could (and should) be useful beyond FRS. Rhetorical studies should make use of the methodology, much as this volume does, in order to prioritize rhetorical practices and further our theories and understandings of how rhetorical ecologies impact our practices and challenge us to think beyond the approaches that have become so central to our field and thus to our understanding of rhetoric. This is not to criticize those approaches or claim that they have not yielded necessary advancements in rhetorical thought but, instead, to emphasize that as soon as an approach becomes central to our understanding, it also limits what we are able to see on the periphery.

MAPPING FEMINIST RHETORICAL LANDSCAPES

The connections this collection creates are possible because of the contributors' ability to build on decades of previous feminist, rhetorical, and feminist rhetorical scholarship. As this scholarship demonstrates, the terms *feminism* and *rhetoric* both have rich histories of their own. Along with bell hooks, we see feminism as "a movement to end sexism, sexist exploitation, and oppression," and we stress, as hooks does, that feminism is not antimale but is antisexism and recognizes that people are "socialized from birth on to accept sexist thought and action."[11] Additionally, we believe feminism is necessarily plural and multivocal, and like Karen A. Foss, Sonja K. Foss, and Cindy L. Griffin, we see this multiplicity as a strength that "is rooted in choice and self-determination and does not prescribe one 'official' position that feminists must hold."[12] *Feminist Connections,* then, intentionally places multiple feminisms into discussion, recognizing that while feminism has often been understood as a set of discrete movements (or waves), it can also be useful to study these multiple feminisms as related, interdependent, and interactive.

Definitions of rhetoric are also multiple and multivocal. Rhetoric has always been about communicative acts and the search for knowledge, though our conceptions of what counts as communicative action and knowledge change. In the introduction to *The Rhetorical Tradition*, Patricia Bizzell and Bruce Herzberg note that rhetoric has accumulated varying definitions, including but not limited to "the practice of oratory; the study of the strategies of effective oratory; the use of language, written or spoken, to inform or persuade"; and "the study of the relation between language and knowledge."[13] They ultimately conclude, however, that rather than try to find one ultimate definition, it is better to try to understand how our always evolving definitions of rhetoric respond to and influence the field.[14] Like Bizzell and Herzberg, *Feminist Connections* both resists settling on a single definition and highlights the ideological dimensions of rhetoric: "Knowledge and belief are products of persuasion, which seeks to make the arguable seem natural, to turn positions into premises—and it is rhetoric's responsibility to reveal these ideological operations."[15] Douglas Eyman, in his exploration of the term *digital rhetoric*, explains that Bizzell and Herzberg's definition appeals to him because "it does not situate rhetorical power within a specific medium of communication (e.g., print or speech); rather it highlights the relationship between rhetoric and knowledge production and meaning-making, not just as a mechanism for persuasion."[16] By tracing how rhetorical practices function in different media, this collection investigates how rhetorical power manifests in a variety of communication mediums while recognizing that rhetoric has the ability to produce, reveal, and conceal ideology.

Perhaps the understanding of rhetoric that best fits our collection comes from Robert Davis and Mark Shadle: "In a technological age, rhetoric emerges as a conditional method for humanizing the effect of machines and helping humans to direct them. In a multicultural world, rhetoric is a practice of understanding that uses differences to generate more inclusive forms. . . . Rhetoric is a syncretic and generative practice that creates new knowledge by posing questions differently *and uncovering connections that have gone unseen. Its creativity does not exclude or bracket history but often comes from recasting traditional forms and commonplaces in new contexts and questions*" (emphasis added).[17] Such a generative understanding of and approach to rhetoric encourages this collection's contributors to enact this creative uncovering of connections. Indeed, by considering the importance of technology alongside the unavoidable impact of human difference on rhetorical practices, the chapters in this collection increase our recognition of how the past, present, and future of rhetoric are always already bound to one another—and how rhetorical practices can never truly be understood in isolation from their predecessors or their progenies.

As FRS scholars have considered the relationship between gender and rhetorical practice, they have drawn on the rich, individual, evolving meanings of the terms *feminism* and *rhetoric*. Speaking to what feminism and rhetoric share and could offer one another, Lisa Ede, Cheryl Glenn, and Andrea Lunsford have argued that both fields highly value process, which "signals a larger commitment to linking theory with practice, to recognizing and valuing local and applied knowledges," and that both fields "share a long-standing concern for public values and the public good, for creating spaces within which human subjectivities, at least potentially, can be realized, celebrated, and expanded."[18] Additionally, Lindal Buchanan and Kathleen J. Ryan outline six ways to enact feminist rhetorics. This collection primarily attends to the second ("a theoretical mandate, namely, exploring the shaping powers of language, gender ideology, and society; the location of subject[s] within these formations; and the ways these constructs inform the production, circulation, and interpretation of rhetorical texts"); third ("a practice, a scholarly endeavor capable of transforming the discipline of rhetoric through gender analysis, critique, and reformulation"); and sixth ("a political agenda directed toward promoting gender equity within the academy and society").[19] By enacting this theoretical mandate while considering technology and practicing gender analysis and critique, we hope to encourage members of our field who do not identify as feminists or who do not do feminist work to start to promote gender equity by not just reading and citing work that considers gender and other forms of difference more frequently but also by understanding that even if gender appears absent, it is always impacting rhetorical practices and thus should be recognized in all of our theories of rhetoric. That is, *feminist rhetorical research is rhetorical research*.

Like much FRS work, this collection seeks to enact what Barbara Biesecker calls a "gender-sensitive history of Rhetoric"[20]—one that seeks to understand women's differences while recognizing how those differences enable and constrain women's rhetorical action.[21] As Eileen E. Schell points out, the work of feminist and womanist scholars of color encouraged this intersectional emphasis within feminist rhetorical scholarship in the 1990s.[22] And yet, while the authors in this collection attend to how categories of social difference beyond gender (such as race, sexuality, and religion) shape the rhetorical work of the feminist rhetors discussed, as editors we also remain mindful of critiques charged against the concept of intersectionality. As Rosemarie Tong and Tina Fernandes Botts explain, intersectionality has been critiqued because "the implication is that the categories of race, gender, class, sexuality, and even religion or nationality are problematically based in second-wave notions about clearly defined races, genders, and so on. Race and gender cannot 'intersect,' on this view, unless the theoretical (and actual) boundaries between different races and genders are fairly clearly defined in the first place."[23] Therefore, while recognizing that people face unique oppression based on their intersecting marginalized identities, our collection also invokes interstitiality, as explained by Tarez Samra Graban in the foreword. Interstitiality, as Tong and Botts clarify, has

> been offered in place of intersectionality as an organizing concept to explain the complex web of sociohistorical and sociolegal forces at work in the creation of identity, particularly as it is shaped by oppression. Interstitiality means different things for different feminists. For some, the concept invokes the ill-defined but nevertheless existent space between the existing identity categories of race, gender, and so on. For others, it highlights the unlimited number of identity categories that can overlap and interact in the formation of identity. Perhaps, however, intersectionality and interstitiality are not incompatible concepts and can be understood as different names for the same phenomenon. Interstitiality seems to add to intersectionality, however, an emphasis on the nonessential nature of any singular group identity marker.[24]

Thus, the destabilizing nature of RTM encourages both interstitial and intersectional ways of seeing, helping researchers divert their focus from singular and essentialized identity markers. Such an interstitial approach seeks the spaces between such markers, spaces where rhetorical practices repeat despite being hidden by categories of difference.

Feminist Connections also contributes to the growing research on social movement rhetoric (SMR). In their summary of SMR, Robert Cox and Christina R. Foust conclude that "a robust theory of the efficacy or impact of rhetorical acts in oppositional struggles holds the greatest promise for continued development and contribution of [SMR] scholarship . . . beyond simple accounts of 'resistance' lies the possibility of understanding the relationships among discursive acts, power, and the sources of social and political transformation."[25] By exposing feminist rhetorical connections across centuries, *Feminist Connections* showcases relationships among discursive acts and power while considering the efficacy of feminist rhetorical practices. Additionally, the collection considers how SMR (and specifically feminist rhetoric) adapts and evolves over time, space, and media with the goal of dismantling oppressive systems of power as they transform and insidiously mask their oppression.

Indeed, *Feminist Connections* is unique in its nonlinear consideration of a social movement's rhetoric. Certainly, we could understand suffrage as a social movement distinct from radical lesbian feminism, and such distinctions have been useful in previous scholarship. However, such an approach ignores the complexity of the feminist movement in order to focus on a discrete moment that is easier to study. In contrast, this collection recognizes that the feminist movement encompasses a number of sometimes conflicting social movements but that SMR can benefit from a study of the movement's rhetorical practices across time. Like Sharon McKenzie Stevens and Patricia M. Malesh's 2009 *Active Voices*, our collection "treat[s] social movements as fallible, human, dynamic collections of people."[26] Doing so means studying the rhetoric presented to the public and the rhetoric presented to other members of the movement. Placing these conversations next to one another allows us to see the importance of rhetoric to social movements. *Feminist Connections* illustrates how rhetoric is not only necessary to spur public social change but also necessary within social movements as the members reflect on, critique, and reconsider the movement's own beliefs and actions.

RHETORIC AND MEDIA

Importantly, *Feminist Connections* also recognizes that media shape the ways rhetors enact and deliver their rhetoric to a variety of publics. As Anne Frances Wysocki argues, "what any body is able to do—and how any one body differs from other bodies in its affective and physiological capabilities—cannot be disentangled from the media we use or from the times and cultures in and technologies with which we consume and produce texts."[27] While both historical and digital rhetorical scholarship have attended to the entanglement of media with bodies and the times and cultures in which they exist (e.g., nineteenth-century scholarship's focus on the printing press and digital scholarship's attention to new media), *Feminist Connections* brings these usually separate conversations together, which changes the way media is discussed by allowing for a richer understanding of rhetorical practices and important new discoveries about the relationship between rhetoric and media.

Although scholars such as Tarez Samra Graban; Jessica Enoch, Jean Bessette, and Pamela VanHaitsma; and Gail E. Hawisher and Cynthia L. Selfe have sought to bridge the historical and the digital in rich and provocative ways, such work remains rare. Further, in the digital humanities, the digital has primarily been understood as a method, and many of the feminist rhetorical projects that have come out of the digital humanities have been related to archival projects and concerned with the act of recovering and sharing historical texts through digital methods and media.[28] Other FRS scholars have recognized the rarity of work that bridges the historical and digital. For instance, three of the four "new horizons" that Jacqueline Jones Royster and Gesa E. Kirsch identify at the end of *Feminist Rhetorical Practices* explicitly call for FRS scholars to pay more attention to technology and the digital, and Buchanan and Ryan identify "gendered rhetorics in digital environments" as one of several topics that are not as present in their *Walking and Talking Feminist Rhetorics* as they would like.[29]

A primary goal of *Feminist Connections*, then, is to place the digital and the historical in conversation with one another in order to better understand the relationship between rhetoric and media. *Feminist Connections* combines the digital and the historical in order to uniquely consider media (from print to digital and everything in between), uncovering how feminists reuse and revise rhetorical practices while revealing the ways media shapes and influences those revisions. Consequently, our contributors attend to media's impact on recurring rhetorical practices. While the goals of our collection led us to direct our contributors to consider the role of media after initially identifying rhetorical connections, chapters' later pathways vary, determined by the authors' own observations and values and their attention to the impact that identity, nationality, location, and more have on rhetorical practices.

Feminist concerns dominate these later pathways, though this collection's rhetorical discoveries are, as mentioned previously, applicable beyond FRS. While many studies have paid attention to rhetoric and media, the chapters in this collection consider how a range of media shapes specific rhetorical practices, contributing to an enhanced understanding of the complex relationship between rhetoric and media. Although this collection considers feminists' uses of rhetorical practices, the practices themselves are not limited to feminists, and consequently, the implications discovered therein should be attended to by rhetorical studies at large. Indeed, *Feminist Connections* identifies new and expands on old rhetorical patterns and modes of engagement, creating frameworks that allow for a fuller theorization of how rhetorical practices evolve over time, how media influences rhetorical strategies and devices, and how our scholarship is improved by considering the historical and digital as always already interconnected.

ARRANGEMENT

As we read proposals and then chapters connecting historical and contemporary feminist rhetorical practices, we identified three feminist rhetorical frameworks: revisionary rhetorics, circulatory rhetorics, and response rhetorics. These frameworks emerged out of the proposals. As we read, we noticed them being referenced but not explicitly named; therefore, we decided to name them and group the chapters accordingly to highlight common feminist rhetorical practices within the frameworks. By organizing chapters into these three frameworks, we highlight rhetorical patterns in order to create new theories of feminist rhetorical practice. Just as individual chapters are not limited by a focus on time period, the three sections privilege connections in rhetorical practices and therefore disrupt a more typical collection organization that might have grouped chapters by rhetor or purpose. In order to make these connections explicit, each section begins with an introduction that theorizes the feminist rhetorical framework and links the chapters in that section.

Arranging an edited collection is difficult for anyone, particularly for feminists wanting to promote equity while questioning binaries and resisting rote categorization. This work is also difficult for rhetoricians because any organizational scheme imposes terministic screens by focusing attention on certain aspects while also deflecting others or hiding them from view.[30] Therefore, while we have carefully considered how and why to arrange the chapters in our collection, we also want, as Joy Ritchie and Kate Ronald wanted for their edited collection, for "readers to find their own connections . . . to gather these rhetorics together in their own view and use them to create and to reimagine rhetorical history and their own rhetorical practices."[31] While we created these frameworks for generative purposes, we hope our readers will read beyond and between our frameworks in order to identify their own.

We begin with Revisionary Rhetorics, a section where authors take up a well-established move within FRS: looking with fresh eyes, through a lens focused on gender, in order to re-vision rhetorical practices and understand them differently, particularly by expanding their scope. In rereading feminist and/or technological narratives, the chapters in this section encourage an ethics of care in order to offer models and/or cautionary tales that draw attention to overlooked moments and effects of past feminist rhetorical action and benefit future feminist rhetorical study and practice.

The Circulatory Rhetorics section addresses questions related to delivery and distribution. Drawing connections between feminist rhetorical strategies of the past and those of the present, the authors in this section consider the ways rhetorical messages are always already caught up in networks of encounter and interaction through the processes of circulation. More specifically, the chapters in this section point to important questions regarding the ever-shifting relationships between rhetors, audiences, and the affective, amplified nature of media.

In Response Rhetorics, the final section, contributors consider how members of marginalized groups respond to audiences with power, both within and outside of feminist movements. The chapters in this section discuss how anonymity, perceived failure, repetition, and narrative allow rhetors without power to persuade unreceptive audiences and encourage them to listen.

While we are pleased with the diversity of this collection, we recognize that many important areas of concern are not addressed in the following pages. We are particularly aware of the lack of Indigenous and immigrant voices, the absence of chapters focused on trans and gender nonbinary people, a failure to attend to physical ability and neurodiversity, and a scarcity of voices from beyond the United States. Further, as three white, cis women with US citizenship, we are keenly aware that our own subjectivities keep us from seeing other important areas of inquiry. As we gain distance from this work, we will continue to consider how RTM can be more inclusive and therefore produce more responsible research and activism. Additionally, we look forward to learning from how other scholars choose to enact and/or modify RTM beyond this collection.

CONNECTING SCHOLARSHIP AND PUBLIC ACTION

Feminist Connections further takes up what Royster and Kirsch saw on the horizon of FRS by continuing to push feminism and rhetoric to cross one another's borders, particularly by recognizing that within existing FRS scholarship, there are borders between feminist historiographic work and feminist digital work. While not the only way to do so, *Feminist Connections* serves as one way to reach what Royster and Kirsch have identified as an ambitious threefold challenge for FRS: "to enhance our capacity to build a more richly endowed knowledge base, carry out a more inclusive research agenda, and generate greater, more inclusive interpretive power."[32] Indeed, by approaching rhetorical practices transversally, RTM provides greater interpretive power by exposing connections and disconnections that may not have been otherwise evident, creating a more richly endowed knowledge base. As you read through this collection, we hope that you, too, will engage with the questions that started and sustained this project:

How have contemporary feminists adapted or remixed earlier feminist rhetorical strategies?

How has a specific (proto)feminist rhetorical strategy manifested itself in different times and/or places?

How have feminist conversations evolved, mutated, or changed as a result of technological advances such as the popular printing press, the television, or the internet?

How have the ways feminists communicate with one another changed as a result of technological advances?

How have technological advances influenced the opportunities and limitations for feminist organizing, protest, and action?

How have feminists of different time periods, spaces, and locations found ways to have conversations with those whose experiences do not mirror their own and/or with those who challenge dominant feminist discourses?

How have feminists developed rhetorical spaces and tactics to foster, challenge, and/or alter feminist conversations?

How have rhetors used (proto)feminist rhetorical action to address issues related to identity and embodiment? And how do technologies contribute to producing and shaping knowledge about these issues?

How have global projects and/or issues influenced feminist rhetorical practices, both historically and in the present day?

The identifying and theorizing of recurrent rhetorical practices found in this collection provide a model for broadening our rhetorical vision and illustrate how such a broadened vision is generative for both theory and practice. And while the theoretical and practical implications apply to all rhetoricians, *Feminist Connections* is particularly useful for rhetoricians concerned with feminist activism and social movement rhetorics. Since we began working on this collection, we have witnessed the separation of immigrant children from their parents; the erosion of reproductive rights; attacks on the trans community; continued state violence against black, migrant, and Indigenous bodies; an increase in white nationalism; the dismissal of sexual assault allegations against men in power; the US government's refusal to acknowledge human impact on the environment; and any other number of terrifying realities in our world. Consequently, the implications uncovered here should guide those of us in FRS and rhetorical studies more broadly as we craft activist rhetorics during a time when academics cannot ethically remain behind academia's hallowed yet insular walls.

Notes

1. Throughout this chapter, we use the phrase *rhetorical practices* as an umbrella term that includes rhetorical strategies and rhetorical devices.

2. For instance, the suffragists' rhetorical strategy employed both logical and pathetic appeals via their reliance on the rhetorical device of juxtaposition (figure I.1).

3. Alison Piepmeier, *Girl Zines: Making Media, Doing Feminism* (New York: New York University Press, 2009).

4. *Oxford English Dictionary*, s.v. "transversal," accessed September 25, 2018, http://www.oed.com.

5. Pelin Tan, "Decolonizing Architectural Education: Towards an Affective Pedagogy," in *The Social (Re)Production of Architecture: Politics, Values and Actions in Contemporary Practice*, ed. Doina Petrescu and Kim Trogal (New York: Routledge, 2017), 78.

6. Pelin Tan, "Transversal Materialism: On Method, Artifact, and Exception," in *2000+: The Urgencies of Architectural Theory*, ed. James Graham (New York: Columbia University Graduate School of Architecture, Planning and Preservation, 2015), 200.

7. Tan, 200.

8. Wendy Hesford, "Global Turns and Cautions in Rhetoric and Composition Studies," *PMLA* 121, no. 3 (2006): 796.

9. See Rebecca A. Dingo, *Networking Arguments: Rhetoric, Transnational Feminism, and Public Policy Writing* (Pittsburgh, PA: University of Pittsburgh Press, 2012); and Mary Queen, "Transnational Feminist Rhetorics in a Digital World," *College English* 70, no. 5 (2008): 471–89.

10. Jacqueline Jones Royster, "In Search of Ways In," in *Feminine Principles and Women's Experience in American Composition and Rhetoric*, ed. Louise Wetherbee Phelps and Janet Emig (Pittsburgh, PA: University of Pittsburgh Press, 1995), 389.

11. bell hooks, *Feminism Is for Everybody: Passionate Politics* (Cambridge, MA: South End Press, 2000), viii.

12. Karen A. Foss, Sonja K. Foss, and Cindy L. Griffin, *Feminist Rhetorical Theories* (Thousand Oaks, CA: SAGE, 1999), 3.

13. Patricia Bizzell and Bruce Herzberg, *The Rhetorical Tradition: Readings from Classical Times to the Present*, 2nd ed. (Boston: Bedford/St. Martin's, 2001), 1.

14. Bizzell and Herzberg, 1.

15. Bizzell and Herzberg, 15.

16. Douglas Eyman, *Digital Rhetoric: Theory, Method, Practice* (Ann Arbor: University of Michigan Press, 2015), 17.

17. Robert Davis and Mark Shadle, *Teaching Multiwriting: Researching and Composing with Multiple Genres, Media, Disciplines, and Cultures* (Carbondale: Southern Illinois University Press, 2007), 103.

18. Lisa Ede, Cheryl Glenn, and Andrea Lunsford, "Border Crossings: Intersections of Rhetoric and Feminism," *Rhetorica: A Journal of the History of Rhetoric* 13, no. 4 (1995): 404.

19. Lindal Buchanan and Kathleen J. Ryan, introduction to *Walking and Talking Feminist Rhetorics: Landmark Essays and Controversies*, ed. Lindal Buchanan and Kathleen J. Ryan (West Lafayette: IN: Parlor Press, 2010), xiii.

20. Barbara Biesecker, "Coming to Terms with Recent Attempts to Write Women into the History of Rhetoric," *Philosophy and Rhetoric* 25, no. 2 (1992): 156.

21. Biesecker, 157. While Biesecker uses the term *woman*, we want to be clear that we do not wish to suggest a focus only on biological women, and we promote K. J. Rawson's call to critically examine the category of woman. See K. J. Rawson, "Queering Feminist Rhetorical Canonization," in *Rhetorica in Motion*, ed. Eileen E. Schell and K. J. Rawson (Pittsburgh, PA: University of Pittsburgh Press, 2010), 39–52.

22. Eileen Schell, introduction to Schell and Rawson, *Rhetorica in Motion*, 14.

23. Rosemarie Tong and Tina Fernandes Botts, *Feminist Thought: A More Comprehensive Introduction*, 5th ed. (New York: Westview Press, 2018), 129.

24. Tong and Botts, 129.

25. Robert Cox and Christina R. Foust, "Social Movement Rhetoric," in *The SAGE Handbook of Rhetorical Studies*, ed. Rosa A. Eberly, Kirt H. Wilson, and Andrea A. Lunsford (Thousand Oaks, CA: SAGE, 2009), 622.

26. William DeGenaro, "Politics, Class, and Social Movement People: Continuing the Conversation," in *Active Voices: Composing a Rhetoric for Social Movements*, ed. Sharon McKenzie Stevens and Patricia M. Malesh (Albany: State University of New York Press, 2009), 199.

27. Anne Frances Wysocki, introduction to *Composing (Media) = Composing (Embodiment): Bodies, Technologies, Writing, the Teaching of Writing*, ed. Kristin L. Arola and Anne Wysocki (Logan: Utah State University Press, 2012), 8.

28. Moya Z. Bailey, "All the Digital Humanists Are White, All the Nerds Are Men, but Some of Us Are Brave," *Journal of Digital Humanities* 1, no. 1 (2011), http://journalofdigitalhumanities.org.

29. Buchanan and Ryan, introduction, xv; see also Jacqueline Jones Royster and Gesa E. Kirsch, *Feminist Rhetorical Practices: New Horizons for Rhetoric, Composition, and Literacy Studies* (Carbondale: Southern Illinois University Press, 2012).

30. We are certainly not the first set of editors to call attention to such difficulties; see, for example, Janet Emig and Louise Wetherbee Phelps, introduction to Phelps and Emig, *Feminine Principles and Women's Experience*, xi–xviii; and Joy Ritchie and Kate Ronald, introduction to *Available Means: An Anthology of Women's Rhetoric(s)*, ed. Joy Ritchie and Kate Ronald (Pittsburgh, PA: University of Pittsburgh Press, 2001), xv–xxxi.

31. Ritchie and Ronald, introduction to *Available Means*, xxvii.

32. Royster and Kirsch, *Feminist Rhetorical Practices*, 134.

PART ONE

REVISIONARY RHETORICS

Kerri Hauman

Feminist rhetorical work is often described with a lengthy list of verbs with the prefix *re*. Joy Ritchie and Kate Ronald provide a selection of these terms in the introduction to their collection of women's rhetorics: we recover, retell, reclaim, reconceptualize, reconceive, re-present, regender, and revise. In fact, most of this *re* work functions in service of the final word here: revision. As such, the framework of *revisionary rhetorics* is likely the most recognizable framework for feminist rhetorical studies (FRS), which has a long history of re-visioning historical rhetorical practices to recover and account for women and their rhetorical work within powered, gendered systems.

In her landmark revisionary FRS work *Rhetoric Retold*, Cheryl Glenn notes that Douglas Ehninger issued the inaugural call for revisionary histories of rhetoric in "On Rhetoric and Rhetorics" in 1967. FRS scholars have certainly heeded this call to focus on revisionary histories; Jessica Enoch even goes as far to claim that the prevailing exigencies for feminist historiography in rhetoric are "to challenge and revise the rhetorical tradition."[1] Twenty-five years after Ehninger's call, Jacqueline Jones Royster and Gesa E. Kirsch highlight the role revision and revisioning continue to play in FRS via the second section of their text *Feminist Rhetorical Practices*, titled "Re-Visioning History, Theory, and Practice," which surveys more than thirty years of FRS scholarship. This first section of *Feminist Connections* both acknowledges and builds on the fact that revision is something FRS scholars have been doing for decades in order to expand the definitional and locational scopes of rhetorical action.

The OED's definition of the prefix *re* provides a fitting explanation of why feminist scholars undertake this *re* work: *re* is "prefixed to ordinary verbs of action . . . sometimes denoting that the action itself is performed a second time, and sometimes that its result is to reverse a previous action or process, or to restore a previous state of things."[2] FRS scholars have been visioning for a second (or more) time in order to reverse the understanding created by previous scholarship, which was that the scope of rhetoric was limited to persuasive action by privileged (i.e., white, wealthy, land-owning, able-bodied, cis, heterosexual) men, and to instead create scholarship that restored women to their rightful place in the stories we tell about rhetoric across time and space. As K. J. Rawson points out in both his chapter "Queering Feminist Rhetorical Canonization" and his *Peitho* conversation with Patricia Bizzell, FRS scholars must continue this project of re-visioning in order to produce scholarship that rightfully expands from focusing on women, which has almost exclusively meant cis women, to focusing on gender in a way that challenges a binary view of gender and is better in line with feminism and gender theory developments "that are flourishing in queer studies and elsewhere, inside the academy and out."[3] The chapters in *Feminist Connections* do not make Rawson's recommended moves to question the category of woman and carefully interrogate gender as explicitly or often as we would like; however, Kellie Jean Sharp's chapter in this section explicitly looks to queer theory to broaden the scope of FRS scholarship, which we see as an important taking up of Rawson's call. Sharp's work, along with the rest of the chapters not only in this section but in the entire collection, performs the important work of both connecting to and departing from the more well-told, well-known histories of rhetoric.

The chapters in this section build on strong FRS revisionary work and, importantly, account for many of the complexities rhetorical scholars have been urging us to pay attention to. For instance, David Gold argues that our revisionary work must "not simply recover neglected writers, teachers, locations, and institutions, but must also demonstrate connections between these subjects and larger scholarly conversations"; must "better incorporate recent advances in recovery work, thus beginning with the assumption of a complex, multivocal past as our starting point for historical inquiry"; and must "recognize a more fluid interaction between ideology and pedagogy, resisting the temptation to reinscribe easy binaries, taxonomies, and master narratives, even when countering them."[4] The authors in this section do indeed focus on larger scholarly conversations and this complex, multivocal past in order to resist easy binaries, taxonomies, and master narratives. For example, both Tara Propper's and Jill Swiencicki, Maria Brandt, Barbara LeSavoy, and Deborah Uman's chapters follow Leah DiNatale Gutenson and Michelle Bachelor Robinson's call to consider how technology "'races' our thinking about the past and requires that we take an active role in joining and expanding future conversations."[5]

Turning to Enoch's discussion of the revisionary work of FRS scholarship is helpful in considering how this work of revisionary rhetorics is similar to and different from previous FRS scholarship. In her discussion of re-visioning the aims of feminist scholarly work, Enoch presents two new methods that could allow feminist rhetorical scholars "to see a more broadly conceived telos for feminist scholarship: historiographic research that interrogates the complicated imbrication of rhetoric, gender, and history."[6] As Enoch suggests can be done by work that "releases hold of the rhetorical tradition to consider what else a feminist historiography might do if it does not work towards canonical revision as its ultimate goal," the work in this section seeks to add to a growing body of work that considers "how categories of race, class, physical ability, and sexuality complicate and enhance understandings of the rhetorical process of gendering and vice versa."[7] Our goal is not revising the canon but rather, as explained in the introduction, finding connections we previously could not see because they were obfuscated by habitual practices of focusing on time, content, and media and because we held largely separate(d) conversations about feminist historiographic rhetorical work and digital feminist rhetorical work. Thus, our understanding of both the old and new is revised by the uncovering of connections between the two.

With our own slightly re-visioned goals, the authors in this section honor and expand on the rich history of re-visioning in FRS. The section begins with Swiencicki, Brandt, LeSavoy, and Uman's chapter "Seneca Falls, Strategic Mythmaking, and a Feminist Politics of Relation." In using RTM, they consider their own contemporary enactments of some of the rhetorical practices from the 1848 Women's Rights Convention at Seneca Falls and turn a critical eye on these practices that were used to position Seneca Falls as an origin story of feminist history. Swiencicki, Brandt, LeSavoy, and Uman argue that feminist rhetorical historiographers have an important role to play in "promoting intersectional, reparative places of feminist inquiry and coalition." The authors focus their discussion on how they have shaped their own rhetorical approaches (which are grounded in what Aimee Carrillo Rowe calls a "politics of relation") in holding Seneca Falls Dialogues (SFD)—an event that has occurred biannually since 2008. They conclude with a comparison of their own work with SFD, digital and analog, to digital strategies used on Twitter after the 2016 presidential election that decentered Elizabeth Cady Stanton and Seneca Falls in order to "[complicate] history, [create] reparative spaces, and [forge] alliances that could not happen in one era but can be actualized now, in all their productive tension."

Next, Propper's chapter, "Epideictic Rhetoric and Emergent Media: From *CAM* to BLM," explores the ways that Pauline Hopkins's work in the *Colored American Magazine* and various visitors' contributions to the #SayHerName tribute page on the Black Lives Matter website "reveal a unique interrelation between emergent forms of media, social mobilization, and public memorialization." Propper re-visions epideictic rhetoric to expand its scope and demonstrate how viewing revisionary and epideictic rhetoric together can provide a framework that allows us to uncover histories of marginalized communities and then use those to develop new methods for community building. In her analysis and comparison of the recovery and memorialization work achieved by Hopkins and #SayHerName contributors, Propper is careful to recognize differences between the two media platforms while using the connections she uncovers to reveal how black women in the nineteenth and twenty-first centuries have relied on the same rhetorical practices in order to navigate racist structures.

Narratives of technology, according to Amy Koerber, typically exclude technologies women have historically had access to, and she argues that a feminist rhetoric of technology would correct for this exclusion by expanding the definition of technology to account for reproductive and domestic technologies. Koerber notes that feminist historians and feminist scholars in other disciplines have recovered stories of early female inventors ignored by mainstream history and have worked to expand definitions of technology, and she urges feminist rhetorical scholars to view these revisionist approaches as models.[8] Thus, the final two chapters in this section demonstrate how feminist rhetoricians can re-vision historical narratives of rhetoric and technology.

Although they do not address reproductive and domestic technologies, Risa Applegarth, Sarah Hallenbeck, and Chelsea Redeker Milbourne take up Koerber's larger call for revisionist approaches to technology by reexamining language they refer to as *recruitment tropes*, language that was historically used to attract women to the technologically driven fields of telegraphy and stenography. In their chapter, "Recruitment Tropes: Historicizing the Spaces and Bodies of Women Technical Workers," Applegarth, Hallenbeck, and Redeker Milbourne urge feminist rhetoricians to consider how re-visioning historical narratives surrounding the language of these recruitment tropes might provide cautionary tales about current technological narratives of coding, which they argue parallel their historical case studies in initially appearing to "upset existing gendered, raced, and classed hierarchies . . . only to reassert these hierarchies over time," particularly through a neoliberal discourse of empowerment.

In the final chapter in this section, "Take Once Daily: Queer Theory, Biopolitics, and the Rhetoric of Personal Responsibility," Sharp takes up Koerber's call for revisionist approaches to technology that account for reproductive technologies. However, Sharp extends this focus not just to reproductive technologies but also to technologies related to sex and sexuality more broadly through her discussion of the birth control pill and Truvada, a pre-exposure prophylaxis (PrEP) drug used to prevent HIV. In her exploration of "the relationship between pharmacological discourse and fantasies of sex and sexual liberation," Sharp also revises the notion of recovery so familiar in feminist rhetorical studies in order to look beyond the straight, cis man/cis woman binary in both her use of queer theory and her discussion of a technology most commonly associated with gay men. While re-visioning the historical narrative about the birth control pill as a cautionary tale to consider how the ways we talk about and understand Truvada might shape current and future conceptions of bodies, identities, and sexuality, Sharp productively connects conversations in FRS and queer studies by asking questions like "How does discourse shape politics? How might discourses shape our very bodies? Our sexualities? How does the way we talk about sex influence the kind of sex we have or do not have?"

Ultimately, in the Revisionary Rhetorics section of our collection, the authors join a lineage of feminist rhetorical studies scholars who look with fresh eyes. The chapters in this section provide FRS scholars with additional models of revisioning intended to build on and reckon with past feminist rhetorical action as well as cautionary tales intended to benefit future feminist rhetorical actions.

Notes

1. Jessica Enoch, "Releasing Hold: Feminist Historiography without the Tradition," in *Theorizing Histories of Rhetoric*, ed. Michelle Ballif (Carbondale: Southern Illinois University Press, 2013), 58.

2. *Oxford English Dictionary*, s.v. "re- (prefix)," accessed January 7, 2018, http://www .oed.com.

3. K. J. Rawson, "Queering Feminist Rhetorical Canonization," in *Rhetorica in Motion*, ed. Eileen E. Schell and K. J. Rawson (Pittsburgh, PA: University of Pittsburgh Press, 2010), 52.

4. David Gold, "Remapping Revisionist Historiography," *College Composition and Communication* 64, no. 1 (2012): 17.

5. Leah DiNatale Gutenson and Michelle Bachelor Robinson, "Race, Women, Methods, and Access: A Journey through Cyberspace and Back," *Peitho* 19, no. 1 (2016): 87.

6. Enoch, "Releasing Hold," 72.

7. Enoch, 72.

8. Amy Koerber, "Toward a Feminist Rhetoric of Technology," *Journal of Business and Technical Communication* 14, no. 1 (2000): 65.

1

Seneca Falls, Strategic Mythmaking, and a Feminist Politics of Relation

Jill Swiencicki, Maria Brandt, Barbara LeSavoy, and Deborah Uman

Seneca Falls—the town, the 1848 Women's Rights Convention, and the iconic suffrage leaders—persists as a meaningful signifier of feminist political action. As journalist Amanda Hess observes of Hillary Rodham Clinton's turn to suffrage after the 2016 democratic primary, "When she clinched the Democratic nomination for president—the one she would formally accept the following month, dressed in suffragist white—Clinton called back to the convention of 1848, where 'a small but determined group of women, and men, came together with the idea that women deserve equal rights.' The feminist project started there, Clinton implied, and she was going to finish it."[1] In her campaign, Clinton invoked the mythic Seneca Falls, New York, creating a lineage for such contemporary political projects as equal pay, reproductive freedom, and access to affordable health care. Such origin myths are an important way feminist connections are made across places and time periods.

Seneca Falls can serve to legitimate present-day political action.[2] Yet as a terministic screen, it also deflects and silences other aspects of women's history, particularly through its insistence on single-issue politics of race and gender. In her book *The Myth of Seneca Falls*, historian Lisa Tetrault chronicles the historiographic practices that occurred for the 1848 convention to become Clinton's feminist origin point. For example, toward the end of her decades of activism and writing, Susan B. Anthony filled her Rochester, New York, neighborhood with smoke that billowed for days as she burned her expansive archive of suffrage artifacts from groups across the country and from decades of struggle to win the vote. In a conscious act of erasure, she destroyed the diversity of activism, knowledge, and practices of many organizations so that her own three-volume opus, *History of Women's Suffrage*, would be the definitive account of what was in fact a dispersed, often intersectional, multigenerational, multiplatformed activist achievement.[3] In Anthony's history, Seneca Falls emerges as the origin point of women's rights activism despite the fact that she did not attend that 1848 convention,[4] and despite the multiple locations and ideologically diverse participants in the struggle that preceded it, contested it, and formed after it.

Challenges to the Seneca Falls origin myth that Clinton invoked came briskly after her loss in the 2016 presidential election. After the international Women's March on January 21, 2017, articles and messages circulated on social media that identified white feminists as a strained locus of allyship and liability in the growing postelection resistance movement. One of them, a meme circulating on Facebook and attributed to Raka Ray, names "white feminism" as the key impediment to robust resistance. This claim is supported by the fact that 94 percent of black women who voted cast their ballot for Clinton, and 53 percent of white women who voted cast theirs for Trump.[5] "To my white friends demonstrating today," says Ray in their meme, "do not forget that white feminism is white supremacy. Do not forget that Susan B. Anthony was a racist that argued for suffrage on the grounds that white women are more valuable than any black person. . . . Donald Trump is President because of white supremacy, and if there's one thing white women have proved time and again, it's that they will always prioritize their race privilege over solidarity with women of color. If you want to be an ally, the first step is to never forget."[6] To move an antiracist feminist agenda forward in a repressive presidential era, Ray insists, we cannot replicate single-issue, white liberal feminist activism that elevates the rights of the most privileged over the rights of all. In Susan B. Anthony's name, Ray invokes historical betrayals, when white feminists left behind the agendas of women of color to make legislative gains, and Ray argues that we have to understand how feminists structured their platforms for rights in the past so we do not repeat these mistakes. Ray disrupts traditional ways of understanding feminism as a unified, coherent march toward freedom and justice, challenging feminism to be more expansive not just in its focus but also in its modes of communication and storytelling.

In this chapter we join scholars and activists in asking what roles feminist rhetoric historians can play in "never forgetting"—in promoting intersectional, reparative places of feminist inquiry and coalition. We examine our collaborative attempt to return to Seneca Falls and create a critical, experimental, feminist space of knowledge-making through what we call the Seneca Falls Dialogues (SFD). We cofounded the biennial SFD a decade ago when members from the Rochester chapter of the American Association of University Women, the Seneca Falls community organizing group Women's Institute for Leadership and Learning, and women and gender studies (WGST) faculty from five colleges in the Rochester region organized the 2008 Seneca Falls Dialogues, a meeting timed to commemorate the 160th anniversary of the 1848 Seneca Falls Convention. The SFD does not sponsor presentational formats during the breakout sessions but specifies in its "call for dialogues" that session organizers create activities, problem-solving settings, working groups, and other practices that create possibilities for social justice outcomes. As WGST faculty, we were eager to draw on the history and location of Seneca Falls to gather with community members, artists, businesspeople, politicians, activists, teachers, researchers, and students to sponsor intersectional projects and conversations and to support existing and nascent activist work. Four SFD gatherings followed with hundreds of participants at each event.

Rather than perpetuate the myth of Seneca Falls, the goal of the dialogues is to engage in strategic mythmaking: making feminist connections—in a contested, mythic space—that account for and acknowledge past injustices and engage in activities that create different, more just relations. Abandoning feminist spaces that are compromised by past race, class, gender, and generational betrayals misses an opportunity to do better this time around. We attempt this process because we teach feminist rhetorics, and important literacy and rhetorical work happened in Seneca Falls: over the two-day-long 1848 convention, three hundred attendees held what could be called an extended writing workshop, as Elizabeth Cady Stanton read her "Declaration of Sentiments," and attendees like Frederick Douglass and Lucretia Mott revised it, using lofty debate, heated dialogue, and tedious wordsmithing to come to consensus on a manifesto that included, among other things, the formal demand for the right to vote. We return to local history to understand the core practices of the 1848 convention and to revise and transform them for new ends. In the following pages, we critically reflect on two whole-group activities we engaged in at the 2016 Seneca Falls Dialogues: one activity involves returning to sacred suffrage texts to examine and remake them; the other involves returning to the open dialogue format for cross-generational political discussion. These activities attempted to create what Aimee Carrillo Rowe calls a "politics of relation," which asks us to examine "how we may hold ourselves accountable for who we are (becoming, as a function of belonging), and the collective conditions out of which our agency, experience, and consciousness emerge."[7] As our discussion of these activities and our concluding dialogue will show, we have yet to bridge what seems like incommensurate worlds—Clinton's mythic, enduring Seneca Falls and Ray's racist, exclusionist Seneca Falls. Indeed, our work in strategic mythmaking aims not to perpetuate these memory wars and divisions, but to create the potential for a "power-attentive intimacy" that may confront and remake past feminist relations.[8]

TOWARD A POLITICS OF RELATION

The Seneca Falls Dialogues are two days of concurrent sessions of group discussion, activist work, and coalition-building, along with whole-convention dialogues and featured speakers. During the two October days of the SFD, participants meet in the Wesleyan Chapel, site of the 1848 convention; we also meet in the Seneca Falls community center, the historic Gould Hotel, and the visitor center of the Women's Rights National Historical Park, effectively integrating our concurrent sessions throughout the town's entire main street. Residents of Seneca Falls and those visiting the national park sometimes wander into our sessions and stay. The power of place resonates in these gatherings. Throughout the two days, participants can be found trying to describe the feeling of "being part of history," and the feeling of history saturating our activities. History, for many, is in fact a feeling, an association or affiliation with original artifacts and locations: seeing copies of the "Declaration of Sentiments" and "Resolutions" documents and the minutes from the original 1848 convention, interacting in the Wesleyan Chapel itself, or standing at the actual podium where Elizabeth Cady Stanton and other revered figures stood. This experience of being part of history is seamless for some but fraught for others. Indulging in the feeling of mythic memory can circumscribe critical reflection and even transgression. How we produce historical memory in our activities and in the structure of the SFD therefore functions as an important record of how we understand and remake the past.

Producing historical memory involves, as Carly S. Woods notes, a clear purpose in our own motives in the work of rhetoric. She argues for "the synergistic relationship between rhetorical history and intersectional research," insisting that "rhetorical historians are not simply cartographers who locate women frozen in time on an already printed map of rhetoric. We are travel companions who study the movement of people and discourses across space and time."[9] Woods, Cindy L. Griffin, Karma R. Chávez and other feminist rhetoricians are working with the theories of feminist solidarity and cross-racial feminist "bridge work" begun in Cherríe Moraga and Gloria Anzaldúa's *This Bridge Called My Back*, Anzaldúa and AnaLouise Keating's *This Bridge We Call Home*, Chandra Talpade Mohanty's *Feminism without Borders*, and Rowe's *Power Lines*.[10] In her essays on the subject and in her book, Rowe examines cross-racial feminist alliances in higher education in order to identify reparative practices across social differences. Rowe critiques identity politics and the "politics of location" as getting in the way of reparative practices because of their fixed, self-focused notions of identity.[11] Rowe argues that a feminist politics of location represents "a particular set of modes of belonging—to whiteness, to other women as lesbian, and to US citizenship, for instance—without interrogating the conditions that enable, or would potentially disrupt, those sites of affective investment."[12] Influenced by the work of Chela Sandoval on feminist methodologies of the oppressed, Rowe sees feminist location analysis as returning too often to a liberal focus on the individual, and on a single axis of identity that requires multiple displacements of experience, history, and place.[13]

A politics of relation, on the other hand, focuses attention on the "power transmitted through our affective ties."[14] It foregrounds how "the subject arrives again and again to her own becoming through a series of transitions—across time and space, communities and contexts—throughout the course of her life . . . constituted not first through the atomized self, but through its longings to be with."[15] In a feminist politics of relation, "belonging precedes being," where feminist subjectivity is actively constituted "not first through the 'Self,' but through its own longings to be with."[16] Rowe's premise is that alliances in feminism are forged in uneven power relations, in structural inequalities, and in histories of marginalization. She aims "to render these conditions visible in order to enable the formation of critical agency, in the form of new modes of accountability for one's location."[17] It is the way Rowe's work helps us enact "structures of accountability . . . [in] who one talks to, and writes for and with" that is most useful for the SFD and our own relationships.[18] M. Jacqui Alexander, in her book *Pedagogies of Crossing*, calls this practice one of "how to disappear the will to segregation" through "appropriate ceremonies of reconciliation that are premised within a solidarity that is fundamentally intersubjective."[19]

The location of Seneca Falls matters, as do the identities and allegiances of its participants. What matters most, though, is the way that we build a politics of relation through the historic spaces and texts of that iconic suffrage meeting. What are our affective ties to this history? To each other in this endeavor of dialogue? What practices could the SFD engage in that would be reparative across our differences, and awaken common areas of commitment and engagement? Feminist rhetorical work like Rowe's—work that theorizes a way forward in coalition struggles and intersectional alliances—is particularly inspiring. So too are the stories and case studies of such attempts. Such stories need to accompany the many calls for intersectional rhetorical practice so we can understand what happens in flawed, fraught, caring lived attempts at a politics of relation. To contribute to this effort, in the following pages we reflect on two practices from the 2016 SFD that brought participants together to reconsider the "sacred text" of the 1848 suffrage meeting—the "Declarations of Sentiments." We also include a reflection on how, even with our best attempts at cross-racial and cross-generational dialogue, epistemic privilege can prevail.

ACTIVITIES FEATURING A "SACRED TEXT"

The "Declaration of Sentiments," authored by Elizabeth Cady Stanton, is the sacred text of the 1848 Women's Rights Convention. Literacy researcher Sylvia

Scribner argues that some texts are imbued with sacredness, as cultures fix values, "special virtues," core beliefs, and ideals not only in their key documents but also in the literate members who interact with and interpret those texts.[20] They do the cultural work of centering and decentering values and naturalize ideas as fixed and completed conversations instead of as available for dialogue or open questions. In the 2018 SFD we used the "Declaration of Sentiments" to create a conversation about feminist identity formation then and now. Knowing that unity can be a silencing tactic,[21] we experimented with this text in order to create a new, more inclusive awareness.

Such an approach is novel when we consider that the "Declaration of Sentiments" intended to unify the suffrage platform and identity. Its form is modeled on the Second Continental Congress's Declaration of Independence of 1776, with its template of repeated wrongs and usurpations and its chronicle of rights demanded. The "Declaration of Sentiments" intentionally reroutes the male-dominated rhetoric of the United States' origin story by calling its truths "self-evident," by claiming that "all men *and women* are created equal," and by asserting that among "certain inalienable rights" for women are "life, liberty, and the pursuit of happiness." In doing so, the "Declaration of Sentiments" self-consciously positioned itself both in the trajectory of US political texts and as a meaningful, foundational departure from these texts. Both the "Declaration of Sentiments" and the 1848 convention recognized the need for an activist community, expressed the desire for a common activist agenda, and appeared as retrospectively natural continuums of American ideology inevitably marching toward universal suffrage and an ongoing campaign for equal rights under the law.

Historically, the attempts at unification through the 1848 declaration failed early on. Tetrault observes that the "Declaration of Sentiments" did not circulate and gain momentum in suffrage meetings in the antebellum period, and at a suffrage convention a few years later, a proposal to resuscitate it was voted down.[22] It was not until an 1873 National Woman Suffrage Association Meeting that the declaration was revived, not by Stanton but by Susan B. Anthony, as a way to commemorate the 1848 convention and begin the work of memorializing and mythologizing that meeting as the origin of the women's suffrage movement.[23] Less a text that circulated in order to do work in suffrage, the declaration stands as a manifesto revived in an attempt to consolidate dispersed, multiplanked women's rights activity into the Seneca Falls myth.

Given this history of the document's circulation, a feature of each SFD is an invitation to critically engage with the "Declaration of Sentiments." We engage it as a *boundary object* that can mediate and structure a politics of relation. Étienne Wenger calls boundary objects crucial parts of learning environments, "artifacts . . . and other forms of reification around which communities of practice can organize interconnections."[24] In this case, strategic mythmaking is taking a sacred text and engaging it as a boundary object, a mediating force in relations, expertise, and motives. Wenger explains, "when a boundary object serves multiple constituencies, each has only partial control over the interpretation of the object. For instance, an author has jurisdiction over what is written, but readers have jurisdiction over what it comes to mean to them. Jurisdiction over various aspects of a boundary object is thus distributed among the constituencies involved, and using an artifact as a boundary object requires processes of coordination and translation between each form of partial jurisdiction."[25] If Stanton had jurisdiction in her 1848 document, jurisdiction now is purposefully made as an open question, one that can be productively explored to clarify values, beliefs, and feminist goals for the present time. Boundary objects as described by Wenger become what Rowe would call "power lines," conduits for seeing relations across difference, location, time, and identity; shared reflection in that moment can repair and remake relations.

During the first evening of the 2016 SFD, documentary filmmaker and media studies professor Leah Shafer invited all the participants into the Wesleyan Chapel for what became a kind of feeling experiment: to collectively recite the "Declaration of Sentiments" and understand the extent to which we can feel and speak its history as a collective in 2016. Close to a hundred of us were filmed reading lines like, "He has made her, if married, in the eye of the law, civilly dead," "he has denied her the facilities for obtaining a thorough education—all colleges being closed against her," and "having deprived her of this first right of a citizen, the elective franchise, thereby leaving her without representation in the halls of legislation, he has oppressed her on all sides."[26] The experience of attempting to unify the group's voice through the collective recitation raised the question: who is the "her" Stanton refers to in this document? In unstructured conversations after the filming, some participants revealed that they cried while reciting the declaration, experiencing an identification with the "her" and with a feeling of history that achieved—through personal risk and sacrifice—real, tangible legal, political, and social gains for women. In the plea for the "her" of the declaration, participants see and feel the bedrock liberal arguments for equality that women have benefitted from since their circulation.

But many others talked about experiencing a withholding—the catch and the ambivalence—when the "her" did not align with them. How does it feel, after all, in 2016, to read the line, "he has withheld from her rights which are given to the most ignorant and degraded men—both natives and foreigners"?[27] Much of the racially, religiously, class-, age-, and ability-diverse group felt distanced from or repulsed by these words that clearly see women as white, available for the subjectivity of citizen, with interests that are hostile to immigrants and those indentured or in bondage. Some of these lines further marginalize black women and those with whom white suffragettes could have partnered to raise all marginalized subjects into multiple enfranchisements. It is this persistent need to rank and order the routes to equality and franchise that this construction of "her" refuses to acknowledge. A few years after the 1848 convention, in her stump speeches across the country, Elizabeth Cady Stanton was unequivocal about suffrage priorities: "I say, no; I would not trust him [black men] with all my rights; degraded, oppressed himself, he would be . . . despotic." On immigrants and voting rights, Stanton argued that "[the] safety of the nation as well as the interests of women demand that we outweigh this incoming tide of ignorance, poverty and vice, with the virtue, wealth, and education of the women of the country."[28] The passage of the nineteenth amendment did not enfranchise all women, as many women of color fell under southern state discrimination practices that denied them access to civic voice.[29] "Over time," Hess observes, "these racial contours would harden into lasting institutions."[30]

Leah Shafer's act of filming a recitation of the "Declaration of Sentiments" in collective voice, and hearing and feeling the resistances, acts of complicity, and acts of transgression revealed our need not to make the SFD a "lasting institution" of liberal feminist assumptions. It is no wonder that, in the discussions after the recitation, some participants said they refused to recite altogether, folding their arms and staying silent. A recitation that seems to constrain our differences actually opened the possibility for deep awareness and even what Rowe calls "differential consciousness." She argues that a politics of relation must invite participants to develop not individual consciousness, a sense of a solitary self-seeking rights and justice, but practices that "frame consciousness itself as a collective process," as "functions of belonging."[31] New modes of empathy can emerge by not reifying the meanings of the declaration but by experiencing each other in the acts of recitation and reflection. Shafer's digital mediation of the recitation experience helped the "Declaration of Sentiments" become a boundary object where epistemic conflicts could be productively revealed and examined. It allowed us to "release hold" of its canonical and sacred status and move to, as Jessica Enoch argues, "interrogat[e] the dynamic relationships among rhetoric, gender, and history."[32]

Because the SFD was occurring two weeks before the 2016 presidential election, we experimented with a second boundary object: a "Declaration of Presidential Sentiments," a large, wall-sized, empty poster with pens attached where participants were invited to respond to Hillary Rodham Clinton's presidential campaign, her platform, and the historical significance of her nomination. In inviting responses, the SFD was not endorsing Clinton's campaign but was making space for participants to respond collectively to this campaign's historical significance while interjecting their voices in response to its political complexity. That is, we hoped to understand the degree to which Clinton's campaign reinvested

Seneca Falls as a popular imaginative touchstone while giving voice to some of the narratives that this "myth" has suppressed since its construction.

Throughout the two days of the SFD, participants would write on the giant poster as they moved from one activity to another, some writing directly to Clinton, some writing general critique and observations to the SFD participants. Our completed "Declaration of Presidential Sentiments" reflected the diversity of the group and offered no unified view. If the 1848 convention forced common ground, our poster board of comments about Clinton's candidacy captured differences about the election with no attempt to resolve them. Some participant statements reflected liberal feminist responses to Clinton's candidacy, stating, "my daughter says thank you," or quoting appreciatively from the original "Declaration of Sentiments," or demanding "Equal Pay for Women!" Some statements on the poster board reflected more intersectional feminist requests, demanding that Clinton "be conscious of race, class, and gender . . . in public policy" or that she remember that "Black Lives Matter, Palestinian Lives Matter, Impoverished Lives Matter, Incarcerated Lives Matter!" One participant quoted activist bell hooks: "Hillary is the embodiment of the white-supremacist, capitalist patriarchy." Another wrote, "I want a dyke for president!" rejecting norms that still structure the presidential political imaginary. Several "Bernie for President" comments were dispersed throughout the poster as well, redirecting the focus of the activity to keep progressive pressure on the Democratic Party. A final category of statements was persistently flip, even dismissive, as represented by the comment: "You go Chillary, knock back a beer for me." The responses in total extended the trajectory of liberal feminist goals enshrined in Seneca Falls, such as nationwide support for the Equal Rights Amendment (ERA) and the desire for our "daughters" to inherit a better world, even as they exposed resistance to this enshrinement by opposing white, nationalist, capitalist hegemony.

This outcome is productive in that the SFD's "Declaration of Presidential Sentiments" poster gives voice to divergent politics that resist consensus, revisiting some of what was erased in the 1848 declaration. However, the project also reflects the degree to which discord resists unification and the realization of a shared agenda, thereby risking irrelevance. The document's printed explanation states that conference organizers would mail the resulting comments to Clinton on Inauguration Day, and the inscriptions themselves address Clinton as if she were our future president. With Clinton's November loss, however, this mailing never occurred. The document includes multiple perspectives on how to use the power of the White House, but it does not bear out those perspectives, reflecting how claiming diversity as an organizational goal sometimes challenges that same organization's ability to articulate and/or realize other goals. As a boundary object more indicative of a participatory culture of play, nonhierarchy, and collaboration, as opposed to an antebellum podium culture of unity, hierarchy, and individual authorship, this iteration of the declaration became an important point of connection for our varied allegiances and desires. For now, the poster will be donated to the Seneca Falls town archives, and photos of it will be placed on the SFD website, as a document that captures the varied feelings of feminists in the central New York region on the eve of the election.

When we think about Tetrault's conclusion that the "Declaration of Sentiments" has silenced other manifestos, other histories, we look forward to centering other artifacts for relational and coalitional consciousness-raising in future SFD meetings.[33] Mohanty argues that feminist imagined communities must be organized less around similarity and more around struggles for social justice.[34] The 2020 SFD, for example, will ask participants to decenter the "Declaration of Sentiments" through weaving practices—digitally and in print. The declaration will be provided alongside many other manifestos—the Combahee River Collective's statement, the Say Her Name statement, the Black Lives Matter platform, and NoDAPL divestment toolkits and political speeches, to name a few. Making an archive of such missions and manifestos, we will invite participants to engage in what Tarez Samra Graban calls "epistemic reconstruction,"[35] using the design modalities of their choosing to create artifacts that give context, engage comparison, find absences, silences, overlaps and ideological fissures, unlikely collaborations, and activist ways forward. A design activity that weaves ideological threads of liberal feminism, like the 1848 declaration, with varied related and divergent decolonial, antiracist, feminist discourses, helps produce new, intentional documents that clarify needed action, maintain or juxtapose tensions, and raise awareness of repeating histories that no longer serve intersectional social justice goals.

ACTIVITIES FEATURING DIALOGUE

The final morning of the conference convenes all participants in a large dialogue focused on a theme with leaders on that topic present for opening remarks and conversation. The 2016 whole-group dialogue increased tensions rather than strategically negotiating them, revealing the difficulties of cross-generational, cross-racial dialogue about our shared political futures. With an eye to the 2016 presidential election, the Sunday dialogue featured four women active in politics, including Congresswoman Carolyn Maloney and Trudy Mason, vice chair of the New York State Democratic Committee, who served as the moderator. Each woman spoke of her challenges and successes through several decades of work in the political sphere, offering models for moving beyond self-doubt and for persevering in elected office despite powerful forces that keep women from entering politics in the first place.

Toward the end of the dialogue, a black student from a local college asked about "the place of women of color in the feminist political work" described by the panelists. Maloney responded by highlighting the importance of the ERA for all women. She argued that the legislation would not discriminate and would indeed, given the larger wage gap faced by black and Latina women, create more significant economic benefits for women of color than for white women. Mason followed this remark by referencing this country's first woman to run for the Democratic nomination for president, Congresswoman Shirley Chisholm, who she described as her "friend and mentor," and she reminded the participants that Chisholm said she identified being female as more of a "handicap" than being black.[36] Two problematic rhetorical moves happened in this exchange. Both could be understood through the concept of epistemic privilege, which Belinda A. Stillion Southard defines as knowledge acquired through oppression that offers a speaker a privileged space to speak.[37] Maloney, in her seventies and having represented New York's twelfth district for decades, reflected a liberal feminism that enshrined the vantage point of her own experience and an abiding faith in the ability of the law to make real social change. Her epistemic privilege came from what Stillion Southard would call "humiliation," a sense of unequal treatment that Maloney tried to remedy through legislation on issues ranging from moving the monument to Anthony, Stanton, and Sojourner Truth from the basement of the US Capitol to the Rotunda, to addressing the severe human trafficking problem in the downstate New York region.[38] As important as these approaches are, the younger participants of color were treated not as co-participants in dialogue—the space where the imagined community of feminists is made—but as subordinate, passive recipients of benefits bestowed by Maloney's generation. The place of young participants was to appreciate the ongoing efforts to advance this legislation, a stance that is patronizing rather than alliance-building. Further, in invoking Shirley Chisholm, Mason suggested that students of color abandon their questioning stance and be "like Chisholm," to see gender alliance as trumping racial identity and alliance. Invoking Chisholm reifies black responses to discussions of the ERA and misrepresents Chisholm's own complex responses to that legislation.

Stillion Southard's research on the contrasting, contentious intergenerational voting rights philosophies of Elizabeth Cady Stanton and her daughter Harriot Stanton Blatch helps us critically reflect on this SFD exchange.[39] Stillion Southard asks, after reading the letters that Blatch sent to her mother about the unique knowledge working-class and immigrant women bring to the political sphere, "What if a rhetor asserts one's epistemic privilege only to displace the epistemic privilege of another?"[40] Jacqueline Jones Royster, in her critique of feminist rhetorical history, might call this occurrence an example of the context of "deep disbelief" that functions to "short-circuit a more inclusive knowledge-making process and limit the impact of challenges, however large or small, to predominant interpretive frameworks" within feminism.[41] Epistemic privilege enacts, in the case described above, the "ideological recentering of whiteness";[42] it is a corrosive thread that weakens power lines across feminist difference.

Nevertheless, the student persisted. Trying to disrupt the "deep disbelief" dismissal she received, she introduced herself to Mason after the large dialogue ended, hoping for a fuller response to her question. Instead, she received what could be seen as another lecture. One SFD organizer felt compelled to intervene, rearticulating the student's concerns and asking for specifics. Mason turned her attention away from the student and to our conference organizer, suggesting that her style of addressing the student's question is part of her way of talking "as a Jew from New York," then turned the conversation again to her close friendship with the late Chisholm as evidence that she understands and is sympathetic toward the perspective of black women. Eventually the exchange ended, and the student's question went unanswered a second time. While the session called itself a dialogue, key, influential participants reinforced rather than productively engaged power differentials along lines of race, authority, and age without providing space for listening, dissent, inquiry, alternative histories and narratives, and disagreement. Mason attempted to naturalize her resistance to dialoguing with the student by finding common ground with the conference organizer as Jewish women from New York, further excluding the student and positioning her as an outsider. Christine Keating might call this practice "compensatory domination," a practice in which members of a group "consolidate, exacerbate, or enable forms of inter-group and intra-group hierarchies . . . in order to engender acquiescence to political or institutional authority."[43] In intervening on behalf of the student, our conference organizer was aware of exercising her white privilege, assuming that she could shield this student from further harm, and that the student's concerns would be taken more seriously if an older woman spoke them; in so doing, the organizer occupied the role of the supposed savior rather than an ally. She interrupted without asking, and by trying to speak for, she instead spoke over. Stillion Southard observes that "when a rhetor aims to recognize the epistemic privilege of others—that is, the ability of others to possess a unique knowledge of oppression—the rhetor's voice can take precedence, while the oppressed can be objectified as the topic of conversation."[44] Yet, where face-to-face dialogue ended, a digital dialogue took its place in the months after the SFD. It was actually on Facebook where reparative practices continued among five of the people present for that encounter. While Mason and the student were not part of the message exchange, several of the observers to the exchange were able to identify problems, offer critique, and clarify practices for future dialogues.

Dialogue is a kind of liberal, rational-critical hope, a hope that rational critical discourse can achieve consensus, can negotiate differences with enough back and forth.[45] Dialogue in this particular instance served to amplify difference and silence already marginalized voices. Although the 1848 convention was just that—firmly rooted in the power of dialogue to achieve consensus, revise needed documents, and draft petitions, news articles, resolutions, and minutes—it was also a place to learn through back and forth what the body actually believes, where thought boundaries take shape. Persisting through the limits of dialogue is challenging, and Stanton herself eventually strained against the mode. Decades after Seneca Falls, not only did Stanton find conventions and their reliance on dialogue too rehearsed and repetitive, the format struck her as old-fashioned. On the burgeoning postwar lecture circuit, Stanton could earn a living and develop her philosophical ideas and political arguments without hindrance. "So long as people will pay me $75 & 100 every night, to speak on my own," Stanton quipped, "there is no need of my talking in Convention."[46]

While the above exchange at the SFD whole-group dialogue highlights what can be problematic about dialogue as a place to enact a politics of relation, we want to be mindful of its pitfalls while trying to reinvigorate it through intersectional awareness. Liberal feminism is a rational, reform-based approach to equality.[47] There is much about liberal feminism that we are indebted to, as Maloney and Mason made clear; suffrage and women's right to divorce and own property are just a few tangible outcomes that we can attribute to early liberal movements. We are caught in the very structures and logics tied to liberal feminist equality measures such as voting rights, education and pay equity, and reproductive health access. Liberal feminists are in many ways rule mongers—glued to patriarchal codes where women's civic entitlements are measured against standards of men. In talking with the student after the second attempt at dialogue, we were reminded that "feminism is a formation continually in process. Its production as an inclusive space is contingent upon the imaginary of those involved in the struggles under its name. When feminists become blocked around issues of power, it is in large part a question of a blocking of the feminist imaginary— perhaps . . . being too invested in hegemonic forms of power, or a lack of literacy in the realms of the heart."[48] Digital spaces for reflection and critique during and after the SFD are creating better structure for the dialogues we engage in and may help mitigate the kinds of gatekeeping some feminists remain invested in while keeping participants listening, engaging, and working in collaboration. Creating space to reflect on what happened during dialogue, and clarifying the purposes and intended outcomes are the metacognitive accompaniments from which dialogue benefits.

There are moments in feminist history when we need to engage origins and their myths, however flawed, and we can use them to create the feminist connections we need for the present time. We live in Rochester, New York, and we were among the over ten thousand people who converged on Mount Hope Cemetery to visit Susan B. Anthony's grave in the twenty-four hours surrounding the

2016 presidential election. It was clear then that people needed to use this figure and her space to make feminist connections. At the same time, on Twitter,
as news of people flocking to Anthony's grave circulated, feminists engaged in a
digital expansion of this memorializing, helping people find the graves of Ida B.
Wells in Chicago, Illinois, of Sojourner Truth in Battle Creek, Michigan, and
of Anna Julia Cooper in Raleigh, North Carolina. As a single suffrage origin
point in Rochester became a web of memorial suffrage locations through Twitter, feminists promoted the diversity and scope of voting rights history. Those
tweets and retweets made feminist connections across differences around Election Day; they did not denigrate Anthony or Stanton but instead determinedly
decentered them and Seneca Falls and expanded locations for feminist commemo-
ration and voting rights activism. These digital strategies go hand in hand with
and embolden the site-based work of the Seneca Falls Dialogues: complicating
history, creating reparative spaces, and forging alliances that could not happen
in one era but can be actualized now, in all their productive tension.

Anthony and Stanton's version of Seneca Falls in 1848 remains a powerful
narrative that contemporary activists continue to employ even as it sidelines
other narratives that could have emerged in its place. If Frederick Douglass, Ida B.
Wells, or even Lucretia Mott had emerged as canonized storytellers of women's
rights instead of Stanton or Anthony, the origin story of American feminism
would likely have included a fiercer stance against racism, a more ardent effort
toward black suffrage, a broader reach toward racial inclusivity. As Sally Roesch
Wagner has noted, if Indigenous activists were engaged as allies, and if suffragist arguments such as those from Matilda Joslyn Gage had taken hold, the story
of American feminism might have rooted itself more locally than nationally, or
might have emphasized the democratic, decolonial influences of the Iroquois
Confederacy on suffrage.[49] The ongoing challenge for the SFD, therefore, is to
employ the story of Seneca Falls without once again compromising those other
priorities and other histories, to understand the value of unification while advocating contemporary, intersectional feminist voices all attempting to advance
their own individual and sometimes conflicting agendas. Combined, the geographic Seneca Falls and the digital spaces generated at and after the Seneca Falls
Dialogues make this work possible; our strategic mythmaking both draws on the
materiality of place and interrogates and transforms the epistemic privilege of
that place, valuing the interstitial spaces that contemporary, intersectional feminist connections require.

Strategic mythmaking, then, acknowledges the myth of Seneca Falls and its
symbolic status as enduring and effective feminist activism. But it does so in order to sustain feminist regional meetings that examine, revise, and remake those
power lines in light of injustices and exigencies now. Normalizing discourses and

exclusionary practices exist beside our aspirational, relational practices, and it is our ability to identify, acknowledge, and adjust that will move us forward. Calling attention to the tension between *location*—an uncritical space of veneration—and *relation* allows collaboration and consensus to emerge. Creating structures of accountability and habits of multiple awareness—in other words, to be part of a practice while simultaneously reflecting on it and making adjustments for right action—is the work of feminist connections.

Notes

1. Amanda Hess, "How a Fractious Women's Movement Came to Lead the Left," *New York Times*, February 7, 2017, https://www.nytimes.com.

2. Lisa Tetrault, *The Myth of Seneca Falls: Memory and the Women's Suffrage Movement, 1848–1898* (Chapel Hill: University of North Carolina Press, 2014), 8.

3. Tetrault, 182.

4. Tetrault, 2.

5. Hess, "How a Fractious."

6. Raka Ray, "To My White Friends Demonstrating Today," digital image, meme, January 17, 2017, https://me.me.

7. Aimee Carrillo Rowe, *Power Lines: On the Subject of Feminist Alliances* (Durham, NC: Duke University Press, 2008), 15.

8. Rowe, 73.

9. Carly S. Woods, "(Im)Mobile Metaphors: Toward an Intersectional Rhetorical History," in *Standing in the Intersection: Feminist Voices, Feminist Practices in Communication Studies*, ed. Karma R. Chávez, Cindy L. Griffin, and Marsha Houston (Albany: State University of New York Press, 2012), 91.

10. Woods, 9; and Cindy L. Griffin and Karma R. Chávez, introduction to Chávez, Griffin, and Houston, *Standing in the Intersection*, 1–31. See also: Cherríe Moraga and Gloria Anzaldúa, eds., *This Bridge Called My Back: Writings by Radical Women of Color*, 2nd ed. (New York: Kitchen Table/Women of Color Press, 1983); Gloria Anzaldúa and AnaLouise Keating, eds., *This Bridge We Call Home: Radical Visions for Transformation* (New York: Routledge, 2002); Chandra Talpade Mohanty, *Feminism without Borders: Decolonizing Theory, Practicing Solidarity* (Durham, NC: Duke University Press, 2003); and Rowe, *Power Lines*.

11. Aimee Carrillo Rowe, "Be Longing: Toward a Feminist Politics of Relation," *NWSA Journal* 17, no. 2 (2005): 18.

12. Rowe, 18.

13. Griffin and Chávez, introduction, 3–4.

14. Rowe, "Be Longing," 16.

15. Rowe, *Power Lines*, 27.

16. Rowe, "Be Longing," 17.

17. Rowe, 18.

18. Rowe, 24.

19. M. Jacqui Alexander, *Pedagogies of Crossing: Meditations on Feminism, Sexual Politics, Memory, and the Sacred* (Durham, NC: Duke University Press, 2005), 18.

20. Sylvia Scribner, "Literacy in Three Metaphors," *American Journal of Education* 93, no. 1 (1984): 20.

21. Rowan Grigsby, "So You Think You Know a Thing: Feministing 201," *CrossKnit* (blog), January 24, 2017, https://crossknit.wordpress.com.

22. Tetrault, *The Myth of Seneca Falls*, 16.

23. Tetrault, 70–71.

24. Étienne Wenger, *Communities of Practice: Learning, Meaning and Identity* (Cambridge: Cambridge University Press, 1999), 105.

25. Wenger, 108.

26. Elizabeth Cady Stanton, "Declaration of Sentiments" (speech, Seneca Falls Woman's Rights Convention, Seneca Falls, NY, July 19, 1848).

27. Cady Stanton, Declaration.

28. Tetrault, *The Myth of Seneca Falls*, 19.

29. Tetrault, 192–93.

30. Hess, "How a Fractious."

31. Rowe, *Power Lines*, 43.

32. Jessica Enoch, "Releasing Hold: Feminist Historiography without the Tradition," in *Theorizing Histories of Rhetoric*, ed. Michelle Ballif (Carbondale: Southern Illinois University Press, 2013), 60.

33. Cricket Keating, "Building a Coalitional Consciousness," *NWSA Journal* 17, no. 2 (2005): 85–103.

34. Discussed in Keating.

35. Tarez Samra Graban and Patricia Sullivan. "Digital and Dustfree: A Conversation on the Possibilities of Digital-Only Searching for Third-Wave Historical Recovery." *Peitho* 13, no. 2 (2011): 2.

36. Shirley Chisholm, *Unbought and Unbossed* (Washington, DC: Take Root Media, 2009), 20.

37. Belinda A. Stillion Southard, "A Rhetoric of Epistemic Privilege: Elizabeth Cady Stanton, Harriot Stanton Blatch, and the Educated Vote," *Advances in the History of Rhetoric* 17, no. 2 (2014): 158.

38. Stillion Southard, 159.

39. Stillion Southard, 157–78.

40. Stillion Southard, 159.

41. Jaqueline Jones Royster, *Traces of a Stream: Literacy and Social Change among African American Women* (Pittsburgh, PA: University of Pittsburgh Press, 2000), 254.

42. Kim Marie Vaz and Gary L. Lemons. "'If I Call You, Will You Come?' From Public Lectures to Testament for Feminist Solidarity," in *Feminist Solidarity at the Crossroads: Intersectional Women's Studies for Transracial Alliance*, ed. Kim Marie Vaz and Gary L. Lemons (New York: Routledge, 2012), 3.

43. Qtd. in Vaz and Lemon, 14.

44. Stillion Southard, "A Rhetoric of Epistemic Privilege," 173–74.

45. Joan B. Landes, "The Public and Private Sphere: A Feminist Reconsideration," in *Feminism: The Public and the Private*, ed. Joan B. Landes (New York: Oxford University Press, 1998), 142.

46. Qtd. in Tetrault, *The Myth of Seneca Falls*, 53.

47. Rosemarie Tong and Tina Fernandes Botts, *Feminist Thought: A More Comprehensive Introduction*, 5th ed. (New York: Westview Press, 2018), 11–13.

48. Rowe, *Power Lines*, 43.

49. Sally Roesch Wagner, "The Iroquois Influence on Women's Rights," in *Indian Roots of American Democracy*, ed. Jose Barreiro (Ithaca, NY: Akwe Kon Press, 1992), 115–34.

2

Epideictic Rhetoric and Emergent Media

From CAM *to BLM*

TARA PROPPER

THE NIGHT OF JULY 13, 2013, Alicia Garza wrote a Facebook post in response to the acquittal of George Zimmerman for the shooting death of seventeen-year-old Trayvon Martin in Sanford, Florida. Garza, who was working as a special projects director for the National Domestic Workers Alliance in Oakland, California, described the post in an interview for the *New Yorker* as a "love letter to Black people."[1] Affirming her community's frustration with "how little black lives matter" in public culture, Garza demanded her readers "stop giving up on black lives," reiterating in her final comments that "our lives matter."[2] Garza's friend Patrisse Cullors, a teacher at Otis College of Art and Design in the Public Practice program whom Garza met at a conference for activists in 2003, shared the message, adding the hashtag #BlackLivesMatter. The post garnered immediate currency on social media, sparking the attention of Opal Tometi, the executive director of the Black Alliance for Just Immigration in New York City, who volunteered her own expertise in creating a more cohesive digital platform.

While all three women are considered cofounders of the Black Lives Matter (BLM) movement—a movement that now includes a network of more than thirty local chapters mobilized against police brutality and unfair sentencing laws, and emboldened by increased reporting on cases of state violence against marginalized and minoritized populations (Michael Brown, Eric Garner, Freddie Gray, Tamir Rice, Walter Scott, Sandra Bland, Philando Castile, and Alton Sterling)—they champion a horizontal ethic of organizing, which advocates a chapter structure focused on local contexts and events. Garza asserts that "the model of the black preacher leading people to the promised land isn't working" and draws from the legacy of female black civil rights activists such as Ella Baker, who emphasized community outreach and local collective organizing.[3] Crediting social media as a principal organizing tool for reporting on local events and mobilizing grassroots campaigns, Garza explains that "technology has really changed

the game in terms of how people participate and what they decide to participate in."[4] Cullors also emphasizes new media as instrumental in making visible
the violence perpetuated against marginalized and minoritized communities, as
she notes that "on a daily basis, every moment, black folks are being bombarded
with images of our death. And after a while it does something to your psyche. . . .
It forces black folks to really deal with the reality of how oftentimes painful it
is to say out loud, 'we might die.'"[5] Although such imagery confirms a legacy of
racism and systemic oppression, it can serve as a powerful stimulus for activism.
That is, such imagery operates as a visual testament of racial violence and public
memorialization of the lives lost as a consequence of racist ideology. As Tometi
suggests, public memorialization—or the act of making publicly visible those
who have been rendered invisible—can alter how we value and legislate on behalf of marginalized and minoritized communities. Explaining why she initially
became involved with the project, Tometi recalls, "I felt a sense of urgency about
the next steps we could take together to change the story."[6]

What I find interesting about Garza's, Cullors's, and Tometi's sentiments is
that they reveal a unique interrelation between emergent forms of media, social
mobilization, and public memorialization. The very phrase "Black Live Matters"
began as a media-specific form of virtual representation (i.e., a Twitter hashtag), which later evolved into an activist movement that shed light on the violence black bodies face in public spaces while simultaneously memorializing victims whose stories have gone unannounced. Despite the digital nature of BLM's
creation, though, I argue that Garza's, Cullors's, and Tometi's activism reflects a
much longer history of black women's use of emergent media and public memorialization as a means of interrogating *and* participating in the public spaces, resources, or spheres of representation that were historically denied to black citizens. More specifically, I demonstrate how modern, digitally focused activist
projects resonate with the rhetorical practices and discursive features of turn-
of-the-century black feminist periodicals, which sought to reaffirm the role that
black women have played as active participants within the public sphere and
civic life. Similar to Jill Swiencicki, Maria Brandt, Barbara LeSavoy, and Deborah
Uman's investigation in this collection—which explores how feminist historians
can promote intersectional dialogue that brings to light diverse and possibly
conflicting histories—this chapter demonstrates how emergent media (i.e., periodical presses and digital platforms, respectively) can provide the foundation
for rethinking what constitutes "the public" by narrating the untold stories of
those who have been ostracized from this arena.

In order to achieve this goal, this chapter first examines Famous Women of
the Negro Race, a syndicated column written and edited by Pauline Hopkins
for the *Colored American Magazine* (*CAM*) from 1901 to 1904 (figure 2.1). I
demonstrate how turn-of-the-century periodicals used the unique affordances

FIGURE 2.1. The cover of the July 1902 *Colored American Magazine.*
Digital Colored American Magazine, http://coloredamerican.org/.

of newly established printing technologies—which at the time included more
visually elaborate layouts inspired by halftone printing practices—to undertake
a process of historical recovery that allowed marginalized communities to position themselves within a commonly shared public sphere. In doing so, I highlight how these periodicals exhibited a particular version of epideictic rhetoric
insofar as they undertook a community-building process that sought to reclaim
the public sphere for marginalized and minoritized groups whose legacies were
previously unannounced or silenced. Furthermore, these periodicals sought to
teach their readership how to speculate new avenues for civic participation based

on these recovered histories. Put differently, these periodicals memorialized the unspoken legacy of influential black women as a means of instructing a diverse readership to reenvision black women's participation in the public sphere and spur activist mobilization for future progress.

The next section of this chapter examines the Say Her Name movement, which is an ongoing peer-sourced webpage running on the BLM website that commemorates black women who have been killed by racial violence.[7] I argue that the Say Her Name project builds on many of the same rhetorical features illustrated in *CAM* and, by extension, uses the act of public memorialization as a means of interrogating the discriminatory practices that attempt to regulate minority bodies in public spaces while also spurring social mobilization in response to this discrimination. However, locating commonalities between *CAM* and Say Her Name does not mean that these two organizations are participating in the exact same forms of social activism, nor are they responding to the exact same historical circumstances. Rather, finding connections between *CAM* and Say Her Name underscores how activist movements have used the advantages and unique features of emergent media technologies to reclaim the public sphere for black women and people of color, respectively, via the act of public memorialization. This act of reclamation, in turn, can help clarify how emergent media shapes the rhetorical practices activist groups use to participate in dynamic forms of community building while reaffirming the oft-unspoken heritage of black women's contributions to social progress.

Ultimately, the goal of this examination is to chart how marginalized and minoritized writers have taken advantage of emergent media platforms to diagnose hierarchies of power within the public sphere as well as recuperate the "lost" or "erased" histories of traditionally silenced communities within these power arrangements. I highlight how epideictic rhetoric can be a useful framework for better understanding the ways in which media-based activism undertakes the work of questioning who does (and does not) count as legitimate members of the public. However, I would like to first discuss how contemporary interpretations of epideictic rhetoric resonate with the theme of revisionary rhetoric. Making connections between epideictic and revisionary rhetoric not only highlights the community-building aspects of these discursive practices, it also demonstrates how we can apply these practices to print and online media.

EPIDEICTIC RHETORIC, REVISIONARY PRACTICES, AND FEMINIST MEDIA ACTIVISM

Drawing on the work of Dale L. Sullivan, Henrietta Rix Wood explains that epideictic rhetoric is "determined by a constellation of purposes, including education, preservation, and celebration."[8] These functions serve to identify a fundamental value system that connects members of a community. Therefore, the chief purpose of epideictic rhetoric is community action and organization. Richard Graff and Wendy Winn further reaffirm these community-building features, defining epideictic rhetoric as "argumentation that seeks to reaffirm agreements on values, its chief outcomes being the strengthening of community bonds, and by extension, the laying of grounds for future appeals to action."[9] Graff and Winn suggest that community action requires first articulating the shared community values presupposing and inspiring such actions. Thus, "epideictic serves an educational function in the sense that its practice occasions the enacted display and observation of virtue."[10] Moreover, such displays of value work to forge community affiliation and identity, renewing the humanity of community members. As John C. Adams writes, "The excellence exhibited in the humanity of those praised not only is revealed for acknowledgement, but it becomes a common point of identification, which, at minimum, enables recognition that one of 'us' exemplifies virtue. The recognition may induce pride in one's community and inspire auditors with a sense of their potential to also act virtuously."[11] In this formulation, the work of epideictic rhetoric is twofold, as it not only identifies and acknowledges the central value system connecting members of a community but also reveals how such a value system can inform future community actions and identification. More specifically, epideictic is instructive insofar as it "displays" values that unite members of a community and presents arguments about how these values might operate in future contexts.

Epideictic rhetoric's emphasis on community building and appeal to future possibilities or applications of communal value systems can function as a productive complement to revisionary rhetoric's emphasis on acknowledging communities who have been historically silenced or overlooked. In *Revisionary Rhetoric, Feminist Pedagogy, and Multigenre Texts*, Julie Jung suggests revisionary rhetoric is "committed to listening to those voices which are too easily silenced and often reside on the margins/borders. Furthermore, it is a rhetoric concerned with the hard work of (re)reading in order to hear those perspectives that are easily ignored on first reading."[12] In this sense, revisionary rhetoric can help us push back on canonized versions of history that attempt to obfuscate, victimize, or criminalize marginalized and minoritized experiences. The "hard work of (re)reading" is not a linear, one-step process, though, seeing as revisionary rhetoric "is a rhetoric that demands both to be heard and responded to."[13] In identifying the imperative to both be heard and respond, Jung touches on the pedagogical underpinnings of revisionary rhetoric and, by extension, the common foundation that revisionary practices share with epideictic rhetoric. On the one hand, revisionary rhetoric teaches us how to listen for the erased histories of marginalized communities and respond to these unspoken stories. On the other hand, epideictic rhetoric teaches us how to create new communal affiliations and speculate how the values inherent to these communities can function in future scenarios. When viewed together, revisionary and epideictic rhetoric can grant the tools for teaching us how to recover the unspoken or silenced history of marginalized communities, how to derive new methods of community building in response to these newly recovered histories, and how to speculate the ways in which the values inherent to these newly recovered histories can function in future scenarios. Hence, viewing revisionary and epideictic rhetoric in conjunction with one another vis-à-vis their shared pedagogical dimensions can offer a framework for better understanding how we can not only memorialize the erased histories of marginalized communities but also, in reclaiming these erased histories, find new ways of deriving communal affiliations in the future.

While coupling the pedagogical elements of both revisionary and epideictic rhetoric can help us establish a framework for better understanding the impact of reclaiming erased histories in order to speculate new communal affiliations, I also want to be sensitive to the nature of the primary texts that are examined here. That is to say, the following sections of this analysis will demonstrate how epideictic rhetoric (which has traditionally been considered an oratorical genre) operates in print-based activist media that uses public memorialization as a means of questioning the hegemonic regulation of the public sphere and public history. Consequently, I briefly review how scholars have discussed the public nature of activist media and how activist media can allow marginalized or minoritized communities to access, reconstruct, and intervene in public political life and discourse. As Jacqueline Jones Royster explains in *Traces of a Stream*, activist media "has served as a constant forum for the voices of African Americans to be heard. They have constituted a counterforce to the more dominant 'official' voices that define the public agenda in a manner that usually excluded African American interests."[14] The correlation these media outlets forged between space and representational discourses has maintained particular currency within feminist circles throughout the twentieth century, as modern feminisms have aimed to expand how marginalized and minoritized identities acquire—*and have historically acquired*—legibility within and across personal, professional, and public landscapes. In "Constructing Difference in Public Spaces," Susan Ruddick refines the relationship between public space and social identity, arguing that "public spaces can disturb our conventional hierarchical notions of scale," specifically geographic scale, "becoming at once local and national spaces for the construction, mediation, and regulation of social identities."[15] Ruddick posits that media is a "critical tool in instructing the public" how to imagine and evaluate these identities, including intersections among race, class, and gender categories. Ruddick's analysis places into focus the instructive quality of public writing and media activism, particularly with regard to marginalized and minoritized identity construction and racial resignification.

In short, epideictic rhetoric, revisionary practices, and activist media all share a common interest in instructing a readership how to reenvision new forms of communal affiliations from both a historical and a future-looking perspective *and* reenvision the spaces said communities have (or will) traverse. Underscoring these shared pedagogical dimensions is not meant to over-simplify the similarities between these three interpretive frameworks. Instead, my goal is to highlight how the community-building features of these frameworks are inseparable from the pedagogical goal of teaching a readership how to think differently in response to hearing the unspoken histories of silenced communities *and* how to act differently as we move toward a still-unrealized future where these silenced communities finally have a voice. In other words, to ignore the pedagogical features of epideictic rhetoric, revisionary practices, and activist media is to run the risk of undercutting how these ideas can coalesce in such a way that initiates real-world mobilization. With these ideas in mind, I turn to *CAM* and, eventually, the Say Her Name project in order to demonstrate how both of these outlets instruct readers to reimagine black women's historical role in public life.

VISUALIZING BLACK WOMEN'S CONTRIBUTIONS IN *CAM*'S FAMOUS WOMEN

In the March 1901 issue of the *Colored American Magazine*, Pauline Hopkins chronicled the life of Edwin Garrison Walker as part of her Famous Men of the Negro Race series. As a preface to her article, Hopkins included a selection from Tennyson's "Ode on the Death of the Duke of Wellington." The final lines of that selection read: "He is gone who seemed so great / Gone; but nothing can bereave him / of the force he made his own. / ... / And he wears a truer crown than any can weave him."[16] Although the project of recovery, of "weaving crowns" to honor the dead, cannot fully grasp or articulate the "force" of the life lived, Hopkins included Tennyson's poem to argue that it, nevertheless, was the necessary work of those dedicated to the "education and advancement of ages yet unborn, as well as the benefit of the present generation."[17] Endeavoring to make publicly visible to the ages yet unborn and present generation the invisible history of black experience in America, Hopkins provided her readers with not only a historical literacy missing from mainstream media outlets but also a visual context for complicating dominant portrayals of black identity (as many of her biographical sketches included illustrations and/or photographs of her featured men and women). Aiming to make black subjectivity intelligible within mainstream media, Hopkins offered a new interpretive frame for reading and recognizing black identity within dominant discursive and visual regimes.

While the Famous Men of the Negro Race and Famous Women of the Negro Race columns both adjusted the lens through which to acknowledge public actors and their contributions to society, Hopkins's treatment of black women offered a more collective portrait of public subjects, relying less on individual contributions to race history (as was typical for her Famous Men sketches). In an advertisement for the twelve-part Famous Women series, black women are grouped into eleven categories: abolitionists, educators, vocalists, instrumentalists, elocutionists, artists, medical practitioners, legal practitioners, businesswomen, literary workers, and club women. The advertisement notes that the "position occupied by the negro woman in this country is peculiar; she is constantly called upon to combat not only caste, but disbelief, among the whites, in her morality, and in her possession of any of the gentler virtues of womanhood."[18] Arguing that there was "no denying the overwhelming social and civil influence of women," the advertisement stresses that such women were central to the progress of the race. "Without these women, the education of the men and the wonderful changes wrought by emancipation would go for nothing."[19] Accordingly, black women's work was exemplary insofar as it contributed to the public good through public education and outreach.

The first installment of Famous Women chronicled "Phenomenal Vocalists," including sketches of Elizabeth Taylor Greenfield (1824–76), Madame Annie Pauline Pidnell (1834–1901), and Anna Madah (1855–1929) and Emma Louise (1857–1901), also known as the Hyers Sisters. Noting that "negro song... [was] the only original music of America," Hopkins positioned each woman's story within the larger canon of musical art and tradition.[20] Referencing early Egyptian, Grecian, and Roman musical traditions, Hopkins regarded the unacknowledged black artists who "labored in the rice swamps of the South" as the forebears of the American musical canon. Hopkins suggested that black music was distinguished by its closeness to land and nature. Accordingly, such proximity to land and landed cultures translated into a closeness to the history of such lands. "The genius of music, supposed to be the gift of only the most refined and intellectual of the human family, sprang into active life among the lowly tillers of the soil and laborers in the rice swamps of the South. The distinguishing feature of Negro song is its pathos and trueness to nature. It is the only original music of America, and since emancipation has become a part of the classical music of the century."[21] As evinced in Hopkins's emphasis on land and landed history in this profile, as well as in her other biographies, there is a noticeable sensitivity to the physical places staging the accomplishments and activism of black women. Presenting Lawrence W. Rosenfield's views on epideictic, Margaret LaWare writes, "epideictic brings together a community to witness the present, illuminating the community's inherent reality—its humanity and its relationship to a particular place, making visible the previously invisible ... [and] replacing the urgency for action with an urgency for recognition."[22] Hopkins's epideictic rhetoric is marked by its negotiation with physical places and locations. Underscoring both the spatial and temporal connections elucidating black presence in the public sphere, Hopkins's profiles offer a verbal and visual mapping of women's collective struggles to garner recognition in this sphere of influence. It is therefore each woman's negotiation with place and location, and particularly her capacity to garner public visibility within these physical and virtual environs, that Hopkins deems praiseworthy.

In addition to focusing on women's place in the public sphere, Hopkins's biographies highlighted the interrelation of racism and sexism. For example, in the second installment of Famous Women, entitled "Some Literary Workers," Hopkins profiled Phillis Wheatley, Francis Grimke, and Ida B. Wells. Criticizing the "gag law" imposed on women who do not remain "silent," namely club workers and writers, Hopkins notes, "We know that it is not 'popular' for a woman to speak or write in plain terms against political brutalities, that a woman should confine her efforts to woman's work in the home and church."[23] Hopkins then chronicles the stories of women who have not subscribed to these "popular" precepts, granting Ida B. Wells the most space in her column. Referencing Wells's cross-Atlantic antilynching speaking tour, Hopkins describes Wells as an "acknowledged power upon the public platform."[24] Hopkins focuses her analysis on Wells's reception as a public speaker. "Miss Ida B. Wells, an American colored lady from Tennessee, pleaded the cause of her race on Tuesday evening last. After lecturing successfully in Edinburgh and Glasgow, she passed onto the chief English provincial towns, and then to London. . . . Nothing more harrowing has been for years related from a Glasgow platform than the narrative she gave of the cruelties and outrages perpetrated upon her people."[25]

Hopkins treats the physical distance Wells has traveled from her humble beginnings in Memphis as a credit to her success as a public speaker. However, as Hopkins emphasizes, the distances Wells has traveled from her hometown do not minimize her connection to such spaces. Rather, Wells's public works have broadcasted the racial discrimination characterizing such places. In telling *her* story, Wells not only reinterprets these spaces of the past but also (through her activism) intervenes in how such spaces are managed and governed.

Momentarily interrupting Hopkins's sketches are portraits of black community activists, including teachers, artists, politicians, and librarians. For example, the July 1902 installment of Famous Women—"Educators"—features portrait images of Joan Imogen Howard and her mother, Joan L. T. Howard (figures 2.2 and 2.3). Focusing on Joan Imogen Howard's accreditation from New York University (Howard received a "Masters in Pedagogy") and her experiences teaching grammar in New York schools, the article emphasizes the importance of familial support. The portrait images of both women appear in the middle of Hopkins's copy—a common design feature distinguishing many of Hopkins's columns. In other words, while individual pages of *CAM* are dedicated to long-form articles and reviews, portraits of black women are positioned throughout the magazine. This collage-like or quilted quality is especially prevalent in the Famous Women series, providing a visual testament to black public lives and experiences.

FIGURE 2.2. Joan Imogen Howard, pictured in Pauline Hopkins's column Famous Women of the Negro Race in the July 1902 issue of *Colored American Magazine*. Digital Colored American Magazine, http://coloredamerican.org/.

By accessing and revising the public record to account for black women's histories and biographies, the pages of *CAM*, and particularly Pauline Hopkins's Famous Women of the Negro Race column, made black women's experiences of concern to everyone—a gesture that not only treated black women's issues as part of public concern but also revised who "everyone" implied when referring to members of the public and affirmed black women's role as participants in civic life. Reading Hopkins's Famous Women column as epideictic discourse affords a

oping along their own lines. Then, when they have fought their fight and won their way up, where they can stand on an equal footing with us, let us consider their admission."

In the discussion of the color question, Miss Jane Addams (Hull House, Chicago) aroused the most interest by declaring herself a partisan of colored clubs and holding the opinion that "no race can uphold a race integrity apart from other races, and that it lies with the stronger people to stand with the weaker." The final call for the previous question carried the amendment by an overwhelming vote.

The power of organization among women is a sociological study. Women were narrow mentally; it is supposed that they have been broadened by their educational opportunities and their growing influence which has, hitherto, commanded the respect of the world. We had hoped that as a race, we should receive the fair treatment, the sympathy, the loyalty, that their reputation guaranteed, but the Biennial at Los Angeles has given us a rude awakening.

"They find their fellows guilty of a skin
  Not colored like their own, and having power
To enforce the wrong, for such a worthy cause
Doom and devote them as their lawful prey."

At the World's Congress of Representative Women from all Lands, in 1892-3, under the superintendance of such women as Mrs. Potter Palmer, Mrs. Charles Henrotin, Mrs. May Wright Sewall, Mrs. Avery, Miss Frances E. Willard, and others, such notable women of color as Frances Ellen Harper, Fanny Jackson-Coppin, Annie J. Cooper, Fanny Barrier Williams, and Hallie Q. Brown, delivered addresses which drew the eyes of the entire world upon them and their race.

In connection with the same great Exposition, Miss Imogen Howard, as we have stated in the above sketch, was signally honored by being appointed a member of the Board of Women Managers of the State of New York, for the Columbian Exposition, the only Negro so honored by any other State. Miss Howard's peculiar fitness for the position to which she was called, added additional lustre to her fame, and her race stepped up a rung on Ambition's ladder.

In Massachusetts, we may mention that, added to her fame as a teacher and lecturer, Miss Maria L. Baldwin has for years been a member of the Cantabrigia Club of Cambridge, than which no wealthier, no more highly cultured, no club of wider fame exists in the entire country. No token of esteem has been too high for this club of noble-minded women to bestow on their admired colored member.

In connection with the famous Boston Political class under its president, the great parliamentarian, Mrs. Harriet P. Shattuck, we may mention the fact that Mrs. Mary J. Buchanan, a beautiful and cultured woman of color, has

JOAN L. T. HOWARD
(Mother)   *See page 206.*

FIGURE 2.3. Joan L. T. Howard, pictured in Pauline Hopkins's column Famous Women of the Negro Race in the July 1902 issue of *Colored American Magazine*. Digital Colored American Magazine, http://coloredamerican.org/.

more expansive view of how marginalized and minoritized communities have renegotiated this form of public speech. While Hopkins's biographies do not advocate a return to preestablished community values and goals—which is how epideictic rhetoric has been treated in classical rhetorical study—they do serve to renew a sense of community among marginalized bodies, not only making black women's stories legible to a wider public sphere but also recovering the embodied experiences of black women in such a way that instantiated shared community values, which, in turn, emphasized community organization and local activism. Hopkins's column is far from the Aristotelian view of epideictic as overly sentimental ceremonial speech, and is instead concerned with "refounding and renewing a sense of community by invoking the values and virtues underwriting the community."[26] Ultimately, Hopkins's histories serve to reimagine the public record not as a coherent and homogeneous chronology but, rather, as a stratified and deeply contested genealogy that encompasses the diverging experiences of marginalized and minoritized communities. Consequently, Hopkins's column challenged and unsettled established historical conventions—conventions that eroded or erased the lived experiences of black women—while highlighting community development at a local level.

PUBLIC MEMORIALIZATION AND MOURNING IN CONTEMPORARY MEDIA

Pauline Hopkins's Famous Women series publicized the lives, biographies, and histories of black women and, in doing so, undertook a particular form of public memorialization that could be used to teach readers about the role of black women in a commonly shared public history. In this section, I explore how the Say Her Name project engages in a similar type of public memorialization. However, I do not want to simply point out commonalities between Hopkins's articles and the activist undertakings of Say Her Name. Rather, I want to demonstrate how the Say Her Name project builds on the same rhetorical practices deployed in *CAM* while simultaneously adapting these practices to the unique structural features of contemporary digital media platforms. Whereas Hopkins's articles used individual biographies as a way to reimagine black women's role in public history and the public sphere, the Say Her Name project engages in crowd-sourced and multimodal forms of archiving black women's experiences in the public realm as a means of spurring social activism. In order to further explore how, exactly, the Say Her Name project extends and evolves the epideictic features and community-building goals exhibited throughout *CAM*, I first examine how the BLM movement and website use public memorialization as a means of social mobilization.

Much of the copy found on the BLM website, which relies on user content and participation, documents the consequences of racist ideology and the psychic cost associated with the systemic devaluing of black life in mainstream culture. The site's mission statement explains that "#BlackLivesMatter is an online forum intended to build connections between Black people and our allies to fight anti-Black racism, to spark dialogue among Black people, and to facilitate the types of connections necessary to encourage social action and engagement."[27] Employing epideictic rhetoric to assign value to historically devalued and dehumanized lives, bodies, and communities, the website memorializes vic-

FIGURE 2.4. Say Her Name splash page. Black Lives Matter Global Network, http://sayhername.blacklivesmatter.com/.

tims of systemic racism through the recirculation of stories and imagery documenting the violence perpetrated against black bodies, exposing the racial hierarchies implicit in the inhabitation of public space. The virtual public square through which BLM activists organize and mobilize offers an intersectional and nonhierarchic access point for reinventing public inhabitation and representation (a project similarly taken up by the editors of *CAM* a century earlier).

Like the editors of *CAM*, who reappropriated black visibility within the public square, BLM activists recover and resequence stories about black lives using social media publicity. While the BLM hashtag serves as a decentralized mode of tagging and sorting media information, the website acts as an aggregate of peer-sourced reporting and commentary. Thus, by virtue of its wide engagement with a diverse readership, the site operates as a digital archive that features the stories, lives, and experiences of marginalized and minoritized communities.

The BLM website not only draws connections between incidents of state aggression, assault, and racial violence, but it also attempts to recover women's stories that have not garnered public attention. Remaining sensitive to the ways in which racial discrimination overlaps with other socially inscribed prejudices, such as classism, sexism, homophobia, and transphobia, BLM's "About" page (as of 2017) asserts the following: "[BLM] goes beyond the narrow nationalism that can be prevalent within some Black communities, which merely call on Black people to love Black, live Black and buy Black, keeping straight cis Black men in the front of the movement while our sisters, queer and trans and disabled folk take up roles in the background or not at all. Black Lives Matter affirms the

FIGURE 2.5. Say Her Name splash page. Black Lives Matter
Global Network, http://sayhername.blacklivesmatter.com/.

lives of Black queer and trans folks, disabled folks, Black-undocumented folks,
folks with records, women and all Black lives along the gender spectrum."[28] In
keeping with this mission, the site features a memorial to black women and
femmes, which was created as part of the national Say Her Name day of action
for Sandra Bland, who died in police custody after being held for three days for
a traffic violation. Prominent on the site's carousel banner, the tribute features
"women and femmes" who are "no longer with us, and/or those who inspire us
in our everyday lives," as the site asks users to "upload an image, graphic, or photograph of someone you want to lift up, using either #SayHerName for those
who have been taken from us or #InHerHonor for those who are still with us
or passed from natural causes."[29] The top of the page includes tabs labeled "add
your tribute," "view the toolkit," and "join the action," which allow users to not
only review supplemental material about the Say Her Name day of action (as
well as instructional information about how to interface with the website), but
also build their own public, online memorials (figure 2.4). If users scroll down
the page, they see a collage of portraits of black women and femmes, including a
brief biography of each story (figure 2.5). Similar in nature to Hopkins's Famous
Women of the Negro Race column, the site highlights community participation
and outreach over individual accomplishments. For example, performer Macy
Gray is recognized for her outreach as a "mental wellness advocate and youth

activist," while her accomplishments as a vocalist are not mentioned.[30] Famous women such as Toni Morrison, Maya Angelou, and Betty Shabazz appear alongside community activists and mothers, as well as victims of police violence. For example, Toni Morrison's photograph and biography appear next to that of Kim Milan, the executive director of The People Project, which is an advocate group for queer and trans communities. Both Morrison and Milan's biographies sit below the portrait images of Sandra Bland, LaNiya Miller, Ashaunti Butler, and Domonique Battle—young women who were killed as a consequence of police pursuit. The collage or quilted style of the images and biographies reflects BLM's horizontal ethic of care, which reads each story as a singular node in a network of collective resistance and action.

Recovery through collective mourning, which characterized the earliest iterations of BLM's activism, is evinced in the tributes to Bland, Miller, Butler, and Battle. Although Sandra Bland's story derived moderate media attention, the drowning deaths of Miller, Butler, and Battle were not widely reported. Alongside each woman's photograph, there is an account of her passing. According to the account, Miller (fifteen), Butler (fifteen), and Battle (sixteen), of St. Petersburg, Florida, "drowned in a retention pond off of Gandy Blvd. after being pursued by county and city police for allegedly stealing a car from a local Walmart Market. More than 15 trained police officers ended up on at [sic] the scene, yet the car sank and the girls drowned in less than six feet of water."[31] The account goes on to question whether "officers actually exhausted all options in saving the girls" and asserts that "regardless of the assumed crime, regardless of their actions, LaNiya, Ashaunti and Dominique were kids who deserved to be saved. We stand in solidarity with their mothers, families and friends in demanding justice for them."[32] Because users are in charge of uploading, designing, and composing the tributes, there is no standard method for chronicling each story, as reports range in length and detail. For example, a post memorializing Rekia Boyd is just one line long: "Dante Servin fatally shot an unarmed twenty-two-year-old, Rekia Boyd in 2012. He has decided to resign from the force rather than fight to retain his job."[33] The sparseness of the reporting offsets the largeness of the corresponding image, which is a screenshot taken from a mobile phone. Another tribute, entitled "Derrinnishia Clay and Too Many Others," features a video compilation of the stories of Sandra Bland, Ahjah Dixon, Rekia Boyd, Kindra Chapman, Islan Nettles, Gynnya McMillan, Symone Nicole Marshall, Derrinnishia Clay, LaNiya Miller, Ashaunti Butler, and Domonique Battle— women and femmes who were killed in police custody or pursuit. The video compilation begins with audio from Malcolm X's "Who Taught You to Hate Yourself" speech, which reads "the most disrespected person in America is the black woman. The most unprotected woman in America is the black woman. The most neglected person in America is the black woman" (figure 2.6).[34]

FIGURE 2.6. Still from the video montage "Derrinnishia Clay and too many others." Black Lives Matter Global Network, http://sayhername .blacklivesmatter.com/.

The only consistency among the threads are the numerous headshots and family photographs that accompany the stories, providing a visual reference for each tribute. Presenting readers with various combinations of image and text, the page invites readers to make meaning from a range of cultural and media references, including hashtags, hyperlinks, social media sites, screenshots, slideshows, and other digital material. This multimodal reading experience is also shaped by the various linkages and relationships one might find between different media genres, such as video, sound, still images, and copy. Yet what is most noteworthy about the Say Her Name page is the way in which it requires readers to scroll or click through multiple women's and femmes' stories before arriving at one single tribute. The collage layout provides neither a table of contents nor a reference sheet for finding each story. Such a reading experience can be both aesthetically and psychically overwhelming, as readers are exposed to a multitude of narratives punctuated by accomplishments—à la Toni Morrison's or Maya Angelou's literary successes or Betty Shabazz's academic and activist accreditations—and tragedy, which is exacerbated by the age range of the victims chronicled (the youngest victims are teenagers). However, each tribute offers a visual and textual testament to black life, suffering, and progress, restoring the public record to account for incidents of violence that fall outside of mainstream media's gaze and, as Cullors noted, "changing the story" by moving beyond black criminality.

CONCLUSION

The two case studies explored in this chapter, Pauline Hopkins's Famous Women of the Negro Race column and BLM's Say Her Name project, reveal how activists can undertake unique forms of community building and social engagement by using the specific affordances of different platforms (e.g., new printing technologies at the dawn of the 1900s, and interactive digital media in the contemporary era) to reclaim oft-silenced histories and teach readers how to envision new methods for community building or activism based on the recovery of said histories. The rhetorical practices of these activist undertakings help create "an expansive revisionary space" where "differences can be heard, explored, and understood."[35] In exploring such differences, readers and writers of these texts are required to contend with the inevitable divergences and disconnections between grand narrative and lived or embodied histories. Thus, the rhetorical strategies examined in this chapter provoke a process of divergence that requires readers of multigenre texts to recognize difference without erasing it or rendering it publicly invisible. In recognizing such differences, readers are compelled to (re)read the public sphere in light of those who have been historically excluded from it as well as those who are still struggling to establish themselves as legitimate members within it.

To conclude, this examination has traced a very brief historical lineage of marginalized and minoritized communities that have appropriated emergent forms of media for the purposes of challenging hegemonic understandings of history and legitimacy in the public sphere. Because there are obvious differences between *CAM*, which was a printed monthly magazine, and the Say Her Name project, which is an ongoing digital project without a centralized editorial staff developing and designing its own copy, this study is not suggesting that the two media platforms are one and the same in terms of how they organize, analyze, and display information for a readership. Additionally, this study is not asserting that the online presence of Say Her Name (and, by extension, BLM) is a direct result of the media activism of black women at the turn of the century. To do so would run the risk of either instrumentalizing *CAM* as the only frame of reference for understanding the activist media strategies of BLM or, conversely, instrumentalizing BLM as simply a tool for further extending the historical lineage and impact of *CAM*. Rather, this research seeks to draw connections between *CAM*'s recovery of black women's histories and biographies, the public memorialization of black women's stories through Say Her Name, and the unique ways in which these two undertakings deploy the same core rhetorical practices.

Despite the interventions and social mobilization fostered by these undertakings, media-based activism has often been met with hostility in mainstream culture, and black women activists have borne the brunt of this aggression. Hopkins was forced to leave her post as editor of *CAM* after it came under the control of more conservative-leaning editors and owners, such as Booker T. Washington. Meanwhile, Garza, Cullors, and Tometi have also received a fair amount of skepticism from conservative-leaning analysts in mainstream culture, which is best characterized by the All Lives Matter countermovement. Attempting to override BLM's initiatives to focus on specific marginalized and minoritized populations, the All Lives Matter countermovement reflects an ongoing defensiveness about which communities derive value from and are rendered visible within mainstream culture. Yet feminist media activists then and now have been able to navigate such hurdles by appropriating technologies of literacy, including mass media and social media outlets, to recuperate a history of black stories, experiences, and activism, allowing readers to see themselves as part of a larger public sphere of actors.

Notes

1. Jelani Cobb, "The Matter of Black Lives," *New Yorker*, March 14, 2016, http://www.newyorker.com.

2. Cobb.

3. Cobb.

4. Elle Hunt, "Alicia Garza on the Beauty and Burden of Black Lives Matter," *Guardian*, September 2, 2016, https://www.theguardian.com.

5. Rahel Gebreyes, "Patrisse Cullors Explains How Social Media Images of Black Death Propel Social Change," *Huffington Post*, October 9, 2014, http://www.huffingtonpost.com.

6. Collier Meyerson, "The Founders of Black Lives Matter: 'We Gave Tongue to Something That We All Knew Was Happening,'" *Glamour*, November 1, 2016, https://www.glamour.com.

7. Say Her Name, although discussed here specifically in relation to BLM, was launched by the African American Policy Forum (AAPF) and the Center for Intersectional and Social Policy Studies (CISPS). See "Fill the Void. Lift Your Voice. Say Her Name," *African American Policy Forum*, accessed December 1, 2019, https://aapf.org/shn-moms-network; and Liz Lane's chapter in this volume (chapter 7).

8. Henrietta Rix Wood, *Praising Girls: The Rhetoric of Young Women, 1895–1930* (Carbondale: Southern Illinois University Press, 2016), 58.

9. Richard Graff and Wendy Winn, "Presencing 'Communion' in Chaim Perelman's New Rhetoric," *Philosophy and Rhetoric* 39, no. 1 (2006): 51.

10. John C. Adams, "Epideictic and Its Cultured Reception," in *Rhetorics of Display*, ed. Lawrence J. Prelli (Columbia: University of South Carolina Press, 2006), 259.

11. Adams, 296.

12. Julie Jung, *Revisionary Rhetoric, Feminist Pedagogy, and Multigenre Texts* (Carbondale: Southern Illinois University Press, 2005), 13.

13. Jung, 13.

14. Jacqueline Jones Royster, *Traces of a Stream: Literacy and Social Change among African American Women* (Pittsburgh, PA: University of Pittsburgh Press, 2000), 219.

15. Susan Ruddick, "Constructing Difference in Public Spaces: Race, Class, and Gender as Interlocking Systems," *Urban Geography* 17, no. 2 (1996): 142.

16. Alfred Tennyson, "Ode on the Death of the Duke of Wellington," qtd. in Pauline Hopkins, "Edwin Garrison Walker," Famous Men of the Negro Race, *Colored American Magazine* 2, no. 5 (March 1901): 358.

17. Hopkins, 358.

18. "Announcement for 1902," *Colored American Magazine* 4, no. 5 (April 1902): 413.

19. "Announcement for 1902," 413.

20. Pauline Hopkins, "Phenomenal Vocalists," Famous Women of the Negro Race, *Colored American Magazine* 4, no. 1 (November 1901): 46.

21. Hopkins, 3–4, 46.

22. Margaret LaWare, "Encountering Visions of Aztlan: Arguments for Ethnic Pride, Community Activism, and Cultural Revitalization in Chicano Murals," *Argumentation and Advocacy* 34, no. 3 (1998): 140.

23. Pauline Hopkins, "Some Literary Workers," Famous Women of the Negro Race, *Colored American Magazine* 4, no. 4 (March 1902): 277.

24. Hopkins, 279.

25. Hopkins, 280.

26. Rob McCormack, "Epideictic Rhetoric: Renewing Vision, Vibe and Values" (presentation, Australian Association of Teachers of English National Conference, Darwin, Australia, 2006).

27. "Black Lives Matter: Art," *Black Lives Matter*, accessed October 30, 2017, http://art.blacklivesmatter.com.

28. "About," *Black Lives Matter*, accessed October 30, 2017, https://blacklivesmatter.com.

29. "#SayHerName," *Black Lives Matter*, accessed October 30, 2017, http://sayhername.blacklivesmatter.com.

30. "#SayHerName: Macy Gray," *Black Lives Matter*, accessed October 30, 2017, http://sayhername.blacklivesmatter.com.

31. "#SayHerName: LaNiya Miller, Ashaunti Butler and Domonique Battle," *Black Lives Matter*, accessed October 30, 2017, http://sayhername.blacklivesmatter.com.

32. "#SayHerName: LaNiya Miller, Ashaunti Butler and Domonique Battle."

33. "#SayHerName: Rekia Boyd," *Black Lives Matter* accessed October 30, 2017, http://sayhername.blacklivesmatter.com.

34. "#SayHerName: Derrinnishia Clay and too many others," *Black Lives Matter*, accessed October 30, 2017, http://sayhername.blacklivesmatter.com.

35. Jung, *Revisionary Rhetoric*, 3.

3

Recruitment Tropes

Historicizing the Spaces and Bodies of Women Technical Workers

RISA APPLEGARTH, SARAH HALLENBECK,
AND CHELSEA REDEKER MILBOURNE

IN RECENT YEARS, OPPORTUNITIES TO learn coding have expanded exponentially. Once the province of self-taught computer geeks and computer science majors at universities, coding has been made widely accessible via for-profit and nonprofit organizations, many of which specifically target women and girls with their lessons. From Girl Develop It to Skillcrush to Black Girls Code, these organizations often announce a social mission as well as a vocational one. For example, Black Girls Code seeks "to grow the number of women of color working in technology and give underprivileged girls a chance to become the masters of their technological worlds."[1] Similarly, Girl Develop It promises "to create a network of empowered women who feel confident in their abilities to code and build beautiful web and mobile applications."[2] The plethora of coding programs offers a clear exigence for instruction, suggesting that, with the right training, women might finally move from the margins of tech activity to the center.

We argue that coding organizations' claims about the promise of coding opportunities for women may be premature. Though this expanding profession will undoubtedly continue to offer qualified women employment, the cultural status and reliable compensation their work currently enjoys is hardly assured. As we demonstrate through historical case studies, technical professions often appear to upset existing gendered, raced, and classed hierarchies in their early incarnations, only to reassert these hierarchies over time. In the case of coding, such hierarchies reemerge through the neoliberal emphasis on guiding individual decisions and cultivating labor "choices"; as Rebecca A. Dingo argues, such frameworks isolate workers from larger economic and material contexts of exploitation and make it difficult to detect and disrupt patterns, causes, and effects.[3]

We consider two historical contexts in which American women gained access to fields that, like coding, were understood by their contemporaries not only as harbingers of an exciting technological future but as catalysts of important changes in the gender order of their times. Telegraphy and stenography emerged in the late nineteenth century as technical professions accessible to women eager for higher pay and class advancement, but in both cases, women recruited to these professions found that their very presence feminized the fields, prompting a loss of prestige and decline in compensation. Both industries thus failed to deliver on their promise to women. Though the downward trajectory of women's status within these fields may be attributed to a lack of adequate training, the calcified gender norms of an earlier era, or external structural demands on women workers' lives, we suggest that this trajectory was in part facilitated through the rhetorical gendering of work, workplaces, and working bodies.

The rhetorical means by which spaces—especially spaces of work and labor—become gendered has long concerned feminist historians of rhetoric.[4] Major workplace renovations that initially accommodate women often eventually serve to exclude them, as Jordynn Jack and Jessica Enoch have demonstrated in relation to women factory workers during and after World War II.[5] Our cautionary tales of telegraphy and stenography draw on and extend this scholarship, urging circumspection about this contemporary moment in which coding is posited as a new frontier for large-scale, middle-class, technical employment for women. We suggest that recurrent patterns of recruitment that construct the figure of the ideal worker (the telegrapher, the stenographer, the coder) often reinscribe gendered hierarchies within burgeoning professions. Contributing to this collection's efforts to highlight rhetorical strategies that recur across time and context, we demonstrate how recruitment tropes—direct and indirect appeals about the promise of a given profession—become a mechanism for transforming a prized technical literacy into a deskilled, low-status, low-pay complement to a more exclusive domain of technical labor.

Recruitment discourse, we suggest, contributes to gendered divisions within emerging professional fields, including divided tasks, skills, and training requirements, and the situating of male and female workers differently within the physical workplace itself. Labor historian Ruth Milkman has referred to this process as sex-typing, or categorizing women's professional work as distinct from men's, for instance by linking women's work to domestic labor or reframing it as suitably less demanding than work performed by men.[6] Recruitment tropes encourage precisely such sex-typing; they undermine equity by reinforcing broader cultural narratives about women's and men's divergent capabilities and priorities. In what follows, we examine the patterns of workplace gendering that occurred in the cases of telegraphy and stenography to shed light on the contemporary moment in which coding may succeed in recruiting women to gainful employment while failing to secure their equal opportunities within a respected profession. We offer strategies for feminist rhetoricians to disrupt, in the future, this pattern of discourse that reinforces gendered subordination and marginalization.

GENDERED RECRUITMENT AND TELEGRAPHIC SPACES

Although would-be inventors had tinkered with telegraphy for decades, the telegraph age officially began in 1844, with Samuel Morse's successful transmission of "What hath God wrought?" from Washington, DC, to Baltimore, Maryland. Telegraphy thereafter revolutionized communication, transforming commerce, journalism, politics, and American culture. By the 1870s, operators trained in Morse code and the principles of electricity were highly sought in cities around the world. In the rush to fill jobs, newly formed telegraph companies looked to women and men alike as prospective operators. In 1869, the Western Union Telegraph Company opened a school for women at New York's Cooper Institute; by the turn of the twentieth century, the Young Women's Christian Association was offering telegraphy instruction for free in many large cities.[7]

Prospective women telegraph operators were often recruited to the field with promises of ease and comfort. Like today's advertisements promising rewarding careers with little preparation, recruitment materials for and newspaper articles about women telegraph operators highlighted the short length of necessary schooling for aspiring telegraphers, the minimum skills needed to be successful, and the relatively high pay enjoyed by practitioners. For instance, one commentator reported that Morse code only "requires from three to six weeks to learn," and that the career provided a "comfortable" income to someone with "a fair knowledge of orthography, arithmetic, geography, and ordinary mechanical ability."[8] Another article noted that, "after a few months [of] patient study," a woman "can be sure of earning a salary sufficient to provide her with good clothes and a good lodging." The author added that "most women telegraphers are usually very sure that they like their work and would not change places with any saleswoman in the country employed at the same pay."[9] These sorts of statements constitute a trope of *ease*, intended to make telegraphy appear accessible to potential operators who might otherwise have been daunted by the prospect of working with a new, masculine technology.

The trope of ease contributed to the sense that women were suited only for the lowest echelons of the profession and suggested that their training would allow them to fulfill a predetermined and uncomplicated role, rather than participate in the creative and ongoing development of an emerging field. Additionally, such statements suggested that women's employment in telegraphy would be temporary rather than permanent—entry-level work that would end in marriage rather than promotion. As one columnist put it, women would "accept terms inferior to men because they need support only until the marriage state provides it."[10] The Cooper Institute's school for women accepted only students of premarriageable age, seventeen to twenty-four.[11] Styled as a skill easily learned for comfortable steady wages and embodied by the young woman telegrapher in need of only a few years' work, telegraphy quickly established a gendered hierarchy.

Additionally, recruitment efforts relied on a trope of *support* in which women were situated strictly in support roles, as reliable and tractable entry-level assistant operators. For example, in an 1870 catalog of *How Woman Can Make Money*, Virginia Penny cited a (presumably male) telegraph office supervisor in Cleveland, who saw women's "usually reliable habits, their ability to abstract and concentrate thought upon their engagements, [and] their greater patience and industry" as reasons to hire them into the field.[12] Similarly, an 1869 article in the *Journal of the Telegraph* announced that "the girls ... will ultimately make a mass of sober, steady, quiet, practical, and expeditious operators"; they "cannot steal as much and as successfully as men," or "so readily waste money" or "so easily invest stolen funds without detection" because they possess "more fidelity, more patience, more tractability."[13] The positioning of the ideal female telegrapher as serious and reliable—but not brilliant nor innovative—functioned to oppose the technical labor of women and men.

If women's recruitment into the profession cast their ostensibly innate propensity to obey and endure tedium as valuable workplace qualities, men's recruitment to the same jobs valued their inborn drive to innovate and advance. Male telegraph operators were often styled as future leaders or innovators for whom telegraphy offered an uncommon education and a stepping-stone into other endeavors. As a 1907 *Washington Times* article put it, "Many men who are famous today in their several walks of life had their first opportunity to prove their worth because chance had made them telegraph operators and because they had the energy and the brains to make the most of the opportunity thus opened to them."[14] Featuring images of prominent former telegraph operators ranging from Andrew Carnegie to Thomas Edison, the article offered telegraphy as a substitute for traditional education, arguing that "operators who handle commercial messages can get the foundation of a business education from the very reading of the telegrams passing through their hands, and many a good newspaperman, whose schoolboy days ended with the eighth grade, has been graduated from the press association wires."[15] In this way, the role of telegraph operator was rhetorically constructed along two radically different lines that had implications for men's and women's prospects for advancement and compensation.

If recruitment discourse situated female and male telegraphers differently, the vast geographies of telegraphy networks and the spatial arrangements of telegraph offices reinforced these differences. Women operators were encouraged to work in rural areas, where the content and pace of message exchange ostensibly necessitated less skill. The Cooper Institute required female students to "pledge themselves in advance to accept situations away from the city when offered,"[16] while Penny reported that most women "telegraph in small towns, where there is not much to do."[17] This arrangement contributed to a gradual differentiation of labor among women and men, as men working in urban areas were more likely to be exposed to business and political messages, to experience a faster pace of exchange, and ultimately to receive disparate pay based on perceived differences of skill.[18]

Additionally, Shirley Tillotson notes that even in urban offices, women telegraphers were often spatially segregated from their male counterparts.[19] One of Penny's informants described an ideal urban office arrangement as having "a clerk to receive and deliver communications, and the corps of operators and writers, composed exclusively of females, in an adjoining or upper room, apart from public inspection."[20] Though this ideal was not uniformly realized, the increasing complexity of telegraphy led to gender-based specialization by the 1890s; men were often assigned to political or commerce desks, while women were charged mostly with personal or local messages.[21] Like the delegation of women to rural areas, the situating of bodies in demarcated roles and spaces within the office made arguments about the different skill levels of (gendered) workers more difficult to unseat. For instance, an Idaho newspaper article offers the narrative of an "old telegraph operator" frustrated by the proliferation of underskilled women: "I never knew but three first-class lady operators in all my life," two of whom, he allows, are "employed by the big press association, whose wires are worked at a killing pace."[22] The operator provides evidence of these women's skill by referencing their busy work locations, locations few women were given the chance to occupy. He continues: "All the heavy circuits are manned by men . . . The fact is, women can't work the heavy circuits. They are not built that way, I suppose. They do good work on the lighter circuits, but invariably become 'rattled' when put to work on quadruplex or fast wire."[23] Spatial arrangements both generated and confirmed such assessments of women's inherent skills, naturalizing a gendered hierarchy of work within telegraphy.

The discourses surrounding the emergent field of telegraphy thus recruited women but also resigned them to the lowest-status, lowest-paid, and least-promotable ranks of the field. Efforts to promote telegraphy among women hinged not on arguments that women and men shared skills or propensities but on arguments that each was suited to a different aspect of the work. Accordingly, women and men were assigned different responsibilities, which shaped their experiences and confirmed existing ideas about women's limitations.

GENDERED HIERARCHIES AND STENOGRAPHIC STRUGGLES

Like telegraphy, stenography was a rapidly growing field of work in the 1880s, newly available to women. Secretarial work, male dominated for most of the nineteenth century, was understood as highly specialized and well paid, but bureaucratic expansion and new communication technologies gave new importance and complexity to workplace communication, prompting employers to hire "large staffs of typewriting operators, stenographers, clerks, and bookkeepers, who often came from working-class backgrounds."[24] These shifts "confounded efforts to maintain clerical employment's middle-class image" and threatened its masculine alignments.[25]

Stenography, like telegraphy, relied on a trope of *ease*. Commercial training schools and publishers of shorthand training manuals promised prospective stenographers quick professional returns. The Chicago University of Commerce, for instance, advertised shorthand "taught by mail—in 18 easy lessons!"[26] A similar 1911 vocational pamphlet argued that any girl who "hopes to succeed in stenography" needs only "good eyesight, good hearing and a good memory."[27] These minimal requirements describe the embodied demands of most professional pursuits of the period, and indeed stenography gradually became less distinct as a profession and more akin to a skill or literacy that clerical workers would employ in a range of more specific occupations across a variety of workplaces, like today's HTML or PHP. Frances Perkins's 1910 vocational guide characterizes stenographic training as an asset for entry-level employment in fields as diverse as banking, civil service, literary publishing, advertising, and translating,[28] and Helen Hoerle, in her 1935 *The Girl and Her Future*, sees stenography as "an entering wedge" for more specific opportunities.[29]

Recruitment tropes were crucial in addressing anxieties about the disappearance of a professional and masculine secretariat, staging a struggle between capable, highly specialized male stenographers and feeble female stenographers. As in telegraphy, women were often figured as temporary employees in the field, but they were also represented as intellectually or physically unfit for long-term employment. An 1887 opinion piece, for example, published in the *Boston Globe* and reprinted in *Stenography*, contrasts the man who "goes into [stenography] for his life work" with the "Lady Stenographers!" before whom the "spectre of matrimony stands" to curtail professional dedication.[30] Women are not only temporary but inferior employees for this writer. They "expect to understand" what they transcribe and so are less effective at the task of reducing themselves "to the position of a machine"; "if they drop a word or a part of a sentence they attempt to supplement it from their own fund of knowledge, and in the process of supplementing they ignore the present and soon become inextricably embarrassed."[31] In addition, "the average woman's strength" is taxed by the "physical requirements of an active, conscientious stenographer typewriter and telegrapher"; "her head, her back, are liable to ache. Sitting in a cramped position causes her pains in the chest," and "exposure to the rains, and under a burning sun is likely to give her a thousand and one ills to which her particular kind of flesh is heir."[32]

Responses to "Lady Stenographers!" countered its claims with descriptions of the workplace that reveal the unstable gendering of this emergent profession. For instance, "One of the Incompetents," a female stenographer, wrote in to say, "I do not believe that the average lady stenographer has any reason to envy any of her sisters" in other vocations. She compares her employment favorably with that of "the average lady book keeper, perched upon a high stool, with large and cumbersome ledgers and journals to manage, with long rows of eye-tiring and brain-wracking figures to add, and wearisome and perplexing trial balances and statements to prepare; or the average school teacher with multitudinous exercises and examples to look over and correct . . . or the average shop-girl, obliged to stand on her feet all day long subject to the whims, caprices and even insults of careless and selfish shoppers."[33] Casting other fields of employment dominated by women as more physically taxing than stenography, this writer argues for her profession as "more congenial, more remunerative, and less fatiguing and exacting" than its alternatives.[34]

Amid unsettled arguments about the desirability and efficacy of female stenographers, sex-typing of stenography unfolded in similar fashion to that of telegraphy—through internal hierarchies. Court reporting was masculinized and elevated in status while business stenography was feminized and deskilled. A 1920 vocational guide evidences the rarefication of courtroom stenography: "Out of the great army of stenographers, very few, not more than one in a thousand, become shorthand reporters."[35] Although shorthand reporting and stenography demanded familiarity with the same equipment; employed the same systems of notation; and necessitated equal accuracy, speed, and sustained concentration, the two fields emerged as distinct. Court reporting was thus characterized by tropes of *intensity* and *exclusivity*, ascribing excitement, urgency, and greater pay to stenography carried out in judicial space, where high stakes attended accurate transcriptions of proceedings. Male stenographers often described their work as a rare skill set inseparable from legal action, asserting that "the decision of a case rests upon the stenographic report,"[36] and that "frequently a human life has depended upon the accuracy of the court reporter's record."[37] The same 1911 vocational pamphlet that depicts stenographic work as only moderately demanding portrays court reporting as an exclusive domain reserved for "only the exceptionally expert" who can expect a high salary "proportionate to the ability required."[38] These distinctions helped maintain the high pay, high status, and masculine purview of court reporting, even as court reporting remained supportive in precisely the same ways business stenography was—underscoring the power of recruitment discourse to shape identical work as different when gendered.

In response to this sex-typing process, recruitment discourse from the 1920s reflects an altered set of concerns among women stenographers, who counteracted the gendered dynamic that cast them as transferrable labor, interchangeable in the eyes of their male bosses, by discounting ideas of stenography as quick to learn and easy to master. For instance, "The Stenographer's Ten Commandments," a 1922 article published in *Independent Woman*, attempts to reclaim the skill and challenge involved in stenographic work. Commandments such as "Thou shalt be able to write short-hand and to typewrite at least at the rate of 200 words per minute" and "Thou shalt be able to interpret and translate 57 varieties of English and be familiar with all slang phrases"[39] emphasize the technical demands of stenography, while other commandments imply critique of the implicitly gendered rules governing the treatment of stenographers by male bosses: "Thou shalt have nothing more important than the one man's work, for he is very sure no one is so important as he," and "Thou shalt not argue—he is always right."[40]

The emergent field of stenography was, then, a scene of forming and transforming hierarchies. Even as recruitment discourse largely functioned to characterize the business stenographer as an unskilled and interchangeable female worker, deserving of lower wages than her masculine court reporter counterpart, women stenographers sought to reframe the field of business stenography as characterized by a complex range of often hidden intellectual, legal, financial, technical, embodied, and interpersonal work.

GENDERED FIT AND COMPUTER PROGRAMMING

More than a century after the emergence of telegraphy and stenography, proponents of computer programming, or coding, reiterate familiar recruitment tropes, claiming that the demand for technical workers outpaces current supply and that women are needed to fill well-paid positions that can be attained with minimal training. Compared to those of the late nineteenth and early twentieth centuries, contemporary recruitment materials are less likely to reference the delicacy of female bodies or women's limited capacity for rigorous intellectual work, although beliefs about essential gender differences continue to circulate—as the 2017 Google diversity memo controversy highlighted.[41] Nevertheless, the recruitment discourse surrounding coding still emphasizes women's embodied and cultural fit within the field. Our historical case studies demonstrate that technical education does not simply teach neutral bodies how to effectively and efficiently complete technological tasks, but it also rationalizes why certain populations are temperamentally and physically suited to certain work, and it advises job seekers about how to arrange their bodies and behaviors to integrate within existing work environments.

Although coding currently enjoys high status as a skilled technical profession, recruitment efforts to fill positions with women and nontraditional workers suggest that this field, like telegraphy and stenography, is likely to face feminization attendant with deskilling and decompensation. Indeed, the field has already experienced issues with recognizing the contributions of its workers. The first programmers (working on ENIAC, the Electronic Numerical Integrator and Computer, in the 1940s) were women, selected from a pool of human computers who calculated ballistic trajectories by hand during World War II. Despite the complexity of the programming task undertaken by these women, their labor was ultimately classified as support work in service of hardware design.[42]

Subsequent recruitment tropes in the field have emphasized *opportunity*, touting the availability of jobs and the promise of stable middle-class incomes. For example, the organization Women Who Code, a global nonprofit that facilitates meetups for women in tech, describes the software development field as "one of the fastest growing job sectors in the world economy," one that is "projected to grow by 23%" and offers careers that pay "a median income that is 42% higher than other jobs."[43] Similarly Hackbright Academy, a women's software engineering bootcamp, offers a "12-week accelerated software development program," whose 2014–15 cohort boasted a "99% Graduation Rate," a "$92K Average Salary," and "90%+ Job [Placement] Within 6 Months."[44] This emphasis on ready employment and quick trainability is, again familiarly, a mask for material divisions that fissure the technical labor force.

Sanguine predictions of employment opportunities are accompanied by tropes of *fit* that suggest women with limited coding experience might find the profession to offer a sense of belonging. Skillcrush, for example, a female-led coding instruction company, invites women who "like to make things: to build furniture, knit cozy sweaters, throw a ceramic mug," to consider courses and a career in web development.[45] Another Skillcrush program suggests that front-end web design is a potential fit for those who doodled in middle school "and still [get] warm fuzzies when [they] smell a fresh box of crayons."[46] The examples of crafting and doodling characterize activities typically gendered feminine as a bridge to industry metaphors of web development as building or creating, inviting women to see their (feminine) hobbies as an indication of (masculine) professional potential. Although the computer science industry has a history of using hobbies (e.g., video games and electronics) as on-ramps to advanced education and employment, the association of feminized hobbies with coding employment can impact the perception of women's computer skills and competence. For instance, as Milkman argues, midcentury claims that World War II factory work was similar to cooking, sewing, or embroidery helped characterize technical labor as suitable for women but did not ultimately assist women's long-term advancement in technical fields.[47]

Coding recruitment sex-types not simply through tropes of biological or deterministic *fit* but also through tropes of *ease*, including programs that highlight the flexibility of tech work and the compatibility of coding with childcare. For instance, Skillcrush characterizes web design and development as career paths

THREE MONTHS TO A MORE LUCRATIVE & FULFILLING CAREER OR YOUR MONEY BACK.

You deserve to have a creative, exciting job that makes you WANT to get out of bed in the morning. You deserve to work hard and make enough money to take care of yourself. You deserve to have the flexibility to prioritize your family when they need it, without worrying that your job hangs in the balance.

There are currently **681,059 high-paying OPEN jobs** in tech. What are you waiting for?

FIGURE 3.1. Website promotion for Skillcrush programming courses, 2017. Skillcrush, https://skillcrush.com/.

that offer a double bonus of better pay and flexible work schedules. This message is shown in visual form on the company's website, which depicts a young woman working on her computer while holding a baby on her lap (figure 3.1). The image is accompanied with the following text: "You deserve to have a creative, exciting job that makes you WANT to get out of bed in the morning. You deserve to work hard and make enough money to take care of yourself. You deserve to have the flexibility to prioritize your family when they need it, without worrying that your job hangs in the balance."[48] This message offers coding as an empowering alternative to the inflexible, low-paying jobs that are often available to women juggling work and childcare. The image and its accompanying text, however, overlook the possibility that such overt framing—coding: so easy you can do it while tending children—can contribute to the deskilling of a field.

This characterization is explicit in the website's user testimonials. Women identified as "Freelance Web Developers" stress the viability of combining coding work with childcare; one woman claims that she "decided to learn to code so that [she] could supplement [her] husband's income while working from home AND homeschooling [their] four kids.... [Her] work is steady and [her] current hourly rates are 4x higher than in any of [her] previous jobs, and over twice as much as [her] husband makes!" Another testimonial states that the best feature of coding is "the flexibility that this line of work entails—I make my own schedule, so I get to stay home with my little ones AND take frequent dance breaks in my living room."[49] Even if web development does provide higher wages and worker flexibility at present, depictions that characterize women's paid labor as easily happening alongside unpaid caregiving devalue women's skilled labor and lead to its entrenchment within the lower tiers of computer programming hierarchies.

In stark contrast to Skillcrush's projected narratives of coding as easily attained and comfortably combined with childcare, the experiences of its founder, Adda Birnir, illuminate an alternative narrative of women's entry into technical professions. According to the company website, Birnir decided to learn coding after she was let go from a job as a project manager at a digital agency during the 2009 economic downturn; in a "tough economic climate, if you didn't have hard technical skills, you were expendable." Learning to code was neither simple nor speedy: "I started with one teeny tiny small step: I learned digital skills. It wasn't easy. Or fast. I didn't do it in two weeks, or even two years. (I'm still learning new things every day!) But that decision—to gain clear, marketable, digital skills—changed everything. Suddenly, I could execute. If I had an idea, I could make it happen."[50] While Birnir's narrative argues that someone without previous experience can develop technical know-how, it also offers a more demanding account of learning coding skills. The educational process is represented as a lengthy time investment and as an ongoing activity that continues after initial employment. As such, this language does a better job of maintaining the value of the learned technical skills, and it trades on the current high status of coding to argue for the founder's identity as a skilled worker.

A similar narrative strategy for addressing nontraditional workers' ability to fit into industry is shown in the website for Hackbright Academy, a software engineering bootcamp for women. The recruitment discourse found on the website relies on timeline chronologies that demonstrate a transition to coding work from unconventional work histories and majors ranging from dental hygiene to social work.[51] Each timeline details a different student's educational, professional, and personal path into the field, but each follows the same trajectory: a young woman pursues a career path with intellectual and educational promise, becomes frustrated with the lack of opportunities or low pay, learns computer coding at Hackbright Academy, and ends up with an entry-level software developer position. These timelines show women from a variety of educational backgrounds with different reasons for learning to code; mention of their hobbies serves not to qualify them through tangential gendered affinities but instead to show diverse interests like swing dancing, reading, baking, and traveling. This characterization resists the deskilling of entry-level employment and instead represents the field as more expansive and capable of appealing to those with disparate interests and educational backgrounds.

One critique of the Hackbright Academy timelines, however, is that they do not extend far enough; they stop once women attain an entry-level job in the field. Consequently, the women represented are all fairly young and in the early stages of their career. Disparities in employment, pay, and opportunities emerge more noticeably once women are in the field, and thus recruitment discourses that stop at hiring do not convey an accurate picture. Problems women face later in their careers are addressed by some organizations such as Women Who Code: "women who are mid into their careers are leaving tech at 56%, a rate higher than man [sic]. One reason is that women have a much lower chance of being promoted. As a result, we focus on changing the perception of the industry by highlighting the achievements and success of the diverse array of engineers that work in these professions."[52] This focus on both the leaky bucket and the leaky pipeline problem is addressed through the organization's mentorship programs, alumni network connections, newsletters profiling women in tech, and local and national events—strategies that are also used by other coding programs targeting women. This approach seems like a promising step that can support women who are considering joining or who have already joined the field while not overly relying on recruitment tropes that gender women's labor, either as feminine work similar to historical labor practices or as less valued service work that is overlooked by those in the upper strata of computer coding.

CONCLUSION

Using Rhetorical Transversal Methodology to read across divisions of time and context, we can better see how the historical cases of telegraphy and stenography offer a timely warning to professions currently recruiting women and other marginalized employment groups into emergent fields like coding. Even with admirable intentions, such organizations potentially harm the long-term employment opportunities for nontraditional workers by typifying particular bodies, gendered or otherwise marked. Even if some might find the comparison between coding and, say, crafting as a welcoming sign that they are capable of succeeding in the field, historical cases show that such comparisons ultimately devalue women's technical skills and are easily overwritten by alternative characterizations if doing so becomes expedient. Tropes that emphasize the ease of learning new skills or the ability for workers to quickly take on entry-level work, likewise, are linked with larger patterns of deskilling and devaluing. Together with other rhetorical and material forces, these tropes diminish women's work by categorizing it as support, making it less likely that women workers are assigned challenging work that can develop their skills, and ultimately positioning these workers as less deserving of pay increases or promotions. Although the details of sex-typing women's work change across time and occupation, consistent patterns make it more difficult for women to overcome characterizations of their technical skills as easily acquired, linked to domestic or low-skilled work, and well suited to part-time or temporary work. As this collection demonstrates, however, the identification and naming of such patterns provides a path toward modifying and challenging them in the future.

Our recruitment tropes in coding and earlier technical fields reinforces Kristine Blair's argument about the role of narrative in technofeminist research. Blair emphasizes the power of narratives to articulate rich and complex relations with technology, yet she cautions against generic formulations that can solidify simplistic or problematic accounts of women's technology use.[53] Offering appealing and coherent but oversimplified narratives about particular workers, recruitment tropes can function as what author Chimamanda Adichie describes as a "single story": dangerous because of their incompleteness and because they have the capacity to "make one story become the only story."[54] In order to disrupt the single story, organizations that seek to support women must do as Adichie suggests and strive to make visible other, more complex and even conflicting narratives of historical and contemporary women in the field. Building on and extending the approach taken by Women Who Code, these narratives should celebrate individuals with diverse personal and employment backgrounds at multiple stages in their career trajectories—offering a sort of feminist consciousness-raising regarding the present and history of women in technology. Making such histories available, even in recruitment discourse, is a vital step toward making women's lived realities and technical contributions visible, not just to other women thinking about joining or already working in the field, but to all those in a position to hire, work with, or promote individuals from nontraditional groups.

One might argue that our call for representations of diverse women at various career stages is an unrealistic requirement for recruitment discourse, which attempts to cast the field in as favorable a light as possible. However, given the historical and contemporary lack of detailed, heterogeneous narratives of women later in their programming careers, recruitment materials are some of the most visible and circulated accounts of women in the workforce. Hence attending to the narratives that recruitment tropes enable ought to be a priority for those seeking to diversify the industry at all levels, rather than just at the bottom. Organizations that claim to have a social mission have a responsibility to offer more nuanced portraits of what women experience in the field and to highlight innovative work not mentioned elsewhere. Recruitment materials can thus be privileged rhetorical spaces in which to argue for women's suitability and benefit to a field that has a fraught history with hiring and retaining members from underrepresented communities. Rather than offering generalizations of women en masse, we need to gather more histories of women in tech in order to make women's presence visible, distinct, and representative of the multiple ages, skill levels, backgrounds, and career trajectories possible within the field of computer programming.

More broadly, as feminist rhetoricians we must be wary of how recruitment tropes sometimes draw loosely from feminist discourses of empowerment but produce long-term effects that are disempowering. Recruitment strategies that situate workers at the bottom rungs of a professional hierarchy may eventually be deployed in the service of neoliberal arguments placing responsibility for professional advancement solely in the hands of workers themselves, rather than in the social and political structures that surround them. And as Rebecca A. Dingo has suggested, even seemingly stable rhetoric can evolve to serve unintended ends despite the best intentions of the organizations in which it originated.[55] Even if coding organizations consciously work to support diverse student populations, they are still enmeshed in broader economic, institutional, and political networks that can undercut local efforts. And although no organization can anticipate all of these effects, coding initiatives would benefit from taking a longer view of the terms by which they recruit new students, taking care to offer not just a foot in the door, but the tools needed to get to the top floors.

Notes

1. "What We Do," *Black Girls Code*, accessed November 15, 2017, http://www .blackgirlscode.com.

2. "About," *Girl Develop It*, accessed November 15, 2017, https://www.girldevelopit.com.

3. Rebecca A. Dingo, *Networking Arguments: Rhetoric, Transnational Feminism, and Public Policy Writing* (Pittsburgh, PA: University of Pittsburgh Press, 2012), 10–11, 116–17.

4. Jordynn Jack, "Acts of Institution: Embodying Feminist Rhetorical Methodologies in Space and Time," *Rhetoric Review* 28, no. 3 (2009): 285–303; Jessica Enoch, "A Woman's Place Is in the School: Rhetorics of Gendered Space in Nineteenth-Century America," *College English* 70, no. 3 (2008): 275–95; Roxanne Mountford, *The Gendered Pulpit: Preaching in American Protestant Spaces* (Carbondale: Southern Illinois University Press, 2003), 16–39; Sarah Hallenbeck and Michelle Smith, "Mapping Topoi in the Rhetorical Gendering of Work," *Peitho* 17, no. 2 (2015): 200–225.

5. Jack, "Acts of Institution"; Jessica Enoch, "There's No Place Like the Childcare Center: A Feminist Analysis of <Home> in the World War II Era," *Rhetoric Review* 31, no. 4 (2012): 422–42.

6. Ruth Milkman, *Gender at Work: The Dynamics of Job Segregation by Sex during World War II* (Urbana: University of Illinois Press, 1987), 3.

7. "More Women Telegraphers," *Marble Hill Press* (Marbel Hill, MO), July 3, 1901, image 2, Library of Congress: Chronicling America database.

8. Virginia Penny, *How Woman Can Make Money* (Springfield, MA: D. E. Fisk, 1870), 101–2.

9. "More Women Telegraphers."

10. "Telegraph School for Women," *Journal of the Telegraph* 2, no. 2 (January 15, 1896): 42, Hathitrust Digital Library.

11. "Teaching Girls the Art of Telegraphy," *Journal of the Telegraph* 2, no. 2 (May 1, 1869): 122, Google Books.

12. Penny, *How Woman Can Make Money*, 101.

13. "Teaching Girls the Art of Telegraphy."

14. "The Man behind the Telegraph Key," *Washington Times*, October 13, 1907, image 5, Library of Congress: Chronicling America database.

15. "The Man behind the Telegraph Key."

16. "Teaching Girls the Art of Telegraphy."

17. Penny, *How Woman Can Make Money*.

18. Shirley Tillotson, "We May All Soon Be 'First-Class Men': Gender and Skill in Canada's Early Twentieth-Century Urban Telegraphy Industry," *Labour/Le Travail* 27, no. 27 (1991): 102.

19. Tillotson, 102.

20. Tillotson, 101.

21. Tillotson, 102.

22. "More Telegraph Schools for Women," *Idaho Semi-Weekly World*, April 26, 1892, image 2, Library of Congress: Chronicling America database.

23. "More Telegraph Schools for Women."

24. Carol Srole, *Transcribing Class and Gender: Masculinity and Femininity in Nineteenth-Century Courts and Offices* (Ann Arbor: University of Michigan Press, 2010), 6.

25. Srole, 6.

26. "Become an Expert Stenographer," *Popular Mechanics*, October 1912, 33.

27. *Stenography and Typewriting* (Boston: Vocation Office for Girls, 1911), 4, Harvard Library Digital Collections, Women Working, 1800–1930.

28. Frances Perkins, *Vocations for the Trained Woman: Opportunities Other Than Teaching* (Boston: Women's Educational and Industrial Union, 1910), 30–31, 188–89, 244–45, 256, 261–62.

29. Helen Hoerle, *The Girl and Her Future* (New York: Random House, 1935), 38 and 177.

30. "Lady Stenographers!," reprinted from the *Boston Globe*, *Stenography* 1, no. 12 (December 1887): 145.

31. "Lady Stenographers!"

32. "Lady Stenographers!"

33. "Women as Stenographers," letter to the Editor, signed "One of the Incompetents," *Stenography* 2, no. 1 (January 1888): 8.

34. "Women as Stenographers."

35. Catherine Filene, *Careers for Women* (New York: Houghton Mifflin, 1920), 456.

36. Filene, 456.

37. Harriet Roebuck, "Court Reporting," *Independent Woman* 5, no. 2 (1922): 11, Gerritsen Index.

38. *Stenography and Typewriting*, 6.

39. "The Stenographer's Ten Commandments," *Independent Woman* 4, no. 4 (1922): 8.

40. "The Stenographer's Ten Commandments."

41. Daisuke Wakabayashi, "Contentious Memo Strikes Nerve inside Google and Out," *New York Times*, August 8, 2017. The Google diversity memo controversy refers to an internal memo, subsequently made public, that critiqued Google's strategies for improving its workforce diversity. The memo's author, James Damore, cited essentialized differences between men and women, including "personality differences," as a reason for women's low representation in technical and leadership roles within the company. Damore, "Google's Ideological Echo Chamber: How Bias Clouds Our Thinking about Diversity and Inclusion," July 2017.

42. Jennifer Light, "When Computers Were Women," in *Women, Science, and Technology: A Reader in Feminist Science Studies*, ed. Mary Wyer, Mary Barbercheck, Donna

Cookmeyer, Hatice Örün Öztürk, and Marta Wayne, 3rd ed. (London: Routledge, 2014), 67.

43. "About," *Women Who Code*, accessed March 10, 2017, https://www.womenwhocode.com.

44. "Outcomes," *Hackbright Academy*, accessed March 10, 2017, hackbrightacademy.com.

45. "Programs," *Skillcrush*, accessed March 10, 2017, https://skillcrush.com.

46. "Programs."

47. Milkman, *Gender at Work*, 59–61.

48. "Programs," *Skillcrush*.

49. "Programs."

50. "Programs."

51. See, for example, "Hackbright Alumnae Showcase: Alisha Lopes" (August 27, 2019), and "Alumna Spotlight: Hat Hartling Shares Her Hackbright Experience" (December 19, 2018). These and other alumni stories are featured on the blog page of *Hackbright Academy*, accessed December 1, 2019, https://hackbrightacademy.com.

52. "FAQ," *Women Who Code*, accessed March 10, 2017, https://www.womenwhocode.com.

53. Kristine Blair, "A Complicated Geometry: Triangulating Feminism, Activism, and Technological Literacy," in *Writing Studies Research in Practice*, ed. Lee Nickoson, Mary P. Sheridan, and Gesa E. Kirsch (Carbondale: Southern Illinois University Press, 2012), 63–72.

54. Chimamanda Adichie, "The Danger of a Single Story" (filmed July 2009 at TEDGlobal in Oxford, UK), TED video, 18:35, https://www.ted.com.

55. Dingo, *Networking Arguments*.

4

Take Once Daily

Queer Theory, Biopolitics, and the Rhetoric of Personal Responsibility

KELLIE JEAN SHARP

IN THE 2016 *RHETORIC REVIEW* article "Queer Rhetoric in Situ," Jean Bessette claims that queer theory—unlike other similar theories that took root in mainstream academia around the same time—"has had some trouble picking up steam in rhetorical studies."[1] Bessette believes the reasons for this difficulty lie in oppositions in methodology and goals: that queer theory is often ahistorical, and it is invested in a rejection of normativity (a concept that Bessette reminds us is defined differently in different contexts). Following Jacqueline Rhodes and Jonathan Alexander, Bessette recognizes the changes in "the fields of rhetoric, composition, and communication" that have been brought about by "feminist thinking, critical pedagogies, and postmodernity in general," whereas "attention to sexuality has been spotty at best."[2] I agree that the incorporation of queer theory into rhetoric has been slow; however, much of the work coming out of queer theory has given attention to the questions raised by rhetorical studies. In fact, many of the same impulses toward historicizing that motivated interest in rhetoric are also prominent in scholarship labeled queer theory.

Whereas rhetorical studies focuses on rhetorical acts, queer theory is driven by inquiry into desire and fantasy. The differences in investigation and methodology between rhetorical studies and queer theory often have to do with the differences between discourse and fantasy, persuasion and seduction, reason and feeling. What I explore here is the relationship between pharmacological discourse and fantasies of sex and sexual liberation. As Tim Dean concludes in his article "Mediated Intimacies," "Broader ethical questions about the expanding medicalization of sexuality—and about what it means to have our erotic lives mediated by pharmacology—remain under-examined."[3] What Bessette along with Dean puts into focus is the interrelationship between ever-shifting sexual discourse and sexual fantasy. In other words, discourses inform our fantasies, and our fantasies inform discourse, particularly in the realm of sex and sexuality.

A shared investment in the idea of mediation allows for a fruitful exchange between feminist rhetoric and queer theory. I suggest that recent developments in queer theory—particularly in the area of biopolitics—have given due diligence to some of the same questions that feminist rhetorical studies is invested in exploring. These questions include: how does discourse shape politics? How might discourses shape our very bodies? Our sexualities? How does the way we talk about sex influence the kind of sex we have or do not have?

The history of oral contraception and continued conversations about its use and access provide valuable lessons in contemporary discussions of sexual revolution and, in particular, the use of preventative medications like PrEP (Truvada), used to prevent the contraction of HIV. Working at an intersection of queer theory and feminist rhetorical studies, I analyze some means by which the birth control pill has mediated current understandings of gender and sexuality in order to gain insight into the potential of other medications such as Truvada to influence bodies, identities, and sexualities now and in the future. In this analysis, I engage with queer methods that "question the origins and effects of concepts and categories rather than reify them in an allegedly generalizable variable-oriented paradigm, because these categories do not always align with lived experiences."[4] Also as part of my methodology, I look across time and borders in order to establish the various ways in which pharmacological interventions of the body shape discourses and are constituted by discourse.

BIOPOWER AND THE MEDIATION OF SEX

In the introduction to the collection *Body Talk*, the editors Mary M. Lay, Laura J. Gurak, Clare Gravon, and Cynthia Myntti situate the work within the "conflict of medicine, technology, and culture" that Michel Foucault calls biopower.[5] Moreover, they identify the process of normalizing as an important function of biopower. They write, "Normalizing, operating on both the level of the individual and on the level of population, creates and perpetuates a distinction between the normal and abnormal, and, because the normal is always defined in contrast to the abnormal, experts are continuously identifying new abnormalities."[6] Normativity and queerness might often be employed in order to define one another, but they are not exclusively defined in terms of each other. Feminist theory similarly defines itself against normativity working at the service of patriarchy. What *Body Talk* elucidates is the common investment of both feminist rhetoric and queer theory in tracing normalizing discourses in order to understand the functions of certain ideologies (patriarchal, heteronormative, racist, transphobic, and so on).

Another common ground for both feminist rhetorical studies and queer theory is the investment in the idea that all sex is mediated. Sex is mediated by a variety of technologies: computers, pills, online forums, syringes, pregnancy tests, cameras, condoms, and so forth. Rhetorical studies is careful to point out the various ways in which mediation forms discourse as well as the political effects of certain kinds of mediation. Tim Dean—in both "Mediated Intimacy" and the preceding *Unlimited Intimacy*—examines the ways in which sexuality for cis men who have sex with cis men is mediated through medical discourses, the rhetoric of safe sex, pornography, and political discourses surrounding HIV/AIDS. Dean writes, "Our sex is hypermediated by technologies—pornographic as well as pharmaceutical—that give biopower full access to our bodies and their desires in the service of economic profit."[7] Work at the intersection of technology, rhetoric, and sexuality helps reveal the potential for our bodies and desires to be shaped by institutions that determine how such technologies are used and who has access to them.

Here I would like to establish some of the historical and theoretical context in which the specific iterations of biopower that I will be discussing have been constituted. Biopolitics is interested in the politicization of the body and the extension of state power over individual bodies. Theorists of biopolitics have traced the development of populations and the regulation of bodies through war, camps, biotechnology, and state-sanctioned violence. Following philosophers like Foucault, Deleuze and Guattari, and Agamben, Paul B. Preciado's work at the intersection of queer theory and biopolitics has been some of the most rigorous, seductive, and exciting investigations into the politics of the body and sexuality in recent years. In *Testo Junkie*, Preciado frames the invention and dissemination of oral contraception in the United States by discussing the visibility of women in the beginnings of World War II to the first years of the Cold War. He claims that this era constitutes "a moment without precedent for women's visibility in public space as well as the emergence of visible and politicized forms of homosexuality in such unexpected places as, for example, the American Army."[8] With their move further into the public and professional spheres, women and queer people have experienced increased surveillance that reaches into private lives and domestic spaces.[9]

Preciado brings to bear the relationship between nationalistic developments in the midcentury and the restructuring of gender roles and the sexual values that came along with them. He writes, "Alongside this social development, American McCarthyism—rampant throughout the 1950s—added to the patriotic fight against communism the persecution of homosexuality as a form of antinationalism while at the same time exalting the family values of masculine labor and domestic maternity."[10] This development is important from queer and feminist perspectives because it brought new political considerations into domestic spaces, and from a rhetorical studies perspective because it takes into account the context in which new arguments for sexual liberation arose.

THE PANOPTIPILL

These shifts in the political and domestic landscape laid the ground for new ways for biopower to function in people's everyday lives. Developed after a mistake made by Gregory Pincus at G. D. Searle and Company laboratories in 1951, the oral contraceptive pill arrived within this context to further disrupt conversations about reproduction and women's sexuality. Although many saw the Pill as a liberating resource for women to control their own bodies and reproductive processes, Preciado complicates this idea by pointing out the ways in which the Pill also offered a new form of bodily surveillance. According to his analysis, the contraceptive pill "enables the entrance of synthetic hormones (and therefore endocrinological and governmental birth control techniques) into the domestic space, which becomes a consumption/production knot within the pharmacological network."[11] With the entrance of synthetic hormones and antiviral drugs into social and sexual processes, "biopower extended its reach inside human bodies via drugs that regulate sexuality at the molecular level."[12] The reorganization and regulation of bodies and sexuality comes with major shifts in discourse. Such shifts in our understanding of power and its relation to pharmaceutical intervention has had some unintended effects such as the rise of the antivaccination movement and the return of the popularity of unsanctioned forms of treatment such as herbalism.

The forms of surveillance that developed along with the pharmaceutical intervention of the contraceptive pill are such that government regulation of the body is less visible. In fact, Preciado and others have pointed out that the Pill allows for a kind of self-surveillance that puts the individual in the role of *both the person doing the surveilling and the person being surveilled*. Preciado writes, "The Pill works according to what Maurizio Lazzarato, following Deleuze and Guattari, calls the logic of 'machinic enslavement.' . . . It is no longer necessary to shut up individuals within state institutions in order to subject them to biochemical, pedagogic, or penal tests, because experiments on the living human being can now be carried out at home, in the valuable enclave of the individual body, under the watchful, intimate supervision of the individual herself. And all of it happens *freely*, by virtue of the sexual *emancipation* of the controlled body. The biopolitical promise of governing *free* bodies that Foucault identified is here fully accomplished" (emphasis in original).[13] By making adjustments on the level of the individual endocrine system, the Pill allows the individual to feel in control of these adjustments and encourages them to continue to choose to take the product. Meanwhile, large-scale social projects like population control, sexual education, reproductive health, and so forth no longer fall completely under the purview of the government or social agencies but are reabsorbed into the domestic space. Moreover, as people are choosing to take the product, there is less pushback or feeling of intrusion. "If panopticism still functions in the 21st century," writes Dean, "it is because we have swallowed it whole in the name of health."[14]

While people worry about disclosing personal information on Facebook, they are walking around in their daily lives with fitness trackers, calorie trackers, period trackers, and alarms to remind them to take their medication. These trackers are on their phones and watches, documenting large quantities of information about their bodies, and making this information available to the corporations that make the trackers, watches, and phones.[15] Meanwhile, while abdicating responsibility over these issues, governments and companies are still in control of these bodies because they control the knowledges and discourses associated with hormonal birth control: what information the consumer has access to, what kind of testing is done to assure the safety of the product, how the product is sanctioned, where the product can be accessed, how it is covered under insurance or not, and what side effects are important enough to highlight in product literature.

What is the point of the Pill if not to give people who may become pregnant agency over their own reproduction? Preciado and Elaine Tyler May suggest that the pill has been part of a larger social program with goals beyond the individual body. In *America and the Pill*, May writes about the justifications for the development and proliferation of the birth control pill: "By reducing the population, it would alleviate the conditions of poverty and unrest that might lead developing nations to embrace communism, and instead promote the growth of markets for consumer goods and the embrace of capitalism. The pill would also bolster the 'nuclear' family. . . . It would foster planned and happy families—the key to social order."[16] Wrapped up in the promotion of the Pill were nationalistic and capitalist values that promote regulated family planning.

However, lest we forget, the Pill was much anticipated as the solution to many problems: some capitalist, some scientific, some feminist, and others patriarchal. Some of the leading champions of women's reproductive rights truly believed that oral contraception would be a tool—if not *the* tool—of a sexual revolution. Similarly, women throughout the United States without clear political ties to the reproductive rights movement were more than ready for the Pill when it finally arrived on the market. As May explains, "women wasted no time demanding prescriptions," and this demand came as "a surprise to doctors, who normally told their patients what to take, rather than the other way around." The rates for women using the pill were significant, with 1.2 million American women taking the Pill every day within two years of its approval. In a decade, it would become "the most popular contraceptive in the country, used by more than 6.5 million married women and untold numbers of unmarried women."[17]

The reason why people, particularly women's rights advocates, thought of the Pill as a magic bullet to cure the ills suffered under patriarchy is understandable: women had long been aware of their position of being reduced to their reproduction value, and oral contraception offered an easy and discrete way to regulate their ability to prevent pregnancy without major interference from anyone other than perhaps their doctors or pharmacists. Cis women no longer had to rely on a partner to provide contraception or navigate the often-uncomfortable (and historically taboo) situation of discussing contraception with a partner at all.[18]

WHAT THE BIRTH CONTROL PILL SAYS

In "Toward a Posthuman Perspective," Sarah Hallenbeck suggests a shift away from feminist rhetorical methodologies that focus on "*woman-as-rhetor* exercising deliberate, strategic agency against her world, rather than within it" (emphasis in original),[19] and toward a feminist materialist methodology that "can enable feminist rhetoricians to make significant headway in the project of identifying the conditions under which gender norms and differences are generated and circulated, as well as understanding what forces might be drawn together to promote their transformation."[20] Given that many cis women consume oral birth control on an everyday basis, the Pill is a useful subject for analysis using such a methodology. Here I would like to examine the Pill as a rhetorical actor and not just a subject of discourse.

The Pill was already highly politicized by multiple competing discourses before it even hit the market. Strategies for attaining reproductive rights for women were various within the early women's rights movement. Whereas Margaret Sanger hoped for the birth control pill, other writers and activists set their sights on more comprehensive goals. According to May, "Margaret Sanger expressed her hopes for a 'magic pill' to prevent pregnancy as early as 1912 when she was thirty-three years old."[21] However, some radical activists like Victoria Woodhull and Emma Goldman fought against the family and legal structures that dictate the social conditions under which pregnancy and child-rearing occurs. Some wanted to do away with the category of marriage, wanted further acknowledgment and compensation for women's labor, and advocated for "voluntary motherhood."[22] These goals, however, were not as well received by the public as the birth control pill was. May claims that "few of the pill's earliest advocates saw its potential to liberate women. Women, however, saw it as precisely that."[23] Although Sanger's views on the Pill were not necessarily shared by her scholarly and activist peers, cis women in the general public found the rhetoric of the birth control pill persuasive.

While many women embraced the opportunity to use oral contraception, the increase in demand for the Pill was met with backlash by medical professionals. In the late nineteenth century, policies emerged limiting access to birth control and abortion; these policies were "promoted largely by the emerging medical profession, whose mostly male practitioners sought to take control over the process of pregnancy and birth from midwives and lay healers."[24] However, a most likely unintended consequence of the introduction of the birth control pill in the United States is that it "empowered women to make demands on their physicians."[25] As people began to understand more about the birth control pill, they started to realize that (although it solved certain social and medical problems that had primarily impacted women's lives) it created new problems for the people who took it. This realization led to demands for more agency over the research, development, and discussion of the pill. While such people have sought discursive and political control over the birth control pill since it became available, the medical industry, the pharmaceutical industry, insurance companies, and various government entities have consistently held that power.[26]

The contraceptive pill "was a direct result of the expansion of endocrinological experimentation and triggered a process of development of what could be called, twisting the Eisenhower term, 'the sex-gender industrial complex.'"[27] Put into this context, the Pill seems less empowering than many women had hoped. The synthetic manipulation of the endocrine system has the potential to reshape society, human bodies, and, in particular, human reproduction. Although this manipulation has many affirming effects for humans, notably for trans people, Preciado suggests such an expansion in endocrinological experimentation has also led to new ways of colonizing/controlling bodies in service of the state.

Currently, most birth control pills are small and packaged in a container that tells the user which day of the week to take each pill. Most such packages include pills that do not contain any hormones—these are taken during menstruation in order to maintain the habit of taking a daily pill. Although birth control pills have usually been developed to allow for a twenty-eight-day cycle, some result in only a few periods per year. In "Packaging the Pill," Patricia Peck Gossel discusses the design elements of the DialPak, the first "'compliance package' for a prescription drug—one that is intended to help the patient comply with the doctor's orders."[28] Introduced in 1963, DialPak included the slogan "the package that remembers for her" in its ad campaign.[29] Like the recognizable birth control pill packaging seen in popular culture today, the DialPak resembled a makeup compact, the face of a clock, or the dial of a rotary phone. The implications of the design of DialPak and subsequent birth control pill packaging are that pharmaceutical companies are concerned about women taking the pills properly, that women want their birth control to allow them the semblance of a "natural" cycle, and that women are concerned about the discreteness of the packaging. This tendency toward the discrete can also be seen in all of the ways in which tampon companies have encouraged women to hide their menstrual paraphernalia. The design elements convey the idea that the Pill should be incorporated into a user's everyday life but should not be seen by other people.

Another rhetorical element of the Pill can be found in all the desired side effects drug companies have advertised. Hormonal birth control has resulted in a refeminization of women; as Preciado explains, "contraceptive pills for cisfemales are presented as instruments of beauty and feminization—a molecular supplement for osmatic refeminization." Another goal for many companies that produce birth control is to develop a pill based on "'selective estrogen receptor modulators' (SERMs) that will lower the risk of breast cancer—similar to butter that lowers cholesterol levels or methadone as a substitute drug that reduces heroin addiction."[30] Such goals have wide-reaching effects on women's bodies and, in turn, the category of woman itself.

As ideas about desirable side effects develop, so too does the category of womanhood and the bodies associated with it. Pharmaceutical companies have also developed birth control pills "for the cosmetic production of femininity." Along with the regulation of menstruation and birth control, various "issues" for conforming to mainstream ideals of femininity such as acne, hirsutism, and small breasts are now being targeted by such pills. Others promise weight loss and reduced water retention because of antimineralocorticoid properties.[31] Simultaneously, such pharmaceuticals appeal to and create a normative femininity for their (mostly) cis women users. Thus, the Pill says it can be an even better kind of magic pill than Sanger imagined; it can be the kind of product that Kim Kardashian might advertise for on her Instagram page. It can be a pill that does it all for femme women: it removes hair, it gives you better boobs, it gives you a better figure, it clears your skin, and, of course, it keeps you from getting pregnant. It might even stop you from having to have a period every month. Such a pill could keep a cis-hetero woman attractive to a heterosexual man throughout a large portion of her adulthood.

But the Pill also says that some women's needs and lives are more important than others. As many scholars and journalists have written about before, the trials that led to the approval and distribution of oral contraception were executed unethically in Puerto Rico in the 1950s and 1960s. Researchers Gregory Pincus and John Rock assumed that women in Puerto Rico would be more willing and compliant. Also, they "believed that if poor, uneducated Puerto Rican women could use the pill, anyone could."[32] Again, they encountered problems getting women to agree to and follow through with the testing. These issues were understandable given that many of the women did not even know what the Pill was for. After the continued trouble of finding women who would tolerate the Pill's side effects, they took up the strategy of finding populations that could be forced to participate in the testing. Thus, they began studying the use of the Pill by women in a Massachusetts mental asylum as well as those enrolled in medical school in San Juan, where students were forced to take part on threat of expulsion. These women were not told what the Pill was for, that they were part of a clinical trial, or that the treatment was experimental; instead, "they were supposed to shut up, take their medicine, and submit to frequent, invasive medical exams."[33]

Women of color, poor women, women seeking education, and women being treated for mental illness were all uninformed and nonconsenting participants in the creation of the now ubiquitous birth control pill. Whereas Pincus and Rock found it acceptable to test on vulnerable women without informed consent, they had rejected the idea of birth control for men early on because they "believed women would tolerate side effects better than men, who demanded a better quality of life."[34] Inherent in the rhetoric and strategy of the birth control pill was the idea that reproductive health was a woman's responsibility and that men's health and comfort was more important than women's. Also inherent was the idea that scientists and researchers have the authority to determine the uses and values of the Pill—and that women (particularly poor women of color) do not.

The racist, ablest, sexist, and eugenic history of the Pill's development was directly tied to the early advocacy of people like Sanger. She "promoted the idea of a simple contraceptive that would be entirely controlled by women, but held to the belief that the medical profession should regulate and dispense contraceptives."[35] The compromise of women's agency over their own bodies as well as the acquiescence of power over the Pill to the medical establishment revealed Sanger's priorities in the realm of reproductive rights: population control was more important to her than were women's rights. Sanger even attacked some of the very strategies that aligned with the radical socialism she once believed in, saying that they promoted "the procreative instinct" that was "allowed to run reckless riot through our social structure."[36] She also claimed that social programs "turn into subsidies for the perpetuation of the irresponsible classes of society."[37] Concerns about population control played a major part in the birth control pill's development. Although women saw in it the potential for more control over their bodies, the Pill also represented an increase in biopolitical control and a move away from more comprehensive social reform.

PrEP AND THE RHETORIC OF PERSONAL RESPONSIBILITY

There are historical and discursive links between oral contraception and the HIV PrEP pill. In 2004, Gilead Sciences synthesized a drug that has been marketed under the name Truvada and also called PrEP (pre-exposure prophylaxis). After clinical trials, this drug became the first widely used HIV prevention medication. Truvada was still slow to be adopted due to questions raised by the AIDS Healthcare Foundation and other advocacy groups about the drug's cost, potential side effects, and potential to encourage the spread of other STDs and create a drug-resistant strain of HIV. The conversation around PrEP has had interesting parallels to those about the birth control pill decades earlier. Dean writes, "A pair of doctors in New York, together with one of the best mainstream journalists (Donald McNeil, Jr, of *The New York Times*), all observe similarities between the public debate surrounding 'the Pill' half a century ago and that around PrEP today."[38] Moreover, as Preciado points out, developments in hormonal birth control have superseded other pharmacological goals such as "the urgent need to develop methods of prevention of, or a vaccine against, the HIV virus."[39]

As established earlier, contemporary sex is mediated by what Preciado calls the sex-gender industrial complex. In Preciado's analysis of synthesized testosterone and other synthetic hormones, this concept encompasses the multinational corporations that fund medical research, universities, governments, militaries, the pharmaceutical industry, advertisers, and medical professionals, among others. After the genocide of neglect perpetuated by world governments during the HIV/AIDS world epidemic starting before the 1980s and continuing still, Truvada has become "perhaps the most decisive form of mediation for gay men in the United States today."[40]

Gilead Sciences, worth about $87 billion as of 2017, was founded in 1987, and HIV/AIDS-related products remain a central part of its business.[41] Like many large corporations, Gilead has ties to the US government and military. Donald Rumsfeld became a board member in 1988, was appointed Gilead chairman in January 1997, and only left the board in January 2001 when George W. Bush appointed him as US secretary of defense.[42] Cynicism about Gilead's corporate interests has been one of many negative responses to PrEP among leaders in gay communities and HIV/AIDs-related groups. Questions about its effectiveness, cost, availability, and side effects have emerged as have looming concerns about the pill as a strategy for sexual health and disease prevention. In "Why Is No One on the First Treatment to Prevent HIV?" Christopher Glazek explains,

> Critics have questioned PrEP's safety, efficacy, and cost, and have accused the government of colluding with the drug manufacturer at the expense of public health. Regan Hofmann, the former editor-in-chief of *Poz*, a magazine for people living with AIDS, called PrEP a "profit-driven sex toy for rich Westerners." Michael Weinstein, the head of the AIDS Healthcare Foundation (A.H.F.), the world's largest AIDS organization and the primary-care provider for more than two hundred thousand patients around the world, predicted a public-health catastrophe. "The applause for this approach shows just how disposable we consider the lives of gay men," he wrote.[43]

However, advocates for the drug claim that it helps people have agency over the health of their own bodies. In an interview with Mike Miksche for *Slate*, physician David C. Knox claims that Truvada users are "taking charge of their sex lives and sexual health" as they "are getting STI and HIV testing every three months." This "increased personal responsibility" comes with more intensive monitoring.[44] Although concerns about the drug's effectiveness and often-prohibitive cost loom large in discussions of PrEP, health officials have encouraged its use among at-risk populations.

WHAT THE TRUVADA PILL SAYS

During the summer, cities in the United States sport banners that remind citizens to "PrEP for pride," meaning that people whose sexual activity might put them at risk for contracting HIV—particularly cis men who have sex with cis men—should prepare for Pride Week by going on the drug. Like with the birth control pill, Truvada users are encouraged to use it daily, even if one may not be planning to have sex or engage in other activities that risk infection. Another ad campaign encouraging PrEP use bears the tagline "F*** without fear." This ad taps into a common theme in discussions surrounding PrEP use: that it might liberate gay men from the fear of HIV/AIDS and allow them to have freer sex. On the blog *My PrEP Experience*, Truvada user Joel Alcaraz writes, "I still deal with my fear of HIV, but I don't see it as a death sentence anymore. I've become more open to the idea of dating POZ men . . . people in our community have issues with the morality of the pill. Just as the right has issues with birth control and the HPV vaccine. It will only promote more whoredom they say. Men who said they were not at risk, contracted it, now spout the 'condoms only' argument."[45] Discussions like these—about the morality of PrEP—are tied up with respectability politics, a response to the shame historically linked to gay identity, and mistrust of medical officials in the wake of the AIDS crisis.

As I write this chapter in November 2018, a new advertising campaign for Truvada has launched. Although Gilead has maintained that Truvada was not developed as a money-making venture, the company's recent efforts to market the pill have been incredibly profitable. Fittingly, one of the commercials being broadcast features a trans woman saying, "I'm on the pill." "But it's not birth control," continues a man in the next scene. According to Michela Tindera, the commercial, "aptly titled 'I'm on the Pill,' is part of a marketing push that has helped turn the use of Truvada for preventing HIV into a $1.3 billion block-buster, almost 5% of Gilead's annual sales." This move is "a big reversal for Gilead, just three years ago the company said using Truvada to prevent infection with the virus that causes AIDS did not represent a commercial opportunity." However, the development of this new marketing campaign followed a fall in Gilead's sales, and the company has spent an estimated $13 million to broadcast the commercial in prime-time spots.[46]

Using the familiar rhetoric of being "on the Pill," the commercial solidifies the ideological connections between the birth control pill and Truvada that Gilead wants us to have. Like being on birth control, being on the Truvada pill is supposed to imply agency over one's own body and, thus, sexual liberation. These pills are something that a person both *takes* and is *on*. The latter language implies that a person is following a particular program or going through a physical change, like one might be "on a diet" or "on their period." The large-scale results of this program, however, are yet to be seen. Will it eradicate HIV or simply allow institutions more control over who contracts it and who doesn't? Will it allow people more sexual freedom or create new medical barriers for those who have historically been left behind by health care and medical research?

Central to the conversations surrounding both of these pills is an appeal to personal responsibility and a conflation of the isolating task of taking medication with the state of having agency over one's body. These conversations highlight the potential effects of discourse on our bodies and communities because these pills have been ubiquitous mediating factors for sex. My analysis here is not concerned with whether individuals should take these medications—the positive effects that the birth control pill and the PrEP pill have had for many humans are undeniable—rather, it is a caution against relying on one resource or tactic in the fight for sexual liberation. Centralizing these pills as forms of mediation can help us to think about them and their roles in our lives and communities more critically and with more nuance. The successes of such medication can obfuscate the bodily agency and control over sexual health that we relinquish in the age of advanced biotechnology.

Like the birth control pill, Truvada as a form of mediation of sex and bodies should remain suspect. This need for caution is especially true as long as it is tied up with the capitalist aspirations of pharmaceutical corporations and subsidized by the very government that ignored the spread of HIV when it was mostly impacting queer and poor communities. Although these pills have allowed some individuals more freedom over their sexual choices, their failure to bring about sexual liberation for people regardless of social standing is a significant lesson in the continuing fight for liberatory sexual politics in an age of increased pharmacological control. A lasting and equitable sexual revolution cannot be bought or sold.

Notes

1. Jean Bessette, "Queer Rhetoric in Situ," *Rhetoric Review* 35, no. 2 (2016): 148.

2. Bessette, 148.

3. Tim Dean, "Mediated Intimacies: Raw Sex, Truvada, and the Biopolitics of Chemoprophylaxis," *Sexualities* 18, no. 1/2 (2015): 232.

4. Matt Brim and Amin Ghaziani, "Introduction: Queer Methods," *WSQ: Women's Studies Quarterly* 44, no. 3–4 (2016): 16.

5. Mary M. Lay et al., eds., *Body Talk: Rhetoric, Technology, Reproduction* (Madison: University of Wisconsin Press, 2000), 4.

6. Lay et al., 5.

7. Dean, "Mediated Intimacies," 239. See also Dean, *Unlimited Intimacy: Reflections on the Subculture of Barebacking* (Chicago: University of Chicago Press, 2009).

8. Paul B. Preciado, *Testo Junkie: Sex, Drugs, and Biopolitics in the Pharmacopornographic Era* (New York: Feminist Press, 2013), 26.

9. Such surveillance is important to keep in mind as we consider the increasing emphasis on sexual pedagogy in the domestic space vis-à-vis pornography and internet-based exchanges. As Tim Dean, Linda Williams, and others have noted, the increased availability of porn has had a significant impact on the way in which people learn about sex and sexual health (especially in light of the recent rise in abstinence-only sexual education in US public schools). This abstinence-only focus means that much of sexual education is happening in domestic spaces, in "private," but simultaneously under surveillance by corporations and government agencies that have often unencumbered access to data regarding private citizens' personal internet use.

10. Preciado, *Testo Junkie*, 26.

11. Preciado, 173.

12. Dean, "Mediated Intimacies," 236.

13. Preciado, *Testo Junkie*, 206–7.

14. Dean, "Mediated Intimacies," 238.

15. Apple is currently working with Stanford University to use such data to study irregular heart rhythms. See Robbie Gonzalez, "Apple's Heart Study Is the Biggest Ever, but with Catch," *Wired*, November 1, 2018, https://www.wired.com.

16. Elaine Tyler May, *America and the Pill: A History of Promise, Peril, and Liberation* (New York: Basic Books, 2010), 3.

17. May, 1–2.

18. Historically, this partner was most likely a cis male.

19. Sarah Hallenbeck, "Toward a Posthuman Perspective: Feminist Rhetorical Methodologies and Everyday Practices," *Advances in the History of Rhetoric* 15, no. 1 (2012): 9.

20. Hallenbeck, 21.

21. May, *America and the Pill*, 18.

22. Hallenbeck, "Toward a Posthuman Perspective," 15–16.

23. May, *America and the Pill*, 16.

24. May, 4.

25. May, 16.

26. May, 5. Cis men still hold most of the control over biomedical research and medical care. Even with the rise of women in the medical sciences, there has been a significant backlash. As Kristin E. Kondrlik writes in chapter 6 in this volume, women in medicine have been scapegoated by people within their own profession who cite gender shifts in medical staff as the primary reason for issues within the field. Furthermore, there is a continued perception that qualities and behaviors that are gendered feminine are unfit for the medical professional.

27. Preciado, *Testo Junkie*, 28.

28. Patricia Peck Gossel, "Packaging the Pill," in *Manifesting Medicine: Bodies and Machines*, ed. Robert Bud, Bernard Finn, and Helmuth Trischler (Amsterdam: Hardwood Academic, 1999), 105.

29. Gossel, 107.

30. Preciado, *Testo Junkie*, 217–18.

31. Preciado, 218–19.

32. Bethy Squires, "The Racist and Sexist History of Keeping Birth Control Side Effects Secret," *Vice*, October 17, 2016, https://www.vice.com.

33. Squires.

34. Squires.

35. May, *America and the Pill*, 21.

36. May, 19.

37. May, 20.

38. Dean, "Mediated Intimacy," 236.

39. Preciado, *Testo Junkie*, 221.

40. Dean, "Mediated Intimacy," 228.

41. Statistic from *Forbes*, accessed June 2017, https://www.forbes.com.

42. Gilead, "Donald H. Rumsfeld Named Chairman of Gilead Sciences" (press release, January 3, 1997), http://www.gilead.com (removed from website by 2019).

43. Christopher Glazek, "Why Is No One on the First Treatment to Prevent H.I.V.?," *New Yorker*, September 30, 2013, https://www.newyorker.com.

44. Mike Miksche, "Worried About That PrEP-Resistant Strain of HIV? The Doctor Who Discovered It Has Some Advice," *Slate*, March 3, 2016, http://www.slate.com.

45. Joel Alcaraz, "Joel—'I was still scared, but something funny happened . . . ,'" *My PrEP Experience* (blog), 2015, http://myprepexperience.blogspot.com.

46. Michela Tindera, "Gilead Said PrEP Was 'Not a Commercial Opportunity.' Now It's Running Ads for It," *Forbes*, August 7, 2018, https://www.forbes.com.

PART TWO

CIRCULATORY RHETORICS

JESSICA OUELLETTE

IN *NETWORKING ARGUMENTS*, REBECCA A. DINGO reminds feminist scholars that inquiring into the process of circulation can allow us "to see how rhetorical meaning is not always stable," how rhetorics "shift and, thus, have drastically different material effects."[1] This section addresses this notion of rhetorical shifting—the varied, overlapping kairotic encounters that emerge through and from circulation. In bringing a feminist lens to what Laurie E. Gries termed in 2015 *circulation studies*—rhetorics in motion—the authors in this section offer nuanced theoretical and methodological interventions into what is becoming a new, burgeoning area of study.[2]

Over the course of the 2010s, many scholars in rhetoric and composition have theorized circulation as part of an intentional mode of rhetorical delivery, and thus rhetorical deliberation.[3] However, when considering circulatory rhetorics, especially within contemporary media, notions of delivery and distribution are challenged and confounded due to the fact that the rhetorical situation becomes less situational and more ecological.[4] Catherine Chaput, who argues for a transsituational view of rhetorics in motion, states that "Rhetorical circulation gives up the causal relationship between rhetoric and materiality, believing instead that rhetoric circulates through our everyday, situated activities and does not exist in one place: it is always passing through, but it is never located."[5] As the authors in this section demonstrate, circulation is a process through which various and, oftentimes, conflicting intentions and goals come into contact with each other, creating new meanings and new kinds of knowledge. For example, one might circulate an image on a social media site with a particular rhetorical purpose in mind; that image, as it moves and becomes enmeshed in other kairotic moments, may get recirculated as part of a meme or alongside a caption that conflicts with the goals of the image's original message. In other words, the potential effects of circulation within a digital space are not just determined by the relationship between a writer and a reader; rather, those effects are caught up in larger rhetorical networks of encounter and interaction—networks that are constantly changing and shifting due to the amplified and affective nature of the Web's speed and scale.

For feminist rhetorical studies (FRS), and for this collection more specifically, the concept of circulatory rhetorics speaks to the evolving nature of rhetorical *encounters* and *interactions*—what Jacqueline Jones Royster and Gesa E. Kirsch define as "the social networks in which women connect and interact with others and use language with intention."[6] The chapters in this section investigate those interactions and intentions through analyses of the rhetorical practices and strategies employed by and between feminists of different spaces, places, and eras.

In considering circulation as a kind of rhetorical action, this section highlights the ways different kinds of media shape and influence both the potentialities and limitations for such action to occur. As many of the authors in this section point out, contemporary media, particularly Web 2.0, functions as a network of user-generated content—the "writeable" phase of the Web. Moreover, the Web not only facilitates and encourages participation, collaboration, and information sharing, it is driven and run by such content. This phase of the Web has demanded new ways of thinking about rhetorical strategies. The speed of information; the nature of remixing and citation; and the ability to instantaneously respond, modify, and copy are just a few of the changes significant to how we might reimagine rhetorical action within contemporary media. In addition, the time-space compression of digital communication is, in fact, one reason why we might view the Web as a space where our everyday interactions and conversations happen transnationally and where those interactions and conversations, as they circulate, have transnational effects.

Indeed, some of the authors in this section take up questions related to the transnational, revealing how rhetorics, in their travels, attract and magnify the influences of inheritances, past experiences, and surroundings—on both local and global scales. It is from these surroundings that rhetorics gain the power necessary to effect change within these networks, and it is also from these surroundings that rhetorics end up (re)producing and becoming embedded in discourses of power that ultimately undermine or remove their potential for effecting change.

While all the chapters focus on the digital technologies of the Web, particularly the ways in which the circulatory and participatory nature of digital spaces has led to greater levels of interconnectivity among feminists, these chapters also recognize that the contemporary forging of feminist networks, connections, and coalitions in digital environments is made possible by reflecting on, remediating, and revising feminist rhetorical strategies of the past. Indeed, while advanced technologies and information systems have completely altered traditional systems of production and communication, the authors in this section call attention to the ways in which feminist rhetorical strategies evolve and shift and are always already situated within a rich history of feminist rhetorical practice and activism. In the words of Royster and Kirsch, circulatory rhetorics simultaneously embody and expose the "connections among past, present, and futures in the sense that the overlapping social circles in which women travel, live, and work are carried on or modified from one generation to the next and can lead to changed rhetorical practices."[7]

This section begins with a critical investigation into one of the most commonly used methods in FRS: the interview. In her chapter "She's Everywhere, All the Time: How the #Dispatch Interviews Created a Sisterhood of Feminist Travelers," Kristin Winet considers the use of the interview in digital environments as a way for feminist travelers to intervene in the larger discourse of travel and, more importantly, as a way for feminists to debunk the colonialist ideologies that undergird the popular genre. Winet's cogent analysis of a series of conversations between feminists about their travel experiences situates the interview as both a historical feminist methodology and an ever-evolving genre that, when used in digital spaces, can function as a networked site of resistance and revision.

Following Winet, Kristin E. Kondrlik's chapter "From Victorian Novels to #LikeALadyDoc: Women Physicians Strengthening Professional Ethos in the Public Sphere" explores the ways in which professional women physicians have been able to insert their voices into the male-dominated field of medicine through textual engagement with popular media. In comparing feminist rhetorical strategies employed in Victorian novels to the digital feminist interventions used on Twitter, Kondrlik exposes how feminists envision(ed) the rhetorical role of distribution and circulation in both different and similar ways across space and time. Liz Lane's chapter "Feminist Rhetorical Strategies and Networked Activist Movements: #SayHerName as Circulatory Activist Discourse" bridges contemporary feminist activist rhetorics in digital spaces with the feminist activist rhetorics that took place during the 1960s. Lane not only illustrates the sustained use of storytelling and call-and-response strategies over different periods of time, she highlights both the limitations and affordances of technology—specifically the role digital media plays in amplifying and circulating feminist messages.

The last chapter in this section foregrounds the role of circulatory rhetorics within a transnational context. In her chapter "From US Progressive Era Speeches to Transnational Social Media Activism: Rhetorical Empathy in Jane Addams's Labor Rhetoric and Joyce Fernandes's #EuEmpregadaDoméstica (I, Housemaid)," Lisa Blankenship addresses the transnational by drawing parallels between the feminist rhetorical practices of women from different national locales and different time periods, and with access to different material spaces (speeches versus hashtagged digital messages). Her chapter ends with a call for feminist rhetoricians to develop an attuned sense of rhetorical empathy for others' experiences regardless of the materialities surrounding either's position. Thus, these authors suggest that feminist rhetoricians need to begin developing new theories and frameworks to address this new rhetorical landscape.

In sum, the chapters in this section consider the ways in which feminist rhetorical notions of circulation and networks evolve and change depending on their material contexts and environments. Furthermore, these chapters point to the need for rhetoricians to begin looking at circulation as something more than just a form of delivery and/or distribution—as a process enmeshed in and integral to all aspects of writing and rhetorical engagement. While attending to the rich history of feminist rhetorical practices, the authors in this section call attention to the ways in which those practices have been recycled and revised for contemporary media. Indeed, the Web's global reach and immediate, fast-paced communicative features have enabled feminists to engage in various kinds of social activism. More importantly, though, these chapters remind us that those modes of engagement—and the processes of circulation and feminist networking—stem from a long history of feminist rhetorical work.

Notes

1. Rebecca A. Dingo, *Networking Arguments: Rhetoric, Transnational Feminism, and Public Policy Writing* (Pittsburgh, PA: University of Pittsburgh Press, 2012), 7.

2. Laurie E. Gries, *Still Life with Rhetoric: A New Materialist Approach for Visual Rhetorics* (Logan: Utah State University Press, 2015), xix.

3. J. E. Porter, "Recovering Delivery for Digital Rhetoric," *Computers and Composition* 26, no. 4 (2009): 207–24; Barbara Warnick and David Heineman, *Rhetoric Online: The Politics of New Media* (New York: Peter Lang, 2012); Jim Ridolfo, "Rhetorical Delivery as Strategy: Rebuilding the Fifth Canon from Practitioner Stories," *Rhetoric Review* 31, no. 2 (2012): 117–29; Jim Ridolfo and Danielle N. DeVoss, "Composing for Recomposition: Rhetorical Velocity and Delivery," *Kairos: A Journal of Rhetoric, Technology, and Pedagogy* 13, no. 2 (2009), http://kairos.technorhetoric.net.

4. Jenny Edbauer, "Unframing Models of Public Distribution," *Rhetoric Society Quarterly* 35, no. 4 (2005): 5–24.

5. Catherine Chaput, "Rhetorical Circulation in Late Capitalism: Neoliberalism and the Overdetermination of Affective Energy," *Philosophy and Rhetoric* 43, no. 1 (2010): 20.

6. Jacqueline Jones Royster and Gesa E. Kirsch, *Feminist Rhetorical Practices: New Horizons for Rhetoric, Composition, and Literacy Studies* (Carbondale: Southern Illinois University Press, 2012), 101.

7. Royster and Kirsch, 23.

5

She's Everywhere, All the Time

*How the #Dispatch Interviews Created
a Sisterhood of Feminist Travelers*

KRISTIN WINET

> Solidarity is not the same as support. To experience solidarity, we must
> have a community of interests, shared beliefs and goals around which
> to unite, to build Sisterhood. Support can be occasional. It can be given
> and just as easily withdrawn. Solidarity requires sustained, ongoing
> commitment.
>
> —bell hooks

A FEW YEARS AGO, I was writing a profile piece on a well-known writer whose
work I deeply admired, for a collection on contemporary American writers. With
the help of the collection's publisher, I contacted her agent, introduced myself,
scheduled the call, and scoured the internet to learn everything I could about the
woman whose work had convinced me that a writer could blend creative non-
fiction and travel writing in ways I could have never imagined. As I studied the
ways interviewers asked questions and the ways she answered them, I prepared
my own list, hoping I had put together questions that would elicit something
new. In my mind, I'd downplay her first job writing music reviews for a local
newspaper; I'd find out how she got her first story published in the *New Yorker*;
I'd ask her how she took notes on her travels and turned them into elegant essays.
Minutes before the interview, I got up and did a few stretches to shake loose the
nerves; thirty seconds before the interview, I cleared my throat and hit record.

The interview was a spectacular disaster. When the writer picked up, she
couldn't hear my voice on the other end and repeated the word "hello?" six times
before I realized I hadn't actually plugged in my headphones. When I plugged
them in, a loud squealing noise erupted on the other end, likely from the effect
of plugging the headphones into the socket while on a call. The call itself didn't

go much better: I asked the same question twice; one of her dogs barked the whole time; and I mixed up the names of two of her former husbands. She answered my questions the way any sane person might answer personal questions over the phone with an inept stranger: politely and awkwardly. She even repeated lines taken directly from other interviews I'd read. By the time the phone call ended, I was deflated. Not only had I stumbled through the interview but I felt like I had uncovered nothing new at all. In fact, when I finally met her in person at a literary event years later, I was too embarrassed to mention that we'd actually "met" before. Instead, I took her out to dinner, and we ate oysters and talked about the limitations women in the travel industry face in comparison to their male colleagues.

The barking dog notwithstanding, I've had time to consider what went wrong, and now that I've done plenty more interviews (and even been interviewed a few times myself), I believe I know what happened: I had done the interview for all the wrong reasons. I hadn't come to the interview from a place of what Jacqueline Jones Royster and Gesa E. Kirsch call *strategic contemplation*, a feminist rhetorical practice that is both internal and reflexive, providing space for the researcher to engage with her own embodied experiences while also moving her toward a place where she can consider the contextual, cultural, and lived experiences of both researcher and researched.[1] I had done the interview from a place of selfishness. I'd been so consumed with the idea of talking to a famous writer and so concerned about conducting the perfect interview that I'd forgotten why I'd done the interview in the first place: to fill in the gaps between her abundant online interviews, many of which were published in a traditional question-and-answer format and which often circulated the same answers. To put it simply, I hadn't thought through my research—I had simply copied someone else's methods.

In the days that followed, I started transcribing our conversation, a tedious process that made me think more deeply about the popularization of the interview not as *method*, but as *genre*.[2] After all, I had been reading plenty of interviews online in their transcribed question-and-answer (Q&A) format. Plus, as a feminist scholar and writer whose interests lie in challenging the ways we think and write about spaces of otherness, I believe that it is critical to contemplate who is authorized to speak, what we are authorized to say in the presence of others, and how and why women have historically used particular methods to gather and spread information. The interview—judging by my first experience— seemed to me to be *anti*feminist, a discursive practice designed to mask our unfamiliarity with each other under the garb of a falsely intimate conversation. As I began considering the ways in which media have impacted feminist rhetorical strategies, however, it occurred to me that though genre studies has asked us to question how forms of knowledge operate in the world, little has been done with regard to the interview as a potentially fruitful gesture toward feminist community building. It got me thinking: could question-and-answer interviews (otherwise known as conversations with predetermined ends) be a feminist act, one that could promote what Lisa Blankenship calls in her chapter *rhetorical empathy*, a stance that keeps with the woman-centered and feminist political philosophy that the personal is always political?

Despite the fact that writers as far back as Plato have published dialogues as manuscripts in their own right, very few texts before the mid-1850s adhere to the "journalistic interview's matrix"—genre conventions that include a Q&A format, a clear distinction between an interviewee and an interviewer, and a relatively short time to publication.[3] These conventions indicate to me, however, that instead of simply being designed to obtain information, the interview could work to build relationships through a cultivated conversation. As a writer and blogger, I recognize that this kind of relationship building is no more prevalent and necessary than in digital spaces, where writers rely on readers to sustain them and to build communities around their shared ideas, ideologies, and interests. Bloggers, regardless of subject matter, use interviews extensively, not only to enhance their own ethos to boost readership and gain traction via shares on social media but also to add relevant voices from the field and provide content that relates to the thematic bent of their site. As popular site *Problogger* advises, using interviews as content provides a conduit for helping "build relationships with other experts in your niche, provide your audience with different perspectives, and encourage influencers to promote your blog."[4] Because niche travel blogs are becoming increasingly important,[5] when interviews do function as content, they typically appear with a brief biographical introduction (tailored with information relevant to the site) and a list of Q&As broken up with photos (ostensibly provided by the interviewee), the answers in paragraph form.

The interview as genre is unmistakably prevalent in the world of travel blogging, a world that comprises a niche-heavy discursive community in which the white, male, Western traveler is still the standard to which the industry is judged.[6] When female voices do enter, such as on popular sites and in online communities like Girls LOVE Travel (GLT), they tend to do so in ways that downplay difference and celebrate what Alison Jaggar calls a Western feminist discourse that projects an unhelpful "global sisterhood."[7] However, though these obstacles certainly exist, there are also spaces of opportunity to break these tendencies. In this chapter, I draw on the rich and complicated discourse of travel in order to investigate one such site where the interview series is used as a place to discuss the gendered, racialized, embodied experience of travel, and, as site creator Bani Amor (who uses the nongendered pronoun *they*) writes, to "decolonize" travel from its problematic history using the interview series as a strategic way to construct a new community of traveler.[8] Though rhetoric and composition studies have begun extending current theories of digital publics to argue for, as

Linh Dich writes, a broader, more inclusive framework that understands online writing environments as "simultaneous and overlapping community and public imaginaries for writers who may need to have multiple audience orientations in order to articulate their experiences," considering the networked potentials of a feminist travel blog is critical feminist work.[9] Therefore, while I do believe that as feminist rhetoricians we must look to the past—and to the complicated discourses that have emerged from that fragmented past(s)—to "imagine a future worth working toward as a more inclusive enterprise," I also believe that we can celebrate the accomplishments of emerging communities.[10]

By drawing on Carmen Kynard's observation that computers and composition have often underscored the power that the dominant gaze has on writing and rhetorical choices and acts,[11] this chapter explores how Amor's #Dispatch interview series actively promotes contemporary feminist travel conversations by helping participants affirm their voices in the face of a highly influential dominant discourse of colonialism and by creating a community of travelers with their own set(s) of issues, revelations, and joys related to the act of traveling. By briefly tracing the generic history of the interview in light of feminist historical practices and rhetorically analyzing two of Amor's interviews in concert with each other, we can see that the #Dispatch series counters colonial travel discourses and lays the groundwork for building an online community of feminist travelers. Ultimately, by considering the interview as *genre* as a feminist rhetorical gesture that can foster a space for coalition building, we can see how it holds the potential for bolstering important discourses in travel media, enabling what Amor calls a "decolonized" feminist travel story to emerge and encouraging greater attention to and circulation of these voices.

RECONSIDERING THE INTERVIEW'S ROOTS:
FROM *METHOD* TO *GENRE*

The term *interview*, which derives from the early sixteenth-century French word *entrevue*, suggests "to see or have a glimpse at each other" and is perhaps one of the most controversial genres in terms of the politics of narrative.[12] This controversy notwithstanding, because interviewing is such an ancient and complex activity, a brief outline of its genealogy *as genre* since the nineteenth century can be helpful for understanding why it has transitioned so enthusiastically to digital spaces. As method, interviewing is at least as ancient an act as writing itself; it has been used in medicine, education, law, business, and journalism to gather information, to share knowledge, and to acquire expertise.[13] In most journalism circles, scholars typically associate the interview with a masculinist tradition, recalling the likes of Plato's dialogues with Socrates (the earliest predecessor in the Western imagination) and, as Jerome Boyd Maunsell suggests, the "table talk" sessions of the sixteenth to nineteenth centuries, in which "an illustrious writer's informal sayings were noted by a friend, relation, or fellow writer of some kind" as men sat around a table.[14] Citing Martin Luther's 1566 *Table Talk* as a critical precursor to the modern format, he argues that the interview as genre is a special form of autobiography "heavily based on conversations" and "arranged within the biographer's wider narrative."[15] From here, many scholars agree that the interview in its current form (as a Q&A conversation between interviewer and interviewee) emerged most significantly alongside nineteenth-century American journalism, specifically in the fields of criminal investigation, political reportage, and the "human story." Because the term *interview* did not officially appear in American newspapers until 1867, many attribute its development as a genre to this time period.[16]

However, an increasing number of scholars believe that we need to widen our understanding of the genre of interview to include more than these specific precursors. In her study of travel essays written in the 1750s by Archbishop Timothy Gabashvili, Paata Natsvlishvili urges journalism scholars to consider texts like his—which, like his travel essay "Mimoslva," involved recording dialogues and publishing them as text—as early predecessors of the genre as well. She argues that despite the fact that time to publication was longer than the genre normally allows (it was simply impossible for Gabashvili to disseminate his conversations), his work fits the journalistic interview's matrix just as much as American newspaper conversations did in the nineteenth century. Black studies scholar Carston Junker also argues for this widening, reminding readers that slave narratives were often generated as interviews, albeit "against a Eurocentric background," with a "presumably white default location" and in a style that robs the interviewee of narrative authority and upholds power differentials.[17] Because genres tend to appear as normative frameworks (also known as "habits or rituals that work"), ideologies are easily naturalized, making these ideologies, as Jessica Ouellette writes in her study of feminist blog networks, difficult to *see*.[18] By acknowledging the ideological problems that can be inherent to a genre, we may find it easier to "question further the potentialities for and limitations of transnational feminist communication and activism within digital spaces," a critical task in feminist rhetorical studies.[19]

Given these political underpinnings of the interview, it might seem odd at first that a social activist like Amor would choose to use the interview to promote a message of inclusivity, but because the format is commonly accepted in the blogosphere, we can more readily see why they chose to organize and publish their interview sessions in this way. However, as Harsha Walia purports, social activists should not "just be present for blockades or in moments of crisis but instead sustain a multiplicity of meaningful and diverse relationships on an ongoing basis."[20] Because social activism—and, in this case, the decolonization of travel culture—is a movement and not a single moment, we must be willing to, as Cindy Milstein notes in her work *Taking Sides,* "locate ourselves within the context of colonization in complicated ways—frequently as simultaneously oppressed and complicit."[21] It is therefore no surprise that Amor utilizes the interview as a tool toward, as they coin it, the "decolonization of travel culture," because the series presents an opportunity to rupture the colonial underpinnings by inserting fresh, previously silenced voices into the conversation. Plus, as Carolyn R. Miller and Dawn Shepherd claimed as far back as 2004, digital activists turn to the space of the blog because of the public's massive failure to realize and promote effective forms of democracy.[22] Though the viability of this assertion has since been questioned,[23] Miller and Shepherd still maintain in later work that, as Ouellette writes, the blog holds potential to "express discontent with mainstream media's voiceless and impersonal (dis)connections with its readers and to offer an 'alternative voice'" that might reach readers hungry for change.[24]

CIRCULATING IN CYBERSPACE:
THE #DISPATCHES IN CONVERSATION

In many ways, *Everywhere All the Time* looks like plenty of other websites in the blogosphere: it has a title in the top left-hand corner, a standard three-column layout that comprises a larger middle space for main content and two smaller sidebars, and content that includes favorite or popular posts, quotes, social media handles, and tag clouds. Underneath the title appear the words "decolonizing travel culture," indicating to readers that the site is not written for the average traveler or reader but rather for an elevated, educated readership that is already aware of the discourse surrounding contemporary feminist conversations. The sidebars are filled with feminist content: quotes from Gloria Anzaldúa, bell hooks, and Edwidge Danticat; a crass advertisement from the early 1900s with a white woman photographing a black South African baby; and links to articles Amor has written, such as "Ten Travel Books by People of Color." The tag clouds include words like feminism, feminist, genderqueer, global, imperialism, intersectionality, and privilege, as well as identity initialisms like LGBT, POC, QPOC, and QTPOC. These important textual and visual cues, more than being a visual poster wall of Amor's interests, indicate what communications scholar Catherine Schryer calls a kind of "reflection." Using the idea of Bakhtin's *chronotope* to emphasize that "every genre expresses space/time relations that reflect current social beliefs regarding the placement and action of human individuals in space and time," she argues that the imposition of one's beliefs and images on a blog is "profoundly ideological" and responds to the *kairos* of the moment.[25]

Though a full visual rhetorical analysis of the site exceeds the confines of this chapter, a closer look at Amor's photography and biography is worthwhile because these elements shape the ethos of the site as feminist space and praxis. At first glance, Bani Amor's photograph and short biography fulfill many of the likely expectations of travel blog readers: a medium close-up headshot of the writer and a three-sentence biography. However, what is not at first apparent is that Amor undermines the predictable travel blog, in which the writer posts a headshot of themselves from somewhere "exotic" (to Western readers) and lists a number of travel accomplishments (with active verbs: danced, ate, hiked, etc.), adventures, and countries traveled to demonstrate their innate cosmopolitanism. In the place of these expected elements, they write, "Bani Amor is a queer travel writer, photographer, and activist from Brooklyn by way of Ecuador," immediately situating themselves as having identities shaped by two continents, and they follow with, "they've been published in *Bitch Magazine* and *Apogee Journal*, among other outlets," alerting readers that Amor has the credibility to do this kind of interrogating.[26]

The interview series on *Everywhere All the Time* appears on a subpage that is linked from the main header on Amor's main site and is simply listed as Dispatches (without the hashtag). When readers click on the link, they are taken to a page framed by a photograph of a hiker strolling along a mountainous path next to a river. Because the figure is not facing the camera and is bundled up in a billowy raincoat, black pants, and oversized backpack, the hiker's gender is not discernible. Though the context for the photo is unclear, it is reasonable to imagine a photograph of an able-bodied person in motion against a landscape on a travel blog. Under the photograph and page title, they describe the exigency for the series, focusing primarily on the fact that the topics they cover and questions they ask are not currently valued or acknowledged in the "mainstream travel space." As they write, "I've been chatting with travel writers and personalities of color about their experiences navigating the media industry and the globe with an intersectional lens, exploring themes like power, privilege, place, identity, microaggressions, hustling and the creative process, which are rarely touched on in the mainstream travel space. If you'd like to get involved, get in touch!"[27] There is much to unpack in these two sentences. As with the rest of their site, Amor is careful to demonstrate the level of informality that characterizes their mixed style of the familiar and the academic. By using the verb *chat* (and verb phrase "I've been chatting") over a more formal option like *discuss* or *interview*, they attempt to neutralize any feelings of uncertainty or insecurity readers might have. Following this opening, they use the travel-themed verbs *navigating* and *exploring* to imply a kind of wading through a network of discourse that is unnecessarily difficult to traverse. They emphasize the fact that the writers and personalities of color interviewed on the site are moving through the world "with an intersectional lens" and an eye toward considering how power, privilege, place, identity, and microaggressions (a term that is not explained to readers but rather assumed to be understood) play into the larger travel experience. The nominal phrase "which are rarely touched on in the mainstream travel space" stresses how Amor's site departs from the traditional travel blog in an attempt to bring to the surface previously marginalized voices that are not touched on in the genre's typical space(s). In Amor's mixed style, they make sure to add that the interviews cover "hustling and the creative process" as well, a signal that indicates that the readers are interested creatives themselves.

Though they have done over twenty interviews, some of which deal with travel writing specifically, I focus here on only two. These two interviews, together, begin unraveling—even decolonizing, to use Amor's word—travel *culture*, or, as I conceive of it, a broad set of social behavior and cultural norms found in particular human societies. Cognizant of our habit of always keeping our past close as we imagine new presents and futures, I think of the limited perspectives we have on women's and minoritized people's travel experiences and, thus, the importance of this work. Alongside the eighteenth- and nineteenth-century narratives of such privileged Western women as Lady Mary Wortley Montagu (who traveled in Turkey) and Flora Tristan, we can see celebrations of a differently privileged female experience from people (not all of them women) who deal with exile, foreignness, and embodiment in compelling ways.[28] I focus on the following two interviews in an attempt to demonstrate how the #Dispatches eschew the idea of a Western, global sisterhood and instead invite a network of travelers to more deeply consider the raced, sexed, privileged, and cultural implications wound up in the complex web of contemporary travel culture and the language we use to describe it.

India Harris: "How Not to Do Travel Writing: A Glossary (pt. 1)"

In a brief, italicized introduction to this first interview, Amor writes that India Harris is "a 30-year-old Black Lesbian hailing from her mother's womb in Washington D.C. and currently living in Brooklyn, NY." By foregrounding her age, race, and sexuality in this first sentence, Amor interrupts the assumption that travelers are homogenous and instead reminds readers that our intersecting identity markers inform the ways in which we experience travel and participate in its culture. At the end of the biography, Amor adds that Harris's travels involve "learning about the culture, history and lives of people of African descent in each country she visits" and that "far too often, the contributions/life breath/existence of Indigenous people and people of African descent are erased from the world's narratives." What this explanation demonstrates is Amor's subject position as a researcher who is interested not in the mainstream travel story but rather in those who have been, as they note, "erased" from a global narrative about travelers. From the title of the #Dispatch, readers can assume that Harris will be providing an alphabetical list of words to avoid in talking or writing about travel, a fact furthered by a quote from fifteenth-century Antonio de Nebrija: "language has always been the perfect instrument of empire." From this first moment, Amor has framed the discussion and articulated a few key principles, namely language's power to obscure others' stories.

Like all the #Dispatches, Harris's interview reads less like a static Q&A done over email asynchronously and more like a curated conversation, one focused on teasing out themes related to Amor's stated goal of decolonizing travel culture. The structure of the interview, that of a back-and-forth dialogue about a prior conversation, appears to be both planned and spontaneous, suggesting that interviewer and interviewee agreed on an initial script but allowed for dialogue to meander. Much like Maunsell suggests in his analysis of literary interviews, this technique limits the autobiographical sketch of Harris (which is, I think, deliberate) and instead puts the focus squarely on Harris's ideas about the colonizing rhetoric of travel writing. This move sets up the reader's expectations that they will receive not an autobiographical sketch of the interviewee and her life but rather a snapshot of an ongoing feminist conversation. As Maunsell writes, interviews (like this one) that play with the play-script form can "offer an unusually focused forum for the discussion of a writer's ideas, especially when directed by an astute interviewer. They operate as autobiography, and often simultaneously as criticism."[29] In the interview with Harris—with its subtitle, "A Glossary"— the criticism takes the form of an alphabetical listing of words that often tossed around when discussing travel.

Amor's desire to resist the larger narrative of mainstream travel culture is clear in the way they develop each conversation's specific theme. In the case of Harris's interview, they mention the goal outright in the third question: "When I think about decolonizing travel culture with a specific focus on travel writing," they write, "and envision what justice in that space would look like, it begins with reclaiming sovereignty over the language used to describe POC, our lands and culture around the world." This goal, to reclaim language, is undertaken over the course of the conversation, as they go through, at Amor's guidance, their co-created list of words that invoke colonialism in travel writing. After Amor poses one open-ended statement meant to establish the context of the interviewee and her life, they start with a contextual frame, letting readers know that "we came up with the ABCs of f***ed up language in travel writing together. Before we get into it, can you share a little on why you think something like this is necessary?" The first of these two sentences, which begins with the inclusive pronoun *we* and ends with the adverb *together*, situates Harris and Amor in a community. Harris's response, which describes a time she was preparing for a backpacking trip and had trouble finding travel blogs by people of color, continues to help guide the conversation. In lamenting that many of the blogs she found were riddled with words like *authentic, exotic, g*psy, native,* and *tribal,* she realized that these words are often "misappropriated by leisure travelers as moniker or identities to take on which, because of their privilege, is seen as something positive, while nomadic peoples throughout the world face discrimination." As is common practice in the series, this controversial comment sparks Amor to respond with a resound-ing "Yes," a follow-up comment about what decolonized travel writing might look like, and a question about how Harris feels about Amor's "fav" word: A for authenticity. In the community-building initiative of the #Dispatches, small acknowledgments like inclusive pronouns, references to previous conversations, cocreated lists, words of positive reinforcement, and abbreviated expressions cre-ate an environment that seems less sterile and more inviting.

Amor's goal of bringing to the surface previously marginalized voices that are not touched on in the genre's typical space(s) follows here as they and Harris deconstruct, together, their opinions on words like *authenticity, backpacking, col-orful,* and *discover,* among others (they get as far as the letter G in this particular post). Though the space of this chapter limits a lengthier analysis, we can see the power of the conversational Q&A as Amor and Harris discuss the implications behind the word *authenticity* and consider "what's wrong" with a lot of the words they will be discussing. With Amor steering the direction of the conversation and Harris providing both lengthy commentary and shorter affirmations of Amor's commentary, the exchange is paradigmatic of the #Dispatches. Harris responds to Amor's question about authenticity by arguing that it is, first and foremost, "a social construct." She explains by defining it, stating that "in order for something to be 'authentic' it is inherently setting up a standard in which something else will be measured against it." Amor interrupts, as they often do at points where a di-gression or further explanation would be useful, adding that the "something" to which Harris refers is likely "something out of the white/Western imagination." While this sentence fragment is short, the aside works to keep the interview on track by encouraging Harris to reflect on how the white/Western imagination might have shaped the way many travelers view culture as authentic. Harris re-acts positively to Amor's prompting, fleshing out her definition by including an example of how travelers to large cities in Mexico or Kenya, upon seeing mem-bers of the community using smartphones and laptops, will complain that "it is not authentic" and head off to a rural place in search of an Indigenous popu-lation that can satisfy their desire for authenticity. Amor responds by claiming that "this [example] sets up what's wrong with a lot of the words we'll be discus-sing—what we recognize as The Standard." By keeping their purpose transpar-ent and by using Harris's life experiences and scholarly interests to add a voice to the conversation, Amor redirects, again, the conversation toward an analysis of poorly used words in travel discourse and implores readers to check their own privilege(s) and strive for more equitable language choices.

Pooja Makhijani: "People of Color with Western Privilege"

Pooja Makhijani's interview begins with a short biography that introduces her accomplishments as a writer, emphasizing that she writes children's books, essays, and articles and has bylines in such powerhouse publications as *New York Times*, *Serious Eats*, and *Washington Post*. Though this publication record certainly helps establish her ethos in the industry, her credibility is even more solidified by the revelation, early in the interview, that she is a South Asian American woman who was born in New York City and raised in suburban New Jersey, and who now lives with her partner in Singapore. By foregrounding the multiple identities of a well-known author to their readers, Amor positions Makhijani as a feminist ally, one whose subject position is diverse and multiple. At Amor's probing, we also learn that Makhijani considers herself not necessarily an expatriate but rather an "economic migrant," an "American (Westerner)" with an incredible amount of Western privilege, should she choose to claim it. Though these details of her personal life and story are not included in the biographical sketch (unlike with Harris), the early revelation of these diasporic identities helps develop the narrative of a community of travelers with multiple racial, cultural, and historical communities and invites feminist readers from various backgrounds to be part of the conversation. It also provides a natural entrance to this #Dispatch: Amor introduces Makhijani to the community and uses her life experience(s) to more fully consider the use and political underpinnings of words like *expatriate*— words that are charged with the benefit of Western privilege.

In similar style to Harris's interview, Makhijani's interview centers on asking readers to consider their language choices. In one section, Amor cuts to the heart of the #Dispatch after Makhijani admits that she and her partner prefer the term *economic migrant* to the more privileged *expat*, sharing their thoughts that the current vocabulary used to identify moving bodies is not only insufficient but full of implicit bias. In the relatively short exchange that follows, Makhijani affirms Amor's statement with a resounding "Yes!" and a story about how two of her favorite writers, Laila Lalami and Teju Cole, addressed the problem in a Twitter exchange. Lalami tweeted that "you're a 'migrant' when you're very poor; 'immigrant' when you're not so poor; and 'expat' when you're rich"; Cole added "'émigré' if you have a PhD." Amor does not respond overtly to Lalami and Cole's definitions, instead opining that they decided a while ago that "to be an expat means to hold privilege in the trifecta of class, race and place" and that there are racial hierarchies at work for people of color as well. Makhijani then both affirms and complicates Amor's statement, starting with an exclamatory

"I totally agree!" and then continuing for four paragraphs about how her US passport and American accent have afforded her a great deal of power and privilege in Asia and illuminated the concept of whiteness in a way "[she] never would have conceived of had [she] not moved overseas." This kind of critical engagement with language and the politics of identity, along with a heightened sense of the fluidity of language and the fluidity of the power its uses represent, can, as Royster and Kirsch write, "help us see how traditions are carried on, changed, reinvented, and reused when they pass from one generation to the next" and, in this case, to see "how ideas circulate not just across generations but also across places and regions in local, global, and transnational contexts," allowing us to envision more diverse perspectives.[30]

In order to provide evidence for her claims, Makhijani seizes the autobiographical component of the interview to share two anecdotes that represent the ways in which micro- and macroaggressions play out (and how they dissipate and disappear) in her everyday life in Singapore. In the first example, she laments that before people see her American passport, they often ask her and her partner whether they had an arranged marriage (to which she comments with an informal, parenthetical "WTF?" signaling her own disbelief). In the second, she chronicles how common it is for friends from India to be rejected, ignored, or treated poorly by landlords, bartenders, servers, and retail clerks. She adds (with a comment that she is a "t-shirt/jeans/flats/no makeup/no jewelry kinda gal") that she can tend to receive poor service as well—until, that is, she puts on her "best loud, friendly American twang." These anecdotes serve two purposes. On the one hand, they are relatable and necessary, a welcome pause in an otherwise heady debate about the connotations afforded to words that travel writers use uncritically every day; and on the other, they keep the interview semiautobiographical—a necessary nod, as Maunsell argues, to the requirements of the genre as most recognize it. Therefore, because the interview balances between the conversational and the theoretical, Makhijani emerges as both a member of the feminist travel community (the face of a perspective on an issue of relevance, that of whether we can all be "expats") and a traveler asking hard questions about what it means to be embodied.

CONCLUSION: #DISPATCH(ES) AS IMPLICATIONS FOR COMMUNITY BUILDING

As a travel writer and feminist, I remain interested in the rhetorical implications of interview series like Bani Amor's, and I continue to wonder how using interviews might help shape a more nuanced, more inclusive perspective on the dominant travel narrative. The story of the interview series is a tale of circulation, of solidarity, of positioning, and of community building in a networked environment that looks, on the surface, radically changed from our traveling foremothers. I align it with the kind of feminist epistemology proposed by such scholars as Alison Bailey, as it offers options for "destabilizing the center" of the hegemonic stories that seem to be ever present in tourism discourse and that often silence, discipline, and constrain critical counterstories.[31] Keeping in mind that, as bell hooks writes, we do not need to share common histories, have collective antimale sentiments, or even have among us similar experiences, cultures, or ideas to create solidarity or sisterhood, I recognize our continued need to be "united in our appreciation for diversity, united in our struggle to end sexist oppression, [and] united in political solidarity."[32] As the creation and promotion of public discourse relies on the rhetorical practices communities use to respond to a shared exigence, we must critically examine the ways in which our everyday communities use interview series to ideologically shape, constrain, and ignite social relations in digital spaces.

Though some might say that Amor's site is isolated to diverse travelers who already believe and embody the kind of traveling the site promotes, we must also remember that coalition building in both historical and contemporary society often begins in what Jane Mansbridge calls "protected enclaves," where groups can explore ideas and arguments in safer environments.[33] A personal blog, in this case, can provide this kind of curated safety. Though counterpublic theory scholar Karma R. Chávez attests that these enclaves are most often "spaces of withdrawal" because the activists have suffered harsh treatment or high levels of oppression or crisis, I believe that if we look to the past and consider the spaces where most women's work has been done—churches, domestic spaces, and collectives—we can also see the potential of such spaces of withdrawal.[34] What sets Amor's site apart from being simply a space of withdrawal is that it also engages with those who strive for a more equitable travel discourse, as reader comments on the #Dispatches reveal. Sara thanks Amor and Harris for "sharing [their] perspectives and wisdom" and adds that she will be keeping the list close by every time she blogs; Allison mentions that "this helps [her] monitor [her] own writing and try to find a voice that is sensitive to the people and places [she] want[s] to write about"; and Elizabeth admits that she shared the post and used it to "revise [her] entire blog and also really think about its direction and the kind of space [she] want[s] [her] writing to occupy." Alyssa adds that "despite being a POC, I can't say I haven't been guilty of some of these things in my own travel writing" and wants to know how we, as feminist writers and travelers, do what needs to be done. Though I agree with Alyssa's lament that the people who really need to be reading lists like these probably are not the ones reading them, I also believe that, through the #Dispatches, these kinds of conversations are working to strengthen a community of feminist travelers.

As we continue to study the implications of new and emerging writing practices on the internet, it is more important than ever to remember that, as Paula

Mathieu and Diana George write, "successful circulation of public writing is not achieved by going it alone, but through networks of relationships, in alliances between those in power and those without, through moments of serendipity."[35] Though their work is centered on innovative grassroots media and not necessarily on online communities, what they ultimately argue is something that Amor seems to understand well: "public writing relies on networks of collaboration and community action to circulate, find readers, and keep an issue alive."[36] Publishing a conversation between fellow travelers about complex issues in our globalized world is one such way to reach an increasingly diverse population and serve the needs of travelers who have, for a long time, felt as if their stories did not match the dominant narrative. The interview as a genre has its own ideological, historical, and cultural implications, and sites like *Everywhere All the Time* are using it not only to provide interesting content to readers but also to promote a specific political agenda and connect feminists in a more inclusive community of travelers. As feminist rhetorical practices continue to evolve and connect feminists across distances both real and imagined, Royster and Kirsch's words should continue to inform our research and study, reminding us that as we shift attention to feminist rhetorical practices "that may have escaped our attention, that we may not have valued (and therefore neglected to study)," we will begin to see critical engagement in "ever-vibrant, interlinking social circles" in ways we couldn't have previously imagined.[37]

Notes

1. Jacqueline Jones Royster and Gesa E. Kirsch, *Feminist Rhetorical Practices: New Horizons for Rhetoric, Composition, and Literacy Studies* (Carbondale: Southern Illinois University Press, 2012), 89.

2. For a fuller discussion of genre and its performative role in public spaces, see Anis Bawarshi and Mary Jo Reiff, eds., *Genre and the Performance of Publics* (Boulder: University Press of Colorado, 2016). Similar to what I argue here, the collection contends that understanding genres requires us to move beyond our conception of genre as merely a social way of organizing information and toward genre as a dynamic performance with sometimes unintended rhetorical effects.

3. Paata Natsvlishvili, "For the Genesis of Interview as a Genre," *European Scientific Journal* 2 (2013): 385.

4. Kerry Jones, "6 Tips for Hosting an Interview Series on Your Blog," Darren Rowse, *Problogger* (blog), accessed June 21, 2017, https://problogger.com.

5. Dan Saltzstein, "Travel Blogging Today: It's Complicated," *New York Times*, July 26, 2013, https://www.nytimes.com.

6. Gwyneth Kelly, "Travel Writing Doesn't Need Any More Voices Like Paul Theroux's," *New Republic*, September 11, 2015, https://newrepublic.com.

7. Alison Jagger, "Globalizing Feminist Ethics," in *Decentering the Center*, ed. Uma Narayan and Sandra Harding (Bloomington: Indiana University Press, 2000), 10.

8. To see Bani Amor's website in its current form, please see *Everywhere All the Time*, https://baniamor.com.

9. Linh Dich, "Community Enclaves and Public Imaginaries: Formations of Asian American Online Identities," *Computers and Composition* 40 (2016): 87.

10. Dich, 101.

11. Though Carmen Kynard's essay "Writing while Black" focuses primarily on black discourse in first-year academic writing, her assertion that the dominant gaze exerts immense power over the choices writers make is well suited in this context as well. See Kynard, "Writing while Black: The Colour Line, Black Discourses and Assessment in the Institutionalization of Writing Instruction" *English Teaching* 7, no. 2 (2008): 4–34.

12. Carsten Junker, "Interrogating the Interview as Genre," in *Postcoloniality-Decoloniality-Black Critique: Joints and Fissures*, ed. Sabine Broeck and Carsten Junker (Chicago: University of Chicago Press, 2014), 326.

13. Natsvlishvili, "For the Genesis of Interview," 384.

14. Jerome Boyd Maunsell, "The Literary Interview as Autobiography," *European Journal of Life Writing* 5 (2016): 26.

15. Maunsell, 26–27.

16. Natsvlishvili, "For the Genesis of Interview," 385.

17. Junker, "Interrogating the Interview," 326.

18. On "habits or rituals that work," see Paré, Anthony. "Genre and Identity: Individuals, Institutions, and Ideology," in *Rhetoric and Ideology of Genre: Strategies for Stability and Change*, ed. Richard Coe, Lorelei Lingard, and Tatiana Teslenko (New York: Hampton Press, 2002), 57–72.

19. Jessica Ouellette, "Blogging Borders: Transnational Feminist Rhetorics and Global Voices," *Harlot: A Revealing Look at the Arts of Persuasion* 11 (2014), http://harlotofthearts.org.

20. Harsha Walia, "Moving beyond a Politics of Solidarity toward a Politics of Decolonization," *Colours of Resistance Archive*, 2012, http://www.coloursofresistance.org.

21. Cindy Milstein, *Taking Sides: Revolutionary Solidarity and the Poverty of Liberalism* (Oakland, CA: AK Press, 2015), 46.

22. Carolyn R. Miller and Dawn Shepherd, "Blogging as Social Action: A Genre Analysis of the Weblog," in *Into the Blogosphere: Rhetoric, Community, and Culture of Weblogs*, ed. Laura J. Gurak et al. (Minneapolis: University of Minnesota, 2004), University of Michigan Digital Conservancy, http://hdl.handle.net/11299/172818.

23. For further reading on Miller and Shepherd's more recent work on genre and blogging, see their essay "Questions for Genre Theory from the Blogosphere," in *Genres in the Internet: Issues in the Theory of Genre*, ed. Janet Giltrow and Dieter Stein (Amsterdam: John Benjamins, 2009), 263–90.

24. Ouellette, "Blogging Borders."

25. Catherine Schryer, "Genre and Power: A *Chronotopic* Analysis," in Coe, Lingard, and Teslenko, *Rhetoric and Ideology of Genre*, 84 and 95.

26. Bani Amor, "About," *Everywhere All the Time*, accessed January 22, 2019, https://baniamor.com.

27. Bani Amor, "Dispatches," *Everywhere All the Time*, accessed January 22, 2019, https://baniamor.com.

28. Mary Louise Pratt, *Imperial Eyes: Travel Writing and Transculturation* (London: Routledge, 1992), 164.

29. Maunsell, "The Literary Interview," 26.

30. Royster and Kirsch, *Feminist Rhetorical Practices*, 101.

31. Alison Bailey, "Locating Traitorous Identities: Toward a View of Privilege-Cognizant White Character," *Hypatia* 13, no. 3 (1998): 32.

32. bell hooks, *Feminist Theory: From Margin to Center* (London: Routledge, 2015), 67.

33. Jane Mansbridge, "Using Power/Fighting Power: The Polity," in *Democracy and Difference: Contesting the Boundaries of the Political*, ed. S. Benhabib (Princeton, NJ: Princeton University Press, 1996), 46–60.

34. Karma R. Chávez, "Counter-Public Enclaves and Understanding the Function of Rhetoric in Social Movement Coalition-Building," *Communication Quarterly* 59, no. 1 (2011): 2.

35. Paula Mathieu and Diana George, "Not Going It Alone: Public Writing, Independent Media, and the Circulation of Homeless Advocacy," *College Composition and Communication* 61, no. 1 (2009): 144.

36. Mathieu and George, 145.

37. Royster and Kirsch, *Feminist Rhetorical Practices*, 101.

6

From Victorian Novels to #LikeALadyDoc

Women Physicians Strengthening Professional Ethos in the Public Sphere

KRISTIN E. KONDRLIK

IN EARLY 2016, THE BRITISH medical profession was in the midst of a staffing crisis. Crunched by an aging population and government austerity, Britain's National Health Service (NHS) struggled to negotiate a contract with junior doctors, physicians who had completed their degrees but not postgraduate training. Negotiations stalled over overtime compensation for work in "unsocial hours": weekend hours and hours worked between 7:00 p.m. and 7:00 a.m. on weekdays. On January 4, 2016, the British Medical Association established three strike dates. The first strike, on January 12, disrupted nonemergency medical care in Britain for twenty-four hours.

Under the threat of a second strike, the *Sunday Times* published an editorial on January 17 by writer Dominic Lawson, "The One Sex Change on the NHS That Nobody Has Been Talking about." Lawson asserted that the labor shortfalls in the NHS were a result not of tightening budgets but of gendered shifts in medical staffing. Lawson argued that "increasing numbers of female graduates will create a major shortfall in primary care provision."[1] According to Lawson, women physicians harm the NHS because they prioritize family over their careers and are therefore resistant to working unsocial hours. Lawson diagnosed such resistance as a symptom of the "feminisation" of British medicine—a turning away from "masculine" prioritization of professional over personal obligations. Rather than recognizing the complexity of the NHS's issues, Lawson presented his readers with a view of physicians that was born of archaic gender norms: women connected to home and men connected to profession.

The women Lawson discussed in his editorial struck back. Physician Rachel Clarke created the Twitter hashtag #LikeALadyDoc to engage directly with Lawson's characterization of women physicians. Posting a photograph of Lawson's article, Clarke wrote, "Dominic thinks we're the problem. Really? Try saying that while I'm cardioverting you. #likealadydoc" (@doctor_oxford, January 17, 2016). Referencing cardioversion, a procedure to correct abnormal heartbeats, Clarke noted that the supposed differences between men and women physicians fall away in practice. Clarke's tweet won support from male and female physicians alike; many responded by adopting Clarke's hashtag, #LikeALadyDoc. Some physicians expressed outrage at the article. Others pleaded for greater understanding of the difficulties women physicians face in the workplace. Still others posted pictures of themselves in scrubs, paired with captions rebuking Lawson. These tweets ranged widely in their means of expression, but at their heart, they drew on the affordances of Twitter's multimedia platform to challenge Lawson's criticisms of women physicians.

By engaging with new media outside of their professional duties, these writers joined a national tradition begun by Britain's first women physicians. In the nineteenth century, women doctors presented a challenge to established ideals of gender and work, which confined women to the home. Although women were successful in winning the right to practice medicine in 1876, this legal success did not translate into immediate changes in gender norms. Rather, women physicians, working in a male-dominated field, struggled to win recognition of their authority. The incommensurability of attitudes toward women physicians—of representations of women doctors as contrary to ideal womanhood—created obstacles, and women doctors confronted a resistant public and profession. This continuity of historical and contemporary discourses stands in stark contrast to the discourse surrounding other activist groups such as the Ukrainian FEMEN, which pointedly breaks from traditional and historical feminist discourses.

Where studies of women physicians and ethos, or rhetorical authority, by Carolyn Skinner and Susan Wells focus on women's writing and speaking in professional genres, this chapter centers on how women physicians both in the nineteenth century and today have reshaped their ethos by writing in nonprofessional genres. As do contemporary women, historical physicians and their allies responded to critics by writing for the popular media platforms of their time: burgeoning print culture genres such as novels, memoir, and periodicals. Popular print media allowed women physicians to interact with the broader reading public in ways not possible through their usual professional duties. Thus, female physicians' supporters not only criticized cultural norms that hindered their professional progress but also circulated representations of women as capable physicians, proposing radical alterations to understandings of women's orientation to the public sphere, the public, and the professions. Contemporary physicians using #LikeALadyDoc to dispel outdated gender norms, thus, participate in a historical tradition of using emerging popular media to circulate re-articulations of what it means to be a physician and a woman in a time of shifting gender norms. For feminist rhetoricians, a recognition of this connection calls attention to the abiding power of women's acts of rhetorically aware and genre-aware engagement with popular media, as women across time have used these practices to shift conversations about gender, medicine, and work.

PROBLEMS OF ETHOS FOR VICTORIAN WOMEN PHYSICIANS

Nineteenth-century British physicians, like the women of 2016, faced cultural assumptions that tied women to the domestic sphere. The 1876 legislation that gave women the legal right to become physicians did little to alter restrictive gender norms. The persistence of these norms is reflected in representations of these women in the public sphere. In *Medical Women and Victorian Fiction*, Kristine Swenson notes that writers represented women physicians as unfeminine, weak, and incompetent and, therefore, unfit for medicine.[2] These derogations appeared in professional and popular discourse. In, for example, a speech reprinted in the British medical profession's flagship publication, the *British Medical Journal*, in October 1887, Pierce Adolphus Simpson acknowledges women's "pluck" in winning admission to the profession but argues that "by [her] frame, temperament, and mental constitution woman is not well adapted for medical, far less for surgical, practice."[3] Simpson suggests that women's biological makeup makes them unfit for medicine. Similarly, in 1878, popular satirical periodical *Punch* mocked female physicians in a fictional set of meeting notes of the "Amalgamated Medical Practitioners," a send-up of the British Medical Association. One of the "speakers" notes women physicians' failures as both women and physicians: "Medical studies would tend to destroy female grace and refinement, and all those charms which rendered ladies ornaments of the domestic circle. . . . The faculties of women's minds unfitted them for medical reasoning. Life and death were not to be trusted in their fair but fragile hands."[4] In this text, domestic women—ornaments in society—are graceful and charming, while women physicians only retain their feminine fragility, which makes them dangerous. These and other acts of public writing about women and medicine reinforced skeptical attitudes toward medical women in the latter part of the nineteenth century.

Such suspicion of women physicians was a problem of a distinctly rhetorical nature. In *Health and the Rhetoric of Medicine*, Judy Z. Segal argues that rather than the mere application of scientific theory to the body, "persuasion is a central element in many medical situations" and that medical "experts persuade the public to count some states and behaviors as pathological and others as not."[5] Key to the practice of biomedicine is the persuasion not only of patients, but also of the public and the other professionals, to particular actions or attitudes. Late nineteenth-century medicine was similarly bound up in persuasion. During this period, a female physician's profession involved her ability to persuade patients, colleagues, and the broader public to adopt recommended courses of treatment or of the validity of her readings of the human body—whether in research or in consultations with patients.

Representations of women as unfit for medical practice, however, engendered attitudes that prevented women doctors from enacting such persuasion. Early women physicians in Britain faced a problem of ethos—of the persuasiveness of "character" to an audience. Aristotle delineates three distinct but related aspects of ethos: *phronesis* (the ability to exercise practical knowledge of a subject), *eunoia* (goodwill to community), and *aretē* (excellence or virtue). The possession of these three qualities by a speaker, Aristotle indicates, "is necessarily persuasive to the hearers."[6] Ethos, then, affects the audience's perspective of the speaker. Contemporary rhetorical scholars such as Michael S. Halloran have emphasized the communal nature of ethos. Halloran writes that "the most concrete meaning given for [ethos] in the Greek lexicon is a 'habitual gathering place,' . . . it is upon this image of people gathering together in a public place sharing experiences and ideas, that its meaning as character rests."[7] A speaker's ethos, thus, serves as a point of connection between herself, her audience, and the communities to which the speaker and audience members belong. In the late nineteenth century, women physicians belonged to a number of communities, including that of their profession and the "community" of the general public. Acceptance of a woman physician as a credible and authoritative member of her profession relied in part on her ethos—her ability to persuade audiences of her goodwill to these communities, her good sense and knowledge and practice of medicine, and her good character in her fit into the profession.

Nineteenth-century writers who opposed female physicians attacked each of the three areas of their ethos. Print representations of female physicians frequently undermined their *aretē*. In a striking example, writers to both the *Lancet* and the *British Medical Journal* continued to use the term *medical woman* or *woman doctor* well into the twentieth century, reinforcing the division between doctors and women doctors. Representations also undermined women's *eunoia*. Wilkie Collins, in his 1882 short story "Fie! Fie! or, The Fair Physician," and L. T. Meade and Robert Eustace, in their serials *The Brotherhood of Seven Kings* (1898–99) and *Sorceress of the Strand* (1903), for example, depicted female physicians as unwitting prostitutes or criminals. Finally, many representations undermined women's *phronesis*. In the *British Medical Journal* in May 1892, for example, neurologist James Crichton-Browne argued that women's brains would be overtaxed by education. He wrote that men's and women's brains "are differentiated from each other in structure and function, and fitted to do different kinds of work in the world."[8] Implicit in Crichton-Browne's argument is the need to exclude women from the medical profession, a field requiring intense study and grueling examinations. Each of these critiques of women's ethos centered on their relationships to the public, other women, and their profession—

specifically, on the harm these women would wreak on their communities, male physicians, and their own well-being.

Such representations damaged the public's and profession's attitudes toward medical women. In 1886, physician Sophia Jex-Blake highlights her growing frustration with the effects of these representations: "We are told . . . that nature and custom have alike decided against the admission of women to the medical profession."[9] Echoing Jex-Blake in 1906, female physician M. L. A. Boileau describes meeting acquaintances who believe that women doctors "study just the same things as men—with the nasty parts left out."[10] Boileau's friends view the category of woman doctor as inherently separate from and inferior to that of doctor. Jex-Blake's account reiterates the opposition between women physicians and women's typical place in Victorian nature and custom, and Boileau's acquaintances suggest that only men are truly physicians. Both Boileau's and Jex-Blake's accounts reveal a pervasive uneasiness with women in the medical profession.

These attitudes had consequences for women's careers. Kristine Swenson notes that Britain's first women physicians were restricted to the less prestigious areas of obstetrics and gynecology and steered away from the elite areas of surgery and administration.[11] The *British Medical Journal*, for instance, details a vote for an administrator in Lambeth in 1894. In choosing between candidates, an experienced woman and a less-experienced man, administrators selected the man, arguing that the woman would be better suited for managing a women and children's ward.[12] Doubts about women's place in the medical profession also resulted in their continued exclusion from organizations such as the British Medical Association, the Royal College of Physicians, and the Royal College of Surgeons, which served as social organizations for the profession. Women physicians' professional status, then, was undermined by persistent views of women's unfitness for the category of physician, engendered through attacks on their ethos.

CONSTRUCTING MEDICAL ETHOS THROUGH POPULAR AND EMERGING MEDIA: GENERATION AND CRITIQUE

Contemporary rhetorical scholarship has asserted two ways that individuals such as women physicians can effect changes to their ethos: performative and interactive. The more widely recognized means of shaping ethos is performative. E. Johanna Hartelius, in *The Rhetoric of Expertise*, argues that ethos "is more about performance than about a tacit record of personal excellence."[13] From this perspective, an individual can demonstrate ethos by performing its three aspects in contextually situated discourse. A female physician, for example, could demonstrate *aretē* by competently discussing medicine in professional journals, or *eunoia* by speaking compassionately with her patients or the public.

Defining ethos as merely performative, however, does not fully acknowledge how individuals with restricted access to discursive spaces work around such limitations. Notably, while nineteenth-century men had access to medical associations and journals—professional spaces where a performance of ethos could occur—women's access to these platforms was more circumscribed. As Catriona Blake has noted in *The Charge of the Parasols*, male physicians positioned medicine as a "'community' of men, bound together by a system of exclusive associations, journals and clubs."[14] For decades after their admission into the profession, women were prohibited from membership in prominent medical societies, where physicians performed public orations about their professional practices.[15] Women would occasionally deliver professional talks, but their audiences mostly comprised other women physicians. Additionally, women's access to medical journals where they could perform ethos through writing knowledgeably about medical subjects was limited. Women physicians wrote occasionally about their clinical observations in the *British Medical Journal* and the *Lancet*, but as Blake has noted, editors of these journals often excluded women's voices.[16] Such limitations extended beyond the professional sphere. Consultations with patients, where a physician's ethos could be performed for nonphysicians, were confidential and only rarely discussed in public. As a result of women's isolation in obstetrics and gynecology, these last performances of ethos generally only reached women patients.

In view of such issues of access, especially for historical women rhetors, Carolyn Skinner has advocated an understanding of ethos that moves beyond performance. Skinner, rather, argues for an interactive model. A rhetor's ethos, she notes, can be modified or created outside of contextually situated acts of declamation; specifically, she argues that rhetors and, by extension, other writers and speakers can shape or reshape the ethos of a group by interacting with an audience's existing perceptions of that group.[17] This chapter outlines two specific manifestations of Skinner's initial interactional construction of ethos practiced by the first British women physicians: critical and generative. Writers reshaped medical women's ethos by *criticizing* existing or *generating* new discursive representations of this marginalized group.

One of the major advocates of women physicians encouraged writers to participate in such interactive reshaping of ethos. Writing in 1872, Sophia Jex-Blake states that, for advocates of women in medicine, "a constantly recurring duty will lie before every one who believes in life as a responsive time of action, and not as a period of mere vegetative existence, to 'prove all things, and hold fast to that which is good.'"[18] She declares it "a duty for all . . . to test these statements [against female physicians' experiences and expertise] and to see how far their truth is supported by evidence."[19] Jex-Blake suggests that women physicians and their supporters ought to combat statements against women physicians—including their representation in both popular and professional discourse—by taking their own arguments in favor of women physicians to the broader public.

In the late nineteenth century, writers had the opportunity to critique and generate public discourse in unprecedented ways. Writers and readers inhabited what Laurel Brake, Bill Bell, and David Finkelstein term an "increasingly textual environment."[20] The decreasing cost of paper, increased literacy, and advances in technology allowed for easier circulation of print discourses. Social and political movements exploited the explosion of print culture to sway the public to their causes.[21] Women's political movements made especially quick use of print's affordances. Most notably, as Jane Eldridge Miller has argued in *Rebel Women*, women's suffrage advocates promoted their cause in general-interest periodicals and specialized magazines, created pro-suffrage publications, and published fiction promoting women's suffrage.[22] In this rich print environment, women physicians and their supporters heeded Jex-Blake's exhortation to prove entrenched beliefs about gender and the medical profession through acts of both critique and generation.

Writers circulated critiques of the specter of the female physician through print venues aimed at both their profession and the public. In professional journals, women physicians passionately defended their work. When confronted with Crichton-Browne's assertions about women's brains, for example, Elizabeth Garrett Anderson critiqued his characterizations of women's intellectual limitations as fallacious, citing her own medical training and success. Women physicians also criticized existing representations of the female physician in publications for the general public. Arabella Kenealy's "How Women Doctors Are Made," published in the popular *Ludgate Monthly* in May 1897, dismisses misrepresentations of women physicians. Kenealy notes that women "rank with the first physicians of our time . . . without symptom whatsoever of that 'unsexing' process whereof we have heard so much and have seen less in the ranks of medicine than in any other field of women's work."[23] She opposes accusations of inferior technical skills among women physicians and suggests that medicine does not force them to abandon their femininity in order to succeed. Women physicians, then, critiqued the public's views where the public and other professionals would have easy access to these criticisms.

In order to bolster their ethos, however, women physicians also moved beyond critique; writers *generated* new representations of the woman physician. They crafted and disseminated representations of "real" women physicians that countered existing assumptions about women physicians as dangerously incompetent or unfeminine, even into the twentieth century. In a 1913 issue of the popular *Pall Mall Magazine*, for example, writer Wanda De Szaramowicz describes a "charmingly-dressed woman, with [a] fashionable hat and smart sunshade," and she notes that the average onlooker would be surprised that this fair figure is "the brilliant gynaecologist at a big London hospital."[24] De Szaramowicz expresses disappointment that her fellow Britons find the juxtaposition of femininity and medical skill jarring.[25] De Szaramowicz's article articulates a new possible relationship between women physicians and the community. Women physicians also recounted their own experiences in order to debunk accusations against their medical skill or service to the nation. Caroline Matthews, a physician working on the frontlines of the second Serbian civil war in the 1910s, wrote about her experiences in the periodical *Sphere* and in a memoir, *Experiences of a Woman Doctor in Serbia* (1916). Her writing features graphic descriptions of her medical work at war and of her harrowing experiences as a prisoner of war. Matthews's writing, much like De Szaramowicz's, reenvisions the female physician, rejects assertions about women's weakness, and posits Matthews as a doctor sacrificing her well-being for the health of her nation and its allies.

In the interest of further promoting women physicians in writing, female physicians and their supporters moved into representing women physicians in fiction. Jex-Blake discusses fiction's persuasive and political potential in her 1893 essay "Medical Women in Fiction." Jex-Blake opens her essay with an aphorism from writer Andrew Fletcher: "Let me make the ballads, let who will make the laws!"[26] In the essay from which this aphorism is drawn, Fletcher notes the rhetorical power of poetry in Britain's past: it could influence the public's attitudes more than could legislation.[27] Jex-Blake sees the work being done by the popular fiction of her time as connected to this politically motivating poetry. She writes, "Though Fiction cannot aspire . . . to the position that was held by popular poetry in the Middle Ages, still it may be taken as in some sort its equivalent and successor."[28] Jex-Blake argues that although fiction lacks the cultural cachet that was held by medieval poetry, it is part of the same spectrum: novels possess the potential to sway the opinions of the masses in ways that legal strictures cannot.

Writers used popular novels as vehicles for circulating representations of women physicians. After the legal changes of 1876, the first woman physician to appear in a novel was in Charles Reade's 1887 *A Woman-Hater*. The novel's protagonist rescues talented doctor Rhoda Gale from devastating poverty and employs her to care for his tenants. Reade, known for his novels about social issues, provides a lengthy account of women's fight for medical practice. He depicts Gale as supremely skilled and self-sacrificing. Novels like Reade's, however, while popular with readers, were often lambasted by critics for their focus on political content, rather than on character development.[29] Gale, notably, is only a vehicle for sharing women's struggle to enter medicine. She is an underdeveloped character, prey to the inverse of the sexist tropes Reade sought to dispel: that professionally competent women lack traits of conventional and socially accepted femininity. Despite her competence at medicine, Gale is distinctly and oftentimes garishly unfeminine—uninterested in conventional marriage, masculine, prickly and "unladylike." She is a physician at the cost of belonging to the "community" of women, suggesting an inherent disconnection between conventional femininity and professional medicine.

Crafted by nonphysicians, many other novels featuring women physicians after 1876 struggled to find a balance between representing women's struggles and preserving their ethos. These novels represented women physicians as facing insurmountable social and political foes that kept them from achieving both professional success and personal fulfillment. In the anonymously published *Edith Romney, M.B.* (1883), for example, a woman physician takes up medical practice, only to be sabotaged by her male competitor, Dr. Fane. Romney, as a result of emotional strain, becomes ill with "brain fever," and Fane nurses her back to health. She marries him and abandons medicine. Conversely, G. G. Alexander's 1881 novel *Dr. Victoria* details its heroine's attempts to balance her career with her affection for the wealthy Sir Francis. In the end, Dr. Victoria retains her occupation and encourages Sir Francis to marry her more traditionally feminine cousin. As with Reade's novel, none of these later novels allows a woman to be both talented in her profession and possessing of traditional ideals of femininity; these women, then, were framed as social outsiders—not full members of the communities they served—or as individuals without the fortitude to remain in medical practice.

Women physicians, including Jex-Blake, found such novels troubling. Jex-Blake, in responding to these novels, notes that they fail to reflect her experiences as a woman physician. She notes the "touch of burlesque" in the otherwise "kindly" representation of medical women in *A Woman-Hater* and asserts that *Edith Romney, M.B.* is so foreign to her own experiences that the novel's events "must have been upon another planet."[30] She acknowledges that writers may write whatever they wish about female physicians. She asserts, however, that "the public has a right to require" that representations of female physicians "should not . . . be evolved over a study fire, from the depths of the author's inner consciousness" but rather "should be in some sense taken from life."[31] Jex-Blake, then, encourages writers to more realistically represent women physicians' competence and their responses to the opposition they faced in their professional lives.

In order to combat misrepresentations of their ethos, during the 1890s, women physicians and their supporters generated and circulated representations of women physicians that centered on the difficulties they faced in integrating conventional femininity with their professional ambition—and the ways in which these women could balance what to Victorian Britons were seemingly opposite goals. One such example is medical student and author Margaret Todd's 1892 novel *Mona Maclean, Medical Student*, which details the trials of Todd's eponymous heroine. Mona's friends describe her as clever, cultured, earnest, feminine, and charming.[32] She is not, notably, inhumanly skilled at medicine, as is Reade's Rhoda Gale. At the beginning of the novel, Mona fails her exams—a result of nerves and a lack of preparation, not of a lack of knowledge. Disheartened, Mona leaves medical school and endures her family's scorn for her profession. Her uncle declares, "The very first day I saw your face, I felt sure that you were not the sort to make a doctor. That kind of work wants women of coarser fiber. There is no use trying to chop wood with a razor."[33] In her uncle's and society's views, Mona—feminine, charming, and pretty—is not made of the right material to be a successful physician. In this light, Mona hides her former medical study from her love interest, Dr. Dudley, a male physician. When this concealment is revealed, Dudley rejects her.

Todd's Mona is not flattened by professional or personal setbacks, however, as were Dr. Romney and Dr. Victoria. The events of the novel demonstrate that medical practice is an essential part of Mona's sense of identity and is not at odds with her femininity. Although she demurs, flirting at times with the idea of quitting her studies in order to become a botanist or a clerk, Mona demonstrates her natural aptitude and inclination for medicine by taking on the role of caregiver for numerous people she encounters during her sabbatical—a woman who falls ill at a dance, a friend from medical school, and others—even when she has supposedly abandoned medicine. Mona returns to medical school before the end of the novel, her "nature" overcoming her doubts about her professional skills and her family's assertions about its conflicts with her femininity. At the novel's conclusion, Mona's personal conflicts are also resolved, when she reconnects with Dudley after beating him for a medical prize in physiology. They marry and found a joint practice. Mona, then, unlike her predecessors, joins personal and professional success, combining conventional marriage, feminine personality traits, and medical practice while retaining a positive relationship to the profession and the public.

A few years after Todd's novel was published, Hilda Gregg crafted her own vision of a woman physician with a solid ethos in *Peace with Honour* (1897). Gregg's sister Katherine trained as a physician and undertook missionary work abroad. Gregg's novel details physician Georgia Keeling's travels to Ethiopia with British diplomats. While her novel adopts an adventure plot, including a kidnapping, poisonings, and the discovery of long-dead friends, Gregg—like Todd—incorporates conflicts between femininity and medical practice. Gregg's novel differs from its predecessors, however, in that Keeling is older and more experienced, already having graduated from medical school and lived abroad for many years. Gregg represents Keeling as a level-headed professional, even in dire situations. Keeling successfully cares for her party independently; she amputates a limb, investigates poisonings, and removes cataracts. Her travel companion Lady Haigh notes that the rigor of Keeling's training has strengthened her confidence and her sense of herself as a professional. Haigh asks a fellow traveler, "Is it likely that after going through her training as creditably as she has done, she would ever allow herself to be convinced that it had been impossible or improbable for her to study medicine?"[34] Gregg emphasizes Keeling's fortitude throughout the novel, especially at its conclusion. In a direct reversal of the events in *Edith Romney, M.B.*, male protagonist Dick North, rather than Keeling, succumbs to brain fever after physical and emotional strain, and Keeling nurses North back to health.

Gregg's novel, further, asserts that derogations of women physicians' ethos are outdated. Throughout the novel, North struggles with his affection for Keeling and his hatred of her profession. Other characters berate North for his archaic ideas. North's sister, Mabel, is especially critical of him. She notes that North's ideal woman is subservient, rather than his equal. She asserts that he likes "a woman's eyes to drop before [his], as a sort of unconscious tribute to [his] greatness and [his] glory. A man may look at a woman with the calmest insolence, but she must only steal a glance at his face when he is not looking."[35] North's inability to understand Keeling's profession and her skill becomes a major theme of the novel, only subsiding after his brain fever has led him to rashly break off their engagement, nearly losing her forever. At the end of the novel, however, they are married, and Keeling retains her profession.

Writers such as Todd and Gregg, thus, circulated representations of women physicians that presented them as being good physicians (having *aretē*), being medically competent (exercising *phronesis*), and serving their communities (exercising *eunoia*)—but also as not entirely divorced from conventional femininity, as many of their detractors would have readers believe. These women's reliance on conventional femininity, however, was not without its own issues. Notably, both Todd and Gregg paint a picture of the ideal, feminized woman physician— married, pretty, self-sacrificing for her romantic partner—that may have only deepened the marginalization of women physicians who did not conform to Victorian society's ideals of what a woman should be, do, and look like. Regardless, writing about women physicians in this popular genre brought what might have been insular conversations about women physicians' professional ethos and their relationships to the community and their profession to the general public. These representations offered the reading public diverse perspectives on how a woman might practice her profession in ways that benefitted the community around her, her profession, and herself.

GENERATIVE ETHOS AND CONTEMPORARY MEDICAL WOMEN

While the resistance women faced as doctors in 2016 was less universal than that faced by women physicians at the turn of the twentieth century, both groups faced a problem of ethos. As did early women doctors, contemporary women suffer under the assumption that being a woman ties them more to the domestic than the professional sphere, which undermines perceptions of their dedication to their profession and their credibility with their colleagues and the general public. It should not be surprising, therefore, that contemporary women have drawn on platforms such as Twitter in the same way that their precursors took advantage of the affordances of popular media genres such as novels and periodicals. Twitter is an open-access platform, meaning that the conversation on #LikeALadyDoc was accessible to the public and that tweets could circulate widely. At the time of the controversy around Lawson's article, Twitter allowed individuals to write 140-character messages, though this limit was increased to 280 characters in November 2017, after the initial controversy around Lawson's article had faded. These messages can be paired with images and videos, visible on the "timelines" of users following individuals and curated through the use of hashtags: if users search for or click on a hashtag, they can find tweets tagged with a word or phrase. Thus, the use of a hashtag sorts a tweet into a public collection of similar tweets, which any user can find and respond to. Because women shared Lawson's article with the hashtag, the article was connected to tagged tweets and the conversation surrounding them.

Contemporary women physicians in Britain drew on both critique and generation as they participated in conversations about Lawson's article through #LikeALadyDoc. Many women physicians directly criticized Lawson's characterizations of medical women. They echoed Rachel Clarke's assertions that men and women physicians are equally skilled and deserving of the same respect. Critical care anesthesiologist Maritejie Slabbert writes, "I might be the one resuscitating you in a ditch Dominic Lawson @thetimes #likealadydoc Indefensible sexist hogwash" (@mjslabbert, January 17, 2016). Other physicians note that gendering the professional and domestic spheres only further obscures the problems that the NHS faces. Posting a photograph of herself in a T-shirt with the word HAPPY in pink, intensive care physician Aoife Abbey asserts, "The NHS has problems. My gender isn't one of them. #likealadydoc #pinkwednesday" (@WhistlingDixie4, January 20, 2016). In this short tweet, Abbey notes that Lawson's criticisms are misdirected: the problem is not women's differences from men. Blaming the failures of the NHS on an outdated notion of femininity obscures the causes of its issues. Other writers, such as Johann Malawana, note the counterproductivity of Lawson's gender essentialism, given the current state of the NHS. He writes, "Middle of serious crisis in medical staffing & recruitment. What should we do? Put out sexist articles blaming it on women #likealadydoc" (@johannmalawana, January 17, 2016).

Women physicians also used Twitter to more playfully criticize Lawson's characterizations of women in the medical profession. These women take Lawson's assertions to their absurd ends: blaming women's biology—most often their reproductive organs—for harming medicine. Posting a photograph of herself at work in a hospital, pediatrician Carmen Soto writes, "Sorry ovaries, you'll have to wait. This LTFT [less than full-time] Dr has a 12.5hr shift to do. #likealadydoc

#pinkwednesday" (@gourmetpenguin, January 20, 2016). Soto notes that, even as a part-time physician, she puts her "womanly" priorities—indicated through her reference to her reproductive organs—on hold in order to complete her professional obligations. Emphasizing that her part-time shift is a grueling 12.5 hours, Soto further highlights the groundlessness of Lawson's claim that women physicians are asking to be coddled. Other women noted the absurdity of Lawson's representation of women in the professions. Zoe Norris, a general practitioner, satirizes Lawson's notion of female-coded medicine. Posting a photograph of a pink pen, Norris writes, "My sparkly work pen because if I have to sign prescriptions with a nasty boys['] one I cry all day long #likealadydoc" (@dr_zo, January 17, 2016). Norris mocks the notion that, in seeking more overtime pay for all junior doctors, the British Medical Association is somehow asking for special treatment for women or advocating a weaker, "feminized" medicine. Charline Roslee similarly mocks the notion of weaker or less focused feminized medicine, posting a photograph of herself holding a large orthopedic tool and writing, "Became confused mid Ortho op and tried to give myself a manicure. Then I cried. Blasted ovaries! #likealadydoc" (@hell_on_heels, January 18, 2016). The juxtaposition of the image of Roslee holding the oversized medical device and her assertions that her female reproductive organs confused her into thinking it was a set of nail clippers demonstrates the ludicrous nature of Lawson's characterization of women physicians.

Rather than directly criticize Lawson's article, many other women physicians opted to indirectly contest it by generating and circulating representations of themselves, often retaining a satirical tone. Writers circulated representations of women physicians that reinforced their ethos overall. Many writing to the hashtag, as did Rachel Clarke, pointed out that women are skilled; Clarke, by noting that her skill is indistinguishable from that of her male peers, represents herself and other women physicians as possessing *phronesis*, the ability to wield technical knowledge. Similar to Clarke, emergency physician Louise Cullen notes her practical and intellectual qualifications, sharing a photograph of herself in academic robes and writing, "PhD + FACEM [Fellow of the Australasian College for Emergency Medicine] + Clinical Director + wife and mum of 2 girls + obviously failing as outsourcing meals ... #likealadydoc" (@louiseacullen, January 25, 2016). Cullen represents herself as professionally and personally successful, despite what she satirically pinpoints as her domestic "failure" of having to order in meals. Other physicians focus on women's contributions to the health and well-being of other members of their communities, emphasizing their goodwill or *eunoia*. Kate Prior, an anesthetist, shares a photograph of herself in military fatigues, writing, "Saving lives with a couple of weapons to hand @the times #likealadydoc" (@doctorwibble, January 17, 2016). Prior's circulation of her words and photograph not only connects women physicians with their patients' health but also represents herself as serving the health of the British nation in her work as a physician. Male physicians also contributed representations of women physicians that reinforced their goodwill and their dedication to being the "right" kind of physician. Male junior doctor Dagan Lonsdale notes that, "This weekend, I checked every major decision about a patient with a woman-My consultant. My boss. My role model. #likealadydoc" (@daganlonsdale, January 17, 2016). Lonsdale generates and circulates a representation of a female physician as a mentor shaping the next generation of young (and, in this case, male) doctors, strengthening not only women physicians' *aretē* or competence in their profession but also their *eunoia* or service to their community. Such representations reinforce women's place in the profession, as they demonstrate the benefits these women provide for the various communities they serve as medical professionals and their fitness for the profession.

Many other women physicians crafted and circulated representations of themselves and their personal lives that emphasized their ability to exercise professional ethos and maintain a satisfying domestic life, directly countering Lawson's claims about conflicts between women's home lives and their professions. Lynn Miller, a consultant cardiologist, posted a picture of one of her daughters dressed as a doctor and wrote, "I'm Dominic Lawson's nightmare - a lady doctor with mini lady doctors. Wrecking the NHS #likealadydoc bwahahahaaa" (@LynnGreigMiller, January 17, 2016). Miller relishes serving as a counterexample to Lawson's gender essentialism, as she is both a physician and a mother. Kristen Conrad similarly emphasizes her successful relationship with her children in nonwork hours. Conrad shared a picture of herself playing with her son, both of them with big smiles on their faces, and wrote, "This is what I do when I'm not 'working out of my hours' #likealadydoc #traumamama #ILookLikeASurgeon" (@kc140605, January 21, 2016). Conrad, a trauma surgeon, emphasizes her success in the "other" obligations that supposedly "limit" her professional advancement. Other writers echoed Miller's and Conrad's satirical engagement with Lawson's argument without emphasizing motherhood. Surgeon Roshana Mehdian, for example, notes, alongside a photograph of herself in scrubs, "I can scrub up . . . both the DISHES and for an OPERATION

Though contemporary women's use of Twitter to critique and generate ethos resembles the strategies used by historical women, Twitter's particular affordances shape these interventions. Most notably, contemporary technologies far outpace those of the nineteenth century, allowing for more dynamic conversations about women's representation in cultural discourses. The responses to Lawson's article appeared within hours of its publication, whereas nineteenth-century print responses took days or more to appear. Additionally, where nineteenth-century writers had to work with publishing gatekeepers, any individual with a Twitter account can contribute to #LikeALadyDoc. Thus, Twitter's format allows for a plurality of responses from women of different backgrounds, which means that the women represented by the hashtag demonstrate more diverse relationships to the notion of traditional femininity than either Todd's or Gregg's novels. Twitter also fosters long-term discussion. Long after the 2016 strike concluded, users have continued to use the hashtag to share articles and photographs and offer commentary about current events affecting women physicians.

#LikeALadyDoc is just one example of contemporary women in stereotypically masculine professions using social media to circulate representations of themselves to the general public. In response to other recent sexist remarks, women engineers created the hashtag #ILookLikeAnEngineer, while women scientists created the hashtag #DistractinglySexy. Discussions about women in scientific professions on social media have also highlighted intersectional concerns. On October 9, 2016, Delta flight attendants called for assistance in helping a passenger. Tamika Cross, a black physician, volunteered, but a flight attendant assumed that Cross was not a doctor, as a result of her age and race. Eventually, Cross was allowed to assist, but, infuriated, she posted an account of her experiences to Facebook, noting the "blatant discrimination" she faced as a young black physician.[36] Similar to British physicians, black physicians created a Twitter hashtag, #WhatDoesADoctorLookLike, to discuss medicine and race; physicians posted selfies in scrubs, circulating representations that opposed assumptions that physicians are white and male.

Both nineteenth-century and contemporary women physicians engaged popular media to circulate re-articulations of what it means to be a physician and a woman in a time of shifting gender norms. These two examples not only demonstrate that #LikeALadyDoc is part of a historical tradition of women professionals responding to public resistance through nonprofessional genres; they also emphasize the abiding power of acts of rhetorically aware and genre-aware engagement with the popular media of the day for strengthening women's ethos. By writing for genres that reached beyond their duties as medical professionals, writers of both social media posts in the twenty-first century and of novels and essays in the nineteenth century contributed to ongoing public discourse about gender and medicine and combated the ever-evolving resistance toward women in male-dominated professions.

Notes

1. Dominic Lawson, "The One Sex Change on the NHS That Nobody Has Been Talking about," *Sunday Times*, January 17, 2016, http://www.thetimes.co.uk.

2. Kristine Swenson, *Medical Women and Victorian Fiction* (Columbia: University of Missouri Press, 2005), 87–88.

3. Pierce Adolphus Simpson, "An Address on Post-Graduate Possibilities. Delivered at the Opening of the Medical Classes in the University of Glasgow, October 25th, 1887," *British Medical Journal* 2, no. 1400 (October 29, 1887): 927.

4. "The Fair Sex and the Faculty," *Punch* 74 (January 26, 1878): 34.

5. Judy Z. Segal, *Health and the Rhetoric of Medicine* (Carbondale: Southern Illinois University Press, 2006), 1–2.

6. Aristotle, *On Rhetoric: A Theory of Civic Discourse*, trans. George A. Kennedy (New York: Oxford University Press, 1991), 121.

7. Michael S. Halloran, "Aristotle's Concept of *Ethos*, or if Not His Somebody Else's," *Rhetoric Review* 1, no. 1 (1982): 60.

8. James Crichton-Browne, "The Annual Oration on Sex in Education. Delivered before the Medical Society of London," *British Medical Journal* 1, no. 1636 (May 7, 1892): 949–54.

9. Sophia Jex-Blake, *Medical Women: A Thesis and a History* (New York: Source Book Press, 1970), 4.

10. M. L. A. Boileau, "The Lay Mind," *Magazine of the London School of Medicine for Women* 35 (October 1906): 675.

11. Swenson, *Medical Women and Victorian Fiction*, 132.

12. "Medical Women as Workhouse Doctors," *British Medical Journal* 1, no. 1729 (February 17, 1894): 371.

13. E. Johanna Hartelius, *The Rhetoric of Expertise* (Lanham, MD: Lexington Books, 2011), 12.

14. Catriona Blake, *The Charge of the Parasols: Women's Entry into the Medical Profession* (London: Women's Press, 1990), 24.

15. Women were only admitted to the British Medical Association in 1892 (with the exception of Elizabeth Garrett Anderson, who was admitted in 1873), the Royal College of Physicians in 1909, and the Royal College of Surgeons in 1911.

16. Blake, *The Charge of the Parasols*, 24.

17. Carolyn Skinner, *Women Physicians and Professional Ethos in Nineteenth-Century America* (Carbondale: Southern Illinois University Press, 2014), 40.

18. Jex-Blake, *Medical Women*, 4.

19. Jex-Blake, 5.

20. Laurel Brake, Bill Bell, and David Finkelstein, *Nineteenth-Century Media and the Construction of Identities* (New York: Palgrave MacMillan, 2000), 3.

21. Maria DiCenzo, Lucy Delap, and Leila Ryan note that the multifaceted and broad sweep of print in this period offered social and political movements unprecedented access to the public sphere. See DiCenzo, Delap, and Ryan, *Feminist Media History: Suffrage, Periodicals, and the Public Sphere* (New York: Palgrave Macmillan, 2010), 24.

22. Jane Eldridge Miller, *Rebel Women: Feminism, Modernism and the Edwardian Novel* (Chicago: University of Chicago Press, 1994), 125–62.

23. Arabella Kenealy, "How Women Doctors Are Made," *Ludgate Monthly* 4 (May 1897): 30.

24. Wanda De Szaramowicz, "The Woman Doctor," *Pall Mall Magazine* 52, no. 246 (October 1913): 497.

25. De Szaramowicz, 497.

26. Sophia Jex-Blake, "Medical Women in Fiction," *Nineteenth Century* 33, no. 192 (1893): 261.

27. Andrew Fletcher, *An Account of a Conversation concerning a right regulation of Governments for the common good of Mankind* (Edinburgh, 1704), 10.

28. Jex-Blake, "Medical Women in Fiction," 261.

29. A writer for the *Westminster Review*, for example, expresses his annoyance with Reade, writing, "If Mr. Reade will turn a novel into a pamphlet, he must take the consequences." See "Belles Lettres," *Westminster Review* 108, no. 214 (October 1877): 273.

30. Jex-Blake, "Medical Women in Fiction," 263.

31. Jex-Blake, 261–62.

32. Margaret Todd, *Mona Maclean, Medical Student*, ed. Oliver Lovesy (London: Pickering and Chatto, 2011), 69.

33. Todd, 323.

34. Hilda Gregg, *Peace with Honour* (Boston: L. C. Page, 1902), 38.

35. Gregg, 12.

36. Tamika Cross, "I'm sure many of my fellow young, corporate America working women of color can all understand my frustration when I say I'm sick of being disrespected," *Facebook*, October 9, 2016, https://www.facebook.com.

7

Feminist Rhetorical Strategies and Networked Activist Movements

#SayHerName as Circulatory Activist Discourse

LIZ LANE

> If we can't see a problem, we can't fix a problem. Together, we've come together to bear witness to these women's lost lives. But the time now is to move from mourning and grief to action and transformation. This is something that we can do. It's up to us.
>
> —Kimberlé Crenshaw, "The Urgency of Intersectionality"

FEMINIST LEGAL SCHOLAR KIMBERLÉ CRENSHAW urged the audience of her October 2016 TED Talk to heed her call to action, calling on listeners to remember the lost lives of black women by speaking their names aloud in a dark lecture hall, turning their names into action, and urging listeners to uncover other stories.[1] Crenshaw's call and her audience's response grew from the ongoing Say Her Name social media movement, and they also drew on feminist conversations and historical rhetorical strategies that reflect women's continuing efforts to make their voices heard in often exclusionary spaces. This chapter examines the Say Her Name hashtag movement, analyzing how feminist rhetorical strategies are at play in the multitude of online posts that contribute to archives of networked activist discourse.[2] Social media movements in networked spaces become influential tools of change as they allow everyday online users to access and contribute to a growing corpus of activist discourse across the globe. Though crucial feminist scholarship has uncovered historical rhetorical methods of women's expression,[3] it is vital to study the rhetoric of women's alternative forms of expression in networked spaces to better understand how networked users and minoritized populations share information, seek affiliation, and build communities through relatively accessible technologies.[4] Outside of traditional modes of expression that often silence, erase, and/or misrepresent women's lived experiences,[5] feminist hashtag movements circulate and share activist missions to a widespread network of users engaging with social media posts. Recent feminist social media movements such as Me Too and Yes All Women see online users pursue alternative forms of expression, ranging from bold narratives to artistic representations of experiences, to alter the spread of information about social justice issues on their own terms, echoing feminist rhetorical strategies of the past. In networked spaces, feminist activism represents an extraordinary rhetorical moment of bringing feminist and social justice conversations to emergent audiences to highlight women's lived experiences and everyday struggles with racism, sexism, state-based violence, and LGBTQ-exclusionary harassment. Say Her Name is but one example of a thriving hashtag activist movement driven by a rich history of feminist rhetorical interventions that continues to shape our interconnected rhetorical realities.

This chapter examines the Say Her Name movement as a digital assemblage of activist discourse that echoes historical rhetorical tactics used as discursive amplification methods by women of color. I detail how the Say Her Name movement bridges traditional black rhetorical strategies such as the African tradition of *nommo* (a performative naming tactic),[6] the discursive practice of call-and-response (a circulatory tool), and the Greek storytelling practice *muthos* (a narrative mechanism) with contemporary social media discourse. Additionally, I evaluate how the Say Her Name movement maintains an intersectional feminist mission through these strategies, a mission that directly responds to exclusionary feminist networked social movements. In the following sections, I trace connections between the Black Twitter digital community and historical rhetorical strategies as circulatory entities that enable the Say Her Name movement to sustain itself through a vast network of online users, many of them minoritized citizens.[7] As networked activist movements continue to amplify and spark pivotal discussions about women's material experiences,[8] I argue for an enduring focus on marginalized voices as crucial to understanding feminist activist movements and rhetorical strategies of change.

A CAVEAT ON ETHOS AND POSITIONALITY

It bears mentioning that as the author of this chapter, I am analyzing the Say Her Name movement from a position of a white, cisgender woman often described as middle class. I am by no means an authority on the experiences of women of color. The ethos of my location as author and individual is significant to the perspective I bring to a case study that is very much outside of my personal lived experience, which is why I fully disclose this position for the reader. I draw on Nedra Reynolds's work on ethos and location—namely her framing of writerly ethos as an author's stating "where they are coming from"—to articulate my positioning in analyzing this case study.[9] I approach this investigation from my personal belief in the need for intersectional feminism in all pursuits of feminist studies. I am aware of the delicacy of this topic and its subjects' diverse backgrounds, and I aim to write about the Say Her Name movement as justly as I can. In Reynolds's words, one must be responsible for the ways in which she constructs her ethos: "one who 'sees' must also position her seeing."[10] I strongly believe in the rhetorical power of the Say Her Name movement and its importance in exhuming the experiences of women of color, experiences of women who have often been relegated to the margins or overlooked by concurrent exclusionary feminist movements.

As a white woman, I realize that I can never fully understand the experiences of women of color. I am not a part of this community and cannot write about this movement from a firsthand perspective. Therefore, I can never fully capture the experiences of black women, but in this research, I hope to illustrate the Say Her Name movement's overall rhetorical impact in circulating conversations about how marginalized women participate in activist discourse and are memorialized as a result of this discourse. Far too often, the feminism of white women overshadows, excludes, and exacts tension on other groups, both implicitly and explicitly. Say Her Name represents a unique rhetorical phenomenon that, as I argue below, draws on specific black rhetorical and circulatory tactics that enable it to be an effective networked activist movement in often exclusionary networked spaces. Such rhetorical tactics are often relegated to the margins of history in favor of a Western, white perspective of history and rhetorical tradition. But, as Reynolds argues, the margins represent a vital location for fostering ethos for both individuals and communities.[11] Voices from the margins and those located outside of elite digital and physical geographies embody how discourse within those locations shapes understanding of material lives. It is my aim in this chapter to demonstrate how marginalized voices become powerful in collective, networked activist situations and transcend rhetorical situations through circulatory processes. It is imperative that we look to gender, race, *and* class while studying how technology mediates our lives. Discourse from the margins, in the case of Say Her Name, can exact rhetorical change and contribute a fundamental epistemological perspective on the material lives of black women in our contemporary world. I hope this case study will inspire scholars to expand their study of marginalized populations online, as women of color reclaim power and assert their rhetorical agency in efforts to decolonize exclusive sites of knowledge.

THE EXIGENCE OF #SAYHERNAME

The Say Her Name movement was launched in December 2014 as a joint effort between the African American Policy Forum (AAPF) and the Center for Intersectional and Social Policy Studies (CISPS) with the goal of raising awareness about police violence and anti-black crime against black women.[12] A nonprofit organization, the AAPF "promote[s] frameworks and strategies that address a vision of racial justice that embraces the intersections of race, gender, class, and the array of barriers that disempower those who are marginalized in society."[13] Emerging in the aftermath of the death of Sandra Bland, a black woman who was stopped for an alleged minor traffic violation on July 10, 2015, in Texas, and who later died in police custody under mysterious circumstances, the Say Her Name movement responds to the lack of media coverage that stories such as Bland's often garner.[14] The specific mission of Say Her Name is to "shed light on Black women's experiences of police violence in an effort to support a gender-inclusive approach to racial justice that centers all Black lives equally."[15] As violence against black citizens continues to spark fervent discussion, spurred by social media posts bringing attention to the rate at which black men die at the hands of police, the #BlackLivesMatter hashtag oscillates between being a source through which to break news and an outlet through which to circulate the personal experiences that everyday users write about online. The Say Her Name movement grew as black women began to critique the media for its lack of coverage about violence against black women and LGBTQ+ individuals of color. Over time, the #SayHerName hashtag has been used to highlight stories of violence directed toward black women and trans, gay, and lesbian individuals of color (an accommodation that early #BlackLivesMatter posts did not make).

Circulation and Movements from the Margins

Since the murders of Trayvon Martin and Michael Brown gained international media attention in 2012 and 2014, respectively, social media hashtags that highlight violence or experiences of racial minorities have increased in usage, due in large part to the visibility of the Black Lives Matter movement. Founded by three community activists in the wake of Florida teenager Trayvon Martin's murder,[16] Black Lives Matter offers an online community for individuals interested in civil rights, operates as a platform for spreading information about violence against black people, and encourages awareness of the inequities people of color face in society. Black Lives Matter built an activist network online and off, growing to encompass Black Lives Matter chapters across the world and inspiring constant discourse online using the #BlackLivesMatter hashtag. Through the omnipresence of social media, active or viral hashtags eventually reach online networks that might not otherwise engage in the issue. According to scholar Deen Freelon, the message becomes so exposed through online networks that "yet another killing is more likely to push [marginalized citizens] to social breaking points— the point where they can no longer stay silent" and instead begin to engage with the hashtag.[17] According to the Pew Research Center's 2014 report on minority usage of social media, "women and black Americans dominate social networks: 76 percent of women who are online use social media . . . and blacks are 29 percent of online adults who use Twitter, more than any other racial group."[18] Likewise, there has been a prominent rise in the manner that people of color use social media to spread news and raise awareness for social justice issues. In the wake of heightened Black Lives Matter protests, the Pew Research Center recorded that "68 percent of black social media users reported encountering a significant number of posts about race online, while just 35 percent of white users did. Fifty-seven percent of black users have made a race-related post on a social network, but less than a third of all white users have."[19] Activists and ordinary citizens are now able to more easily "document injustices, spread information, and mobilize the public in real time," turning the traditional Western media news cycle on its head and shaping conversations about police violence to represent those most affected.[20] Thus, the momentum of activist hashtag movements like Say Her Name—from the impetus of a violent act, to online outrage, to mainstream conversation—is a powerful rhetorical occurrence that everyday citizens shape through networked activism.

In July 2016, Minneapolis citizen Philando Castile was shot four times by a police officer during a traffic stop for a broken taillight; his girlfriend filmed the encounter from the passenger seat, using Facebook's live video streaming feature.[21] The act of recording the event and streaming it live, heralded by some as a social version of 911, brought the murder to the attention of audiences beyond social media, establishing an account of "what transpired *before* police or media outlets could establish a narrative."[22] Because the #BlackLivesMatter hashtag was used alongside a hashtag of Castile's full name, Castile's name became a hyperlink that archived news about the event and enabled it to spread across networks. The live streaming feature on Facebook's platform facilitated the event's simultaneous broadcasting and archiving, and the footage was viewed 2.5 million times in the days after the incident.[23] As a kairotic response to the public need to record police and citizen encounters, the American Civil Liberties Union (ACLU) released a mobile app in July 2016 that allows users to record a video, which—when recording ceases either by control or by brute force—is sent directly to the ACLU.[24] Though Castile's murder is not the focus of this chapter, his case points to the crucial role of hashtag movements in making violence against people of color visible through mobile devices and networked activism. Increasingly, and as pieces in this collection illuminate, women have turned to social media to amplify personal experiences of violence or harassment while connecting to a broadly distributed community of other women, which itself is a coalitional tradition.

Say Her Name represents a decentralized network of black women and LGBTQ+ individuals, an intersection of minoritized citizens that make up a large number of online users. Until hashtag discourse became an accessible arena in which to share such information, popular media rarely covered minority vio-

FIGURE 7.1. User-created posters memorializing Sandra Bland, 2015. The posters superimpose the words "Be My Voice" over Bland's mugshot. This image appeared in a tweet from Twitter user Eriana (@envyerie, March 14, 2017).

lence as much as it covers violence against predominately white individuals.[25] Twitter became an effective venue for public protest via social media discourse for both its ease of access via smart phones or internet browsers and its "rapid-fire speech and quick counters to mainstream media's misrepresentation or no representation whatsoever."[26] As communication studies scholar Armond R. Towns argues, black cultural traditions "are not only physical and metaphorical" but also digital. Towns points to the "contradictory, complex nature of Black geographies [and (dis)location]" to illustrate that although an activist movement like Say Her Name "is a communicative, geographic condemnation of White supremacy, it is also given voice via an Internet under Western control."[27] Black feminists operate within the colonized, often homogenous spaces of social media platforms and subvert traditional networked discourse to create a movement representing the material lives of women of color. I look to the Say Her Name movement not only as a unique rhetorical response to amplify how black women experience violence and hate crimes but also as a decentralized intersectional feminist movement that responds to other exclusionary social movements. Say Her Name exacts rhetorical impact because of the movement's call for online users to employ circulatory naming as rhetorical action while affecting the larger cultural narrative about the lived experience of women of color. Bland's case is often credited as the first viral instance of the Say Her Name movement, inspiring online users to share her story through multimodal social media posts ranging from text, to video clips from the arresting officer's dashboard camera, to meme-like images of Bland's mugshot or user-generated pictures that included the #SayHerName hashtag alongside Bland's face (figure 7.1).

The circulation of Bland's image saw many users remix her mugshot or dashboard camera footage to encourage identification with her case, urging others to take action and literally "be [her] voice" to seek justice in her mysterious death. Images like the one shown in figure 7.1 are primed for circulation, inviting users to spread them across their own networks and remix images, text, and hashtags to amplify their message. The shareable function of social media posts and hashtags offers "feminist cultural workers with new ways to upend mainstream narratives and elevate conversations within feminist sphere(s)."[28] The #SayHerName hashtag captures women's material confrontations with everyday harassment and racial discrimination, altering discourse surrounding ongoing events as they occur.

#SAYHERNAME AS ACTIVIST INFORMATION STREAM

Hashtag movements provide users with potential connections and affiliations in extended communities that are united by common values. When users write with or alongside a hashtag movement, they engage with a collective identity that evolves with each post. By their very nature, hashtags are interactive: social media platforms allow users to click into a live archive of topical or "trending" posts, exposing them to information outside their local network or immediate public. Users in turn interact with others in a global network in quite a rapid fashion, contributing to the speed at which networked discourse spreads. This interactive, engaging process creates ever-changing information streams, whose direction is dictated by users and their handling of hashtags, mentions, and networked discourse. Hashtags extend and pluralize conversations, influencing the viral potential and visibility of messages outside of a user's network, circulating a catalog of posts that one can search across platforms. Hashtags turn language into action, working as an interactive, performative, and categorical tool that almost any user with a connecting device and internet connection can use to contribute to or explore the conversation. Much like second and third wave feminists employed women's personal narratives in persuasive texts such as fliers and zines that cataloged broad messages of the feminist activist movement, hashtag movements also use the affective rhetorical tactic of personal narrative to extend women's stories and garner the attention of interested network participants, thereby increasing the movements' circulatory potential.[29] Below, I examine how stories and historical rhetorical tactics are central to the circulatory potential of the #SayHerName hashtag.

Though the hashtag symbol did not originate in or emerge with the social media platform Twitter, the service's users have come to define its contemporary use as a rallying cry, an archival tool, and a signifier of community. Hashtags are often user-generated discursive conventions that are "intended to facilitate the curation of tweets about a particular topic using Twitter's limited search capabilities."[30] Information science scholar André Brock points to the stripped-down design and simple constraints of platforms like Twitter, arguing that "Twitter's minimalism allowed mobile access from the beginning, enabling Twitter users to integrate Tweeting into their everyday communication patterns (similar to the rise of SMS or texting)."[31] Its textual constraints (posts were limited to 140 characters until December 2017, when the limit doubled) and its user-friendly interface, "enabled Twitter to be used on millions of 'feature phones' and smartphones—regardless of operating system or manufacturer." Users can quickly write and distribute a post from nearly any location, an ease that explains why Twitter is often host to citizen-generated breaking news and information, news that eventually circulates through and across networks to other social media platforms. As the editors of this collection aptly described in their call for this collection, "as the technologies delivering feminist messages have changed, feminist rhetorical tactics have often developed upon those that preceded them while, at the same time, giving feminist messages new life." Networked social movements can serve as channels for enacting social change and sustain cultural conversations about social movements. Often, networked activist movements call social media users to take public action, such as by participating in a public protest or flooding a government official's office with calls. Just as organized instances of civil disobedience and sit-ins helped propel the mission of the civil rights era, so too have networked activist movements inspired social media users to employ similar rhetorical strategies, as when Say Her Name was adopted as part of Black Lives Matter protests and (in song form) the January 2017 Women's March.[32] Below, I examine the activist rhetorical strategies apparent in Say Her Name, strategies that were meant to circulate the hashtag rapidly among networks and inspire others to participate in the movement's broader mission.

ACTIVIST RHETORICAL STRATEGIES WITHIN SAY HER NAME: *NOMMO* AND *MUTHOS*

The Say Her Name hashtag movement embodies a set of traits that I define as activist rhetorical strategies—the rhetorical tactics and discursive traits that become part of an activist movement about social or cultural issues in an effort to enact change and raise awareness about a particular cause. Although scholars of activist rhetorics define activism and discuss the power structures that activists aim to dismantle,[33] I argue that the type of activist discourse pertaining to feminist networked movements is more complex than that of traditional activism. Feminist activist movements in networked spaces employ affective discourse and borrow from historical rhetorical tactics to amplify their messages in a crowded digital sphere. Additionally, feminist politics forever exist within complex backgrounds of race, class, and gender identity—adding a unique dimension to feminist activist rhetoric in networked spaces. Collectively, activist rhetorical strategies are kairotic and adaptive, as activist rhetorical strategies see networked users create decentralized protests within online communities as responses to current events—protests made up of networked discourse that continually builds a digital archive of their activism. Users apply activist rhetorical strategies to both rapidly create hashtag movements as instantaneous categorical information reserves and also invite others within (and beyond) their online communities to use the hashtag movements to circulate information through networks. The circulatory power of #SayHerName and other feminist networked hashtags is partly dependent on their genesis in networked spaces, but it also hinges on historical rhetorical strategies often seen in discursive traditions of women's communities. Two historical rhetorical strategies apparent in #SayHerName-tagged posts include the African concept of *nommo* (the generative power of naming something into existence) and the power of affective narrative storytelling, or *muthos*, a classical Greek storytelling concept often likened to "myth" but better understood as meaningful statements or "authoritative speech."[34]

Nommo and *muthos* are crucial in extending the cause and reach of the movement to other online feminist communities and beyond. Activist rhetorical strategies are dynamic, always changing to work within specific kairotic contexts in the hands of users. And just as black women in the civil rights movement deliberately forged collectives as "feminists of color . . . distinct from mainstream white feminist groups,"[35] so too have #SayHerName users drawn on the rich history of performative language in the black tradition; *nommo* reflects the rhetorical power behind the message of the #SayHerName hashtag. *Nommo* urges interlocutors to focus on "the belief in the power of the word," reflecting African societal recognitions of the word as something tied to "the power of literacy," often prohibited from minorities, free and enslaved.[36] Affiliation with these feminist movements is enhanced through networked circulation, revealing and "contesting . . . white-washed accounts of history" to better reflect the complex lived experiences of women of color.[37] When rhetorical strategies like *muthos* and *nommo* appear within writing that users share on social media platforms, hashtags become more than simple messages that reflect a movement's broad mission; they are catalyzed as "tools for affiliation, political-discourse making, and collective identity-informing," rhetorical objects that concurrently shape networked communities and extend their reach.[38] Women who might not otherwise engage in public protests or community organizing identify with a resonant aspect of a hashtag movement and might then participate in the growing discourse of new media activism.

Nommo *and Call-and-Response as Performative Rhetoric*

In networked spaces, call-and-response takes shape in the form of mentions, replies, or reposts—strategies that further amplify user posts and activist rhetorical strategies. Within Say Her Name, *nommo* simultaneously identifies and amplifies the names of these women for rhetorical impact, imploring networked users to repeat and amplify the names of women killed at the hands of state-based violence.[39] Posts tagged with #SayHerName are rooted in rhetorical strategies of call-and-response and the discursive tactic of *nommo*, defined as "the generative and productive power of the spoken word to construct a discursive reality by speaking a name into existence and drawing upon the expressive, powerful nature of a word," providing agency and material existence to words, particularly names.[40] Bland's experience became a rhetorical tool to raise awareness to the great injustice that women of color face. Hashtags like #SayHerName and #SandraBland (and other names turned into hashtags) call out because they want a response; they are structured toward participatory discourse that becomes performative. In the tweets below, users call on others to respond and speak women's names into memory:

> Black women are victims of police violence too. Let's center all lives equally in our movement to combat police violence. #SayHerName (@AAPolicyForum, May 21, 2015)

> Policing gender = police violence vs. Black Trans Women #SayHerName #Duanna Johnson #NizahMorris #IslanNettles #BlackWomenMatter (@dreanyc123, May 20, 2015)

> #SandraBland sister: Keep hashtagging #SayHerName because the minute you forget her name you forget her character (@MSNBC, July 22, 2015)

Nommo is apparent in these three tweets in that users are both speaking black women's names into existence (as seen in the tweets from @dreanyc123 and @MSNBC) and including statements of racial inequalities, pointing to the disparate experiences these women face. MSNBC tweeted a statement from Bland's sister Sharon Cooper during a press conference about Bland's death, propelling Cooper's personal plea to a large audience of mainstream media viewers. Cooper stressed that users should keep using Bland's name as a hashtag, keep using #SayHerName to express their outrage, and keep Bland's case in the news, repeating the name and hashtag to add power to each.

In @dreanyc123's tweet, the names of trans women Nizah Morris, Islan Nettles, and Duanna Johnson become interactive hashtags, clickable links that circulate through networked spaces and gain power through each share, like, or retweet. Here, *nommo* is invitational as well as performative, urging users to echo these hashtagged names, amplify their stories, and learn more about violence against trans women while also adding rhetorical power to their names as actions. Here, *nommo* becomes a circulatory amplification tactic, using the names of trans women to raise awareness about state-based trans violence, adding power through the Say Her Name networked activist movement and illuminating issues of gender policing for a networked audience. As a historical rhetorical tactic in a networked space, *nommo* becomes performative when coupled with hashtags.

In drawing on historical rhetorical tactics from the black tradition, the civil rights movement, and second wave feminism, Say Her Name represents a distinct rhetorical context: women users employ activist strategies and narrative tactics as a sociopolitical tool to memorialize women and create communities.[41] Such strategy echoes historical moments wherein displaced African women developed communities to "recover balance and stability in their lives . . . caring and nurturing for their communities," using networked language to make sense of and change the world around them through connections.[42] In this way, Say Her Name calls on historical sociopolitical tools to memorialize women, care for the black women's community, and powerfully tell women's stories as an act of social justice. Activist strategies, in the context of these networked feminist movements, hearken back to historical rhetorical tactics that have accompanied women's modes of expression for many decades, boldly inserting women's experiences into public consciousness in efforts to raise awareness of the everyday struggle of women rhetors. The African American discursive traditions of *nommo* and call-and-response were instrumental in the civil rights movement and allowed messages of peaceful resistance to spread from protest to protest. Messages were often turned into songs, "form[ing] the communication networks of the movement . . . linking its spirit to centuries of resistance to slavery and oppression," repeated and echoed in cities across the country.[43] Say Her Name amplifies women's experiences while simultaneously highlighting the often complicated and opposing debate about feminism writ large between feminist communities, taking on new contexts with each name and story invoked alongside its hashtag. The movement's user-generated discourse continues to highlight the complex intersections between gender-related issues, class, and differences between white feminists and feminists of color—issues that echo the struggles of the broader feminist movement and ongoing debates about race in our tense political times.

The performative and invitational characteristics of the #SayHerName hashtag "enable Twitter to mediate communal identities in near-real time, allowing participants to act individually yet *en masse* while still being heard."[44] Networked users summon hashtags to request a specific response, asking their audience to take notice of the hashtags employed and respond in kind, "build[ing] consensus either by completion of the original statement or through affirmation of the speaker's intent."[45] In this manner, networked call-and-response evokes a coalitional rhetoric, compelling networked users from myriad racial backgrounds to acknowledge the experiences of women of color—inserting the experiences of women directly into social media and public discourse, demanding action through discourse, and creating an intersectional memorial for individuals affected. Storytelling, though a key factor in the rhetoric of social networks, has always been a crucial element in activist movements, particularly the feminist movement and its affiliated causes. In networked activist spaces, storytelling is a powerful tool for raising awareness to activist issues and igniting social change. On social media, storytelling is performative.

Muthos *and Narrative as Affective Delivery*

Stories in the Say Her Name movement embolden affective responses and personal narrative to proliferate the movement's writing.[46] Affect is the force that spurs and sustains our (online) narratives about our lives and lived experiences, "discursively calling into being further audiences of support."[47] *Muthos*, authoritative storytelling or the act of making meaningful statements,[48] enables narrative to become enhanced with affect in networked spaces, as users turn personal experiences into visible and circulated posts with which others can identify. Traditionally, *muthos* required someone to have a predisposition toward societal power in order to participate in discourse (e.g., one needed to be male and elite to participate in classical Greek forums). Unfortunately, the exclusion of people from public discourse is often a common occurrence, one seen throughout the rhetorical tradition and contemporary public discourse, where women are often silenced or criticized for their methods of expression. With the Say Her Name movement, however, this predisposition to societal power is not needed: I see instances of authoritative speech appearing throughout posts with the #SayHerName hashtag, a reclamation of narrative and discourse to raise awareness about women's experiences. In this way, *muthos* has become a subversive rhetorical tactic to reclaim expression within dominant discourses and assert women's agency through feminist activist movements. Affective narratives figured prominently in previous eras of the feminist movement, as women shared stories of discrimination in the workforce, experiences with sexual harassment, and frustrations with patriarchal traditions at public and private feminist gatherings in efforts to build coalitions.[49] In our networked age, narratives have become a powerful circulatory tool, built from historical rhetorical strategies that ground activist movements in the human experience.

Opportunities to write affectively on social media provide users with the tools to write one's way into becoming whole again, seeking meaning out of violent acts against other women. Sara Ahmed calls this process a "form of self-assembly," a feminist "documentation" process with which women are all too familiar.[50] In this way, affect widens the circulatory potential of hashtag movement posts, inviting other users to participate. Heavily populated social media platforms like Twitter and Facebook are capable of "sustaining and transmitting affect, in ways that may lead to the cultivation of subsequent feelings, emotions, thoughts, attitudes, and behaviors."[51] When affective, narrative-based writing is paired with multimedia images of women's faces and their narratives, the affective power of

FIGURE 7.2. Protest posters showing victims of police violence, their stories amplified and circulated through the #SayHerName hashtag, circa 2015. *Left to right:* Michelle Cusseaux, Rekia Boyd, Kayla Moore, and Shelly Frey. African American Policy Forum, "#SayHerName: Resisting Police Brutality against Black Women," http://aapf.org /sayhernamereport/.

the message increases. As seen in figure 7.2, the image of Shelly Frey, a young mother shot by an off-duty police officer for shoplifting from Walmart, is presented on a large poster board at a public protest alongside images of other black women. Though Frey, Rekia Boyd, and Kayla Moore all died before the Say Her Name movement began, the movement retroactively amplified their stories, combining the hashtag and their images to create a powerful affective visual. Frey's story is summarized on the right side of the poster image, with the date of her death listed on the bottom of the poster. The #SayHerName hashtag and her name are highly visible, completing the visual story for all to see.

The hashtag #SayHerName is now a part of the public cultural conversation about marginalized bodies, representing the erasure of the lived experiences of people of color. The tag's simplistic wording—say her name—implores users to insert individuals' names into discourse, making their names historical markers representative of a memorial for victims of racial or state violence. In this way, *muthos* appears as a call to authoritatively tell the stories of individual women, unapologetically projecting women's names, faces, and stories into and beyond networked spaces. As more social movements begin online, the circulatory potential embedded within networked spaces amplifies individual feelings and experiences, creating a collective network of interactive, emotive responses. The shareable nature of networked posts sustains circulation and archival potential, warranting renewed attention to the potential of rhetorical delivery in our new media age, a time when nearly all are connected through personal social networks near and far.

CIRCULATION AND THE ETHOS OF FEMINIST ACTIVIST MOVEMENTS: LOOKING AHEAD

The use of personal narrative, *muthos*, call-and-response, and *nommo* in networked activist movements builds on rhetorical strategies from previous women's social movements and rhetorical traditions that both sustain and extend the potential of feminist activism. Made apparent through steady user participation with the hashtag #SayHerName, networked hashtags create kairotic, decentralized social movements that circulate feminist activist strategies, highlighting the complexities of contemporary feminist identities. The ongoing rhetorical engagement of the Say Her Name movement shows that activist rhetorical strategies in networked spaces coalesce to illuminate and shape conversations about women's lived experience, building affiliations through rhetorical connections. Such strategies allow movements, stories, and information about women's material lives to become searchable and accessible to interested readers, forever changing how networked spaces alter memory and cultural conversations.

Affiliation hinges on both the geographical and cultural locations from which users originate, affecting their identification with online discourse and the communities where networked movements take place. In the classical Greek sense, the most specific definition of the term *ethos* was "habitual gathering place," the conventional social space where culture unfolded.[52] Yet, these gathering spaces were open only to men and elite members of society—women, slaves, and marginalized citizens were not allowed in common gathering spaces. Online networks represent our modern gathering spaces, places where culture unfolds and discourse spreads, as social networks are where conventional information, everyday writing, and social interactions with acquaintances near and far take place. The communal networks through which we interact online shape our norms, our language, and our interactions with one another offline. The members of these networks, such as Black Twitter, assert ethos by expressing the values of their community and circulating these values through rhetorical strategies such as *nommo* and *muthos*. Hashtag activism works within these communal boundaries of ethos, often representing a nexus of users' locations. As Sherri Williams observes, "when white feminists miss opportunities to stand with their black sisters and mainstream media overlooks the plight of nonwhite women, women of color use social media as a tool to unite and inform."[53] Looking ahead, feminists writ large should work to highlight the plight of minoritized women and marginalized voices, as our connections and intersections are what make us stronger, together. Connections, made by people, give way to dynamic discoveries, as the editors of this collection explore in their introduction, framing Rhetorical Transversal Methodology as one way to forge new connections that can uncover exciting rhetorical potentials. The "transversals between historical feminist and digital feminist work"—to use the editors' language—represent an area rife with discoveries of pivotal rhetorical connections that can teach us much about feminist experiences, knowledge, and potential.

This chapter's brief analysis of the Say Her Name movement illustrates the reach and potential of feminist hashtag movements and activist rhetorical strategies in networked spaces. Historical rhetorical strategies and feminist traditions continue to inform our understanding of feminist rhetoric in historical spaces and contemporary locations. As Crenshaw asserts in her TED Talk, if marginalized women's names and experiences are not visible, we cannot bear witness to the experience. It is our rhetorical duty to amplify, share, and circulate the names and experiences of others who can no longer speak or share their experiences. The medium and mode will continue to change, yet core feminist rhetorical strategies of telling personal stories and uncovering women's experiences will sustain histories of lived experience, archive public events and news, and provide dynamic spaces for users and citizens to engage with issues relevant or important to them.

Notes

1. Kimberlé Crenshaw, "The Urgency of Intersectionality" (filmed October 2016 at TEDWomen in San Francisco, CA), TED video, 18:49, https://www.ted.com.

2. Networked activist discourse, for the purposes of this case study, is defined as activist discourse and content shared through networks. See Manuel Castells's discussion of "a space of flows" in Castells, *Network of Outrage and Hope: Social Movements in the Internet Age* (Hoboken, NJ: John Wiley, 2015), 31. See also Clay Spinuzzi's combined definitions of networks as "made up of telecommunications equipment; complex assemblages of sociopolitically aligned humans and nonhumans; and interrelated, constantly developing, often contradictory cultural/historical activities." Spinuzzi, "Who Killed Rex? Tracing a Message through Three Kinds of Networks," in *Communicative Practices in Workplaces and the Professions: Cultural Perspectives on the Regulation of Discourse and Organizations*, ed. Mark Zachry and Charlotte Thralls (Amityville, NY: Baywood, 2007), 46.

3. Cheryl Glenn, *Unspoken: A Rhetoric of Silence* (Carbondale: Southern Illinois University Press, 2004), xi–xiii.

4. "Relatively" in this context refers to the common, but not ubiquitous, presence of and access to internet connections, smart phones, and connected devices that activist movement participants use when partaking in feminist hashtag movements.

5. Alexah Konnelly, "#Activism: Identity, Affiliation, and Political Discourse-Making on Twitter," *Arbutus Review* 6, no. 1 (2015): 1–16.

6. Shirley Wilson Logan, *"We Are Coming": The Persuasive Discourse of Nineteenth-Century Black Women* (Carbondale: Southern Illinois University Press, 1999), 24.

7. Sherri Williams, "#SayHerName: Using Digital Activism to Document Violence against Black Women," *Feminist Media Studies* 16, no. 5 (2016): 922–25.

8. Amplification is a key rhetorical concept that covers the Greek notion of *auxesis*, related to oratory, and rhetorics of power and autonomy. However, in this chapter, amplification is treated as a method for subverting dominant, silencing power structures and illuminating marginalized voices through circulation and "intensification and dignification," in Kenneth Burke's words. See Burke, *A Rhetoric of Motives* (Berkeley: University of California Press, 1969), 69; Amanda Nell Edgar, "The Rhetoric of Auscultation: Corporeal Sounds, Mediated Bodies, and Abortion Rights," *Quarterly Journal of Speech* 103, no. 4 (2017): 350; and Ian E. J. Hill, "Not Quite Bleeding from the Ears: Amplifying Sonic Torture," *Western Journal of Communication* 76, no. 3 (2012): 220.

9. Nedra Reynolds, *Geographies of Writing: Inhabiting Places and Encountering Difference* (Carbondale: Southern Illinois University Press, 2007), 11–22.

10. Reynolds, 334.

11. Reynolds, 332.

12. Kimberlé Crenshaw and Andrew J. Ritchie, *Say Her Name: Resisting Police Brutality against Black Women* (New York: African American Policy Forum, 2015); see also "Fill the Void. Lift Your Voice. Say Her Name," *African American Policy Forum*, accessed December 1, 2019, https://aapf.org/shn-moms-network.

13. Crenshaw and Ritchie, *Say Her Name*, 30.

14. Mia Fischer, "#Free_CeCe: The Material Convergence of Social Media Activism," *Feminist Media Studies* 16, no. 5 (2016): 756.

15. Crenshaw and Ritchie, *Say Her Name*, 1.

16. Black Lives Matter was founded by Alicia Garza, Patrisse Cullors, and Opal Tometi in 2013, "in response to the acquittal of Trayvon Martin's murderer, George Zimmerman." See "Herstory," *Black Lives Matter*, accessed October 10, 2019, https://blacklivesmatter.com; and Tara Propper's chapter in this volume (chapter 2).

17. Qtd. in Victor Luckerson, "The Mainstreaming of #BlackLivesMatter," *Ringer*, August 16, 2016, https://www.theringer.com.

18. Reported in Williams, "#SayHerName," 923.

19. Reported in Luckerson, "The Mainstreaming of #BlackLivesMatter."

20. Crenshaw, "The Urgency of Intersectionality."

21. Brandon E. Patterson, "Harrowing Facebook Live Video Shows Black Man Dying after Police Shoot Him during Traffic Stop," *Mother Jones*, November 10, 2017, https://www.motherjones.com.

22. Luckerson, "The Mainstreaming of #BlackLivesMatter."

23. Luckerson.

24. "ACLU Apps to Record Police Conduct," *American Civil Liberties Union*, accessed October 10, 2019, https://www.aclu.org.

25. Williams, "#SayHerName," 922.

26. Catherine Prendergast, "Before #BlackLivesMatter," in *Rhetorics of Whiteness: Postracial Hauntings in Popular Culture, Social Media, and Education*, ed. Tammie M. Kennedy, Joyce Middleton and Krista Ratcliffe (Carbondale: Southern Illinois University Press, 2017), 76.

27. Armond R. Towns, "Geographies of Pain: #SayHerName and the Fear of Black Women's Mobility," *Women's Studies in Communication* 39, no. 2 (2016): 124.

28. Sarah J. Jackson and Sonia Banaszczyk, "Digital Standpoints: Debating Gendered Violence and Racial Exclusion in the Feminist Counterpublic," *Journal of Communication Inquiry* 40, no. 4 (2016): 391. See also, in this volume, Bethany Mannon (chapter 13), who explores the circulatory potential of personal narratives for online movements, and Kristin E. Kondrlik (chapter 6), who considers how hashtag communities strengthen their ethos through public engagement.

29. Amber E. Kinser, "Negotiating Spaces for/through Third-Wave Feminism," *NWSA Journal* 16 no. 3 (2004): 127.

30. André Brock, "From the Blackhand Side: Twitter as a Cultural Conversation," *Journal of Broadcasting & Electronic Media* 56, no. 4 (2012): 546.

31. Brock, 536.

32. Katie Presley, "Janelle Monáe Releases Visceral Protest Song, 'Hell You Talmbout,'" *NPR*, August 18, 2015, http://www.npr.org.

33. Symon Hill, *Digital Revolutions: Activism in the Internet Age* (Oxford: New Internationalist, 2013), 15.

34. Beard, Mary. "The Public Voice of Women." *London Review of Books* 36, no. 6 (March 20, 2014): 11–14, https://www.lrb.co.uk.

35. Bonita Roth, *Separate Roads to Feminism: Black, Chicana, and White Feminist Movements in America's Second Wave* (New York: Cambridge University Press, 2004), 1.

36. Logan, *We Are Coming*, 25.

37. Terese Jonsson, "White Feminist Stories: Locating Race in Representations of Feminism in the *Guardian*," *Feminist Media Studies* 14, no. 6 (2014): 1024.

38. Konnelly, "#Activism," 2.

39. Molefi Kete Asante, *The Afrocentric Idea* (Philadelphia: Temple University Press, 2011), 21.

40. Asante, 22.

41. Jacqueline Jones Royster, *Traces of a Stream: Literacy and Social Change among African American Women* (Pittsburgh, PA: University of Pittsburgh Press, 2000), 100.

42. Royster, 99.

43. Thomas Vernon Reed, *The Art of Protest: Culture and Activism from the Civil Rights Movement to the Streets of Seattle* (Minneapolis: University of Minnesota Press, 2005), 2.

44. Brock, "From the Blackhand Side," 539.

45. Brock, 539.

46. Other pieces in this collection, from Skye Roberson (chapter 9) and Bethany Mannon (chapter 13), explore online narratives as persuasive entities that sway others to participate and sustain circulation of a media event in digital spaces.

47. Zizi Papacharissi, *Affective Publics: Sentiment, Technology, and Politics* (New York: Oxford University Press, 2015), 6.

48. Beard, "The Public Voice of Women."

49. Roth, *Separate Roads to Feminism*, 18.

50. Sara Ahmed, *Living a Feminist Life* (Durham, NC: Duke University Press, 2017), 27.

51. Papacharissi, *Affective Publics*, 22.

52. Reynolds, *Geographies of Writing*, 328.

53. Williams, "#SayHerName," 924.

8

From US Progressive Era Speeches to Transnational Social Media Activism

Rhetorical Empathy in Jane Addams's Labor Rhetoric and Joyce Fernandes's #EuEmpregadaDoméstica (I, Housemaid)

LISA BLANKENSHIP

JANE ADDAMS WAS ONLY THIRTY-TWO years old, four years into her work at Hull House, when she delivered a speech on women's working conditions on May 19, 1893, at the World's Columbian Exposition in Chicago.[1] Twenty-seven million people visited Chicago during the exposition, held May 1 to October 30, 1893. It spanned six hundred acres, with representatives from forty-six nations taking part. Over two hundred congresses or conferences were held, by far the most popular of which was the Women's Congress, featuring eighty-one sessions and drawing an estimated 150,000 people, mostly women.[2] The Women's Congress was an unprecedented platform for women to speak publicly on issues of concern to them—the first of its kind in the world. In a small venue reminiscent of an academic conference, a handful of upper-class white women listened to the young Addams, an Illinois state senator's daughter who would give up her wealth and social standing to live and work among poor immigrant families in an exploding industrial neighborhood west of downtown Chicago. Her experience of living among immigrant families in Chicago's nineteenth ward would change her in ways she could not have comprehended when she first moved into Hull Settlement House in 1889. She would go on to found the profession of social work in the United States and was one of the most famous women of her time when she died in 1935, winning the Nobel Peace Prize the year before her death. The stories of the women she worked with changed her and formed her thinking; she relied on them throughout her life to make her arguments for social reform to audiences with backgrounds like hers: privileged women (and men) who were removed from the suffering of working-class people.

A continent away and over a hundred years later, Joyce Fernandes grew up the daughter of a domestic worker in Brazil. She also worked as a maid for seven years before going to college and becoming a history teacher, a profession that she held for five years before pursuing activist work and music full time. Her journey toward becoming a labor and women's rights activist began when a media outlet in Sao Paolo featured posts she had written on her Facebook page in July 2016 about the humiliation she endured in domestic work, as well as the experience of growing up black or *preta* in Brazilian society. The story was picked up soon after by the BBC, and the social media presence she created to share the stories of other women like herself, #EuEmpregadaDoméstica (I, Housemaid), gained over one hundred thousand followers overnight. She combines her activist work on labor with her well-known persona as a rapper, writing, speaking, and making music focused on racism in Brazilian society, and appearing on media as varied as MTV and TED Talks. When the BBC circulated her story, she became known beyond Brazil as well.

Fernandes told the BBC that her goal is to "provoke and give voice to the voiceless . . . the majority of whom are black and . . . do not have anyone to vent to." She has called her Twitter hashtag and Facebook page #EuEmpregadaDoméstica, a place to "expose what is being swept under the carpet," calling for improved working conditions and ultimately an end to domestic service as a "vestige of slavery."[3] She told the BBC she has received thousands of stories, most of which were sent to her by domestic workers' daughters and even granddaughters via email. To date she has posted several hundred of them on the site. She does not post names or images of the women unless they give her permission (usually only first names).

Despite their strikingly different backgrounds and subject positions, Jane Addams and Joyce Fernandes attempt to enact change on a societal level by bringing attention to the very real, personal stories of people caught up in exploitative systems. The comparison I make between the two women hinges not only on their common fight for women's rights and their labor activism but also on their similar rhetorical strategies. Both place themselves within the stories they tell: their own experience becomes an important persuasive element in their rhetorical purposes of bringing greater awareness to abuses of women in domestic work. Neither of them is removed from the suffering they testify to: Addams by way of choice and Fernandes by way of birth and circumstance. Despite the fact that in many ways they could not be more different, and separated as they are by over one hundred years and the revolution of digital media and social media networks, they both rely on elements of what I call rhetorical empathy to enact change:[4]

> Yielding to an Other by sharing and listening to personal stories
> Considering motives behind speech acts and actions

Engaging in reflection and self-critique

Addressing difference, power, and embodiment

I have come to see these strategies as core features of feminist rhetorics, especially those focused on highlighting intersectional power differences. Rhetorical strategies characterized by a strategic kind of empathy are in keeping with a woman-centered and feminist political philosophy that the personal is always political. Empathy is grounded in pathos and the personal, but it has potential for political power as well. The use of the personal in the form of stories disarms an audience through identification ("You're like me on some level") and so helps bridge gaps in understanding across marked social differences. It is difficult enough to understand our own experiences and motives, but stories invite us to imagine what an Other has gone through in ways that other rhetorical appeals cannot.

I imagine rhetorical empathy as both a *topos* and a *trope*: a place one chooses to enter to think about how to approach an Other, and a discourse and embodied rhetoric characterized by listening and the emotions often associated with vulnerability. The tropes and speech acts that result from such a topos are characterized by stories of the Other that resist stereotypes, narratives based on the personal as a way of knowing.[5] Such narratives result from seeing the Other as an individual who is part of a larger system, but an individual nonetheless. Personal narratives, a precursor and integral part of the Me Too movement, are a defining characteristic of feminist rhetoric and have long been used by women for social change. The use of personal narratives makes both the subject of discourse and the audience or interlocutors within discourse vulnerable in some way, creating an opening for (ex)change. Rhetorical empathy can invoke change because it disarms. In Fernandes's words, both women attempt to "humanize[s] the relationship between employers and employees," Addams in the genre of the public speech, commonly used by women in the late nineteenth-century United States, and Fernandes in digital environments of much greater scope than the print media of the Progressive Era.[6] Social media provides a circulatory power and rhetorical velocity to Fernandes's rhetoric and activist efforts that Addams could not imagine (though it is interesting to think about how she would have functioned in contemporary media culture).[7] Social media enables the widespread circulation of the stories and images of the domestic workers and activists Fernandes features on #EuEmpregadaDoméstica. Her rhetorical approach invites viewers and readers to go beyond the binary of images and word and instead to think in terms of what Kristie S. Fleckenstein calls *imageword*.[8] The fact that viewers can scan quickly through these digital, disembodied stories in a passive, voyeuristic consumption of the Other could arguably contribute to the disintegration of empathy and social connection, as Sherry Turkle argues in

Reclaiming Conversation.[9] However, the presence of a discursive community of people writing their emotions and reactions to the imageword compositions on #EuEmpregadaDoméstica creates a participatory, communal aspect that facilitates empathetic responses. The combination of imageword and participatory writing on social media opens a space that is enhanced rather than diminished by its dispersed circulation in digital spaces. Further, social media's reach facilitates a communal experience around shared trauma, as Liz Lane explains in her discussion of *muthos* in the previous chapter: "As more social movements begin online, the circulatory potential embedded within networked spaces amplifies individual feelings and experiences, creating a collective network of interactive, emotive responses."

This chapter explores how rhetorical empathy functions in the labor rights rhetoric of these two complex, compelling women, one hundred years and—in terms of digital technology—light years removed from one another. Both women represent significant milestones for women's speaking out publicly as labor rights advocates: Addams at the first historic gathering to feature women's speeches on a global scale, and Fernandes through the platform of digitized, networked rhetoric on social media, with its instantaneous, global reach. I use the characteristics I associate with rhetorical empathy as an organizational framework to look closely at Addams's Columbian Exposition speech and at the stories of domestic workers Fernandes has curated and brought to international attention.

JANE ADDAMS, FIRST WAVE US FEMINISM, AND WOMEN'S DOMESTIC LABOR

Addams had been invited to speak at a panel at the World's Columbian Exposition on what was beginning to be known as home economics; the respondent to her talk was Mary Hinman Abel, a pioneer of the movement. It is unknown how many people attended the panel, but other panels at the eight-day, first-of-its-kind World's Congress of Representative Women drew as many as three thousand, including seventy-three-year-old Susan B. Anthony, who spoke in favor of labor unions in the main evening session of the following day. The atmosphere of the World's Columbian Exposition—and the Women's Congress—was electric. Politically and rhetorically, the speech marks the beginning of an evolutionary process for Addams on labor reform. Although Addams's panel was focused on home economics, appealing to middle-class white women, she used the opportunity to advocate for changes in the conditions of working-class women, trying to create awareness of the humanity and living conditions of domestic laborers. In 1898 she would deliver a speech to the General Federation of Women's Clubs in Chicago, making many of the same arguments but also calling for government intervention. In 1901 she would help form the Working Women's Association of America Union to help improve working conditions and raise wages; and in

1903 Addams and Mary McDowell assisted in founding the first union for female workers on a national scale, the Women's Trade Union League.[10] While Addams would move toward greater governmental intervention to address social injustices, she maintained her belief throughout her life that true social change could only be accomplished as people were moved in their emotions on a personal level to see the Other as equal within a democracy. She would write in *Twenty Years at Hull House* in 1912 that "social change can only be inaugurated by those who feel the unrighteousness of the contemporary conditions."[11]

Personal Epistemology and Rhetorical Listening: Addams and Hull House

In the speech to the Women's Congress, Addams describes the poor working conditions of domestic workers and portrays them as marginalized members of a democratic society that had become increasingly stratified into classes in the late nineteenth century, a product of the worst aspects of capitalism. Between 1870 and 1902, domestic work was the leading occupation of women; by 1870 one in five Chicago families employed live-in domestic workers, who accounted for 60 percent of wage-earning women.[12] Immigrants and black women composed the majority of domestic workers prior to 1900 (more than half), with the number of black women rising after World War I. Between 1870 and 1902, domestic work was the leading occupation of women in Chicago and the nation. Workers usually were young, single women from working-class families, often newly arrived Irish, German, Scandinavian, or Polish immigrants in the last half of the nineteenth century, and often among the most desperate for employment.[13]

While Addams did not formulate a rhetorical theory in a formal sense, her praxis blurred the lines between theory and practice. Joy Ritchie and Kate Ronald point out that praxis is "a central feature of women's rhetorical practices" and that we should look to praxis as theory.[14] Characteristics of rhetorical empathy appear throughout Addams's public rhetoric, not just forming a strategy for her but rather constituting her embodied identity. Her embodied philosophy/rhetoric of empathy influenced her engagement with what she called the "common life" of working people at Hull House, resulting in her use of an empathetic rhetorical style focused on the personal, and a habit of solving social problems using cooperative methods.[15] In crucial ways Addams's experience at Hull House formed her epistemological framework. As a pragmatist who held that theory should come from experience, Addams formed her beliefs as a result of what she experienced firsthand in working-class neighborhoods.

Addams and her companion Ellen Gates Starr founded Hull House in 1889 in the working-class nineteenth ward just west of downtown Chicago. They based the settlement house, the first in the United States,[16] on the model of Toynbee Hall in London, designed to foster cross-class relationships and "proselytize the humanities" rather than saving souls.[17] Addams's philosophy for Hull House was that it would provide an opportunity for women and men with social capital to work alongside residents in working-class neighborhoods to develop literary, cultural, and practical skills. Addams tells her audience that her arguments for worker reform had come from her personal knowledge of the perspectives of women employed as domestic workers. At the beginning of her speech she announces that "an attempt is made to present this industry from the point of view of those women who are working in households for wages," and that "the opinions in [this talk] have been largely gained through experiences in a Woman's Labor Bureau, and through conversations held there with women returning from the 'situations,' which they had voluntarily relinquished in Chicago households of all grades. These same women seldom gave up a place in a factory, although many of the factory situations involved long hours and hard work."[18]

Her rhetorical style is informed a great deal by her belief in mutual exchange rather than overt persuasion, a belief that undergirded her philosophy at Hull House. Similar to the idea that empathy involves feeling *with* rather than *for* an Other, Addams believed in *being with* people rather than *doing for* them. In this sense she resisted popular, late nineteenth-century notions of the role of what was commonly known as benevolence. Rather than trying to persuade people of her own beliefs, Addams tried to forge greater understanding and connection between people in different social classes and ethnic groups. In this process she realized that the greatest good came from gaining the perspective of the Other, and that within that learning process change occurs, both in the Other, who is persuaded to accept a new perspective, and within the rhetor, who listens to the perspective of the Other. Addams's engagement with working-class struggles at Hull House changed her, and her public rhetoric advocating reform was a result of this change.

Pathos and Story: Personalizing the Impersonal

Addams's speech at the Columbian Exposition, though relatively short and obscure, is a good example of her early rhetoric and is representative of her rhetorical style: as in her longer, more well-known work such as *The Long Road of Woman's Memory* (1916), she relies on her personal experience and on stories to form knowledge and appeal to her audience. In the speech Addams draws from her friendships and daily interactions with domestic workers at Hull House, using personal stories as emotional appeals to humanize the women whom most if not all of her audience employed in their homes.

In "Domestic Service and the Family Claim" and its fuller version, "A Belated Industry," Addams personalizes what had become a considerably impersonal commonplace of middle- and upper-middle-class families employing young women to live full-time in their homes as servants. Faye Dudden makes a compelling argument that prior to the 1830s, young women employed by families for domestic work were considered in many cases to be part of the family, to be "help," eating in the dining room with the other members of the family rather than in a back room or basement, and often being employed only for temporary seasons, such as during a family illness.[19] Furthermore, most domestic workers were native-born women whose families lived in the same community as their employers.

Dudden speculates that a shift toward viewing and treating domestic workers as impersonal employees began around midcentury. As industrial capitalism took hold, work shifted away from the home, men began working outside the home, and rising middle-class women began to be seen as the keepers of the home exclusively. In order to preserve "family time" in the evenings, undisturbed by domestic chores such as cleaning and cooking, the woman of the family would hire and supervise one or more servants. Dudden holds that the shift from workers as "help" to workers as "servants" was "demanding and demeaning, prompting the withdrawal from service of many of the native-born daughters who had been willing to help."[20]

The result was an occupation that required young women to live full-time with a family, often left without any companionship or social outlets, and often treated with disrespect or worse by the woman of the house. In her speech, Addams attempts to humanize the women working daily in the homes of her audience, focusing on the isolation such work produces in young women—her primary argument against the ethically bankrupt system of domestic labor in her society. She points to the hypocrisy of the women in her audience who employ young women and require them to live full-time in their homes, denying the women a chance to have families of their own: "The employer of household labor, in her zeal to preserve her family life intact and free from intrusion, acts inconsistently and grants to her cook, for instance, but once or twice a week such opportunity for untrammeled association with her relatives."[21] She stresses the inconsistencies of the domestic labor model with two biting sentences contained in the Columbian Exposition proceedings but omitted by Addams or her editors in the article published in the *American Journal of Sociology* (and providing a memorable impression of Addams): "So strongly is the employer imbued with the sanctity of her own family life that this sacrifice of the cook's family life seems to her perfectly justifiable. If one chose to be jocose one might say that it becomes almost a religious devotion, in which the cook figures as a burnt offering and the kitchen range as the patriarchal altar."[22]

She describes the changes that she—during her time at the Chicago Labor Bureau—has seen in young women who have worked as live-in domestic workers: "Many a girl who complains of loneliness, and who relinquishes her situation with that as her sole excuse, feebly tries to formulate her sense of restraint and social mal-adjustment. She sometimes says that she 'feels so unnatural all the time.'"[23] Addams goes on to point out that "the writer [referring to herself] has known the voice of a girl to change so much during three weeks of 'service' that she could not recognize it when the girl returned to the bureau. It alternated between the high falsetto in which a shy child 'speaks a piece,' and the husky gulp with which the *globus hystericus* is swallowed. The alertness and *bon-homie* of the voice of the tenement-house child had totally disappeared."[24]

The young women for whom Addams advocates and whose perspectives she tries to represent in "A Belated Industry" become real people, those same people who live and work in the homes of the women in her audience and who suffer under the current system—a system producing bad effects, she argues, not only for domestic workers but also for the women who employ them.

Addressing Injustice and Difference: The Personal in the System

Addams's primary argument in her speech is that the domestic labor system kept alive by the women in her audience suffers from two major flaws: ethical and industrial. In making this argument she focuses on both the personal and the political. The practice of employing young women full-time as cooks and housemaids to keep up an antiquated social system, Addams argues, deprives the women of families of their own and isolates them. On a larger level, she points out that her work at Hull House had shown her that the use of such an ethically compromised model drives young women to work in factories so that the best workers are not available for domestic labor. She positions both the women in the audience and the young women they employ as human beings, individuals, caught in a larger system that was not good, ultimately, for anyone involved.

Addams invites her audience of women who employ domestic help to imagine these domestic workers as fellow wives and mothers trying to run their own households. She compels her audience to think about how difficult household work is for women who work in factories (making the goods that the women in her audience consume on a daily basis) or who help run the households of women who employ them while also attempting to run their own: "The difficulties really begin when the family income is so small that but one person can be employed in the household for all these varied functions, and the difficulties increase and grow almost insurmountable as they fall altogether upon the mother of the family, who is living in a flat, or worse still, in a tenement house, where one stove and one set of utensils must be put to all sorts of uses, fit or unfit, making the living room of the family a horror in summer, and perfectly insupportable in rainy washing days in winter."[25] She describes an immigrant woman living in a tenement whom she had seen "pass by a basket of green peas at the door of a local grocery store, to purchase a tin of canned peas, because they could be easily prepared for supper and 'the children liked the tinny taste.'"[26]

Unlike Joyce Fernandes, Addams never worked as a domestic laborer. She knew women who had and was moved and changed by their stories. Her rhetoric invites the same kind of change in her audience, as they experience someone with whom they could identify—a socially acceptable, upper-class white woman—encouraging them to think of the lower-class women in their homes, cleaning up their messes and helping raise their children, as equal to them and worthy of a better life.

TRANSNATIONAL, DIGITAL ACTIVISM: JOYCE FERNANDES, PRETA-RARA, AND #EUEMPREGADADOMÉSTICA

In the hundreds of stories of domestic workers she has posted on the #EuEmpregadaDoméstica (I, Housemaid) Facebook page, Fernandes humanizes the millions of domestic workers in Brazil who often are rendered invisible or considered less important in society because of their occupation or skin color. In these stories, real women recount their abuses in their own words—or, because many of the women lack the literacy and access necessary to participate on Facebook, in the words of their daughters and granddaughters. Many of these daughters and granddaughters were themselves domestic workers before going to college; their posts indicate they have internalized the stories of their mothers into their own narratives about the value of their lives and the lives of other women of color in their country. The women's stories describe, sometimes in painful detail, the effects of domestic labor—which Fernandes calls modern-day slavery—on their physical bodies as well as their self-esteem and ability to have a decent life of their own while taking care of other women in their society.

Fernandes makes it clear that it is just as important to fight the emotional effects of slavery's legacy as it is the legal and material ramifications, resisting the effects of racism in multiple ways. She proudly celebrates her own body and black identity on her professional Facebook page, which she named after her rapper persona, Preta-Rara. She encourages other young, black women to see their own worth and advocate for those who still suffer under domestic labor abuses, and she shares the stories of other domestic workers on the #EuEmpregadaDoméstica Facebook page. Her performance name is a powerful reclamation of blackness. People with noticeable African features and skin color—those with the darkest skin—are generally referred to (and they identify) as *negro* or *preto* (black). Preta, the Portuguese word for "black," is a reclamation similar to "queer."[27] Rara in Urban Dictionary is "lovable" and "the most beautiful and amazing girl ever."[28] Preta-Rara, then, signifies in English something like "queer, wonderful, eccentric black woman." With her assumed name, Fernandes resists racist assumptions and associations of blackness and fights to redefine what it means to be black in Brazil.

She often begins her posts on #EuEmpregadaDoméstica and her Preta-Rara Facebook page—all of which are written in Portuguese and translated into English below—with the salutation "Estamos juntas, Preta-Rara!" (We are together, Preta-Rara), so that her stage name becomes a communal name for all women like herself in her culture. In a post to the #EuEmpregadaDoméstica Facebook page dated July 25, 2016 (just four days after she had created the page and witnessed its viral launch into worldwide media coverage), she describes the purpose for the site, using the third-person, communal plural to speak on behalf of other women like herself:

> We are together, Preta-Rara!
> Since Thursday, July 21, the hashtag #EuEmpregadaDoméstica (via social media) made us think about the place reserved for black women in this society.... They take care of the sons of others . . . and in most cases receive a low salary. In addition, there are no labor rights such as vacations, annual bonuses, payments for night shifts, overtime, health insurance, transportation vouchers and food stamps. And this reminded us (no big news) of the low position of this job, not being allowed to access living spaces in their own place of employment, not being able to take the main elevator, sit at the table for meals, and eating meals that are different from those of their bosses.

She goes on in the same post to address and resist the low position of black women in Brazil: "And even when we develop or when we insist on leaving these jobs, they intend to point out that the large population of black women - at the base of the social pyramid - should remain there."

Despite the well-earned criticism Facebook has received for promoting political division during the 2016 election in the United States, and for its lack of transparency in describing to users how their information will be used (and sold), the fact is that without Facebook the stories of these women would, in all likelihood, not be told, at least not on the level afforded by social media. Many posts receive several hundred comments, some from people pushing back against her message or expressing disbelief at what she is writing, and many offering support and writing their own messages about family members or friends. The circulatory reach of these posts is multiplied within Facebook's algorithm, which allows users to view comments made by their friends, exposing the women's stories to the social network of the tens of thousands of people who follow her feed. Considering how these posts and stories travel and are dispersed among varied networks and audiences using frames such as circulation and mobility studies is useful in thinking about the role of online networks in social change. The notion of *circulation*—what Laurie E. Gries describes as a key threshold concept for rhetorical studies—alongside a lens of rhetorical empathy provides useful ways of thinking about audience and affect in digital spaces.[29]

Her many audiences include not only other women like herself, whom she encourages to advocate for others who are still in domestic work and shut off from opportunities despite the improvement of labor laws, but also young women in college who are fans of her music. In a post to the #EuEmpregadaDoméstica Facebook page on October 22, 2016, she writes:

> To college students!
> What's the point in gaining awareness from the stories on this page but then going to your fraternity parties and leaving the place a mess because Monday is "Aunty Cleaning" day? And beyond the everyday mess, she is forced to collect cans, used condoms, empty loaded ashtrays, and face the bathroom just as you can imagine right now, and still she's paid R$ 50 for the job. Rethink your life and your ideas, get off the internet and seek change for the world that you always talk about. Where's the real empathy?

This post highlights Fernandes's use of her music platform and status as a rap star to reach audiences who may never be exposed to or interested in labor issues for domestic workers. She asks her audience to try to imagine what life is like for the women who clean up after them in their dorm rooms and apartments while they are partying and going about their lives. The affective power of this post, of course, lies in the fact that she herself has been both the college student and the woman cleaning up, so to speak.

Millions of women in Brazil work as domestic maids, a position typically filled by women of color as a vestige of legalized slavery, and a result of staggering income inequality. US media coverage of the 2016 Summer Olympics in Rio de Janeiro glossed over or failed entirely to account for the country's income inequality or the fact that its crime is historically rooted in the country's history of slavery and continued racism. Media images focused instead on the result of these factors, portraying the city as plagued by crime and pollution, with the Olympic City standing as a staged, security-filled semimirage. Young, dark-skinned boys, shirtless, ran among tourists in city squares, captured on surveillance footage attempting to pickpocket foreigners in town for the games. US Olympic swimmer Ryan Lochte made up a story about being robbed at gunpoint by locals to cover up a night of drunken vandalism.[30] One of the stories behind the crime runs deep. Of the eleven million people brought to the Americas in the Middle Passage, four million ended up in Brazil in its three-hundred-year history of slavery, which ended in 1888.[31] These staggering numbers make the country "the second blackest nation in the world," according to Henry Louis Gates Jr., after Nigeria.[32]

As in the United States, the racism and exploitation that drove slavery in Brazil still exist today. The income and wealth gap between those coded white and those coded nonwhite is staggering: nonwhite people earn only 60 percent as much as white people, who earn 84 percent of total income.[33] Women of color

in Brazil traditionally have worked in disproportionate numbers as domestic laborers, with roots in legalized slavery. Sandra Lauderdale Graham points out that
"in the 1870s, 87–90% of slave women in Rio worked as domestic servants, and
an estimated thirty-four thousand slave and free women labored as domestics.
Thus, Brazilian women in urban centers often blurred the lines that separated the
work and lives of the slave and the free."[34] Today Brazil has the largest number of
domestic workers in the world at six million,[35] almost one in every five women
in the country, the majority of whom are black women with little education.[36]

The hundreds of posts on #EuEmpregadaDoméstica contain story after story
about physical and psychological trauma faced by women in domestic work,
often as a result of the lack of maternity leave or other basic rights enjoyed by
most other workers. The stories on the site describe the isolation—pointed to
by Addams—of young women cut off from normal family life and subjected to
almost unspeakable horror in some cases. In a harrowing post dated August 3,
2016, Fernandes shares a story sent by a woman whose mother was a domestic
worker for decades:

> My mom has been a maid for 40 years and here is the story that left her terrified:
> In 1989 I was two years old and it was typical for maids with children to live
> in their employer's house. One day my mother's boss offered to buy me because
> she couldn't get pregnant, and claimed that my mom wouldn't have resources to
> take good care of a child, being a single mother. She must have thought that my
> mother would accept it just like the other maid did, and the worst thing was that
> the child's mother was still working in the house and kept seeing her son calling
> another woman mother. My mom got scared and left in the middle of the night.

Other stories recount women who were denied water so that they would not
have to relieve themselves, older women who were forced to take the stairs to
upper floors when the service elevator was out (they were barred from using the
main elevator), and women forced to eat off the floor rather than sit at the table
with the family. The emotions these stories elicit, both in the comments of the
posts as well as among the countless more who read and do not post, create a
sense of empathy with women caught in a system with little legal protection and
little respect in society.

Characteristic of empathetic rhetorical practices, Fernandes focuses on the
personal within the systemic; she listens and invites listening (and with it, emo-
tion and a call for social change). In the stories she shares on the Facebook page,
she describes in poignant detail the many abuses done by employers, but she also
resists painting such people as entirely bad, casting them instead as part of a larger,
racist culture. In one of her first posts (July 21, 2016) to #EuEmpregadaDoméstica
she describes how she left domestic work and went to college. The post reads

at first almost like a coded literacy narrative meant to appeal to left-minded, middle- and upper-class women who employ domestic workers. However, by the end of the story there is a sense that she is being sincere: she appreciates and even cares deeply for her former boss. She offers a picture that goes against easy stereotypes of domestic workers, and in doing so she offers an affective appeal, consciously or not, to other women who employ domestic workers:

[**Boss:**] Joyce, I see you taking so long to dust off the shelf and my books, do you like reading?

Me: Yes, I read the Bible a lot.

Boss: I have already caught you hiding and reading my book "Olga." You can take it home to read. Have you ever considered continuing your studies?

Me: Yes, I want to go to college to study history; it's very expensive, and I don't know if I can afford it.

Boss: That's amazing, you will have to read a lot, huh! And you will have a shelf with far more books than the lawyer here. You will get it girl, I'm sure.

(My boss Regina is the only one who encouraged me to study, and when I met her at Gonzaga beach in Santos/SP, I gave her a big hug and said that I was a teacher, and we cried together.)

A number of the women who post responses to the stories on the #EuEmpre gadaDoméstica Facebook page appear from their avatars and rhetoric to be well-educated allies to Fernandes's work, so an attempt to reach out to them as shapers of public opinion and policy among the powerful "white" ruling class makes sense. It is important to stress, however, that Fernandes mixes her graciousness with a great deal of sarcasm, and with anger and confrontation. In a post from July 24, 2016, she highlights the daily consequences of injustices, extreme power, and income inequality:

The G1 website published a story on the #EuEmpregadaDoméstica webpage three days ago.

They talked about the campaign I created and posted a random photo from Facebook, where I'm wearing blue lipstick, sunglasses, and with my black hair up high, reflecting my self-esteem. There were so many racist comments, trying to offend my race, that G1 disabled the comment option at the end of the article.

The Master's House freaked out! We lifted the carpets and showed the dirt and scum that the traditional Brazilian family has been hiding indoors for centuries. That's it! I left a place that many others have left before me, many of them leaving with me, and several ones that will leave soon, because our voice now echoes in the world. And you, sucker racists, won't stop me! AND I'M NOT ALONE, AND HAVE NEVER BEEN! I have several Black Women with me, standing up to it every day and willing to show up, because we are tired of being invisible in this racist society!

Far from covering over the racism that underlies the domestic worker industry in Brazil, in telling these women's stories, Fernandes creates a sense of solidarity among workers themselves and calls out privileged women who benefit from their exploitation.

CONCLUSION: CONNECTING ACROSS DIFFERENCE

Both Fernandes and Addams compel their audiences to view domestic workers as individuals with lives and histories of their own. Jane Addams used rhetorical empathy to appeal to her audience of middle- and upper-middle-class white women to change the way they approached the issue of immigrant women working in undesirable conditions as maids and cooks in their homes. Joyce Fernandes uses elements of rhetorical empathy in the form of stories to create solidarity among workers and move her privileged audience to change. Fernandes's experience as a domestic worker enables her to approach her audience—of other young women like herself and women who employ domestic workers—as one who knows intimately about the suffering and journeys she details. This additional element of her subject position and experience adds power to her rhetorical appeal.

The fact that Addams speaks on behalf of women from a lower social class is not without its problems—far from it. The use of solidarity or empathy by those occupying a dominant subject position could be viewed as, at minimum, patronizing, even when the best of intentions guide them. However, power and privilege are slippery concepts that shift in relation to context: Jane Addams was often denigrated and ignored by men in power because she was a woman, as were first wave feminists when they began speaking up against slavery, and as women have been since then any time they work with men in social movements. An intersectional lens remains useful in thinking about the ways power is relative to social positioning; at the risk of oversimplification, a white woman has less power than does a white man but more power in most cases than do women of color, even more so in Addams's day. Social class and wealth, though, play a tremendous role in how much power rhetors have in any rhetorical situation. As Tarez Samra Graban argues in the foreword to this collection, a lens of interstitiality helps complicate hard and fast lines of identity by acknowledging that identities shift and are relative to each rhetorical encounter we face.

Jane Addams, the daughter of class and racial privilege, gave up her wealth to live among the immigrant women for whom she advocated. While her class privilege and ethnicity/whiteness would always be part of her identity, she attempted to identify as much as possible with the immigrant workers surrounding her. She formed relationships with her neighbors and experienced life in their neighborhoods, including the squalid conditions of daily life in the nineteenth ward in Chicago. Her first taste of fame on a national scale came in 1895, just after the Pullman Strike, when she took a job as trash collection inspector. To ensure the workers employed by the famously corrupt alderman actually collected the trash, which they had failed to do on a consistent basis up to that time, Addams got up each morning at 5 o'clock and walked behind horse-drawn trash wagons in the filthy unpaved streets. A senator's daughter and upper-class woman who would do such a thing drew much more attention than would a woman from a lower-class background, no doubt. Class privilege and whiteness are real in material ways. She used her privilege and acted as an ally to women with less power, as problematic as that relationship was and can be. For her, though, empathy was more than a "strategy" but a way of life that formed a vital part of her identity. In our contemporary moment, this kind of ally role must be framed by deep listening of the sort Krista Ratcliffe advocates.[37] It is vital that people with privilege adopt a stance informed by listening and rhetorical empathy; it is no longer an option. I write this as a queer, white-coded professor with working-class roots who considers it no longer an option for myself.

People in less dominant subject positions are acutely aware of their social roles and positioning, as Jacqueline Jones Royster notes in her article "When the First Voice You Hear Is Not Your Own,"[38] and they must learn early in life to listen to the dominant majority in order to survive. For those with less power within intersectional subject positions, rhetorical strategies characterized by rhetorical empathy can be problematic and can risk further reifying unequal material conditions. This risk is real and should not be ignored; however, as problematic and complicated as it can be, such a stance can offer perspective and strength. Fernandes represents a significant shift within intersectional, transnational women's rhetorical practices: from one relying primarily on women in privileged positions speaking for migrant women and women of color without class privilege, to one that relies on women of color in postcolonial contexts gaining access to cultural capital through traditional and digital literacy, and advocating for themselves, for change in attitudes, practices, and public policy.

Notes

1. Addams spoke on a Friday morning at 10 o'clock, delivering a fairly brief address, a summary of which, entitled "Domestic Service and the Family Claim," was published in the proceedings of the Women's Congress of the Columbian Exposition. A fuller version of her arguments, three times the length of her speech in the congress proceedings, was published three years later in the *American Journal of Sociology*, titled "A Belated Industry." For the purposes of analysis I use this latter version of her speech, as the full contents of her Columbian Exposition speech are included within "A Belated Industry." Jane Addams,

"Domestic Service and the Family Claim," in *The World's Congress of Representative Women*, vol. 2, ed. Mary Wright Sewell (Chicago: Rand McNally, 1894), 626–31; Addams, "A Belated Industry," *American Journal of Sociology* 1, no. 5 (1896): 536–50.

2. The Women's Congress was held in what is now the Art Institute of Chicago, built specifically for the Columbian Exposition and one of only two buildings (the Field Museum being the other) that survives; the rest of the two hundred temporary structures constructed for the fair burned to the ground during the Pullman Strike the next summer.

3. Luis Barrucho, "I Am Housemaid, Hear Me Roar," *BBC Trending*, August 1, 2016, http://www.bbc.com.

4. Lisa Blankenship, *Changing the Subject: A Theory of Rhetorical Empathy* (Logan: Utah State University Press, 2019).

5. Michael Polanyi, *Personal Knowledge* (London: Taylor and Francis, 2012); Evelyn Fox Keller, *A Feeling for the Organism: The Life and Work of Barbara McClintock* (New York: Henry Holt, 2003).

6. Barrucho, "I Am Housemaid."

7. David M. Sheridan, Jim Ridolfo, and Anthony J. Michel, *The Available Means of Persuasion: Mapping a Theory and Pedagogy of Multimodal Public Rhetoric* (Anderson, SC: Parlor Press, 2012).

8. Kristie S. Fleckenstein, *Embodied Literacies: Imageword and a Poetics of Teaching* (Carbondale: Southern Illinois University Press, 2003).

9. Sherry Turkle, *Reclaiming Conversation: The Power of Talk in a Digital Age* (New York: Penguin, 2015).

10. Louise W. Knight, *Citizen: Jane Addams and the Struggle for Democracy* (Chicago: University of Chicago Press, 2005), 391.

11. Jane Addams, *Twenty Years at Hull-House* (New York: Signet, 1961), 393.

12. George J. Stigler, *Domestic Service in the United States: 1900–1940* (New York: National Bureau of Economic Research, 1946), 5.

13. David M. Katzman, *Seven Days a Week: Women and Domestic Service in Industrializing America* (New York: Oxford University Press, 1978), 5. A notable example of an ethnographic exposé on working-class conditions written by an educated member of the middle class is Lillian Pettengill's *Toilers of the Home* (1902), a precursor to such studies as Barbara Ehrenreich's *Nickel and Dimed: On (Not) Getting By in America* (2001). Pettengill was a graduate of Mount Holyoke who in the late 1890s was unable to find employment as a journalist and so went to work as a live-in domestic servant for one year, partly to pay the bills and have a roof over her head and partly to conduct participant-observer research. Katzman calls her monograph on her experience one of the most extensive accounts of a domestic worker in the United States during the late Gilded Age.

14. Joy Ritchie and Kate Ronald, introduction to *Available Means: An Anthology of Women's Rhetoric(s)*, ed. Joy Ritchie and Kate Ronald (Pittsburgh, PA: University of Pittsburgh Press, 2001), xxviii.

15. Xing Lu, *Rhetoric in Ancient China, Fifth to Third Century B.C.E.: A Comparison with Classical Greek Rhetoric* (Columbia: University of South Carolina Press, 1998); Carol S. Lipson and Roberta A. Binkley, introduction to *Rhetoric before and beyond the Greeks*, ed. Carol S. Lipson and Roberta A. Binkley (Albany: State University of New York Press, 2004), 1–24.

16. Knight, *Citizen*, 192. The College Settlement Association (CSA), which comprised

women educated at the Seven Sisters (Smith, Wellesley, Vassar, Bryn Mawr, Mount Holyoke, Radcliffe, and Barnard), established a settlement house in New York City two weeks after Hull House opened.

17. Knight, 170.

18. Addams, "A Belated Industry," 536.

19. Faye E. Dudden, *Serving Women: Household Service in Nineteenth-Century America* (Middletown, CT: Wesleyan University Press), 1985.

20. Dudden, 7.

21. Addams, "A Belated Industry," 543.

22. Addams, "Domestic Service," 627.

23. Addams, "A Belated Industry," 548.

24. Addams, 548.

25. Addams, 547.

26. Addams, 547.

27. Marques Travae, "'Preto' or 'Negro'? In Portuguese Both Mean 'Black,' but Which Term Should Be Used to Define Black People? Ghanaian-Brazilian Man's Video on the Topic Goes Viral," *Black Women of Brazil*, August 3, 2016, https://blackwomenofbrazil.co.

28. *Urban Dictionary*, s.v. "Rara," entry dated August 12, 2003, https://www.urbandictionary .com.

29. Laurie E. Gries, introduction to *Circulation, Writing, and Rhetoric*, ed. Laurie E. Gries and Collin Gifford Brooke (Logan: Utah State University Press 2018), 3–26.

30. Azadeh Ansari and Steve Almasy, "Lochte: 'I Over-Exaggerated' Robbery Story," *CNN*, August 22, 2016, http://www.cnn.com.

31. Lulu Garcia-Navarro, "Photos Reveal Harsh Detail of Brazil's History with Slavery," *NPR*, November 12, 2013, https://www.npr.org.

32. Henry Louis Gates Jr., "Q&A with Professor Henry Louis Gates, Jr.," *PBS*, *Black in Latin America*, November 11, 2015, http://www.pbs.org/wnet/black-in-latin-america.

33. Mara Loveman, Jeronimo O. Muniz, and Stanley R. Bailey, "Brazil in Black and White? Race Categories, the Census, and the Study of Inequality," *Ethnic and Racial Studies* 35, no. 8, published ahead of print, September 23, 2011, https://doi.org/10 .1080/01419870.2011.607503.

34. Sandra Lauderdale Graham, *House and Street: The Domestic World of Servants and Masters in Nineteenth-Century Rio De Janeiro* (New York: Cambridge University Press, 1988).

35. International Labour Office, *Domestic Workers across the World: Global and Regional Statistics and the Extent of Legal Protection* (Geneva: International Labour Office, 2013), 24.

36. International Labour Office, 26.

37. See Krista Ratcliffe, *Rhetorical Listening: Identification, Gender, Whiteness* (Carbondale: Southern Illinois University Press, 2005).

38. Jacqueline Jones Royster, "When the First Voice You Hear Is Not Your Own," *College Composition and Communication* 47, no. 1 (1996): 29–40.

PART THREE

RESPONSE RHETORICS

KATHERINE FREDLUND

IN ORDER TO THEORIZE RESPONSE rhetorics, the chapters in this section use Rhetorical Transversal Methodology (RTM) to consider how those without power use rhetoric to respond to those with power—recognizing that our theories of rhetoric all too often fail to consider how hostile or unreceptive audiences impact rhetorical choices and effects. Indeed, James Berlin explains, "As I have argued repeatedly, rhetorics arise in response to the conditions of power at a particular historical moment, and these conditions are constantly in flux. . . . We have of course much to learn from the history of rhetoric, but one important lesson is that the past is never exactly reproduced in the present. Innovation for its own sake is a mistake, but innovation in response to changing conditions is necessary—particularly if one happens to be a member of a class, race, or gender out of power and out of luck."[1] While all rhetoric arises in response to conditions of power, the chapters in this section consider Berlin's claim that innovative methods of response are particularly necessary as a result of changing conditions and for those who lack power in society. By placing rhetorical responses from different eras into conversation with one another via RTM, these contributions theorize what we have labeled response rhetorics: rhetorics directed at audiences who do not want to listen rhetorically.

George Yoos proposed that we "introduce the label 'rhetorical response' to encompass these traditional rhetorical modes labeled 'exposition' and 'informative.'" At the same time, he distinguishes the aims of rhetorical response from what he had already labeled "rhetorical appeal." He notes that,

> rhetorical response reflects the ordinary use of the term "to explain" to respond to most kinds of questions put to the speaker by his or her audience. For example, we might be asked to explain what something is like, to explain what happened, to explain how something is done, to explain why someone did some-

thing, to explain what caused an event, to explain what something is made of, to explain the relevance of a statement or fact, to explain who did it, to explain what something means, to explain what one is trying to do or say, to explain the logical connections between Statements, and so on. Thus, rhetorical response, as [he has] labeled it, encompasses such modes as narration, description, logical demonstration, definition, telling how something is done, comparison and contrast.[2]

The chapters in this section, however, illustrate that explaining oppression, equality, and civil rights to hostile and/or unreceptive audiences is a challenging rhetorical task that requires ingenuity and skill.

In her landmark feminist work *Man Cannot Speak For Her*, Karlyn Kohrs Campbell explains, "In a social movement advocating controversial changes, failure to achieve specific goals will be common, no matter how able and creative the advocates, whether male or female. . . . As a result, critics must judge whether the choices made by rhetors were skillful responses to the problems they confronted, not whether the changes they urged were enacted."[3] Because the chapters in this section examine how feminists respond to hostile or unreceptive audiences, they follow Campbell's directive to consider rhetorical choices rather than effect, but they also consider how rhetoric can be effective even when it does not achieve the rhetor's goal. If scholars think about rhetoric's effect beyond the rhetor's goal and with less focus on the time directly after delivery, then so-called failed rhetorics can be understood as effective despite not reaching the rhetor's goals immediately. Further, by taking up Krista Ratcliffe's work on rhetorical listening, the chapters also consider how audiences fail, recognizing that for rhetoric to be successful, not only a skillful rhetor but also a rhetorically receptive audience is required.[4]

The examples of feminist rhetoric found in each chapter further indicate that there are a variety of ways to innovate the "ordinary" when responding to power. For example, rather than provide simple one-off narratives, feminist rhetors have used repetition in their storytelling in order to connect to other women's stories (whether by writing "click!" narratives in the 1970s, or, in the twenty-first century, tweeting hashtags and repeating phrases like "me too"). This use of repetition amplifies feminist rhetoric by emphasizing the connections between women's experiences—challenging those that would dismiss one or two accounts by forcing them to grapple with hundreds to thousands of similar accounts of patriarchy, violence, or inequity. Black feminists (in response to white apathy) have been forced to describe the mindset that allows lynching to be accepted as justice rather than simply describing the horrific nature of lynching in the nineteenth century or police brutality in the twenty-first century. Describing the violence or even watching the violence on the internet is unfortunately and horrifyingly not enough. Both in the case of Ida B. Wells and Black Lives Matter activists, black feminists have explained how systemic racism allows for (and even encourages) violence against black bodies and communities, and yet both the justice system and white feminists continue to dismiss or ignore such violence. Thus, feminist rhetorical responses must find ways to first address and then persuade unreceptive audiences, and the chapters in this section provide models of useful strategies for response rhetorics (anonymity, repetition, and narrative) while also recognizing that failure is sometimes inevitable.

This section begins with perhaps the most time-honored female response to patriarchy: the anonymous author. Skye Roberson's chapter, "'Anonymous Was a Woman': Anonymous Authorship as Rhetorical Strategy," investigates how anonymous authorship has functioned historically to protect a woman's (or her family's) reputation and considers how feminists on Reddit have adapted this use of anonymity. Her chapter challenges us to rethink authorial agency in light of digital rhetorical practices, arguing that while anonymity was once forced, it is now used to give women both power and privacy, a privacy that is not forced but chosen. She argues agency is best understood as "the ability to exert authority . . . over the narrative" by controlling the story—both the story being told and the story of the author. She further explains that anonymity is often a subversive choice for women authors. Historically, that subversion meant finding ways to publish when doing so as a woman meant immediate failure or social ostracization. In the present, it means choosing anonymity at a time when social media constantly demands identification. Anonymity, then, is a rhetorical response to power that allows feminists to both have a voice and remain hidden, and such a choice challenges patriarchal concepts of authorship, agency, and audience.

Further challenging our understanding of the relationship between a rhetor and their audience, Tiffany Kinney's chapter, "Tracing the Conversation: Legitimizing Mormon Feminism," focuses on the rhetorical strategies two Mormon feminists (Sonia Johnson and Kathleen Marie Kelly) used as they fought for women's legitimacy within the Mormon faith. Their stories provide further evidence for Campbell's claim that some audiences cannot be convinced no matter the ingenuity of the rhetor's response. Indeed, feminist rhetoric is sometimes destined for failure because certain audiences are simply incapable of rhetorical listening. Still, these feminist rhetorics laid important groundwork that, Kinney argues, led to future feminist victories. Indeed, Kinney's chapter demonstrates how women rhetors can use time-honored and tested feminist rhetorical practices (practices outlined by Carol Mattingly and Roxanne Mountford) to respond to patriarchy within religious groups.[5] Yet the strength of patriarchy, when it is believed to be ordained by God, can resist women's rhetorical use of traditional dress, mimicry of religious leadership practices, and appeals to reason. Still, Kinney argues that despite the excommunication of the two Mormon feminists she discusses in her chapter, the recent changes in LDS practices present a compelling case that these women's rhetorical practices of legitimacy were successful, despite not achieving their explicit goals. Thus, their failure was not really failure at all—it was a chip in patriarchy's armor. A chip that made room for change, however slow and small that change may seem.

Clancy Ratliff's chapter, "The Suffragist Movement and the Early Feminist Blogosphere: Feminism and Recent History of Rhetoric," continues this section by discussing the striking similarities between suffragist cartoons and "Where are the women" blogs and arguing for the studying of recent histories—histories that are important to our understanding of the ways rhetoric and media interact. Her comparison draws attention to feminist and male bloggers' continued use of "caricatures of femininity" in their responses to critiques about women's involvement in politics. Like Kinney, she also discusses failure, noting that the responses to "Where are the women" blogs did not actually increase the number of women bloggers in the early 2000s, when they appeared. She argues that these blogs are worth studying even though they failed, as failure can teach us as much about rhetorical practices and audiences as success can. Ratliff further discusses how women bloggers called out male bloggers' exclusionary tactics (a practice that Paige V. Banaji discusses in very different contexts in the following chapter) and emphasizes the small cultural changes that resulted from these acts of response while uncovering the reasons this response rhetoric failed.

While caricatures of femininity were once useful rhetorical responses for feminists, they were only really ever useful for white women, as these caricatures assume femininity is always already white and (at least) middle class. Thus, Banaji's chapter, "Mikki Kendall, Ida B. Wells, and #SolidarityIsForWhiteWomen: Women of Color Calling Out White Feminism in the Nineteenth Century and the Digital Age," shifts our attention to a study of how response rhetorics work within the feminist movement—specifically when black feminists respond to problematic instances of white feminism. Her chapter considers Ida B. Wells's antilynching rhetoric alongside Mikki Kendall's #SolidarityIsForWhiteWomen, illustrating how black feminists have responded to white feminism through a form of rhetorical response she terms *calling out*. Like the Mormon rhetors in Kinney's chapter, Wells, Kendall, and the thousands of women who tweeted #SolidarityIsForWhiteWomen stories found themselves with a resistant audience. While this resistance could be perceived as a failure to effectively respond to their audience, Banaji uses Krista Ratcliffe's theories of rhetorical listening to argue that the failure is not Wells's or Kendall's; the failure belongs to white feminists, who (quite disturbingly) have refused to listen rhetorically and call out themselves (ourselves) for well over a hundred years. Thus, Banaji's discussion of the white feminist response to Wells and Kendall illustrates the challenge of crafting response rhetorics when audiences refuse to listen rhetorically to stories that challenge their own understanding of feminism, equality, and intersectionality.

Bethany Mannon's chapter, "The Persuasive Power of Individual Stories: The Rhetoric in Narrative Archives," concludes this section with a discussion of personal narrative and storytelling as a rhetorical method of response. Like #SolidarityIsForWhiteWomen, the three examples in this chapter use repetition, inviting many rhetors to use similar narrative structures in order to amplify their rhetoric. The chapter begins with *Ms.* magazine's "click!" moments before considering how *This Bridge Called My Back* remediated the "click!" moment in order to highlight its focus on white feminism and shift attention to women of color's lived experiences. Her chapter considers how feminists have rejected the separation of narrative and rhetoric and, in doing so, crafted response rhetorics that speak to a variety of audiences, including women who do not identify as feminists and white feminists whose rhetorical practices have excluded women of color. Mannon then turns to *My Duty to Speak* (an online storytelling project that calls attention to sexual assault in the military) in order both to illustrate how digital storytelling revises the narrative rhetorical response once more and to identify ways that feminist rhetorical methods of response are useful for other silenced groups.

The chapters in this section ultimately consider how feminist rhetors respond to power by innovating more traditional delivery strategies like identification, narrative, explanation, and repetition. Indeed, feminist rhetors have no choice but to innovate, as traditional rhetorical methods do not allow them to be heard. Yet the chapters in this section also indicate that rhetorical failure is not always a failure on the part of the rhetor. Audiences too often fail rhetorically, and this tendency is particularly true for white feminists. Further, while Campbell encourages us to consider rhetorical choices instead of effect when studying women's rhetoric, the contributors illustrate how studying a rhetoric's effect through the lens of RTM can lead to important developments, particularly when our goals are not only to critique but to improve feminist rhetorical practices. From these chapters, we learn how feminists have delivered response rhetorics by challenging traditional authorship expectations, by using the rhetoric of those in power against them, by asking multiple rhetors to repeat narrative patterns, and by directly confronting those in power. Feminist rhetorical methods of response, then, innovate traditional rhetorical practices in order to respond to audiences that have not agreed to listen. While feminist response rhetorics sometimes fail in the short term, they also succeed; through repetition, amplification, and even anonymity, feminist rhetors have found rhetorical strategies that can make audiences receptive despite their every intention to remain hostile.

Notes

1. Qtd. in Theresa Enos, "Professing the New Rhetorics: Prologue," *Rhetoric Review* 9, no. 1 (1990): 28.

2. George Yoos, "Rhetoric of Appeal and Rhetoric of Response," *Philosophy & Rhetoric* 20, no. 2 (1987): 111.

3. Karlyn Kohrs Campbell, *Man Cannot Speak for Her: A Critical Study of Early Feminist Rhetoric*, vol. 1 (Westport, CT: Praeger, 1989), 2–3.

4. Krista Ratcliffe, *Rhetorical Listening: Identification, Gender, Whiteness* (Carbondale: Southern Illinois University Press, 2005).

5. Carol Mattingly, "Friendly Dress: A Disciplined Use," *Rhetoric Society Quarterly* 29, no. 2 (1999): 25; Roxanne Mountford, *The Gendered Pulpit: Preaching in American Protestant Spaces* (Carbondale: Southern Illinois University Press, 2005).

9

"Anonymous Was a Woman"

Anonymous Authorship as Rhetorical Strategy

SKYE ROBERSON

AUTHORSHIP AND INTELLECTUAL PROPERTY ARE rooted in systems of gendered oppression. The first copyright law, the 1710 Statute of Anne, represented Lockean values of individualism, asserting that texts, and therefore ideas, were forms of property.[1] The notion of text as property encouraged publishers to seek financial gain from reprinting popular texts, arguing classic works like John Milton, for example, could be continuously sold if the author agreed. This legal precedent sparked conversations about the definition of the term *author*. The author was not only the mind behind the text, but the individual who would financially benefit from selling their work. This copyright system was created by men to preserve the sanctity of their ideas, metaphorically mirroring their perceptions of women (and women's roles).[2] Like men did with the texts they created, so too did they control the women in their lives, and they excluded women from sharing (and therefore profiting from) their ideas. However, women found ways to subvert the system that oppressed them.

Writing under male pseudonyms gave some women the opportunity to publish without their identity being uncovered. During the Victorian era, women could achieve literary fame under their real names, but they were constrained by subject matter and exposed to public scrutiny. For this reason, many women authors chose to publish "first-person anonymous," an action that Alexis Easley describes as "both construct[ing] and subvert[ing] notions of individual authorial identity, manipulating the publishing conventions associated with various print media for personal and professional advantage."[3] By publishing anonymously, women could create an authorial identity constructed on a false persona. The Brontë sisters, notable examples from the Victorian era, each wrote under a male name for a time: Charlotte as Currer, Emily as Ellis, and Anne as Acton. Charlotte said of their writing, "we did not like to declare ourselves women, because—without at that time suspecting that our mode of writing and think-ing was not what is called 'feminine'—we had a vague impression that author-esses are liable to be looked on with prejudice."[4] To gain respect and avoid be-ing essentialized as a woman writer, limited by content choices or dismissed as not having literary merit, they chose to write under male names.

The Brontë sisters are just one example in a long history of women writers who chose to publish anonymously or under male pseudonyms, women who included Mary Ann Evans, Alice Bradley Sheldon, and Kristina Laferne Rob-erts.[5] Virginia Woolf speaks to this tradition in *A Room of One's Own*: "Anon, who wrote so many poems without signing them, was often a woman."[6] This line summarizes the ubiquity and secrecy of anonymous women writers, including those who have never had their real name credited to their work. Although the practice of women writing anonymously is most closely associated with the eigh-teenth and nineteenth centuries, it has repeated throughout the modern era in print and digital media.

Digital platforms with the infrastructure for anonymity lend themselves to women writers who want to maintain secrecy through pseudonyms. Websites like Reddit and Tumblr are outlets for women to publish their stories without disclosing their identity because they operate using usernames, whereas social media accounts are linked to real names.[7] Writing under a username potentially shields the author from attacks linked to their identity beyond the screen. While previous research has been done on Tumblr, using anonymously authored blogs as analytical texts,[8] little research has focused on Reddit, although it is similarly a hangout for anonymous women writers. Unlike Tumblr, which is arranged around a community of blogs, Reddit is organized by "subreddits," or themed forums. All content on the site, including the subreddits themselves, is user cre-ated or submitted. Thus, Reddit has become a massive hub worldwide for shar-ing news, stories, and content. The only requirement for making an account on Reddit is an email address. People unwilling to give Reddit their actual email address can use a temporary address fabricated through a fake email generator. The result is a community in which millions of users communicate under a veil of relative anonymity. For subreddits themed around women's issues, anonymity helps women feel comfortable enough to share information about their lived ex-periences. By writing stories under a username, women have a sense of freedom to discuss their opinions without direct backlash in their offscreen lives.

Thus, the practice of women writing anonymously continues because the op-pressive conditions in which women write persist. Using Rhetorical Transversal Methodology (RTM), we can explore the connections between these two mo-ments to reveal the strategies women use to share their stories within misogynis-tic publishing systems. Women writing in the nineteenth and twenty-first centu-ries face systemic oppression that works to silence their voices. In both instances, anonymous authorship is an intentional rhetorical strategy utilized to subvert systems of inequality. The act of using a pseudonym or username gives the author the power to craft an identity separate from the one tied to their real name (and the material conditions associated with it)—potentially giving them a greater sense of agency and liberation than they might have achieved otherwise. The similarity of these rhetorical acts demonstrates how the strategy of anonymous authorship has persisted over time because it is advantageous for women writers. Cases of women's anonymous authorship based on online platforms reveal the potential for silence to be an act of agency rather than subservience, as it is often theorized in feminist scholarship. Whereas silencing can be analyzed rightfully as a tactic of oppressors, examples like those from anonymous authors on Reddit demonstrate how the intentional use of silence can be a method of asserting agency. Although the execution of this strategy of remaining silent is not always effective, its usage demonstrates a divergence in the tradition of anonymous authorship and the way silence is theorized. In this way, RTM allows us as scholars to view the intersecting and diverging paths in women's rhetorical practices from the nineteenth century to today.

This chapter demonstrates how women resist the traditional boundaries of authorship by subverting our ideas about authorial identities, agency, and silence. To do this, I discuss the similarities and differences between anonymous women writers in Victorian-era periodicals and those on Reddit today. To show how authorship has changed, I consider an anonymous Reddit post from the subreddit r/TwoXChromosomes as a case study for women's anonymous authorship. I then read the differences between these two eras through the lenses of agency and silence. The divergence that marks the shift in this anonymous writing from the Victorian era to the present day represents an evolution in agency and voice that stems from the affordances of online forums. Thus, the shift in patterns of women's anonymous authorship is a response to the toxic culture fostered by online forums.

THE EVOLUTION OF ANONYMITY

There are notable similarities between the contexts of women's periodic journalism during the Victorian era and feminist groups on Reddit.[9] In both situations, women use pseudonyms to share their ideas with the public. During the Victorian era, women would leave their writing "unsigned," or without a real name.[10] For online communities, real names are replaced with usernames. Women will sometimes have two accounts, one associated with their identity as a woman and the other left gender neutral, to avoid its user being confronted as a woman. Hallie Workman and Catherine Coleman interviewed Reddit users on the r/TwoXChromosomes subreddit. One user told them, "I feel the need to obfuscate my gender on my primary account because (for example) if my comments on, say, r/gaming got a lot of attention from that community, and someone looked through my history and discovered I was subscribed to a lot of women's subreddits, I worry that I'd be 'outed' as a woman and people would think of my comments/opinion differently."[11] The fear of being "outed" mirrors concerns felt by Victorian women who wanted to keep their writing separate from their domestic lives. Leaving works unsigned or switching between Reddit accounts allows women to use anonymous identities in order to manipulate publishing systems. This anonymity provides a layer of protection that cannot be achieved otherwise.

Public forums are an important space for women's anonymous authorship. Reddit is a massive website with over one million subreddits, the majority of which are publicly viewable. The content of these forums varies—nearly every interest is represented by a community of readers. Public comment sections allow for conversations between users who can debate with each other in real time. This immediacy was not the case in the Victorian era, when conversations were limited by the speed of the publication process. Regardless of this issue of timeliness, journals became venues for anonymous women authors to debate current issues. When the public read these periodicals, they were unaware that the authors were women (unless an author signed her name). The back-and-forth conversations in journals represent a precursor to internet forums. Journals became spaces where discourse could be undertaken in the public eye.

Finally, writers in both situations use their anonymity to engage in feminist discourse. In Victorian-era periodicals, women debated over what Easley calls *proto-feminism*, also known as the Woman Question.[12] Conversations circulated about suffrage, abolition of slavery, and women's changing roles in society. Topics of similar theme appear on r/TwoXChromosomes, which defines itself as "a subreddit for both silly and serious content, and intended for women's perspectives."[13] With over eleven million subscribers as of October 2018, r/TwoXChromosomes is home to advice, personal narratives, and articles about women's rights. While not the only feminist subreddit, r/TwoXChromosomes is notable for being the largest and most active. In both public forums, women used the veil of anonymity to discuss social issues.

Although the two situations have many similarities, the oftentimes toxic culture of Reddit fosters rhetorical responses that diverge from those of the Victorian era. This is not to say that women authors in the Victorian publishing industry did not face misogyny or harassment. However, the fact that Reddit is free, easily accessible, and instantaneous empowers harassers and trolls. Furthermore, the site's liberal policy toward publishable content allows misogynistic rhetoric to flourish.[14] Reddit is a center of nerd culture due to the popularity of niche subreddits, where minute levels of knowledge can be exchanged. Although nerd culture was built around redefining traditional masculinity, it perpetuates and reifies masculine roles based on its treatment of intellectualism as a sport in which traditional yet niche knowledge is valued over emotional, social, or physical intelligence.[15] This description is consistent with Adrienne Massanari's characterization of toxic technocultures as stemming from nerd culture. According to Massanari, toxic technocultures demonstrate "retrograde ideas of gender, sexual identity, sexuality, and race, and push against issues of diversity, multiculturalism, and progressivism."[16] Nerd culture and toxic technocultures have overlapped in several Reddit scandals, including the 2014 Gamergate and the forced resignation of former Reddit CEO Ellen Pao in 2015. Even though Reddit is a large and diverse community of users, there is a vocal contingent that attacks those working toward social progressivism on the website.

Amid Reddit's toxic culture, feminist subreddits like r/TwoXChromosomes craft themselves as spaces for women. In Workman and Coleman's ethnography of r/TwoXChromosomes, they explored the intersection of language and meaning in cybercommunities.[17] When describing the tone of the subreddit, users tended to highlight its friendliness and openness in direct comparison to the rest of Reddit. Respondents described the misogynistic attitudes on other subreddits to explain why they favored r/TwoXChromosomes. The overlap between nerd culture and toxic technocultures creates an environment of fear around identifying as a woman and a feminist. Being "outed" does not just entail having one's ideas dismissed: it describes a process of branding, social isolation, and disgust for those who do not align with white masculinity. Therefore, the fact that r/TwoXChromosomes maintains a vibrant community built on a feminist agenda is an achievement. In a digital space where women and feminists are ostracized, r/TwoXChromosomes provides a space for voices who might otherwise be silenced on Reddit.

Although there are startling similarities between Victorian periodicals and r/TwoXChromosomes, the affordances of online discourse results in differences between the two that show how the anonymous tradition has evolved. The combination of toxic technocultures, feminist communities, and anonymous users provides unique opportunities for understanding one version of modern feminist discourse. Within this context, writers push the boundaries of agency. While silence was once considered an act of subservience, it can also be a liberating choice.

AGENCY AND SILENCE

Voice and silence are often conceptualized as necessarily opposed. Throughout history, women were excluded from participating in public discourse. Silence was forced, not chosen, creating a dichotomy to voice that seems intuitive. Scholars have affirmed this polarizing relationship, discussing the act of "coming to voice" as a critical step toward liberation from oppression. As the association of voice and liberation grew, voice become synonymous with power and agency. Silence was an act of submission or continued subjugation, whereas voice was considered an act of defiance and self-recognition.

However, this understanding of the relationship between voice, silence, and agency has been criticized for its underlying assumptions about women's power and its dismissal of the rhetorical aspects of silence. In *Unspoken*, Cheryl Glenn argues silence, like speech, is a rhetorical act that exists on a spectrum of power and subordination. Silence has often been associated with femininity, "a trope for oppression, passivity, emptiness, stupidity, or obedience."[18] Traditionally disenfranchised groups in a social hierarchy are "muted" by a dominant group, prevented from participating in discourse. Thus, an inability to speak fluently in some social interactions indicates that "silence itself becomes the language of the powerless."[19] However, Glenn argues that silence is more complex than an action of oppressor on oppressed, saying "people use silence and silencing every day to fulfill their rhetorical purpose, whether it is to maintain their position of power, resist the domination of others, or submit to subordination—regardless of their gendered positions."[20] Silence allows rhetorical actors to readjust relations of power. Such silent power plays are sometimes difficult to detect because rhetoric is often associated with verbal communication. Women's uses of silence are not bound to binaries of oppression or easily definable, but they represent the complexity inherent in any rhetorical act.

Compounding these debates further is agency, traditionally defined as an author's ability to claim authority over their choices. Coming to voice is associated with claiming agency, whereas silence or nondirect forms of communication are associated with victimhood or powerlessness. Anonymous writers are often lumped with the latter group—seen as powerless victims—because of an assumption that women are not choosing to be unidentified. This belief is a result of traditional conceptions of women's rhetorical agency at times when many women had no choice but to go unacknowledged. However, equating agency with a sense of visibility dismisses the importance of silence or anonymity as a deliberate rhetorical choice. If agency is an ability to claim authority, then purposefully remaining silent or hidden—exercising one's agency or authority to do so—is an act of power worth equal consideration to that of being outspoken. As bell hooks argues, the notion of silence as a form of submission was created by white feminists to describe their backgrounds in largely WASP households. In black communities (or other ethnic groups), women's voices can be heard. For black women, the struggle was not finding a voice, but rather changing the nature and direction of their voices to speak to outsiders. Describing the oral tradition of black women, hooks writes, "It was in this world of woman speech, loud talk, angry words, women with tongues sharp, tender sweet tongues . . . that I made speech my birthright—and the right to voice, to authorship, a privilege I would not be denied."[21] Not all silent voices are oppressed. Some voices only come alive in the presence of peers and allies, reflecting a decision by the speaker to privilege certain audiences out of necessity or respect.

One goal of feminist narrative research is to challenge these assumptions about voice and agency, which, as Jo Woodiwiss argues, can be done by engaging with storytellers who embody nontraditional experiences and use divergent modes of storytelling.[22] In listening to these stories, the audience does not need to evaluate their factualism but rather examine the rhetorical situation of the storyteller and their motivation for sharing information. By listening without judgment, the audience acknowledges the speaker's value by virtue of them just sharing their experiences. According to Woodiwiss, then, an analysis of narrative should focus less on an evaluation of a story's truth. Rather, an analysis should attend to the speaker's choice of medium for communication and the way their voice and identity are represented through that medium.

Traditional narrative research often involves some line of communication between the researcher and the speaker. Through this contact, the researcher can corroborate elements of the speaker's identity to ensure the validity of the research. Online discourses constructed by anonymous individuals do not have these avenues for verification. A user's history can be tracked by their name, but that information is only valuable if they have revealed information about their real selves elsewhere.

Once doubt is cast on the author's identity, it can be tempting to dismiss their entire narrative as potentially fake because it cannot be corroborated. But to assume the story is fake just because it does not follow conceptions of authorship that privilege ownership and naming is to trivialize the author's experience. Karen A. Foss and Sonja K. Foss articulate the importance of listening in feminist research: "feminist scholars view personal experience as always admissible because they are unwilling to declare some experience to be better than others—to make qualitative judgments about the nature of those experiences."[23] Whether the author is writing about their experience or not, emotional posts speak to a truth beyond the scope of a single narrative. Regardless of the author's real-world identity, their creation has transcended their sphere of influence, and the story is now part of public discourse. Bethany Mannon's chapter in this collection discusses *My Duty to Speak* (an archive creating a shared discourse on assault) as an example of how anonymous narratives contribute to public discourse. As feminist researchers, we should consider the ways anonymity impacts rhetorical choices and audiences, sometimes even allowing for rhetoric to be more powerful than it might be if delivered with a name. Anonymity does not immediately render rhetoric any less powerful.

"PLEASE PLEASE PLEASE GOD VACCINATE YOUR KIDS"

"Please please please god vaccinate your kids" by user u/throwaway44321424 was published on the r/TwoXChromosomes subreddit in January 2017.[24] The text of the post reads as follows (spelling, punctuation, and other errors have not been corrected):

> I'm sitting alone drinking to much again and just need to get this off my chest. Three years ago I had a baby girl, her name was Emily and I loved her more than anything in this entire fucked up world. She was a mistake and I'd only been getting my shit together when I found out I was going to have her. I spent a long time thinking over whether or not I should have her or just abort her because I wasn't bringing her into a good place, but in the end I planned things out and did everything to make sure I could afford her and we wouldn't be living in poverty. I did everything I could for my baby with doctors visits and medicine and working a shit retail job at 8 months pregnant all by myself just so I could bring some happiness into my life. she was born in October and was so so beautiful. I'd messed up a few things in my life but I wasn't going to mess up with her if I could help it.
>
> Then when she was 8 months old, too young yet for an mmr shot? she got sick. She was sick for a while and I'd never seen anything like it. I took her to the doctor. She was in the hospital and she looked so bad, she was crying and coughing and there was nothing I could do. I felt like the worst mother in the world. After I got her to the hospital she got worse, got something called measles encephalitis, where her brain was inflamed. I hadn't believed in god in years but you better believe I was praying for her every day. She died in the hospital a week or so later. I held her little tiny body and wanted to jump off a bridge and broke down in the hospital. The nurses were sympathetic and I was, well I made a scene I'm pretty sure.
>
> I found out later via facebook of fucking course that the neighbor I'd had watch my baby was an anti-vaxxer and had posted photos of her kid sick and other bullshit about how he was fine.
>
> He was fine? He was FINE? My kid was DEAD because she made that choice. I went over and talked to her and she admitted he'd been sick when she'd had my kid last but didn't think much of it. I screamed at her. I screamed and yelled and told her the devil was going to torture her soul for eternity you god loving cunt because she took my baby from me. I'm sure I looked crazy, at the time maybe I was. I'm crying writing this now, and in my darkest moments I'd wished her kid was dead and it makes me feel worse.
>
> I'd like to say I'm doing better but I'm really not. I'm alive, going day to day, trying to be the person I wanted to be for my kid even if my little Emily isn't

here anymore. That's the only thing keeping me going anymore. I don't have anything else left.

Please vaccinate your kids, so other moms like me don't have to watch their baby die. It's not just your choice only affecting your kid, you are putting every child who for some reason hasn't gotten vaccinated in SO much danger. Please please please for the love of god please vaccinate.

EDIT: I spent a long time thinking about if I should edit this, after being horrified that I posted this in the first place and puking and crying. I still can't deal with any of this when not drunk. Thank you to everyone for the support, saying that doesn't really cover how I feel, I'm just glad there are good people out there, and I'm sorry to all of you who have suffered a loss. To everyone who told me I was a murderer, that it was my fault, that I was an awful mother, that my child spending time with a boy who had measles was NOT the reason my baby got measles, that I never should have had a kid because I was poor, and that I should kill myself, I have only one thing to say to you, because anything else isn't worth it: I hope you are happy. I hope you live a long and happy life with people in it who love you and care for you and that you do not suffer like I did. I hope you are loved.[25]

As of October 2017, this post was the eighth most popular post of all time on r/TwoXChromosomes, with over 45,000 upvotes and 3,340 comments. The post is a narrative written from the perspective of a mother mourning her recently deceased daughter, who died from exposure to measles. After her child died, the narrator discovered via Facebook that her neighbor's son had also contracted measles because he had not been vaccinated. The neighbor babysat for the narrator in the past, thus exposing her infant to the measles that would take her life. In the post, the narrator rants about the danger of choosing not to vaccinate, demonstrating how vaccinations are a public safety issue and not a matter of preference. The narrator's style is raw, full of expletives, unflinching in the way it discusses trauma (for example, the author explains she is unable to bring up the subject of her child while sober). Overall, throwaway's story is compelling in its unabashed fury and sadness.

Unlike many Reddit posts, the author leaves the narrative as the last word from her hand. "Please please" is the only post or comment written by this user, including all comments and posts sitewide. Within the user's post, she chooses not to engage with the comment section although her narrative draws a large response from the community. She does add an edited response to the overall community, thanking those who offered their support and shaming users who posted insults or doubted her story. By responding to the post in an overall statement, throwaway carefully controls her identity as an author. She never engages the audience directly in the comments section. If she had made additional comments, she would risk providing hints about her identity, which could risk her anonymity and could make her authorial identity the subject of speculation in the community (more than what already occurs in confession threads). Rather than willingly bringing herself into that conversation the way most traditional authors do (by participating in meta discussions), she responds to the entire community once. Moreover, the lack of account activity means she has the final word on her story; no user can comb through her history and use it to invalidate her experience. Throughout throwaway's rise to popularity on r/TwoXChromosomes, she controls her authorial identity by choosing to distance herself from the community's collaborative engagement and, thus, refusing to succumb to identification.

Across Reddit, "throwaway" accounts are common. Although regular Reddit accounts give the user an ample amount of anonymity, previous posts and comments can give curious people tools to find the poster's identity. When throwaway's story went viral, the Reddit community was quick to search out ways to dismiss it as false, some saying it was impossible for her child to die of measles without media attention.[26] The speed and ferocity of people to criticize her post demonstrates the culture of Reddit. Had she divulged more information by posting on her main account, she likely would have been attacked. Assuming an anonymous identity allowed her to enter and leave the conversation on her own terms.

The name itself, throwaway, is a nod to women writers of the past. The male pseudonyms historical women took are throwaways, meaningless names created to obfuscate their identity. Although some women would choose a pseudonym based on the names of lovers or friends, the name itself has little meaning. It does not represent the woman or her writing, except to a public she cannot directly face. Throughout Reddit, throwaway accounts are used by men and women. People create them to preserve the posting history on their main account. As the name itself suggests, this author's chosen name is a mask within a mask, hiding the user from the Reddit community and any real-life identifiers. A string of numbers are attached to the name throwaway because so many throwaway accounts have been created, and each name must be unique. The name, throwaway, is more than something random the user typed in. It is a gesture toward anonymity, toward an identity existing to do one thing and then be thrown away.

The anonymity Reddit affords, coupled with the life experiences of the user, positions her in a liminal state between her material conditions and virtual freedom. In *Life on the Screen*, Sherry Turkle argues, "when we step through the screen into virtual communities, we reconstruct our identities on the other side of the looking glass. This reconstruction is a cultural work in progress."[27] When a user arrives at the border of a digital space, they bring with them their physical identities and lived experiences. In this way, the user throwaway could not move past her grief without acknowledging it in the digital realm. If her physical identity and experience did not matter, she could slip into her Reddit identity without acknowledging her pain, leaving the "real world" behind. Likewise, the user's digital life is another border where she has the freedom to assume multiple identities. This freedom allows the user to craft their own narrative, real or fictional, about their identity. The borders between physical and digital are fluid, and they position the user as both her physical and nonhuman self. While she cannot escape her material conditions, she can have enough freedom to tell her story without suffering backlash in her material life.

The need for anonymity is a response to both Reddit's culture and the omnipresence of social media. Had the grieving mother written the narrative on a main account, she would risk being harassed by other users. Social media would be an inappropriate place for the narrative. The user would risk being called out, insulted, and shamed for sharing their trauma. Thus, using an anonymous platform like Reddit provided the user with options for controlling her story. If toxic cultures exist online and in the physical world, women will look for spaces to express themselves. Reddit's culture, void of traditional authorship, is also a reaction to the abundance of technology and the freedom alternative identities afford. When all these factors come together, they create new and exciting ways to understand rhetoric.

RETHINKING AGENCY

Throwaway, and other anonymous authors writing in digital spaces, forces a reexamination of agency in the twenty-first century. In an era of social media, when identities are on display for anyone to access, the act of hiding is subversive. Traditionally, feminist rhetorical studies has focused on ways agency is denied to women through forms of social oppression. However, anonymous digital authors exercise their agency by hiding themselves from being discovered, challenging the metaphor of finding voice and the assumptions it entails. The act of hiding is not an action based on submission. Instead, it is a way of controlling identity in a space where identifying as a woman can be weaponized against the user.

The author's ability to separate themselves from their physical being, to assume a temporary identity, gives the author freedom to share stories that might receive negative attention on social media platforms. Anonymous authors do not give their audience an opportunity to exploit their story or their identity. Authors can comment on their story at will or disengage from their temporary Reddit accounts entirely without facing backlash in their real lives. Choosing a throwaway username nods to this freedom by using a word associated with something temporary. It claims power by refusing definition and naming (and thus the possibility of being written off or harassed). This act of identity negotiation and power dynamics indicates a change in the relationship between authorship and agency in the twenty-first century.

This example suggests that agency should be understood as the ability to exert authority, even when invisible, over the narrative. In this way, agency is less about coming into a state of being and more about utilizing available resources to control a story. These resources are akin to Joy Ritchie and Kate Ronald's reclamation of Aristotle's available means, "to mark the ways in which women have discovered various means by which to make their voices heard."[28] Women have learned to persuade with the means available to them, and this flexibility allows women to redefine and subvert traditional argumentation. Similarly, exercising agency over a narrative becomes an act of using available means when the anonymous online author utilizes the affordances of technology. Although this exercise is wrapped in silence and secrecy, making it difficult to analyze, it is no less an act of asserting agency.

This conceptualization of agency encapsulates the anonymity of women writers who used male pseudonyms to advance their careers. Instead of waiting for a time when they could publish under their female names, they used male pseudonyms to subvert a system that would deny them the opportunity to otherwise publish. The ease of manipulating Reddit identities and the "throwaway" pseudonym are all resources u/throwaway44321424 appropriated to retain the privacy of her real-life identity. Anonymous online posters use the tools available to them to control their identities as writers, a power that might have been denied to them had they tried to publish as women. Thus, a pattern of women using pseudonyms to publish is consistent from print to digital media, but women's agency increases as more women have access to power.

As women have attained more social and cultural power, they have more agency in identifying themselves in public spaces. Throughout history, women were not allowed to participate in civic life. During the nineteenth century, the popular press and changing gender dynamics made women's authorship more accessible. The popular press gave women the opportunity to speak in public spaces where they were previously excluded. Despite these advancements, it was better for the well-being of many women to remain anonymous. Gendered divisions in sociopolitical power were still too entrenched for some women to speak freely in public or have a career as a writer under their own name. In these instances, anonymity was a choice made under duress. In the twenty-first century, advancements in technology and women's power further illustrate how silence functions rhetorically. The affordances of online anonymity allow women to use silence strategically. The ability to speak freely or disengage from a conversation illustrates that silence can be a *choice*. While it is certainly true that silence is a spectrum and that some women are still forced into silence, more women have the means to choose silence than ever before. The internet provides the freedom of choice between publishing under a name and doing so under a pseudonym. This freedom provides women with more opportunities to share their stories and decide how they want to represent themselves. For women writers, identification (naming themselves or not) is a rhetorical strategy, one that gives a writer the power to choose how they will interact with their audience after their story becomes public. In an age where digital engagement between authors and audiences happens as soon as the story is published, the choice to disengage and remain silent is an exercise in women's authorial agency.

Notes

1. Mark Rose, *Authors and Owners: The Invention of Copyright* (Cambridge, MA: Harvard University Press, 1994), 4–5.

2. Debora Halbert, "Poaching and Plagiarizing: Property, Plagiarism, and Feminist Futures," in *Perspectives on Plagiarism and Intellectual Property in the Postmodern World*, ed. Lise Buranen and Alice Myers Roy (New York: State University of New York Press, 1999), 113.

3. Alexis Easley, *First-Person Anonymous: Women Writers and Victorian Print Media* (New York: Routledge, 2004), 2.

4. Charlotte Brontë, *Charlotte Brontë's Notes of Pseudonyms Used by Herself and Her Sisters, Emily and Anne Brontë* (Champaign, IL: Project Gutenberg, 1990), 1.

5. These women's chosen pseudonyms were George Eliot, James Tiptree Jr., and Zane, respectively.

6. Virginia Woolf, *A Room of One's Own* (New York: Penguin, 2013), 51.

7. Facebook is a troublesome medium because of its influence and popularity, and the repercussions of membership include invasions of privacy, potential harassment, and negative feelings of self-worth. These problems are compounded by their direct association to the user's physical identity. Users are prompted to fill their profile with facts about their life and even to link their account to their phone number. Facebook also has an "authentic-name policy" that results in banning accounts that are suspected as fake.

8. Akane Kanai. "The Best Friend, The Boyfriend, Other Girls, Hot Guys, and Creeps: The Relational Production of Self on Tumblr," *Feminist Media Studies* 17, no. 6 (2017): 912.

9. For more information about the various periodicals written by anonymous women during the Victorian era, see Alison Adburgham, *Women in Print: Writing Women and Women's Magazines from the Restoration to the Accession of Victoria* (London: Allen and Unwin, 1972); and Hilary Fraser, Stephanie Green, and Judith Johnston, *Gender and the Victorian Periodical* (Cambridge: Cambridge University Press, 2003).

10. Easley, *First-Person Anonymous*, 2.

11. Hallie Workman and Catherine Coleman, "The Front Page of the Internet: Safe Spaces and Hyperpersonal Communication among Females in an Online Community," *Southwestern Mass Communication* 27, no. 3 (2012): 14.

12. Easley, *First-Person Anonymous*, 35.

13. "Community Details," r/TwoXChromosomes (forum), *Reddit*, created July 16, 2009, https://www.reddit.com/r/TwoXChromosomes.

14. Andrew Marantz, "Reddit and the Struggle to Detoxify the Internet," *New Yorker*, March 19, 2018, https://www.newyorker.com.

15. Lori Kendall, "'White and Nerdy': Computers, Race, and the Nerd Stereotype," *Journal of Popular Culture* 44, no. 3 (2011): 507.

16. Adrienne Massanari, "#Gamergate and the Fappening: How Reddit's Algorithm,

Governance, and Culture Support Toxic Technocultures." *New Media and Society* 16, no. 8 (2015): 335.

17. Workman and Coleman, "The Front Page of the Internet," 14.

18. Cheryl Glenn, *Unspoken: A Rhetoric of Silence* (Carbondale: Southern Illinois University Press, 2004), 2.

19. Glenn, 25.

20. Glenn, 153.

21. bell hooks, *Talking Back: Thinking Feminist, Thinking Black* (Boston: South End Press, 1989), 124.

22. Jo Woodiwiss, "Challenges for Feminist Research: Contested Stories, Dominant Narratives, and Narrative Frameworks," in *Feminist Narrative Research*, ed. Jo Woodiwiss, Kate Smith, and Kelly Lockwood (New York: Palgrave, 2017), 15–16.

23. Karen A. Foss and Sonja K. Foss, "Personal Experience as Evidence in Feminist Scholarship," *Western Journal of Communication* 58, no. 1 (1994): 39.

24. Throughout the rest of this chapter, u/throwaway44321424 will be shortened to throwaway.

25. u/throwaway44321424, "Please please please god vaccinate your kids," posted January 2017, r/TwoXChromosomes (forum), *Reddit*, https://www.reddit.com/r/TwoXChromosomes.

26. u/NeverWasNorWillBe, "Woman fabricates story of 8 month old daughter dying of measles-related brain encephalitis. The story made the front page," posted January 2017, r/quityourbullshit (forum), *Reddit*, https://www.reddit.com/r/quityourbullshit.

27. Sherry Turkle, *Life on the Screen: Identity in the Age of the Internet* (London: Phoenix, 1995), 177.

28. Joy Ritchie and Kate Ronald, introduction to *Available Means: An Anthology of Women's Rhetoric(s)*, ed. Joy Ritchie and Kate Ronald (Pittsburgh, PA: University of Pittsburgh Press, 2001), xvii.

10

Tracing the Conversation

Legitimizing Mormon Feminism

Tiffany Kinney

> Women begin to speak and write from a different starting point than
> most men and because they confront fundamental obstacles to being
> accepted as rhetors, women's rhetoric often entails the development of
> alternative communication strategies. This is especially true of ethos
> [gaining authority and developing legitimacy], since it is precisely the
> characteristics of a good speaker that have historically been denied to
> women.
>
> —Carolyn Skinner, *Women Physicians and Professional Ethos in*
>   *Nineteenth-Century America*

Before her excommunication, Sonia Johnson was a fifth-generation
Mormon, who held all the indications of someone living a righteous life—a
mother of four, a faithful wife, and a Sunday school teacher. Johnson was also
a graduate student at Rutgers University, where she became fluent in the language of activism and feminism, knowledge she later used to found an organization named Mormons for ERA (Equal Rights Amendment). After the Mormon Church reacted negatively to her activism, Johnson criticized her church
on gender issues. Subsequently, church leadership started disciplinary proceedings against Johnson for her outcries and for organizing Mormons for ERA.
While she fought for her membership, this fight was short lived, and Johnson
was excommunicated in December 1979. Upon her excommunication, she re-
named her organization Non-Mormons for ERA and continued to advocate
for the ERA and other causes as part of the National Organization for Women
(NOW). Eventually, Johnson became frustrated with the hierarchal nature of
NOW, and she chose to leave the feminist movement altogether.

A year after Johnson's excommunication, Kathleen Marie (Kate) Kelly was born into a Mormon household in Hood River, Oregon. Like Johnson's, Kelly's early life was interspersed with accomplishments inside her faith such as serving a Mormon mission, graduating from Brigham Young University, and marrying her husband in the Salt Lake Temple. While Kelly displayed hints of her commitment to feminism during her undergraduate education, she became more radical and invested in social change when she enrolled in law school at American University. In 2013, Kelly founded Ordain Women (OW), a group that advocates for gender equality in the Mormon Church. With parallels to Johnson's experience, Kelly endured an excommunication trial after founding OW as she was charged with "apostasy," which is "defined [by the Mormon Church] as public advocacy of positions that oppose church teachings."[1] Similar to Johnson, Kelly continued her commitment to feminism upon her excommunication, as a lawyer for Planned Parenthood of Utah.[2] While their paths diverge, as Johnson moves from political activism to separatism and Kelly from religious to political activism, they echo each other in their response to patriarchy and their work for women's legitimacy.

While the time periods are different and the causes have changed, the underlying purpose of Mormon feminism remains the same: its supporters seek legitimacy inside their faith. Yet, the decades separating Johnson and Kelly allowed technological advancements to influence the conversation, causing it to evolve so these women construct arguments about legitimacy using "alternative communication strategies" in differing genres.[3] These arguments take on contrasting shapes depending on the time period in which they are written—as Johnson pens a book in the 1970s and Kelly posts blogs in the 2010s. Despite this generic evolution, Kelly and Johnson use similar devices to forge connections among women and establish Mormon women's legitimacy. In line with pan-historical work by Debra Hawhee, Christa J. Olson, and Alison Piepmeier, this chapter examines how the feminist conversations initiated by Johnson and Kelly respond to women's lack of legitimacy in the Mormon Church.[4] Throughout this chapter, I employ Rhetorical Transversal Methodology (RTM) in order to highlight the similarities—despite time, space, and technological differences—between these religious feminists' efforts to forge a coalition in support of Mormon women's authority.

STRUCTURE OF THE MORMON CHURCH

Founded in 1830 in Fayette, New York, the Church of Jesus Christ of Latter-day Saints (LDS or Mormon Church) has a membership that is today majority female. In fact, Mormon women in Utah make up 60 percent of the local wards, while outside of Utah, Mormon women make up 52 percent of the local wards.[5] Yet despite representing the majority of the membership, women are not welcomed into the church governing councils, such as the General Presidency, Twelve Apostles, or Quorum of the Seventy.[6] Women also cannot participate in the higher authoritative branches of the religion as they are only granted influence over other female church members and children.

The positions Mormon women hold are a type of "second-class" authority, exemplified by the divergent titles given to male and female leaders. In *From Housewife to Heretic*, Johnson describes the hierarchical relationship between male and female leadership roles when she observes that male leaders are given specific titles to exert their authority (e.g., prophet, apostle, elder), while all women use the title of sister.[7] The divergent naming practices for positions of authority break along gender lines and circumscribe the authority of female Mormons. In effect, the naming practices strip women of their authority as all women are addressed by the same title, thereby suggesting they are viewed as equals regardless of their position. The sameness of their titles also renders them interchangeable even though they may hold differing positions with diverse skill sets. The unfairness of these naming practices is further highlighted as these women are embedded inside a hierarchical atmosphere in which men do have titles designating their authority.

In addition, the church leadership is powerful enough to silence any questioning or dissenting responses through excommunication. Johnson depicts the power of the church leadership as such: "when the prophet speaks, the debate has ended."[8] Johnson and Kelly are among many who have been excommunicated because of their public responses to church leadership. Other silenced voices include the September Six, six women and men who spoke out in 1993 about gender inequality in the church. Fawn Brodie, who wrote *No Man Knows My History*, a 1945 biography of LDS founder Joseph Smith, was excommunicated in 1946 for her unflattering depictions of the religious leader.

In a rhetorical situation where one is responding to an institution powerful enough to excommunicate, the necessary response is to establish one's legitimacy, so as to influence the institution from the inside. Other potential responses, like demanding change, lead to excommunication or to the member's leaving the church and do not create change unless a noticeable number defect. As such, legitimation is a necessary response in this context because it is best positioned to ignite some change in an institution led by unquestionable patriarchs—an audience that does not listen rhetorically. And while Kelly's and Johnson's excommunication does represent failure, it is an individual act of failure and does not render the failure of legitimacy as a response to patriarchal institutions. Instead, their excommunication represents the limits of their rhetorical strategies during their respective time periods and in the face of unreceptive audiences. While these strategies failed, Mormon women have started to gain legitimacy through incremental successes since 2015, successes that are part of a larger conversation concerning women's legitimacy arguably that was initiated by Kelly's faith-based actions and Johnson's invention processes.

DEFINING AND EXPANDING LEGITIMACY

From the Latin word *legitimus*, legitimacy is related to *lex* (make legal), but studies on legitimacy often take an extended view and not only examine whether a behavior is codified into secular law but also whether it has garnered societal consensus. Peter Berger and Thomas Luckmann take this extended view to its logical conclusion when they state that "all language is legitimation."[9] This chapter builds on this notion of legitimacy by exploring language that is not found inside a legal tradition but is instead used to gain a form of consensus from a religious audience.

Rhetors from powerful social locations employ various devices to maintain and replicate their legitimacy, while rhetors from social locations without power employ similar devices in an attempt to initially establish their legitimacy. I depart from most of the literature on legitimation in that I do not examine how legitimacy is maintained by those who already have power. Instead I consider how religious women, often part of a marginalized group, respond to an unrhetorical audience, develop their legitimacy, and project their ethos when they are prevented from cultivating it.[10]

The above understanding of legitimacy, as a form of social consensus, is intimately tied to rhetorical notions of authority and ethos. Authority is understood as the embodiment of legitimate power, while ethos hinges on one's character and determines one's authority in a rhetorical setting. If the legitimizing process is successful, then a person or group will encapsulate legitimacy as the authority in that community. And when speaking or writing, they will portray a convincing and believable character or ethos to their audience. Legitimacy, authority, and ethos are used in conjunction with one another, and although these concepts diverge they continue to gain traction among scholars that research how a rhetor engenders legitimacy.

Legitimacy as Rhetorical Response

Legitimacy is used by Mormon women as a response to a patriarchal structure that is powerful enough to excommunicate them for their dissent and silence them because of their social location as women.[11] As such, legitimacy in this context is what James Berlin notes as "the new rhetorics," which "must be grounded in conflict, in dissension, in disorder."[12] By its very nature, legitimacy involves tracing conflict as most groups in power do not grant legitimacy willingly to groups from disempowered social locations.

To understand legitimacy as a form of response, one has to understand the power dynamics between an audience and a rhetor. According to George Yoos, those listening to a response need to be "open to altering their beliefs and/or commitments, and ... should have some need to know what someone else has to say."[13] In the case of Mormon feminism, this audience is other Mormon women, who are "open to altering their beliefs" as they participate in conversations with Johnson and Kelly. This openness is in contrast to the hostility shown by the church leadership toward women's bids for legitimacy. Yet, even the church leadership had "some need to know," because these feminist women were read as publicly challenging their abilities to govern.

Furthermore, Yoos claims "responses . . . furnish audiences with the speaker's beliefs and perspectives on questions . . . thus a rhetoric of response facilitates an audience's *access to a speaker's thoughts and beliefs*" (emphasis added).[14] Yoos's depiction of response as an act of explaining one's position is similar to Antonio Reyes's articulation of legitimacy as an act of justifying one's behaviors, ideas, or thoughts. Yoos also posits that rhetorics of response function by demonstrating "displays of logical *connections between explanations and facts*," displays that require "a speaker respected for expertise and experience" (emphasis added).[15] Both Johnson and Kelly are arguably speakers with some ethos, as both are well-educated women (holding an EdD and a JD, respectively) who serve their faith (as a Sunday school teacher and a missionary, respectively).

The writings of both women function according to Yoos's model of a rhetorics of response, although in different ways. Johnson uses invention processes to allow for "direct access to [her] thoughts and beliefs," while Kelly employs strategic delivery to demonstrate "logical connections between explanations and facts."[16] On the one hand, Johnson reveals her thoughts through her description of her invention process, "hearing into being." According to Johnson, this invention process involves "relearning abilities that the patriarchy says are irrelevant and that it scorns."[17] Johnson's focus on encouraging women to relearn abilities that are not taught to be relevant gives access to her thoughts—specifically, that feminists must challenge the patriarchy by relearning abilities such as listening to their own intuition and valuing other women's experiences. On the other hand, Kelly forges connections between facts and explanations when she is engaging in her strategic delivery. While shaping OW's delivery of its message, she emphasizes that "No. We [OW supporters] will not protest," which she further supports by claiming that OW only applied for a "'free speech' permit because the city of Salt Lake requires it of any large group gatherings in a public space."[18] Kelly draws a distinction between her "faith-based action" and a "protest" because she does not want to risk getting charged by the church with apostasy—defined as public criticism of church policy—public criticism that is typically implied with protesting. Here, Kelly connects her *explanation* that OW is not "protesting" (but is instead participating in a "faith-based action") to the *fact* that Salt Lake requires permits for all large groups, and not only those protesting. Kelly relies on connections between facts and explanations as a response, and she draws these connections when legitimizing women's authority through strategic delivery.

In addition to these responses, Johnson and Kelly chose media that was well positioned to further women's legitimacy in Mormonism—monograph-length books and blogs, respectively. Legitimacy is forged through social consensus, and the public exposure of these documents allowed Johnson and Kelly to build said consensus. Also important was that these texts be able to be easily reproduced, circulated, and distributed through material or digital means soon after their publication because they were responding to an exigency.

Moreover, the media Kelly and Johnson employ are specifically chosen and designed for their receptive audience (albeit an audience that evolved in the decades between them): Mormon women. The medium that each woman chooses is a form of public writing, which allows for mixed settings of consumption (public/private) and circulation between "sisters." Blogs and books are frequently characterized as media exposed to the public through commercial bookstores, online marketplaces, and the internet; this media can be experienced asynchronously in private or public spaces. In particular, Mormon women can experience this media in public spaces by reading it at a bookstore, coffeehouse, and other places outside of their homes, and they can access it on their phones or even through an (ostensibly public) internet forum, where it might be posted by other users. The asynchrony of this media, however, shelters Mormon women even when they access it in public because they can do so individually, not as part of a group, listening to the rhetors in an open, public space, and without the pressure to respond immediately to the rhetors' arguments. Instead, they can read Johnson's books and Kelly's blogs in private—whether inside or outside their homes—and they can secret their consumption, if needed. Furthermore, this option for private consumption gives these women space to parse each argument within the texts in order to rectify it with their personal belief systems. Once consumed, these texts are easily reproduced and circulated among other Mormon women, by mimeographing, xeroxing, and lending books—or by digitally "sharing" a post with a click of a button. Through these acts of circulation, Mormon women have started to amass numbers and build a coalition in support of women's legitimacy. Johnson and Kelly strategically selected their media to address Mormon women through mixed consumption and easy circulation, which in turn strengthened their response by allowing it to reach more women.

Ultimately, Johnson's and Kelly's bids for legitimacy function as a response by addressing an audience (either the open audience Mormon women or an audience that "needs to know," the church leadership), explaining their position (through invention and delivery strategies), establishing their ethos (as educated women serving their faith), and using well-positioned media to speak to Mormon women (to amass support and establish legitimacy).

ANALYSIS: LEGITIMACY IN MORMON FEMINISM

Sonia Johnson: Invention Processes

While she first attempted to legitimate Mormon women inside their faith, after her excommunication Johnson decided to eschew legitimacy in Mormonism and dedicate herself to advancing in the ranks of NOW. Successful in this context, she eventually forewent legitimacy here, as well, because she decided that both structures enforce domination. These dual experiences inspired her to turn to the process of consciousness-raising as invention, so she could work outside of existing structures.[19] Johnson's feminist consciousness-raising is in line with the strategies observed by Karlyn Kohrs Campbell as it fosters "intense moral conflict . . . so that moderate and reformist options are closed to feminist advocates" as they work outside of existing structures.[20] In Johnson's books, especially *From Housewife to Heretic* (1981), *Going Out of Our Minds* (1987), and *Wildfire* (1990), she first attempts to gain legitimacy and later eschews it for less moderate and reformist options.[21]

Using RTM, I first consider Johnson's use of media and its impact on her response before analyzing the rhetorical strategies used within her response. Johnson secured access to commercial presses that would copy typed pages and bundle them into monograph-length books. Most of her early monographs were published through Random House, while her later ones were self-published through her publishing company, Wildfire. These two methods give different forms of legitimacy, with the monographs published by a large imprint suggesting that her words have been vetted by a respected editor in order to be published, while those that she self-published suggested a writer entirely dedicated to her message. This professional attention and the writer's dedication, accompanied by the price a reader pays to access the text, imbue Johnson's words with additional weight.

Furthermore, Johnson's chosen form of media, monograph-length books, influences her response, which hinges on consciousness-raising as rhetorical invention. In her books, Johnson presents complex arguments that articulate her invention processes in ways not easily summarized. This medium allows Johnson the space to provide access to her thoughts, to describe the invention processes, and to inspire the change inherent in these processes. She uses this space to invent consciousness-raising practices that can inspire Mormon women to challenge patriarchal norms. Later, Johnson's monographs become progressively more radical, as illustrated by her move to self-publishing, and by the transition of her ideas from encouraging consciousness-raising to promoting instantaneous change.

As a genre, monographs assume a reader with time to dedicate to personal stories and in-depth processes. Unlike other feminist monographs of the 1970s, Johnson's do not provide worksheets, prompts, or even many examples. She does not want to "stifle women's invention"; instead she welcomes readers to participate by offering descriptions of consciousness-raising practices and instantaneous change. As Katherine Fredlund argues, invention is not only a practice that creates a text but is also a practice that a text can inspire.[22] Because of their length, monographs are the ideal genre for provoking a specific form of invention in their readers: feminist consciousness-raising.

Invention, as consciousness-raising, specifically functions as a response to the patriarchal norms of Mormonism because it provides access to the speaker's thoughts, provokes readers to interrogate their position of inequality, and forges a connection between readers when they recognize their similarities. By themselves, invention processes not directed to raise consciousness do not constitute a response to patriarchy, as Mormon women are frequently encouraged to participate in invention processes through deep contemplation (they keep historical records and write in daily journals). But Johnson transforms these invention processes into a response. She uses *Going Out of Our Minds* and *Wildfire* to inspire and explore consciousness-raising or "system splitting" invention processes, where women are encouraged to interrogate assumed ways of thinking (such as their subordination), to respond by challenging this position, and to then advocate for their legitimacy. While these invention processes do not respond directly to Mormon male leadership, this leadership constitutes a second, "need to know" audience, because it must be aware of conversations that involve Mormons.[23] Yet, these invention processes do respond to the patriarchal norms of Mormonism by addressing an open audience (Mormon women) and inspiring this open audience to invent ways to challenge these norms and articulate their position and its legitimacy.

Johnson explains her take on the feminist process of consciousness-raising that she calls "hearing into being."[24] As a form of consciousness-raising, "hearing into being" requires that a group listen for thirty minutes as one woman thinks and speaks her way through a topic of her choice. Although not based in conversational dialogue, "hearing into being" builds from a similar practice of consciousness-raising as those Bethany Mannon analyzes in her chapter on "click!" moments, as these Mormon women similarly "offered stories and experiences to cultivate new awareness among participants." Johnson reports on the revolutionary upheaval that happens when women engage in this activity. She explains, "being seriously and completely listened to, being genuinely heard, hardly ever happens to women in ordinary everyday life. Many women cry the first time." Here, Johnson provides access to her thoughts by reiterating the importance of this invention process: "this is a powerful process. Being heard in this way lets us peel off the layers of our minds, coming closer . . . to what I call the old wise woman's mind."[25] Hearing into being does not involve dialogue where aggressive voices dominate; instead it permits women to break their silence and invent a way to be heard. By using hearing in being, these women are not only challenging Mormon patriarchal norms for women, they are also imagining a way to advocate for their legitimacy.

After depicting feminist consciousness-raising as an invention process, Johnson realizes that her reliance on a step-by-step process and her faith in a changeable future are examples of patriarchal norms. Therefore, *Wildfire* moves in a different direction and advocates for instantaneous change—change that does not (necessarily) involve the promise of a bright future. Johnson draws attention to the importance of the present when she notes that this "moment is the only time we have."[26] This emphasis on the instantaneous potential of the present is reiterated again when Johnson provides access to her thoughts, by arguing that the "future reality is transformed when we change our feelings about ourselves—and hence our behavior—in the present."[27] Therefore feminists should not rely on a set process; instead, Johnson suggests, they should invent a more equitable world in the present by changing their behavior and feelings about themselves now and in turn challenging their subordination.

Kate Kelly: Delivery Strategies

Kelly delivers her message strategically to advocate for Mormon women as worthy of ordination because they are respectful "prospective elders."[28] As such, delivery functions to cultivate legitimacy in that it involves shaping the OW supporters into prospective priesthood holders, understood as able to hold authority. As Yoos would have it, Kelly's strategic use of delivery through her blog at the website *Ordain Women* is also a rhetoric of response because she employs facts (about the women, relayed through their dress, their actions, and the website's design), and she connects these facts to explanations about the mission of OW (asking for women's ordination). Importantly, Kelly employs this method to strategically adapt to the habitus of the church, an objective that represents her best chance at convincing the male priesthood that Mormon women should be legitimized through ordination.

In line with RTM, I will first consider Kelly's use of blogs as her selected medium and its impact on her response before allowing my observations to create additional pathways of analysis. Kelly writes in digital formats that are self-published and short in length. Her blogs are text based but sometimes include images and feature embedded links to outside websites or downloadable PDFs. Kelly chose to disable the comment feature for the blogs on the OW website, but these blogs can still be shared on all social media platforms. Blogs allow for fast and widespread distribution of her ideas, along with quick responses from her audience (responses that she has tried to limit). This immediacy, ease of distribution, and the possible consequences for publicly asking for ordination influence Kelly's writing, so she delivers her message in a way that is respectful and reminiscent of authority, which effectively represents her adaptation to the habitus of the church's rhetorical authority. By mimicking the church's leadership, Kelly works to cultivate women's legitimacy and to quell any disagreements between members within Mormonism.

Kelly's delivery depicts OW supporters as respectful, prospective priesthood holders, and therefore as representatives of legitimate authority. As such she describes the work completed by OW as "not seeking members or followers. Rather, [OW] provides a space where Mormons can speak about their concerns about gender inequality and hope that the prophet . . . prays about women's ordination."[29] Kelly describes those who make up OW not as followers of OW but as supporters of women's ordination who remain faithful followers of the Mormon Church, and who seek institutional change through the appropriate channels. Kelly is responding to the church leadership by connecting facts about the women, as supporters but not followers, to explanations about OW and its mission to properly request institutional change—again, adapting to the church's habitus of rhetorical authority by emphasizing proper institutional change.

Moreover, shaping OW's supporters into prospective priesthood holders influences OW's online presence, specifically the website design and its participants.[30] Kelly is not the only feminist Mormon to write blogs, as the blog appears the genre of choice for current Mormon feminists. Joanna Brooks notes that "the internet became a major game changer for Mormon feminists . . . women who may have once felt isolated in their congregations . . . [found] a safe space [online] to communicate."[31] To this point, Kelly employs many of the same delivery strategies online that she uses to shape her organization's in-person faith-based actions, and the website imitates other Mormon spaces in its design, in her decision to disallow comments, in its administrative control, and in the published references to Mormon history and symbolism.

The website *Ordain Women* is built from a WordPress template called "Elegant Themes," which primarily involves a color scheme of eggshell with gray lettering. The landing page features a mission statement followed by a grid of profile pictures from the latest supporters to join OW.[32] The website appears dictated by a series of rules similar to those that orchestrate OW's in-person actions. In particular, the commenting function is disabled, and there is no clear way to submit a blog post. Furthermore, the only women frequently published in the blog section are OW's serving board members. Profiles can be submitted by any visitor, but these profiles are only published upon administrative review. And the website features blogs that build from "Mormon approved" historical evidence or reinterpret important symbolism in support of female ordination. Through the design of OW and its website, Kelly is shaping her supporters into prospective elders as she encourages delivering messages that are respectful of the leadership.

Kelly has similar rules for how her supporters will act during their faith-based actions. She encourages OW supporters not to protest, but to cite leadership, express thanks, and seek to listen to and learn from their leaders. Kelly explains that those who want to participate must come prepared in their Sunday best, "as if attending any other session of General Conference."[33] Here, she figures the OW participants as respectful members of the Mormon Church—as these members could literally blend in with other conference attendees. Again, in her rhetoric of response, Kelly establishes a fact—that Mormon women are prospective priesthood holders—and connects this fact to an explanation about why they need to dress as though they can blend in. Additionally, Kelly's effort to dignify OW supporters through dress is clearly tied to an understanding of a rhetor's appearance and hence to delivery strategies. This finding echoes Carol Mattingly's work on nineteenth-century women's dress, when she argues, "clothing and appearance comprised a major component in the ethos women presented."[34] As demonstrated here, dress continues to influence how female rhetors are read and treated by audiences in the twenty-first century, particularly in religious spaces and contexts. With this example, Kelly builds the ethos of those in OW by mimicking the delivery strategies of prospective elders and by enacting a dress code that further adapts to the habitus of the Mormon Church's rhetorical authority.

In addition to dictating their dress, OW requires participants to act as if they are prospective elders, in events that are organized like priesthood meetings. In a post attributed to "admin," the writer details the schedule for the latest faith-based action, a schedule that includes a "welcome message, a prayer, and a hymn before walking together to the Conference Center."[35] With this schedule, the faith-affirming action resembles a typical LDS Sunday service—a service led by male priesthood holders. Through their imitation, OW members indicate that they can perform the same sacred rituals as those completed by the male leadership. Kelly uses demonstrable evidence that these women are delivering a message in ways expected of prospective priesthood holders, and she uses these facts to explain that female members deserve authority because they can perform the same actions as the male leadership. Although Kelly's delivery strategy is ultimately unsuccessful with her all-male audience, it represents her best chance at success, as she connects fact with explanation to adapt to the habitus of the church's rhetorical authority by explaining why these OW members need to act as prospective priesthood holders.

While Kelly has been strategic in her message, she was excommunicated in 2014 in ways reminiscent of Johnson's excommunication. Yet, Kelly's ideas about women's equality in the Mormon Church have led to incremental changes in Mormon women's legitimacy. For example, in 2015, three Mormon women were appointed to general counsels that were previously all male. Also since 2015, Mormon women are no longer prohibited from watching the all-male priesthood session, as a televised version of this meeting is now accessible to them. And in photo spreads depicting the church leadership, female leaders are now featured alongside male general authorities.[36] Since Kelly was excommunicated before these changes occurred, the church would not directly allude to her work. Yet, while the Mormon Church did not state that the inclusion of women was due to OW's faith-based actions, the timing of the changes, so soon after Kelly's excommunication, makes them seem to be related to her work. Overall, OW has yet to achieve its namesake's goal, which means Kelly's results remain mixed, but the conversation surrounding women's legitimacy in the Mormon Church is not over. In addition, the above incremental changes mean that Kelly's strategies for establishing women's legitimacy have been more successful than were Johnson's strategies. Arguably, this success is because Kelly's strategies are less threatening to the church's power structure, as she intentionally adapts to the church's habitus by mimicking authority in her delivery, instead of challenging authority through consciousness-raising activities. Thus, when seeking to establish legitimacy within oppressive institutions, rhetors may have more success if they use rhetoric that mimics the structures of the institution than if they use rhetoric that dismisses such structures altogether.

CONNECTIONS ACROSS TIME

Both Kelly and Johnson employ legitimacy as a response to the Mormon Church, and their rhetorical responses forge connections among Mormon women and motivate them to act. Yet, while Johnson focused on provoking the invention of women's authority and delivering her message through monographs in a way that involves protest, Kelly centered her response using blogs to characterize her supporters as prospective priesthood holders, in line with the ways of authority established by the church. Johnson's and Kelly's rhetoric responds to their different time periods—one rhetor speaks and writes on paper in a time of political and social upheaval, while the other uses digital technology during a time of increased innovation.

Most importantly, the ways Johnson and Kelly employ delivery and invention allow Mormon women to connect and work toward legitimacy. Johnson's invention processes gave Mormon women a space to imagine themselves without oppressive structures, while Kelly's delivery strategies allow Mormon women to recognize themselves as authorities and develop this identity by acting like authorities.

Kelly's and Johnson's responses to the Mormon Church further connect Mormon women by the mere act of inviting them to participate in public gatherings. Johnson and her followers left leaflets in church buildings and used phone trees of members to cultivate a base. Decades later, Kelly wrote blogs to recruit women to Ordain Women's faith-affirming events. Although their strategies for recruitment are different, both women understood—like other marginalized groups before them—that there is strength in numbers.[37] In addition, both women invited Mormon women to get involved by hosting public events such as faith-affirming actions or feminist protests. While they sometimes met with other women in private, Johnson and Kelly understood that they needed to gather in public and that their documents needed to be public in order to cultivate legitimacy.

RESPONDING WITH LEGITIMACY

As a rhetoric of response, legitimacy traces dissension or disagreement (authorizing women) within a specific context (Mormon faith) in which those with authority (male leadership) do not wish to give others power.[38] Advocating for legitimacy is a rhetoric typical among religious female rhetors. As a twenty-first-century Mormon, Kelly employs rhetorical strategies that refract those employed by nineteenth-century Protestant women and eighteenth-century Methodist women. As Lindal Buchanan notes, "delivery has not pertained equally to both men and women . . . as women were . . . prohibited from standing and speaking in public, their voices and forms acceptable only in the spectator role."[39] Religious women were often only allowed to speak in public if they were models of female propriety and received the permission of male leaders. For example, eighteenth-century Methodist women Sarah Crosby and Hester Rogers had to receive permission from John Wesley, the founder of Methodism, to "expound" in public.[40] As such, these female religious rhetors convinced male leaders of their (the women's) ability to engage in public speaking and were permitted to do so (partly) because they performed traditional femininity.

Across centuries, religious female rhetors respond to male authority by following the appropriate conduct of their gender, while simultaneously disagreeing with the limits of their gender. Arguably, this strategy continues to remain useful because it is understood as less threatening to the patriarchal structure. These traditionally feminine women demonstrate their investment in the patriarchal system through *appropriate* gender performance. While they may disagree with the limits of their gender, *how* they do so continues to play into patriarchal expectations of women—as Methodist women *request* permission from male leaders to speak in public or as Mormon women *ask* male leaders to pray for their ordination.

Yet this strategy is contrary to radical rhetors like Johnson and her sixteenth-century predecessor Anne Askew, who not only disagreed with the limits of their gender but performed their gender apart from these boundaries and questioned the legitimacy of the system altogether. While she eventually burned at the stake, Askew used her rhetoric to challenge the boundaries of femininity by claiming a direct connection to God, unfiltered through man. Whereas Johnson questioned the patriarchal system by employing invention processes to raise the consciousness of her female readers, she later eschewed legitimacy in Mormonism and the feminist movement because of their reliance on hierarchy. As such, like Askew before her, Johnson refused to adhere to traditional femininity.

In addition to these historical echoes, Johnson and Kelly illustrate that legitimacy—with its ability to ignite change from within—is a necessary response to a patriarchal force powerful enough to excommunicate. While Johnson and Kelly used different strategies (delivery and invention), they both worked to establish Mormon women's legitimacy.

These two rhetors amassed support by selecting media that enhanced their efforts to establish legitimacy. Blogs and monographs were public forms, easily consumed in a variety of settings and circulated among groups. Johnson's monographs allowed for space where she could provide access to her thoughts, describe consciousness-raising processes, and inspire the change inherent in these processes, whereas Kelly's blog allowed for a tailored form of delivery, in which she could visually shape an argument and disallow comments—effectively "delivering" a message of prospective priesthood holders to church leadership. Kelly also demonstrates connections between explanations and facts by adapting to the habitus of the church's rhetorical authority, as she encourages OW women to "deliver" facts about themselves as respectful followers (through their traditional dress, their actions, and the website's design). Her best chance at convincing the male authority comes in the form of connecting these facts to explanations as to why these women deserve ordination and legitimacy.

Overall, this analysis of Johnson and Kelly indicates that legitimacy can be produced rhetorically through both invention processes and delivery strategies. While invention processes create ways to map long-term change, delivery strategies forge pathways to immediate, incremental changes. Kelly and Johnson may differ in terms of their historical context and the rhetorical strategies they employ, but their similarities complicate the clear separation between the three waves of feminism, especially concerning how these waves pertain to religious women, as both rhetors advocate for the same cause: women's legitimacy.

Notes

1. Associated Press, "Excommunicated Mormon Kate Kelly Loses Appeal, Pledges to Continue Ordain Women Campaign," *Huffington Post*, November 5, 2014, http://www .huffingtonpost.com. Ordination involves granting a faithful member authority inside a religious context. As an ordained member, one is permitted rights, such as the ability to speak directly with God, offer blessings, and preside over meetings.

2. Lindsay Whitehurst, "Court Sides with Utah's Planned Parenthood in Defunding Case," Associated Press, *Business Insider*, July 13, 2016, https://www.businessinsider.com.

3. Carolyn Skinner, *Women Physicians and Professional Ethos in Nineteenth-Century America* (Carbondale: Southern Illinois University Press, 2014), 171.

4. Debra Hawhee and Christa J. Olson, "Pan-Historiography: The Challenges of Writing History across Time and Space," in *Theorizing the Histories of Rhetoric*, ed. Michelle Ballif (Carbondale: Southern Illinois University Press, 2013), 90–106; Alison Piepmeier, *Girl Zines: Making Media, Doing Feminism* (New York: New York University Press, 2009).

5. Peggy Fletcher Stack, "Gender Gap Widening among Utah Mormons, but Why?" *Salt Lake Tribune*, December 22, 2011.

6. These church-wide governing councils make decisions on spiritual matters that affect any member. Often, these all-male councils craft proclamations that guide membership, decide on budgets, and determine programming.

7. Sonia Johnson, *From Housewife to Heretic: One Woman's Spiritual Awakening and Her Excommunication from the Mormon Church* (New York: Doubleday, 1981), 250.

8. Sonia Johnson, "Patriarchal Panic: Sexual Politics in the Mormon Church" (presentation at the meeting of the American Psychological Association, New York, September 1, 1979).

9. Peter Berger and Thomas Luckman, *The Social Construction of Reality* (New York: Anchor Books, 1966), 131.

10. For studies of how the powerful maintain legitimacy, please see: Antonio Reyes, "Strategies of Legitimization in Political Discourse: From Words to Actions," *Discourse & Society* 22, no. 6 (2001): 781–807; and Theo Van Leeuwen, "Legitimation in Discourse and Communication," *Discourse and Communication* 1, no. 1 (2007): 91–112.

11. Although the process of legitimation could lead to further gender equality, some activists claim that cultivating women's legitimacy inside patriarchal structures should not be a part of the feminist cause as it reproduces a structure that is already unequal. I argue that legitimation is important for this kind of feminist work, which focuses on reforming patriarchal organizations in the hope of creating more gender-equitable organizations. It is not my place, as a feminist rhetorical scholar, to suggest how feminist activism should look. Instead I write this piece to parse how feminist activism does look, specifically within the context of the Mormon Church.

12. Qtd. in Theresa Enos, "Professing the New Rhetorics: Prologue," *Rhetoric Review* 9, no. 1 (1990): 10.

13. George Yoos, "Rhetoric of Appeal and Rhetoric of Response," *Philosophy & Rhetoric* 20, no. 2 (1987): 108.

14. Yoos, 113.

15. Yoos, 115.

16. Yoos, 115.

17. Sonia Johnson, *Going Out of Our Minds: The Metaphysics of Liberation* (New York: Crossing Press, 1987), 155.

18. Kate Kelly, "FAQs for the Oct. 5 Priesthood Session Action," *Ordain Women* (blog), September 9, 2013, https://ordainwomen.org.

19. Johnson, *Going Out of Our Minds*, 324.

20. Karlyn Kohrs Campbell, "The Rhetoric of Women's Liberation: An Oxymoron," *Quarterly Journal of Speech* 59, no. 1 (1973): 75.

21. Johnson, *From Housewife to Heretic*, 14–15; Johnson, *Going Out of Our Minds*; Sonia Johnson, *Wildfire: Igniting the She/Volution* (Albuquerque, NM: Wildfire Books, 1990).

22. Katherine Fredlund, "Forget the Master's Tools, We Will Build Our Own House: The Woman's Era as a Rhetorical Forum for the Invention of African American Womanhood," *Peitho* 18, no. 2 (2016): 67–98.

23. Yoos, "Rhetoric of Appeal," 108.

24. Johnson, *Going Out of Our Minds*, 155.

25. Johnson, 133.

26. Johnson, *Wildfire*, 38.

27. Johnson, 48; see also 13 and 197.

28. Kate Kelly, "Join Us Oct. 5th for the Priesthood Session!" *Ordain Women* (blog), September 17, 2013, https://ordainwomen.org. All of Kelly's blog posts analyzed in this chapter were published between 2013 and 2016 on her website, *Ordain Women*. This site had received over three hundred million visits as of late 2018.

29. Kate Kelly, "OW Conversations," *Ordain Women* (blog), August 1, 2014, https://ordainwomen.org.

30. Kate Kelly, "FAQs for the Oct. 5 Priesthood Session Action," *Ordain Women* (blog), September 13, 2913, https://ordainwomen.org.

31. Qtd. in Lorie Winder Stromberg, "Agitating Faithfully," *Ordain Women* (blog), September 30, 2015, https://ordainwomen.org.

32. A blog post by "Caroline" explains that the featured profiles "mirror the Mormon Church sponsored 'I'm a Mormon' campaign, as these Mormons attach pictures of themselves to their statements, a brave move away from anonymity." Caroline, "Mormons Who Advocate for Women's Ordination," *Ordain Women* (blog), March 28, 2013, https://ordainwomen.org.

33. Kate Kelly, "FAQs for the Oct. 5 Priesthood Session Action," *Ordain Women* (blog), September 13, 2013, https://ordainwomen.org.

34. Carol Mattingly, "Friendly Dress: A Disciplined Use," *Rhetoric Society Quarterly* 29, no. 2 (1999): 25.

35. Admin, "Ordain Women Priesthood Session Information," *Ordain Women* (blog), October 5, 2015, https://ordainwomen.org. "Admin" is shorthand for administrator, or one who controls what and when blogs are published. Although anonymous, this "admin" is assumed by many readers to be Kelly, since she created the website, founded Ordain Women, and organized this faith-based action.

36. Peggy Fletcher Stack, "3 Women Appointed to Previously All-Male Mormon Executive Council," *Salt Lake Tribune*, August 18, 2015.

37. Sarah Hallenbeck, *Claiming the Bicycle: Women, Rhetoric, and Technology in Nineteenth-Century America* (Carbondale: Southern Illinois University Press, 2015), 327; Richard D. Fave, "Ritual and the Legitimation of Inequality," *Sociological Perspectives* 34, no. 1 (1991): 21–38.

38. Enos, "Professing the New Rhetorics," 6–7.

39. Lindal Buchanan, *Regendering Delivery: The Fifth Canon and Antebellum Women Rhetors* (Carbondale: Southern Illinois University, 2005), 2.

40. Vicki Tolar Collins, "Walking in Light, Walking in Darkness: The Story of Women's Changing Rhetorical Space in Early Methodism," *Rhetoric Review* 14, no. 2 (1996): 336–54.

11

The Suffragist Movement and the Early Feminist Blogosphere

Feminism and Recent History of Rhetoric

CLANCY RATLIFF

IN AN APRIL 6, 2017, POST on her blog, *Dooce*, commemorating its sixteenth anniversary, Heather Armstrong wrote, "That's right. My blog is old enough to drive a car."[1] The same can be said for my research about blogs, which I started in 2001. At that time, blogging was new, edgier than cutting edge: bleeding edge. The faculty members in my graduate program were skeptical about supporting this research at first, but soon they embraced it. Not long after what we now recognize as the peak of the blog phenomenon around 2005, though, people started asking me, "What's next? Blogging is just a fad; what are you going to do when people lose interest in it and the next new thing comes along?" I didn't like the question, and it took me about a year of reflection to articulate why. Certainly blogging has receded; some have even said that it's dead, though plenty of evidence shows that it's not, such as blogs that have Facebook fan pages, some with hundreds of thousands of likes. What I started saying to those who asked was that I reject the premise of *what's next?*, which is that the most prescient research about the newest media is the most valuable. I agree that *kairos* is one quality of good research in rhetoric; even so, in 2018, we *should* still care what people were doing on the internet in 2004. What we need, I argue, is work in the recent history of rhetoric, work that uses the Rhetorical Transversal Methodology (RTM) employed throughout this volume. There has been great archival research published that connects the historical and the digital, as archives from the distant past are digitized,[2] but we can also study online discourse as feminist histories of rhetoric, not only as digital media artifacts or pedagogical strategies. When we study phenomena as they are happening, we have only the past to compare them to. From 2002 until 2005, I was writing what were effectively scholarly hot takes on blogging. Now, as I reconnect with my materials on gender and blogging, I have not only the distant and recent past to use to understand what was happening rhetorically, I also have everything that has happened since: all the rich and varied use of digital tools by social movements: It Gets Better, Black Lives Matter, Me Too, and others. Also, the scholarship that has been done since then greatly informs my current analysis, especially the 2014 special issue of *Peitho* focusing on digitized archives of the suffragist movement.[3] More importantly, readers of this writing have the benefit of looking both back and forward as well.

Gender and sexism within blogging communities was a topic discussed on blogs from the earliest emergence of the genre. During this time, the notion of "A-list bloggers" also came into being, most of them men who were writing about the aftermath of the September 11, 2001, terrorist attack in the United States. Some of these men would occasionally post blog entries asking, "Where are the women bloggers?" Intermittently, between 2002 and 2005, this viral topic would erupt across blogs: in response to the question, women would post long lists of links to women's blogs and critique both the man who raised the question and the male-dominated blogosphere. The recurrence of the discussion became so commonplace that feminist bloggers gave it the label "Where are the women," even shortening it to WATW. Men would respond to the long lists of links to women's blogs with their opinions as to why women bloggers were not getting noticed, usually framed as explanations of ways women should change their blogging style, not as critiques of how the blogosphere should change to recognize and integrate women. I conducted a historical study of these "Where are the women" exchanges across blogs, with a dataset that includes thirty-three posts by men, sixty-nine posts by women, and thousands of comments on the various posts, written in August 2002, September 2002, March–August 2004, December 2004, and February 2005. In my coding of these posts, I found eighteen categories, most of which cast women bloggers in the familiar stereotypes of maiden and mother. I did a frequency count of the most common categories (table 11.1).

In this chapter, I focus primarily on two of these categories—"women aren't interested in politics" and "women don't have time to blog"—sentiments that echo commonplaces in rhetoric surrounding the suffragist movement. My aim is to present a narrative of the rearticulation of norms of femininity as they occurred in these posts and comments about gender in blogging, caricatures that are surprisingly consistent with those in circulation during the suffragist movement. I provide here a snapshot of the rhetorical context that women bloggers were working within during these early years of blogging. Whether conditions are better or worse for women now is beyond the scope of this chapter and depends on the criteria being used (more exposure to larger audiences, more money made from blogging, less harassment/fewer threats, etc.). During this segment of time, though, over and over, men made (and women responded to) variations of the claims that: (1) women aren't interested in politics; they're interested in babies, fashion, and celebrity gossip; and (2) women don't have time to blog; they're too busy with the house and the kids. The rhetorical strategies the

TABLE 11.1. FREQUENCY COUNT OF THEMES IN "WHERE ARE THE WOMEN" (WATW) POSTS AND COMMENTS

Theme	Number of times mentioned in blog posts	Number of times mentioned in blog comments	Total number of times mentioned
Men and women communicate differently	26	57	83
Caricatures/ Metacommentary about WATW itself	12	66	78
Sex and attractiveness (women should post sexy photos of themselves to get readers)	24	35	59
What is political/ What is a political blog	12	43	55
Women don't have time to blog	6	41	47
Blogroll references (I link to women's blogs/ You don't link to women's blogs)	10	36	46
Women aren't interested in politics	10	28	38

women used in their responses to these claims varied; some posts were straightforward explanations of the lower profiles of women bloggers, and others were more forceful, direct expressions of anger toward the individual men who seemed not to notice women bloggers or who simply dismissed their work. I turn now to the distant past of the early twentieth century, to statements about women during the suffragist movement, and I then demonstrate the relevance to claims about gender in blogging.

GENDER CONSTRAINTS IN IMAGES OF THE SUFFRAGIST MOVEMENT

Rhetoricians have studied the suffragist movement extensively, including the visual rhetoric about women's suffrage at the time. For example, the aforementioned 2014 special issue of *Peitho* is focused exclusively on political cartoons about the suffragists by John T. McCutcheon.[4] These powerful anti-suffragist images negatively affected the movement. In an article from that issue, Kristie S. Fleckenstein writes that almost all cartoonists were men, so there were not many pro-suffrage visual arguments, and she observes the ways that suffragist women were drawn as masculine; men were also drawn, in a speculative world where women could vote, as feminine. Fleckenstein says, "the circulation of the female harridan and the male sissy . . . provides *Tribune* subscribers with visual forms and models by which to perceive and act on his cartoons. These stock characters infiltrated users' cultural imagination and shaped perceptions that, in turn, guided their participatory actions."[5] Those images were part of, to use Fleckenstein's term, a "visual media ecology" that invites the viewer to visualize the issue of suffrage the way the cartoonist has, and through repetition the visual representations train viewers to integrate the images into their perception.[6]

Sarah L. Skripsky shows that McCutcheon's drawings of women figure them as domestic angels not suited for public life, and one example Skripsky cites is "Miss Chicago (Picking a Mayor)—'Eeny, Meeney, Miney, Mo,' Etc.," a 1907 cartoon by McCutcheon.[7] In it, a confused-looking woman stands facing a long line of men. Skripsky writes, "As the title suggests, Chicago is figured as a naive woman, a feminized city unsure about its next leader, and thus choosing one randomly from a line-up of male hopefuls."[8] While this particular cartoon is not specifically about women's right to vote but rather about a city's mayoral election, the image of a woman is associated with not understanding the nuances of politics and the facts and processes of government. Skripsky also points out, however, that "While early McCutcheon cartoons poke fun at the political role of the suffragette-angel, later cartoons show her as a necessary audience and counterbalance for morally suspect politicians."[9] McCutcheon's career as a cartoonist spans the years before and after the Nineteenth Amendment passed, and his visual arguments about women evolved over time.

To build on these analyses of McCutcheon's work, I offer two 1909 political cartoons about the suffragist movement, one by T. E. Powers and one by Merle Johnson. "When Women Get Their Rights" (figure 11.1), created by T. E. Powers and published on January 27, 1909, warns of the deterioration of government if women are allowed to enter it. In this image, one woman sits at a desk. She has a gavel in her hand, and a tag around her neck marks her as the "mayoress." Two other women stand attending her, one with no label, and the other with one reading "Mrs. Mitz." Behind the mayoress stands another woman, whose tag reads "fire com-ess." This last woman says, "My what a stunning gown you have on mayoress—can I have an auto for my department?" "Sure," says the mayoress, who is so impulsive and capricious that she is motivated by unctuous flattery. Woman, then, is not to be trusted in municipal government; a simple compliment on her outfit can affect a city's budget. She puts fashion and vanity ahead of government.

FIGURE 11.1. T. E. Powers, "When Women Get Their Rights,"
Arkansas Gazette, 1909.

Merle Johnson's cartoon (figure 11.2) shows two images: in the top image, a woman is walled into an enclosure. She peers out over the wall, which reads "Women's 'Sphere.'" At her feet behind her are a toy spinning top labeled "gossip" and a doll with an elaborate dress that says "fashion." In the image below it, a woman with a baby in a stroller stuffs a ballot in a box at a voting center, with other women waiting in line behind her to do the same. The caption between the two images reads, "Woman Devotes Her Time to Gossip and Clothes Because She Has Nothing Else to Talk About. Give Her Broader Interests and She Will Cease to Be Vain and Frivolous." This image shows what Skripsky calls the "suffragette-angel" figure, sometimes used strategically within the suffragist movement, who votes, maintains a dainty feminine appearance, and takes care

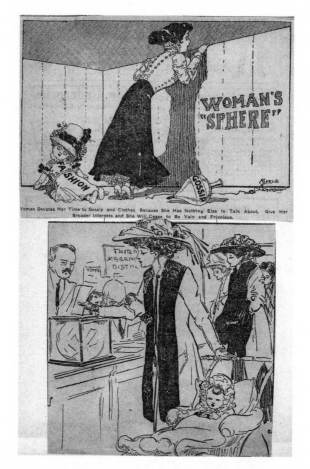

FIGURE 11.2. Merle Johnson, "Woman's 'Sphere'" suffrage cartoons, 1909. Drawings, https://www.loc.gov/item /rbcmiller002064/.

of children at the same time. Overall, in these images we see a conflict between traditional femininity and political participation: mutually exclusive sets of interests in either fashion and gossip or economics and government. This conflict has persisted well into the time of the blogosphere; historical rhetorics are brought clearly to bear in the digital context of blogging.

WOMEN AREN'T INTERESTED IN POLITICS

Some of the "Where are the women" comments display a dismissive attitude, a view of women and their interests as frivolous and silly. John Hawkins, when trying to come up with a list of thirty-five political blogs by women, writes of the exercise: "To be honest, I'm not even sure there are 35 readable blogs written by women on the right [conservative] side of the blogosphere. By the time you get that deep—assuming you don't count male/female group blogs—you'd practically be down to women posting flag cake recipes every two days."[10] In another post, Hawkins explained further: "So let me branch out: Why are comparatively so few female bloggers of note in the political blogosphere?" He continues: "Personally, I have come to suspect it's just a numbers game. On the whole, women aren't as interested as men in politics, so therefore there are a lot less women than men writing about politics, and hence there is a much smaller pool of female bloggers with the talent to move up the ranks. Some people probably won't like that answer, but hey, why aren't there as many women who are sports fans as men? Why are there a lot more women than guys who enjoy romance novels? Maybe it's nature, maybe it's nurture, maybe it's some combination thereof, but men and women on the whole don't have the same level of interest in politics."[11]

Another conservative blogger, Dean Esmay, wrote, "Numerous surveys have been done—if someone wants to get in my face I can produce references—showing pretty universally that women are less interested in politics than men are. Don't talk to me about the exceptions you know, look at the data. Women just aren't as interested or as well-informed on politics, when you look at them as a demographic group."[12] In a 2005 comment at the liberal blog *Political Animal*, a reader posting with the name "Reg" declared that "there are simply less females than males passionate about politics, hence less females blogging. If there is a blogosphere concerned with sales at Nordstroms or Hollywood gossip, that blogosphere will be predominately female."[13] What Hawkins, Esmay, and Reg say is quite similar to the "Woman's 'Sphere'" political cartoon from almost a century earlier. This sentiment was stated over and over by men: there aren't many political blogs by women, because women aren't interested in politics; women are interested in babies, fashion, and celebrity gossip. We might call this sentiment *mansplaining* now. In the blog world of the early 2000s, women faced what Betty Friedan encountered as a freelance writer for women's magazines in the 1950s, if I may digress briefly to the historical midpoint between the suffragists and the bloggers. One male editor told her, "Our readers are housewives, full time. They're not interested in the broad public issues of the day. They are not interested in national or international affairs. They are only interested in the family and the home. They aren't interested in politics, unless it's related to an immediate need in the home, like the price of coffee."[14] Friedan reflects on this encounter: "it was simply taken for granted by editors, and accepted as an immutable fact of life by writers, that women were not interested in politics, life outside the United States, national issues, art, science, ideas, adventure, education, or even their own communities, except where they could be sold through their emotions as wives and mothers."[15]

One might argue that *women aren't interested in politics* is a self-fulfilling prophecy, but feminist bloggers simply rejected the premises of that statement: the narrow assumption that "political" specifically means horse-race election coverage, war, and foreign policy; the mutual exclusivity of politics and other interests; and the implication that men aren't interested in celebrity gossip (indeed, some of what they called "politics" consisted of gossipy posts about sex scandals involving politicians).

Commenter Katherine, in a thread under a 2004 post at *Crooked Timber*, challenges the claim: "The one thing that really drives me crazy in this is the idea that a lack of women political bloggers means that women aren't interested in politics. I really don't think that's true as far as voter turnout, campaigns I've been involved in, etc., all of which are much better indicators of political interest than blogging. There was a survey in my law school that showed hugely different rates of volunteer class participation among men and women. It may be that blogging is another form of 'public speaking.'"[16] Katherine provides a much-needed corrective to the idea that women's alleged absence in political blogging and mass media punditry is indicative of an absence of interest in politics. Blogger zoe kentucky, in a comment at *Political Animal*, builds on this corrective: "there is a shortage of women who are interested/passionate/obsessed with politics? Guess folks around here haven't spent too much time in the non-profit progressive advocacy world in DC—it's pretty much dominated by women."[17] These posts from Katherine and zoe kentucky are examples of counternarrative, a feminist response that Bethany Mannon analyzes more fully in this volume. While the counterargument that blogging is not a reliable measure of women's political interest is a sound one, it did not result in lasting change in the everyday practices of bloggers.

WOMEN DON'T HAVE TIME TO BLOG

Any blogger or casual reader of blogs could make the passing observation that it takes a lot of time to maintain a blog. To have a successful political blog that has an audience of regular readers, bloggers must find material, preferably articles on the Web or other bloggers' posts, to read and comment on in their posts. This preliminary reading alone can entail hours of scouring through periodicals such as the *New York Times*, *New Republic*, *New Yorker*, *Atlantic Monthly*, *Wall Street Journal*, *Economist*, *Boston Review*, *New York Review of Books*, and many others, including government websites and the websites of think tanks. Bloggers must also promote their own blog, and that inevitably means reading other people's blogs and responding to their posts, both in others' comment threads and on their own blog. Bloggers also must respond to readers who leave comments on posts. In addition to this, many bloggers also correspond with readers via email.

Will Franklin, at his conservative blog, *WILLisms*, illustrates the role of *kairos* in the process of responding:

> In blogging, being first is sometimes more important than being best. This very post, for example, is probably about 2 days too late to get much play in the blogosphere, as people have already moved on to other, bigger, better topics.
>
> Blogging is about frantic deadlines. Women, generally, are not.
>
> By the time women have formed a well-developed answer they are comfortable with, it is too late to post about it. Meanwhile, men have answers for everything.
>
> It starts early, too. Little boys are more willing (and faster) to raise their hands and answer questions than little girls.
>
> Later in life, men are inherently more willing to blurt out an answer than women in a group setting. The same goes for blogging, the ultimate group setting.[18]

According to Franklin, women are hesitant, tentative, too afraid of being wrong to keep pace with the rapid-fire momentum of blog discussion. Although the implications of his statement are noteworthy, I am more interested in the point he makes about immediacy as a generic convention of blogs. Not only do bloggers have to respond to and interact with other bloggers, they also have to do so *immediately*. Much of the act of blogging consists of monitoring other people's blogs, waiting for someone else to respond to one's posts, responding to their responses, and responding to other people's posts (in the comments section of their blogs or on one's own blog). Timing, or to use the rhetorical term *kairos*, is quite important; a blogger must be fast on the uptake. Terry Papillon analogizes *kairos* to improvisational musical performance: "Without thinking, one must recognize when an occasion presents itself; one must know what is the best way to take advantage of that occasion; one must know what notes to play and what makes the appropriate style for the occasion."[19] In order to attain the tacit, fluid knowledge of the rhetorical situation that the rhetor must possess to use this facility, the rhetor must devote a great deal of time to studying the speakers, the topics, and the style of the discussions.

The claim *women don't have time to blog* was often uttered in the "Where are the women" threads, usually followed by some version of "because they're too busy taking care of the house and the kids." A colossal body of scholarly literature in anthropology, sociology, women's studies, psychology, and other disciplines examines the division of labor within the home, with child-rearing, cooking, and cleaning expected of women, regardless of other work responsibilities. These studies date back to at least 1898, with the publication of Charlotte Perkins Gilman's monograph *Women and Economics: A Study of the Economic Relation be-*

tween Men and Women as a Factor in Social Evolution. In 1976, Adrienne Rich published *Of Woman Born: Motherhood as Experience and Institution,* based on research in multiple disciplines as well as her personal experience. Other works include Nancy Chodorow's 1978 *The Reproduction of Mothering,* in which she identifies the reproduction of mothering as the girl's identification and continuousness with her mother, and she points to a tendency among girls to see their mothers as role models and, in turn, in themselves a desire to mother.[20] This pattern is a social psychological process that helps keep gender hierarchy in place as long as women are the ones expected to care for children. Parenting and domestic labor, even throughout feminist criticism of their curtailment of women's opportunities, continue to be a fact of life for most women.

The material conditions of blog writing, then, are important: domestic labor is a necessity, and time is a limited resource. Still, many women, even women who bear the sole responsibility of child-rearing and housework, find time to write. Blogging, however, calls for an especially large amount of leisure time. In September 2002, blogger MinuteMan tersely pointed out, "Blogging is a hobby: Men come home from work and blog, women come home from work and mind the kids and the home."[21] This acceptance of the status quo went mostly unquestioned in the posts and comment threads in "Where are the women" discussions, even by women bloggers, whose posts carried a resigned, sometimes sardonic tone, but did not significantly challenge the distribution of labor in the home.

In March 2004, speculating as to the main reason for the underrepresentation of women in political blogging, feminist blogger Laura McKenna cited "Time. I don't have much of it. To do the current events blogs, you need to be able to write quick draw posts with lots of links. And links take a lot of time. Not only do they have to be programmed in, but you need to read around and wade through comments. Women have less free time than men."[22] Rivka, an active woman blogger, adds in a December 2004 comment at *Crooked Timber:* "Large, well-constructed studies consistently demonstrate that women do more housework and childcare than men, and that men have more free time—something on the order of 20 hours per week of additional free time, for men with full-time jobs vs. women with full-time jobs. There's a gender gap in home-related work, which leads directly to a gender gap in the time men and women have to engage in hobbies like blogging. And that gap probably exists regardless of whether women are more 'interested' or 'drawn' to housework—someone's got to do it, after all."[23]

Each of these bloggers agrees that blogging—especially maintaining blogs that are heavily interlinked with others and that display a constant engagement with an audience (required in order to reach a wide readership), as opposed to blogs with only a few posts per week—takes a lot of time. They also point out that blogging is a hobby, suggesting that blogging is not the only hobby women may miss out on due to their increased domestic responsibilities. In a 2005 comment at the conservative blog *La Shawn Barber's Corner*, Karen M. writes: "Obviously, more men have more free time than women, given the statistics on women (generally) pulling more than their fair share of the load in home and family responsibilities," adding that "As for interest in politics, some of the most engaged people I know are my women friends; we talk about political issues all of the time ... but as I said, *they* don't have *time* to blog."[24] The state of domestic labor was unfortunately not problematized by anyone, men or women. Not once in the "Where are the women" threads, even on feminist blogs, did I find any comments challenging men to offer to do any domestic tasks so that their wives would have time to pursue their hobbies. Instead, the comments I read suggested that women's primary responsibility for domestic labor was, to an extent, the unfortunate but natural state of affairs.

Bloggers' material conditions are important, and they can enable or disable participation in public discursive space. In the "Where are the women" threads, a considerable number of women wrote in specific, concrete detail about the physical tasks that consume their days and nights. Leila Abu-Saba, in a 2005 comment at *Political Animal*, reflects on her blogging time: "Right now the kids are watching a little TV after an exhausting birthday party, and my beloved hubbie is playing electric guitar while gawking over my shoulder. I usually blog at night after the kids go to bed, and sometimes during the day when they're at school. Many mommy bloggers do something similar. If I had a full time job along with the one I've got (childcare, cooking and housekeeping) I wouldn't do it."[25]

On a 2005 post on Trish Wilson's blog, *The Countess*, commenter La Lubu also agrees that material conditions matter. She writes, "As far as I'm concerned, they can continue their little circle jerk, and we can continue to do our thing. Speaking for myself, I don't get a whole lot of links (and I kinda like it like that— quality, not quantity!) because I don't post every day. Fact is, I don't always have time to post every day, because there are things I do and like to do besides blog, plus all the mundane stuff (job, cooking, housework, yardwork, etc.) needs to be done too. And I'm a single mom too! So yeah, time is an issue. And I think time tends to be more of an issue amongst women bloggers than men bloggers. The second shift is real."[26] La Lubu's comment calls attention to the argument that women's assumption of domestic responsibilities enables men to participate more fully in blog discussions. Along with blog technology and other new media, this long-established historical circumstance continues. As Seyla Benhabib notes, "the agonistic political space of the [ancient Greek] *polis* was only possible because large groups of human beings—like women, slaves, children, laborers, non-citizen residents, and all non-Greeks—were excluded from it while they made possible through their labor for the daily necessities of life that 'leisure for politics' that the few enjoyed."[27] Both gender and technology have always been part of the history of rhetoric, going in large part unnoticed, but computers and the internet have made them especially visible.

The gender and class inflections of blog participation are apparent in many of the "Where are the women" posts and comments, as exemplified by Susan S. in a 2004 comment at *Political Animal*:

> I don't have a blog, but read and comment on many. At the risk of offending some of you, let me tell you why my women friends aren't into blogs. They don't have time! Most of them aren't into politics either (which drives me crazy) but even the ones who are interested don't have time to sit at the computer and read and write all day long. They are working, volunteering, cleaning house, doing laundry, running errands, etc., and prefer to spend their down time escaping from anything that requires brain power. And who can blame them???
>
> I happen to be very fortunate in that I don't have to work outside the home, I have a housekeeper who cleans my house weekly, and my kids are pretty self-sufficient during daytime hours, AND my husband is very supportive of my political interests. I went to college during the turbulent late 1960s and early 1970s so developed my involvement in politics then. Most of my friends came of age during a much more settled time (the mid to late 1970s) and didn't see a need to know about or be involved in politics and world events.
>
> I get the impression that most bloggers are men who are on the computer most of the time in work-related stuff and blog in between projects; or they are students who have free time between classes.[28]

Susan S.'s comment dramatically demonstrates the zero-sum game at work in the material conditions of blog writing. Time spent blogging must be taken away from other tasks. Susan S. states that her responsibilities are kept to a minimum; she likely does not work outside the home, and she has hired help, older children, and a supportive husband. She suggests that all four of these factors enable her to devote time to active participation reading and commenting on other people's blogs. Susan S. is at a point in her life in which she has time of her own, as well as plenty of money, necessary conditions for writing, as stated by Virginia Woolf in *A Room of One's Own* (1929). Again, what we can observe is the feminist rhetorical response of narrative. It is significant to note here the rhetorical situation of "Where are the women": the audience (those reading the posts and comments by women) was not only made up of the so-called A-list men but also included the many women bloggers and commenters on the blog sites. These narratives about women's material conditions are, I would argue, as much an affirmation and a nod of "I see you" to other women as they are an attempt to educate the men.

Perhaps the most unfortunate consequence of *women don't have time to blog* is what its legitimacy and validity means for those women who desire deeply to participate in political discourse on blogs, but who are prevented from participating as much as they would like, due to the relentless nature of household work. "Speaking as a woman who would love to be a blogger," commenter catjo writes, "before [women] can begin forming our bloggy thoughts," they must "work, take care of the kid(s), do the shopping, cook, clean, plan, plant and tend to the garden, do the laundry, find the missing homework, make the lunches, take the dog to the vet, plan the events, remember the appointments, smooth over the family feuds, clean the fish tank, locate the tax papers from two years ago, volunteer for the school committees, transport the kiddies to all their activities, worry about whether the check will bounce and make sure tomorrow is reasonably together."[29] This comment offers a vivid series of the daunting material conditions that shape the extent to which many women can participate in blog conversations, myself included.

In a comment at the blog *Feministing*, elfy describes in detail the difficult choice she feels forced to make between blogging and child-rearing:

> I have a first-grader son and a husband. All the child-related stuff takes a lot of time and effort, and somehow my husband is the one with more free time to spend. I do not begrudge him that, and he does help out as much as he can, but in certain circumstances it's just less damage control I have to do if I do it myself (let's just say, homework and impatient fathers don't mix well). I know that most of the working women with kids that I know of are in similar situations.
>
> I'd LOVE to be more politically active, but my primary concern is to raise this kid as best I can. (not to say that it is the ONLY goal I have, but that's a lengthy discussion for another time and place). I'd LOVE to have a political blog, but hey, I don't even have time to maintain a personal one, and if I started something public, I'd feel like I have to update it regularly. As of now, I'm amazed at *feministing* people (and others) who have all this time to read news and find great articles so those of us who are busy can still have access to pertinent news.
>
> On the other hand, my husband has time (and energy) to spend online and offline (washing dishes takes a whole less time than making up sentences with spelling words). So, my point is—and again, I do realize that my situation is not universal—maybe women in general just have less time to spend on politics or anything else, especially those who work and take care of children.[30]

Obviously, given that elfy is leaving a comment at a blog, she is able to do a limited amount of blog reading and commenting, but she clearly would like to be more active and engaged in commentary on the news. Elfy suggests that her husband shares a limited amount of the domestic work, but that she takes on the more time-consuming, emotionally and intellectually challenging work of coaching their son with his spelling homework. Elfy is one of many women in the "Where are the women" threads who expresses frustration at their material constraints. The honest reflections from women of the demands on their time were, I would argue, responses to the "Where are the women" situation, that, like the others, did not change blogging practices generally.

WHERE ARE THE WOMEN? CODA

What, then, can we make of the recurring "Where are the women" discussion? It did not come up again after the 2005 iteration, and there was no progressive revolution in blogging, no epiphany about the definition of *political*, and no great paradigm shift to equal representation in the world of blogging. Instead, the media coverage of blogging splintered further into wonk-type bloggers (who would receive press passes to Republican and Democratic National Conventions) and so-called mommy bloggers. Again and again, stereotypes about women and unexamined, unarticulated assumptions about what constitutes a political blog impeded what could have been a thoughtful exchange about gender in public discourse. Shelley Powers, writing in 2005, reflected: "It isn't the posturing, or the anger, or even the language—it is being unseen. It is writing with all your passion and your heart, and you're not heard and you're not seen. Eventually you give up, and you either take comfort from the few that do listen, or you quit. . . . And the men bring up the subject every few months, sigh about how too bad it is, relish their own position, and feel like they've given the women the sop they need. Then they go back to recognizing those who are similar to them. After all, we all like to read those who share the same background as not. Less strain that way."[31] This hardening of enclaves has been parodied by several bloggers. One of the most celebrated of these parodies was by Leigh Anne Wilson, posting under the pseudonym flea, in 2005:

> [A] re-enactment of a phenomenon that happens about every three months or so:
>
> **Popular, Liberal Male Blogger:** Why don't women blog? I've looked on my blogroll and I don't see any women bloggers. Therefore, they must not exist. Women must not be interested in thinky stuff like politics or computers.
>
> **45 Women Bloggers respond in the comments section:** WTF? We all have blogs!
>
> **Liberal, Male Blogger:** I don't mean blogs about tampons. All women do is talk about feminine hygiene products. I mean, Where are all the women who blog about important stuff; the stuff *I'm* interested in.

45 Women Bloggers: You're right. We only talk about feminine hygiene products. Here's more talk about feminine hygiene products: You are a douche.

Liberal Male Blogger: Wahhhh! You're oppressing me! Censorship! My civil rights are being violated!

One Asshole Woman: I am so embarrassed to be a woman right now! Don't you listen to those hairy bitches, Liberal Male Blogger! *I* understand you!

Liberal Male Blogger: See there? One woman has validated me! That means you all are wrong and I am right!

45 Women Bloggers: douche.

Liberal Male Blogger: Wahhhh!

Repeat in three months with a different blogger. I'll point it out next time it happens.[32]

In this caricature, Wilson derides the men's use of "my blogroll" as evidence with which to conclude that few women bloggers exist. She pokes fun at the self-styled pundits by singling out "politics and computers" as subjects that the Liberal Male Blogger is interested in. After the "45 Women Bloggers" respond with their choral "What the fuck? We all have blogs!" Wilson parodies the confused view that Liberal Male Blogger has of the topics many women choose to address, as well as the disconnect between traditional definitions of political— as in the liberal model of public space discussed by Benhabib—and newer, more expanded definitions of political. Issues such as reproductive freedom, childcare, and infant feeding are parodied as "feminine hygiene products." Paige V. Banaji, in this volume, identifies *calling out* as a feminist rhetorical tactic. Banaji is writing about rhetorical situations on Twitter, but women bloggers make similar moves using both anger and parody. Women in this discussion, as it happened over the course of about three years, showed their wit and nuanced thinking, and it is important to point out that the audience of blog readers was varied. While the men, and the mainstream media (which drove the narrative about blogging), did not change their practices in a permanent way, small changes happened: for example, in 2007, presidential candidate John Edwards chose two women as his campaign bloggers: Amanda Marcotte and Melissa McEwan. This decision was progressive at the time; bloggers were invited to the national conventions of both major political parties in the 2004 election and were given White House press passes starting in 2005, but almost all these bloggers were men.

The same year as the last iteration of "Where are the women," some women, tired of not having equal space and time at conventions about blogging such as BloggerCon, formed their own: BlogHer, which has happened yearly from

212 / CLANCY RATLIFF

2005 to the present, longer, it should be said, than BloggerCon, which had its last conference in 2006. At the 2012 BlogHer conference, President Obama made an appearance via Skype. BlogHer has been critiqued for being an overly white, corporate conference, but it has been a yearly opportunity for women bloggers to meet, talk, and collaborate.

CONCLUSION: SUFFRAGISTS AND BLOGGERS

Certainly, much has changed for women since the beginning of the twentieth century. Still, some vestiges of the gender roles dramatized in the visual rhetorical ecology of the suffragist movement have continued to serve as barriers to women's full participation in the public discourse of blogging. Digital feminist spaces are shaped by these historical rhetorics, even from the distant past. Over a decade has passed since the recurring "Where are the women" blog conflicts, and the technology for engaging in public online discourse has changed; blogging has largely, but not entirely, been replaced by social software, particularly visual platforms like Instagram, Snapchat, and Pinterest. With the 2016 US presidential election, the political landscape has changed as well. We have seen large movements of woman-led discourse, such as the Pantsuit Nation Facebook group and the Women's March on Washington and sister marches around the world, and women in particular have played a prominent role in the increase of constituent calls and letters to elected representatives at the state level. A popular meme after the election was a close-up photograph of an eagle staring directly into the camera. Photoshopped onto its head is a pink pussy hat, like those worn during the Women's March on Washington the day after Trump's inauguration. It reads, "In The Resistance, 86% are women. 66% are over age 45. The Resistance is your mom." The rise of blogging happened during George W. Bush's presidency, in what many of us at the time considered, and still do, to be a politically tumultuous period. We didn't know all that would happen a dozen years later, such as the racism and vicious misogyny that would so dramatically resurface, which is in its fullest expression in digital spaces. If "Where are the women" has taught us anything about feminism and public discourse, it is that progress is incremental and fraught. "Where are the women" as a feminist rhetorical effort failed at intersectionality in particular; more inclusive mobilizations such as Me Too not only are more socially just, they make a stronger impact.

Notes

1. Heather B. Armstrong, "Fourteen Hundred and Ninety Point Two," *dooce* (blog), April 6, 2017, https://dooce.com.

2. For more, see Jean Bessette, *Retroactivism in the Lesbian Archives: Composing Pasts and Futures* (Carbondale: Southern Illinois University Press, 2018); Jessica Enoch and Jordynn Jack, "Remembering Sappho: New Perspectives on Teaching (and Writing) Wom-

en's Rhetorical History," *College English* 73, no. 5, (2011): 518–37; Tarez Samra Graban, "Re/Situating the Digital Archive in John T. McCutcheon's 'Publics,' Then and Now," *Peitho* 17, no. 1 (2014): 73–88; Kristie S. Fleckenstein, "Animating Archive and Artifact: An (Anti)Suffrage Caricature in Its Visual Media Ecology," *Peitho* 17, no. 1 (2014): 14–30; and Jim Ridolfo, "Delivering Textual Diaspora: Building Digital Cultural Repositories as Rhetoric Research," *College English* 76, no. 2 (2013): 136–51.

3. Tarez Samra Graban and Shirley K. Rose, eds., "The Critical Place of the Networked Archive," special issue, *Peitho* 17, no. 1 (2014).

4. Graban and Rose.

5. Fleckenstein, "Animating Archive and Artifact," 27.

6. Fleckenstein, 14.

7. Sarah L. Skripsky, "Rereading McCutcheon's Suffrage Plots: Rising Action in the Digital Archive," *Peitho* 17, no. 1 (2014): 46–59.

8. Skripsky, 54.

9. Skripsky, 52.

10. John Hawkins, "There Is No Such Thing as a Glass Ceiling in the Blogosphere," *Right Wing News* (blog), April 12, 2004, https://www.rightwingnews.com.

11. John Hawkins, "Feminist Tweakage in the Blogosphere Version 3.0—The Final Chapter!" *Right Wing News* (blog), April 30, 2004, https://www.rightwingnews.com.

12. Dean Esmay, comment on "Why Don't Chicks Blog?," *Dean's World* (blog), December 18, 2004, http://www.deanesmay.com (site discontinued).

13. Reg, comment on "Women and Blogging," *Political Animal* (blog), February 22, 2005, https://washingtonmonthly.com/political-animal.

14. Betty Friedan, *The Feminine Mystique* (New York: W. W. Norton, 2001), 84.

15. Friedan, 100.

16. Katherine, comment on "Gender and Blogging," *Crooked Timber* (blog), December 18, 2004, http://crookedtimber.org.

17. zoe kentucky, comment on "Women's Opinions," *Political Animal* (blog), February 22, 2005, https://washingtonmonthly.com/political-animal.

18. Will Franklin, "Whither the Female Bloggers?" *WILLisms* (blog), February 22, 2005, http://www.willisms.com.

19. Terry Papillon, "Isocrates' Techne and Rhetorical Pedagogy," *Rhetoric Society Quarterly* 25, no. 1 (1995): 152.

20. For more, see Nancy J. Chodorow, *The Reproduction of Mothering: Psychoanalysis and the Sociology of Gender* (Los Angeles: University of California Press, 1978); Sara Ruddick, *Maternal Thinking: Towards a Politics of Peace* (Boston: Beacon Press, 1989); and Andrea O'Reilly, *From Motherhood to Mothering: The Legacy of Adrienne Rich's "Of Woman Born"* (Albany: State University of New York Press, 2004).

21. MinuteMan, "Ain't No Way to Treat a Lady," *Just One Minute* (blog), September 9, 2002, http://justoneminute.blogspot.com.

22. Laura McKenna, "Why Don't More Women Have Political Blogs?" *Apt. 11D* (blog), March 12, 2004, http://apartment11d.blogspot.com.

23. Rivka, comment on "Gender and Blogging," *Crooked Timber* (blog), December 19, 2004, http://crookedtimber.org.

24. Karen M., comment on "Irony and Kevin Drum," *La Shawn Barber's Corner* (blog) February 23, 2005, http://lashawnbarber.com.

25. Leila Abu-Saba, comment on "Women's Opinions," *Political Animal* (blog), February 20, 2005, https://washingtonmonthly.com/political-animal.

26. La Lubu, comment on "Oh, Not Again! And a Month Early," *The Countess* (blog), February 21, 2005, http://trishwilson.typepad.com.

27. Seyla Benhabib, "Models of Public Space: Hannah Arendt, the Liberal Tradition, and Jürgen Habermas," in *Habermas and the Public Sphere*, ed. Craig Calhoun (Cambridge: MIT Press, 1993), 72–98.

28. Susan S., comment on "X Chromosome Blogging," *Political Animal* (blog), June 4, 2004, https://washingtonmonthly.com/political-animal.

29. catjo, comment on "The Blogosphere," *Political Animal* (blog), June 3, 2004, https://washingtonmonthly.com/political-animal.

30. elfy, comment on "'Where Are the Women Bloggers' Mystery Revealed," *Feministing* (blog), February 22, 2005, http://feministing.com.

31. Shelley Powers, comment on "Women's Opinions," *Political Animal* (blog), February 20, 2005, https://washingtonmonthly.com/political-animal.

32. Leigh Anne Wilson, untitled post, *One Good Thing* (blog), January 29, 2005, http://buggydoo.blogspot.com.

12

Mikki Kendall, Ida B. Wells, and #SolidarityIsForWhiteWomen

Women of Color Calling Out White Feminism in the Nineteenth Century and the Digital Age

PAIGE V. BANAJI

IN 1894, IDA B. WELLS was in Great Britain campaigning against lynching when she was asked about the support her campaign had received from Frances Willard, the internationally known social reformer and president of the Woman's Christian Temperance Union (WCTU) in the United States. Wells answered truthfully, that Willard was not supportive of her antilynching campaign. As Wells described later in her autobiography, "I replied that the only public expression about which I knew [by Willard] had seemed to condone lynching."[1]

Nearly 120 years later, on August 13, 2013, Mikki Kendall, a freelance writer and digital activist, began the hashtag #SolidarityIsForWhiteWomen after noticing the absence of white feminist support for her friend, a woman of color, who had been verbally attacked online by a supposed feminist ally. In Kendall's view, the episode pointed to a much larger issue: "Feminists were, once again, dismissing women of color (WOC) in favor of a brand of solidarity that centers on the safety and comfort of white women."[2]

In these stories, two women of color, separated by over a century, engage in the feminist response rhetoric of *calling out*. Wells calls out Willard, whose reputation as a progressive reformer belied her acquiescence on the issue of racial violence. Likewise, Kendall calls out the white feminists who offer solidarity only for other white women. As Wells's and Kendall's experiences confirm, white feminists, while purportedly advocating on behalf of all women, do not always acknowledge the racial, social, economic, and other injustices that women and men of color face, nor do white feminists always acknowledge the privilege that their race grants them. This issue, termed by some as "white feminism," has gained attention recently through a proliferation of related hashtags (#WhiteFeminism, #FeminismIsForWhiteWomen, #Intersectionality, #SolidarityIsForWhiteWomen); however, while the term is new, the issue is not.

This practice of calling out white feminism has a long history within feminism. Other examples include Sojourner Truth's famous question "Aren't I a woman?" and Frances Ellen Watkins Harper's 1866 speech "We Are All Bound Up Together," in which Harper exclaimed, "I tell you that if there is any class of people who need to be lifted out of their airy nothings and selfishness, it is white women of America."[3] During the second wave of feminism, the Combahee River Collective formed as a response to white feminism. In a statement published in 1977, they claimed, "Black, other Third World, and working women have been involved in the feminist movement from its start, but both outside reactionary forces and racism and elitism within the movement itself served to obscure their participation."[4] This sentiment was put more bluntly by Audre Lorde, who, in her "Open Letter to Mary Daly," asked, "Mary, do you ever really read the work of Black women?"[5] These rhetorical responses to white feminism were echoed in the landmark black feminist collection *This Bridge Called My Back: Writings by Radical Women of Color* (1981), which, as Bethany Mannon argues in this collection, used personal narrative to counter the second wave's focus on white, middle-class women's experiences. These writings responded to white feminism and planted the seeds of third wave feminism, which, emerging a decade later, would seek to be more inclusive. Yet, as is clear through Kendall's experience, the third wave promise of inclusivity has not been fully realized. The issue of white feminism persists.

This chapter seeks to examine white feminism and the interventions made therein by Wells during the late nineteenth century and Kendall in the twenty-first century. Although there are many examples of women of color calling out white feminism throughout history, a comparative analysis of Wells's and Kendall's rhetorics offers particularly keen insights into the recalcitrant issue of white feminism. Kendall's hashtag, #SolidarityIsForWhiteWomen, demonstrates that white feminism is not merely the erasure of women of color's experiences but also the upholding of solidarity for white women *at the expense* of women of color. When juxtaposed with Wells's antilynching rhetoric—which demonstrated how the protection of white women led to racial violence—the white feminist practice of exclusive solidarity is revealed as deeply disturbing.

Like the other authors in this collection, I employ a Rhetorical Transversal Methodology (RTM) to examine the ways white feminism and rhetorical responses thereto cut across temporal divides. Informing my methodology is Krista Ratcliffe's theory of rhetorical listening.[6] Ratcliffe envisions rhetorical listening as a means to "facilitate cross-cultural communication"; I argue that rhetorical listening can also facilitate cross-historical understanding. As Ratcliffe explains, to listen rhetorically, we must "stan[d] under discourses . . . letting discourse wash over, through, and around us and then letting them lie there to inform our politics and ethics."[7] Applying this practice to a cross-historical comparative analysis would entail "standing under" discourses separated by time, listening for the tensions and resonances between them, acknowledging the "(un)conscious presences, [and] absences" that have persisted over time.[8] Further, to listen rhetorically, we must proceed from a logic of accountability, which Ratcliffe defines in terms of an understanding of the relationship between past and present. To "proceed from an accountability logic" is to "focu[s] on the present, with attention paid to the resonances of the past."[9] For feminists to act according to an accountability logic would mean that we acknowledge "how all of us are, at present, culturally implicated in effects of the past (via our resulting privileges and/or their lack)." Accountability logic necessitates an understanding of a history of privilege that informs our own "accountability for what we do about situations now, even if we are not responsible for their origins."[10]

Using rhetorical listening cross-historically, one can uncover persistent assumptions about race and gender that undergird current debates and divisions within feminism. Moreover, listening rhetorically is a practice that often precedes the rhetorical response of calling out. Feminists of color today, like Kendall, read the words and actions of white feminism through the lens of history, and it is through an understanding of the troubling historical legacy undergirding white feminist rhetorics that they expose the problematics of white feminism. Likewise, rhetorical listening is necessary for white feminists if they are going to avoid the perils of white feminism. In order for feminists to move beyond their divisions, we all must better understand and more transparently acknowledge the troubling history that sometimes shapes current feminist rhetorical practices.

In the discussion that follows, I use rhetorical listening to examine the recurring issue of white feminism that both Wells and Kendall seek to expose. First, I examine the ways Kendall's viral hashtag #SolidarityIsForWhiteWomen initiates a collective discussion about the prioritization of white women's comfort and safety over that of women of color. Then I analyze Wells's antilynching campaign, in which she offers an incisive deconstruction of what could be considered the most disturbing manifestation of "solidarity is for white women": the rape myth used to justify lynch law. Both Kendall and Wells use calling out as a rhetoric of response to expose and amplify troubling assumptions within feminism, and (in the penultimate section) I look at these assumptions as they are deployed by white feminists then and now. Finally, I propose calling out and listening as feminist rhetorical strategies necessary for healing divides within feminism. As feminists, we need to call out feminism when it fails to live up to its own standards. At the same time, we need to listen to our rhetorical choices for troubling assumptions, and we need to listen without defensiveness to the critiques of others when our rhetorical choices are called out.

#SOLIDARITYISFORWHITEWOMEN GOES VIRAL

Mikki Kendall describes herself as "a writer, diversity consultant, and occasional feminist." An avid Twitter user and blogger, she writes about issues relating to "intersectionality, policing, gender, and sexual assault," and when her hashtag #SolidarityIsForWhiteWomen went viral, she was thrust into the limelight of digital feminism.[11] When she began the hashtag, it was personal. A friend, Sydette Harry, had been verbally attacked online by former Pasadena City College professor Hugo Schwyzer. Widely known in the feminist blogosphere as a "male feminist," Schwyzer admitted to charges of sexual harassment in 2013. He also admitted to targeting and verbally attacking women of color online. Kendall was incensed by the reaction of prominent digital feminists like Jill Filipovic (of *Feministe*) and Jessica Valenti (of *Feministing*), who are both white, and who were reluctant to condemn Schwyzer when women of color had been criticizing his hypocrisy and racism for years. Kendall argued that Filipovic and Valenti were "complicit in allowing Hugo Schwyzer to build a platform," and they did not "express regret or condemnation for his impact on . . . the women of color he has 'trashed' over the years."[12]

Kendall explained #SolidarityIsForWhiteWomen and its impetus in an online article for the *Guardian*, in which she described the Schwyzer scandal as "the catalyst" for the hashtag. However, as her article makes clear, her hashtag "is about a crucial debate, not a phony professor's meltdown."[13] The Twitter thread that launched #SolidarityIsForWhiteWomen began on August 12, 2013,[14] when Kendall (@Karnythia) commented on a conversation between Harry (@Blackamazon) and Filipovic:

> Convo between @Blackamazon & @JillFilipovic = "your abuser got traction from me until I felt unsafe, so what?" #SolidarityIsForWhiteWomen

> Oh honey, your safety as @Blackamazon was always secondary to @JillFilipovic's comfort. Because #SolidarityIsForWhiteWomen

After two tweets focusing specifically on Harry and Filipovic, Kendall wrote, "I feel a moment coming on . . . Let us commence discussing all the ways that #SolidarityIsForWhiteWomen."

Kendall begins the discussion, tweeting, "#SolidarityIsForWhiteWomen when there is more concern for their tears & comfort than the safety of WOC." With her next tweets she brings in examples—both specific and general—of exclusionary white women's solidarity: the lack of media coverage of the death of Rekia Boyd, a black woman who was shot and killed by an off-duty police officer in Chicago just two months prior; Native American rape victims, whose experiences are ignored and not included in "discussions of #rapeculture"; feminist discussions of misogyny in music that ignore songs like "Brown Sugar" by the Rolling Stones, which capitalizes on a racist misogyny against black women.

Kendall's hashtag went viral as other women contributed to the discussion. In just four days, 75,465 tweets bore the #SolidarityIsForWhiteWomen hashtag.[15] Through the hashtag, Twitter users built a collective argument against white feminism, and they offered evidence to substantiate a variety of supporting claims. A number of users pointed to Miley Cyrus's recent Video Music Awards (VMA) performance in August 2013 as an example of the double standards held for white women: "Miley sticks middle finger up in pics, smokes & wears grills = just her being a kid. Trayvon does it = hes a thug #SolidarityIsForWhiteWomen" (@mixdgrlproblems). Others pointed to evidence of cultural insensitivity and paternalism. Farah (@RoadtoPalestine) wrote, "#SolidarityIsForWhiteWomen is when Femen gets to decide the Muslim women's attire."[16] In other tweets, women of color revealed ways that feminists ignore how both gender and race contribute to oppression. Rania Khalek (@RaniaKhalek) wrote, "#SolidarityIsForWhiteWomen when convos about gender pay gap ignore that white women earn higher wages than black, Latino, and Native men." Likewise, Renee Bracey Sherman (@RBraceySherman) wrote, "#SolidarityIsForWhiteWomen = fighting for #reprorights but saying nothing ab shackling of pregnant & forced sterilization incarcerated WOC." Finally, many of the tweets suggested the complicity of white women in racial oppression. Solidarity is for white women, Kendall (@Karnythia) tweeted, "when you ignore the culpability of white women in lynching, Jim Crow, & modern day racism."

The hashtag #SolidarityIsForWhiteWomen invited women of color to respond collectively to white feminism. By definition, a hashtag is simply a label used to help identify data and facilitate searches. However, on Twitter, hashtags are visible and user driven, and they serve a social function. As linguist Michele Zappavigna explains, a hashtag "presupposes a virtual community of interested listeners who are actively following this keyword or who may use it as a search term."[17] Further, I would argue that the hashtag, in addition to "presuppos[ing] a virtual community," functions as a marker of a conversation and an invitation for users to join the conversation. Kendall (@Karnythia) made her invitation obvious when she tweeted, "Let us commence discussing all the ways that #SolidarityIsForWhiteWomen." Moreover, unlike other related hashtags—for example, #WhiteFeminism or #Intersectionality—#SolidarityIsForWhiteWomen is both a complete sentence and a claim. Thus, users responding to Kendall's hashtag were prompted to engage in a collective rhetoric as each supplied evidence to support Kendall's claim. Under the hashtag #SolidarityIsForWhiteWomen, women of color on Twitter proffered a very convincing case against white feminism as they exposed double standards, hypocrisy, paternalism, the exclusion of women of color, and myopia on issues of race within prominent feminist discourses. Through their collective calling out, they revealed the complicity of white feminists in the reification of racist stereotypes and the persistence of racialized oppression.

WELLS'S ANTILYNCHING RHETORIC

In many ways, the hashtag #SolidarityIsForWhiteWomen describes the critique Wells launched against lynching in the late nineteenth century. Lynching in the South against black Americans had been steadily increasing since the Civil War, peaking in 1892, the year Wells began her campaign.[18] Wells's antilynching writings, while certainly powerful condemnations of lynching, were also broader social critiques that revealed how stereotypes of gender and race contributed to racial violence. In particular, Wells's antilynching rhetoric demonstrated how white women were falsely positioned as victims of sexual assault in a narrative justifying violent acts against black Americans. Wells revealed that, in the post-Reconstruction South, solidarity was for white women. When they cried rape, a lynch mob would rally and commit acts of violence purportedly to secure justice. Solidarity was for white women—but not for women of African descent who had long endured sexual violence perpetrated against them by white men.

The rape myth used to justify lynch law was so deeply ingrained that even Wells, who was outspoken on issues of racism before launching her antilynching campaign, had quietly acquiesced to the inevitability of lynching. As she admits in her autobiography, she, "like many another person who had read of lynching in the South . . . had accepted the idea meant to be conveyed—that although lynching was irregular and contrary to law and order, unreasoning anger over the terrible crime of rape led to the lynching."[19] However, in 1892, an event occurred in her hometown of Memphis that compelled her to start asking questions. On March 9, Wells's friends Calvin McDowell, Will Stewart, and Thomas Moss were the victims of a lynch mob. The three men had been arrested on dubious charges of shooting at "officers of the law." In the night, McDowell, Stewart, and Moss were stolen out of their jail cells by an angry mob, taken outside of town, and "horribly shot to death."[20] McDowell, Stewart, and Moss were respectable members of the community and co-owners of the People's Grocery. Wells recognized that their murders were in retaliation for their success as business owners and the competition their grocery store brought to white-owned businesses. The lynching of McDowell, Stewart, and Moss, "opened [her] eyes to what lynching really was. An excuse to get rid of Negroes who were acquiring wealth and property and thus keep the race terrorized and 'keep the nigger down.'"[21] The event prompted her to launch a systematic investigation of lynching.

After the first three months of her research, Wells discovered that "every case of rape reported in that three months became such only when it became public."[22]

Her discoveries cast doubt on the idea that the crime of rape was the reason for lynching. She wrote the following editorial in her newspaper, the *Free Speech*:

Eight Negroes lynched since last issue of the *Free Speech*, one at Little Rock, Ark., last Saturday morning where the citizens broke (?) into the penitentiary and got their man; three near Anniston, Ala., one near New Orleans; and three at Clarksville, Ga., the last three for killing a white man, and five on the same old racket—the new alarm about raping white women. The same programme of hanging, then shooting bullets into the lifeless bodies was carried out to the letter. Nobody in this section believes the old threadbare lie that Negro men assault white women. If Southern white men are not careful, they will over-reach themselves and public sentiment will have a reaction; a conclusion will then be reached which will be very damaging to the moral reputation of their women.[23]

As Jacqueline Jones Royster argues, this editorial "was incredibly bold, even for an outspoken journalist, because of what it suggested about the 'truth' of lynching. . . . The unstated question was, 'If assaulting white women is a threadbare lie, then what might the truth be?'"[24] The answer was that white women were far from innocent victims. As Wells proved, white women were rarely the victims of sexual assault in these cases. Often they were involved in consensual relationships with the black men who were lynched, often they lied about their relationships in order to preserve their own reputations, and sometimes they participated directly in the lynch mobs. To make this case, Wells provided her audience with a proliferation of carefully narrated vignettes about white women's consensual affairs with black men and their complicity in racial violence. Each story was told with precision, accuracy, and detail; the result was a disturbing account of lynch law in the South.

Royster argues that Wells's case against lynching revealed several deeply ingrained race and gender stereotypes: "White women were pure, virginal, and uninterested in sexual pleasure. They needed and deserved protection. African American women were wanton, licentious, promiscuous. White men (who had obviously engaged in sexual acts with African American women over the decades, given the range of skin colors among African Americans) could not be accused of raping 'bad' women. 'Bad,' amoral women did not need or deserve protection. . . . African American men were lustful beasts who could not be trusted in the company of 'good' women, white women."[25] These stereotypes bolstered the rape myth used to justify lynch law. White women were venerated as pure and virginal. The preservation of this image of white woman from the perceived licentious clutches of black men necessitated the swift, summary justice provided by lynch mobs. Venerated white womanhood was the justification for mob violence.

Unlike Kendall, Wells did not have the affordances of a social media plat-form to deliver her message; however, she was enabled by developments in print technology and an emerging print culture. In late nineteenth-century and early twentieth-century America, "thousands of small presses sprang to life, providing critical outlets for voices raised in social protest, racial and ethnic pride, or ar-tistic experimentation."[26] Jean Marie Lutes argues that the black press was espe-cially noteworthy during this time, launching over twelve hundred newspapers between 1895 and 1915.[27] Wells was a central figure in the rise of black print culture. She edited the Memphis *Evening Star*, and when she was forced to leave Memphis as a result of her editorial in the *Free Speech*, she began writing regu-lar columns in the *New York Age*.[28] Wells used the press as a vehicle to spread her antilynching message, and this effort invited a collective response from other women. It was through her editorials in the *New York Age* that Wells reached prominent black women such as Victoria Earle Matthews and Maritcha Lyons, who invited Wells to give a speech at the Lyric Hall in New York City for 250 black women from across three states.[29] The event raised the money necessary for Wells to publish her first pamphlet, the 1892 *Southern Horrors: Lynch Law in All Its Phases*. Inspired by Wells's speech, Matthews and Lyons formed the Wom-en's Loyal Union of New York and Boston to organize against lynch law and act on behalf of racial uplift. Similarly, Wells's antilynching campaign prompted Josephine St. Pierre to begin the Women's Era Club of Boston.[30] Through the newspaper, her speaking engagements, and her pamphlets, Wells circulated her message, which prompted other black women to organize around her cause.

WHITE FEMINISM, THEN AND NOW

While the truth of Wells's incisive analysis of race and gender prompted black women to organize, her antilynching rhetoric proved a bitter pill to swallow for some white feminists. An illustrative example of the white feminist back-lash against Wells's antilynching campaign was the criticism Wells received from Frances Willard. In their rhetorics of reform, feminists of Wells's era often re-lied on notions of white women as virtuous and morally superior to their male counterparts. As Bonnie J. Dow explains, the rhetoric of Willard "reinforced be-lief that the ascribed feminine characteristics of love, tenderness, forgiveness, and superior morality were the antidote to the sickness created by a ruthless, imper-sonal, competitive, and often brutal outside world."[31] The facts of Wells's anti-lynching case clashed with these notions, and it proved easier for women re-formers to accept the more commonly held belief that black men were a threat to white women than to tackle their problematic conceptions of white womanhood.

In her address to the 1894 WCTU Convention, Willard declared, "It is my firm belief that in the statements made by Miss Wells concerning the white women having taken the initiative in nameless acts between the races she has put an imputation upon half the white race in this country that is unjust, and save in the rarest exceptional instances, wholly without foundation."[32] Temperance women, like Willard, often accepted the rape myth as truth. When this acceptance was coupled with the popular negative stereotypes of black men as sexually aggressive and prone to alcohol abuse, temperance rhetoric became a racist rhetoric, as the words of Willard illustrate: "the problems on their [i.e., white Southerners'] hands is [sic] immeasurable. The colored race multiplies like the locusts of Egypt. The grog-shop is its center of power. 'The safety of woman, of childhood, of the home, is menaced by a thousand localities of this moment, so that the men dare not go beyond the sight of their own roof-tree.'" Appropriating the language of the Bible to compare black men to the plagues on Egypt, Willard employs racist stereotypes to further her temperance argument that men's corruption through alcohol threatened "the safety of woman, of childhood, and of the home."[33]

The WCTU passed an antilynching resolution in 1893. However, such a move was undermined by Willard's continued belief in the rape myth that justified lynching. In her 1893 presidential address at the national WCTU convention, she states, "Our duty to the colored people have [sic] never impressed me so solemnly as this year when the antagonism between them and the white race have [sic] seemed to be more vivid than at any previous time, and lurid vengeance has devoured the devourers of women and children." Although she condemned lynching as lurid vengeance, Willard still believed that black men were "the devourers of women and children."[34] In order for her to renounce the rape myth, Willard would have to relinquish her assumptions about white womanhood and black men. However, she remained blind to the ways that her understanding of race and gender connected to racial violence.[35]

Unfortunately, the gender and race stereotypes informing lynch law still circulate today, even within feminist discourse. Hashtags such as #SolidarityIsForWhiteWomen provide women of color with a way to call out the so-called feminists who employ these stereotypes. For example, Kendall demonstrated how Taylor Swift's 2010 VMA performance, a direct response to Kanye West's stealing the stage during her acceptance of a VMA the year before, is a "coded message" about "the idea of white people feeling violated by black people 'not knowing their place.'" As Kendall wrote, "if this is what happens when someone is rude to a white woman in public, we really haven't come past race at all. Not even a little bit."[36] Likewise, Kendall and other digital feminists of color criticized the creator and star of *Girls*, Lena Dunham, who said that when Odell Beckham Jr. was seated next to her at the 2016 Met Gala, "he looked at me and he determined I was not the shape of a woman by his standards. . . . The vibe was very much like, 'Do I want to fuck it?'"[37] Dunham may have been trying to criticize the objectification of women's bodies and unrealistic standards of beauty often on display at entertainment industry events like the Met Gala; however, her words also revealed the persistence of racist stereotypes that paint black men as sexually deviant and white women as objects of black male lust. Some feminists of color compared Dunham's account of Beckham to the 1955 lynching of Emmett Till, whose accuser admitted in January 2017 that her story about Till's sexual advances was false. In a retweet of the news about Till's accuser, one woman wrote, "This is why Lena Dunham's fantasy about Odell Beckham at the Met Gala is problematic aka people have gotten killed over these kinds of LIES!" (@bevysmith, March 1, 2017). As the tweet succinctly explains, Dunham's account of Beckham reified the same stereotypes unpacked by Wells as underlying the rape myth used to justify lynch law.[38]

By calling out Willard, Swift, and Dunham, feminists of color reveal that white feminism is not simply a matter of white feminists excluding women of color. This issue is persistent and important, but the above examples further reveal the deployment of problematic stereotypes to support purportedly feminist arguments. Willard, Swift, and Dunham rely on conceptions of white women as pure and innocent and black men as sexually deviant; they fail to listen rhetorically to their own rhetorical choices, and feminists of color, who hear these ideological tensions, rightfully call them out.

CALLING OUT AND LISTENING

To improve the health of feminist discourse, I argue that calling out and listening are necessary rhetorics of response to white feminism. To call out involves making uncomfortable truths known and relevant. Wells explained that the goal of her rhetorical endeavors was "to tell the whole truth."[39] In her analysis of Wells's antilynching rhetoric, Shirley Wilson Logan argues Wells used detailed description and repeated examples to "evoke the strong presence" of the issue of lynching and bring it to the attention of "audiences geographically and emotionally removed."[40] Logan draws from Chaïm Perelman and Lucie Olbrechts-Tyteca's definition of rhetorical presence, which they describe as "the displaying of certain elements on which the speaker wishes to center attention in order that they may occupy the foreground of the hearer's consciousness."[41] As Logan argues, "with subjects like lynching, invoking presence was especially important since that which is suppressed becomes very easy to ignore, dehumanize, and rationalize. Presence prevents such suppression because it is not an abstract philosophical construction."[42] Wells exposed uncomfortable truths, including the troubling assumptions about gender and race that undergirded lynch law's rationale and the complicity of white women in racialized violence. Moreover, she exposed these truths in concrete terms that made them uncomfortably real for her audiences.

Likewise, Kendall has exposed and brought presence to uncomfortable truths about current white feminism. On Twitter in 2013, Kendall's rhetoric was limited to posts of 140 characters, making the kinds of detailed descriptions found in Wells's antilynching pamphlets difficult to achieve; however, Twitter enables Kendall to work collectively with other digital feminists of color to bring numerous examples of white feminism to light. In an interview for *Bitch Media*, Kendall explains, "I can't say what will result from #SolidarityIsForWhiteWomen, but I do know that Twitter is changing everything. Now, people are forced to hear us and women of color no longer need the platform of white feminism because they have their own microphones."[43] Arguably, the #SolidarityIsForWhiteWomen hashtag has become a form of solidarity in itself.[44] As a result of the hashtag, women of color have come together to voice their experiences and observations. In the same way that Wells's numerous examples about white women's complicity in racial violence brought presence to the issue of lynching and the false premises on which it was based, Kendall and digital feminists of color have brought presence to the issue of white feminism by collectively voicing multiple examples of exclusion and double standards. The result is a revelation of the truth that audiences "are forced to hear."[45]

The practice of calling out among feminists of color pushes rhetoricians to revise understandings of response rhetorics. Yoos defines *rhetorical response* using the "ordinary use of the term 'to explain' to respond to most kinds of questions put to the speaker by his or her audience."[46] He conceives of rhetorical responses as addressing the *desired* needs of audiences: "They address the curiosity of audiences concerned about various matters. They address questions that an audience is wont to ask speakers about."[47] However, this pattern is obviously not the case with the practice of calling out; Wells and Kendall certainly explain white feminism and its effects, but the impetus for such explanations does not derive from the audience's desire to know or understand white feminism. Rather, through the practice of calling out, audiences are "forced to hear" explanations that make them uncomfortable.[48] The practice of calling out is informed by a power dynamic whereby the speaker, coming from a marginalized position, confronts those who are complicit in her marginalization. As Nedra Reynolds has argued, it is through this kind of confrontational rhetoric that marginalized people can claim rhetorical agency, which she defines as "not simply about finding one's voice but also about intervening in discourses of the everyday and cultivating rhetorical tactics that make interruption and resistance an important part of any conversation."[49] Indeed, calling out seems an important rhetorical tactic for resistance.

Given that the practice of calling out seeks to undermine entrenched power dynamics, it is not surprising that Wells's and Kendall's rhetorics have been met with defensiveness rather than a desire to understand. Just as Wells experienced a backlash to her antilynching campaign from white feminists such as Willard, so has Kendall, who has been characterized as divisive by some digital feminists.[50]

In "Feminism's Toxic Twitter Wars," for example, Michelle Goldberg examines the "toxicity" of Twitter as a forum for feminism, where "feminists are calling out one another for ideological offenses." Goldberg argues that digital feminists have retooled the concept of intersectionality as a mode of "tone policing" and shaming: "Online . . . intersectionality is overwhelmingly about chastisement and rooting out individual sin." The expectation, according to Goldberg, is "that feminists should always be ready to berate themselves for even the most minor transgressions."[51] Goldberg is correct that Twitter can be a vitriolic space; however, her critique replicates the very issue #SolidarityIsForWhiteWomen hopes to address. By painting women of color as divisive interlopers and bullies who invade the "safe space" of white middle-class feminists, Goldberg demonstrates that white women's safety and comfort is more important than the needs and concerns of women of color; the very argument that Kendall is a bully is a case in point for the argument that solidarity is for white women. Moreover, this discomfort, if embraced, could lead to growth within the feminist movement.

In the cases of white feminism discussed here, women fail to listen rhetorically for the problematic resonances of their own rhetorical choices, and they fail again to listen when their rhetorical choices are critiqued. Accusing the critic of being divisive does not contribute to a healthy feminist discourse, nor does being defensive in response to critiques or focusing on the "good intentions" of unwitting offenders. As Melanie Yergeau has written, "*good intentions* is often code for *the feelings of the offender matter more than the realities of the marginalized*" (emphasis in original).[52] Alternatively, rhetorical listening serves as tool for cross-historical understanding and allows the rhetor to hear the resonances of racist and problematic historical legacies in their own rhetorical choices. In particular, given the defensiveness with which some white feminists have responded to criticism, I would point to the importance of embracing what Ratcliffe describes as "a logic of accountability": "Because a logic of accountability focuses us on the present, with attention paid to the resonances of the past, a logic of accountability suggests an ethical imperative that, regardless of who is responsible for a current situation, asks us to recognize our privileges and nonprivileges and then act accordingly."[53] Likewise, this chapter has revealed a need for white feminists to be more cognizant of history, their privileges, and their sometime position as oppressors, and to act accordingly.

The rhetorical methods I have suggested here apply to all feminists. As Kendall notes: "Just as we can all be oppressed, we can all act as oppressors to someone. . . . After all, cis women can and do oppress trans women, white women have the institutional and social power to oppress women of color, able bodied women can oppress people with disabilities, and so on. Oppression of women isn't just an external force, it happens between groups of women as well." As Kendall argues, the sooner feminists confront the forms of oppression that occur within feminism, "the sooner feminism actually becomes a movement that embraces all women."[54] Rhetorically speaking, feminists can confront these realities and potentialities through the practice of rhetorical listening—listening for the resonances of problematic histories and discourses within feminist discourses—and by calling out ourselves and each other when we hear those resonances.

Notes

1. Ida B. Wells, *Crusade for Justice: The Autobiography of Ida B. Wells*, ed. Alfreda M. Duster (Chicago: University of Chicago Press, 1970), 202.

2. Mikki Kendall, "#SolidarityIsForWhiteWomen: Women of Color's Issue with Digital Feminism," *Guardian*, August 14, 2013, https://www.theguardian.com.

3. Frances Ellen Watkins Harper, "We Are All Bound Up Together," in *Proceedings of the Eleventh Women's Rights Convention* (New York: Robert J. Johnston, 1866), Black Past, https://blackpast.org.

4. Combahee River Collective, "A Black Feminist Statement," in *This Bridge Called My Back: Writings by Radical Women of Color*, ed. Cherríe Moraga and Gloria Anzaldúa, 2nd ed. (New York: Kitchen Table/Women of Color Press, 1983), 211.

5. Audre Lorde, *Sister Outsider* (Berkeley, CA: Crossing Press, 1984), 68.

6. Women of color repeatedly call for white women to listen, and it is with this call in mind that I—a white, heterosexual, cisgender, middle-class, able-bodied woman—present this comparative study of Kendall's and Wells's feminist rhetorics. These identity markers have granted me privileges to which neither of my research subjects have had access. However, my privileged status as a white woman does not mean I do not have to engage in the hard and uncomfortable work of talking about race. As Margaret Jacobsen laments, "For too long, the emotional labor that comes with talking about race has been put on people of color. It can no longer be this way." Jacobsen, "White Women, You Need to Talk about Racism," *Bitch Media*, November 14, 2013, http://bitchmedia.org.

7. Krista Ratcliffe, *Rhetorical Listening: Identification, Gender, Whiteness* (Carbondale: Southern Illinois University Press, 2005), 28.

8. Ratcliffe, 29.

9. Ratcliffe, 31.

10. Ratcliffe, 32.

11. Mikki Kendall, "About," *Mikki Kendall: Proud Descendant of Hex-Throwing Goons* (blog), accessed October 10, 2019, http://mikkikendall.com.

12. Kendall, "#SolidarityIsForWhiteWomen."

13. Kendall.

14. Except where otherwise noted, every tweet cited in this chapter was dated August 12, 2013.

15. Susana Loza, "Hashtag Feminism, #SolidarityIsForWhiteWomen, and the Other #FemFuture," *Ada: A Journal of Gender, New Media, and Technology*, no. 5 (2014), https://adanewmedia.org.

16. Qtd. in Erin Gloria Ryan, "Our Favorite #SolidarityIsForWhiteWomen Tweets [Updated]," *Jezebel*, August 13, 2013, https://jezebel.com.

17. Michele Zappavigna, "Ambient Affiliation: A Linguistic Perspective on Twitter," *New Media & Society* 13, no. 5 (2011): 791.

18. Jacqueline Jones Royster, introduction to *Southern Horrors and Other Writings: The Anti-Lynching Campaign of Ida B. Wells, 1892–1900*, ed. Jacqueline Jones Royster (Boston: Bedford/St. Martin's, 1997), 9.

19. Wells, *Crusade for Justice*, 64.

20. Wells, 50.

21. Wells, 64.

22. Wells, 65.

23. Ida B. Wells, *A Red Record: Tabulated Statistics and Alleged Causes of Lynchings in the United States, 1892–1893–1894*, in Royster, *Southern Horrors and Other Writings*, 79.

24. Royster, introduction to *Southern Horrors*, 2.

25. Royster, 30.

26. Jean Marie Lutes, "Beyond the Bounds of the Book: Periodical Studies and Women Writers of the Late Nineteenth and Early Twentieth Centuries," *Legacy* 27, no. 2 (2010): 337.

27. Lutes, 337.

28. Shirley Wilson Logan, *Liberating Language: Sites of Rhetorical Education in Nineteenth-Century Black America* (Carbondale: Southern Illinois University Press, 2008): 103–4.

29. Jacqueline Jones Royster, "A Wells Chronology (1862–1931)," in Royster, *Southern Horrors and Other Writings*, 211.

30. Wells, *Crusade for Justice*, 81.

31. Bonnie J. Dow, "The 'Womanhood' Rationale in the Woman Suffrage Rhetoric of Frances E. Willard," *Southern Communication Journal* 56, no. 4 (1991): 301.

32. Qtd. in Wells, *A Red Record*, 139. Wells quoted Willard extensively in the eighth chapter of *A Red Record*. Willard's comments here can also be found in Woman's Christian Temperance Union, *Minutes of the Twenty-First Annual Convention of the Woman's Christian Temperance Union* (Chicago: Woman's Temperance, 1894), 131.

33. Qtd. in Wells, *A Red Record*, 142. Willard made these comments in an interview with a newspaper reporter.

34. Qtd. in Ruth Bordin, *Frances Willard: A Biography* (Chapel Hill: University of North Carolina Press, 1986), 216.

35. Meagan Parker comes to a similar conclusion about the tension between Willard's adoption of true womanhood and Wells's exposure of white women's complicity in lynching. Parker argues that the Wells/Willard debate exposes competing claims to citizenship by white women and black men. Meagan Parker, "Desiring Citizenship: A Rhetorical Analysis of the Wells/Willard Controversy," *Women's Studies in Communication* 31, no. 1 (2008): 56–78. See also Carol Mattingly for further analysis of the Willard/Wells debate: *Well-Tempered Women: Nineteenth-Century Temperance Rhetoric* (Carbondale: Southern Illinois University Press, 1998), 75–95.

36. Mikki Kendall, "Taylor Swift & Kanye West: White Women, Tears, and Coded Images," *SheKnows Media*, 2010, https://www.sheknows.com (removed from website by 2019).

37. Qtd. in Kiri Rupiah, "The Problem with Lena Dunham, White Feminism, and the Apology Industrial Complex" *Mail and Guardian* (Johannesburg), September 6, 2016, http://mg.co.za.

38. Dunham later apologized on Instagram, saying she had projected her insecurities

onto Beckham and that she "would never intentionally contribute to a long and often violent history of the over-sexualization of black male bodies—as well as false accusations by white women towards black men." (@lenadunham, September 3, 2016).

39. Wells, *Crusade for Justice*, 69.

40. Shirley Wilson Logan, *"We Are Coming": The Persuasive Discourse of Nineteenth-Century Black Women* (Carbondale: Southern Illinois University Press, 1999), 74.

41. Chaïm Perelman and Lucie Olberchts-Tyteca, *The New Rhetoric: A Treatise on Argumentation*, trans. John Wilkinson and Purcell Weaver (Notre Dame, IN: University of Notre Dame Press, 1969), 142.

42. Logan, *We Are Coming*, 74.

43. Tina Vasquez, "Why 'Solidarity' is Bullshit," *Bitch Media*, August 16, 2013, http://bitchmedia.org.

44. See Daniela Ramirez, who questions the degree to which the hashtag creates solidarity. Ramirez, "Has #SolidarityIsForWhiteWomen Created Solidarity for Women of Color?," *Mic*, August 27, 2013, http://mic.com.

45. Vasquez, "Why 'Solidarity' is Bullshit."

46. George Yoos, "Rhetoric of Appeal and Rhetoric of Response," *Philosophy & Rhetoric* 20, no. 2 (1987): 111.

47. Yoos, 112.

48. Vasquez, "Why 'Solidarity' is Bullshit."

49. Nedra Reynolds, "Interrupting Our Way to Agency: Feminist Cultural Studies and Composition," in *Feminism and Composition Studies: In Other Words*, ed. Susan C. Jarrett and Lynn Worsham (New York: Modern Language Association, 1998), 59.

50. See Loza, "Hashtag Feminism," for an analysis of the white feminist backlash to Kendall's campaign.

51. Michelle Goldberg, "Feminism's Toxic Twitter Wars," *Nation*, January 29, 2014, https://www.thenation.com.

52. Melanie Yergeau, "Accessing Digital Rhetoric: Sh*t Academics Say," *Sweetland Digital Rhetoric Collective*, June 17, 2012, http://www.digitalrhetoriccollaborative.org.

53. Ratcliffe, *Rhetorical Listening*, 31–32.

54. Mikki Kendall, "White Feminism and the School to Prison Pipeline," *Mikki Kendall: Proud Descendant of Hex-Throwing Goons* (blog), December 23, 2015, http://mikkikendall.com.

13

The Persuasive Power of Individual Stories

The Rhetoric in Narrative Archives

BETHANY MANNON

GLORIA STEINEM, ELIZABETH FORSLING HARRIS, and Patricia Carbine founded *Ms.* in 1971 to create a forum for women's writing and promote legal, social, and economic equality. The first issue of *Ms.* appeared on newsstands in December 1971. In contrast to its sister magazines, whose advertising and articles perpetuated stereotypes of women as wives, mothers, and uncritical consumers, *Ms.* initiated "a new angle from which to write that began with contributing writer Jane O'Reilly's 'click! of recognition.'"[1] In this and subsequent issues, *Ms.* published readers' personal accounts of recognizing "a patriarchal society in which many assumptions remained unquestioned."[2] Readers sent in their own short personal narratives to make visible the ongoing and ingrained gender inequalities in families, workplaces, and popular cultures. A decade later, *This Bridge Called My Back: Writings by Radical Women of Color* countered the "click!" narrative's tendency to focus on white middle-class women. This multigenre, multivoiced collection, edited by Cherríe Moraga and Gloria Anzaldúa, includes testimonials, poetry, visual art, and personal essays. These acts of self-representation narrate with clarity and immediacy the writers' experiences of selfhood, and they foreground lived experience to theorize oppression and liberation.

In the twenty-first century, affective, immersive digital storytelling projects like *My Duty to Speak* continue this rhetorical practice of organizing multiple voices around activist projects, using the online space to sustain discussions of injustice. Participants understand themselves to be crafting personal testimonies that—as individual and collective narratives—have the potential to address sexism, racism, classism, homophobia, and other forms of oppression. These acts of feminist online self-representation have roots in twentieth-century efforts to collect and circulate personal narratives of women in the United States. Digital storytelling projects recall the "click!" moment; they re-mediate that moment of identification as a click of the mouse that opens a story or joins a discussion forum.

These three sets of texts—the archive of "click!" moments in *Ms.*, the multi-genre personal narratives in *This Bridge*, and the digital storytelling project *My Duty to Speak*—reveal continuities and differences between uses of personal narrative, a vital feminist rhetorical practice. All three collect and "[make] accessible materials for the purposes of research, knowledge building, or memory making," as Jessica Enoch and Pamela VanHaitsma have written.[3] All invite visitors to read and compose stories and responses, and all create meaning from the self-representations of women and girls. All make visible experiences that had previously been invisible to other feminists and to society. By doing so, they challenge dominant discourses in the United States and expand feminist conversations.

I selected *Ms.* letters and *This Bridge* among many possible archives of women's life writing from this period because these collections circulated so widely.[4] Studies of feminist writing and activism in the United States describe them as turning points, and subsequent writers and editors cite them as influences.[5] The same goal of amassing archives of narratives propels digital storytelling projects, and for this reason I chose the form as my third subject. Certainly, a personal narrative rhetoric informs other types of digital writing, like blogs and zines. However, while blogs foreground personal experience, the visions and voices of main authors—as opposed to any number of authors—animate them.[6] Brenda M. Helmbrecht and Meredith A. Love argue that the zines *Bitch* and *Bust* shape a third wave feminist rhetoric by defining readers and participants and using personal narratives.[7] Distinctively, though, digital storytelling has a sustained interest in collecting and circulating narratives, and it explicitly presents lived experience as a source of knowledge and form of activism.

I analyze *Ms.* letters, *This Bridge Called My Back*, and *My Duty to Speak* by locating continuities that point to a rhetorical strategy connecting generations of feminists. A shared regard for the rhetorical power of personal narrative links these three periods in feminist history and makes transformative dialogue possible. However, I also differentiate the forms and uses of personal narrative across these three archives. *Ms.* uncritically advocates for the telling of women's life stories and offers the "click!" moment as a framework for recognizing and recounting experiences of sexism that many men and women previously concealed or dismissed. *This Bridge* contends that the "click!" narrative conceals many stories even as it facilitates identification with others. *My Duty to Speak*, the third collection I study, uses storytelling to intervene in patterns of gendered violence within the US military. This networked online project includes more writers than the previous two and invites more readers to identify with their stories, engaging a more diffuse, ingrained feminism than the earlier collections. While scholars have noted the centrality of personal narrative in women's movements worldwide, little has been said about the ways this rhetorical practice connects generations of feminist activism.

These texts demonstrate that collections of personal narratives function in different ways but serve three goals. First, they testify to gendered violence and oppression and bring visibility to previously overlooked experiences and perspectives. Second, collections that encompass multitudes of voices give evidence of active and growing movements. Third, as a form of response rhetoric, they revisit, revise, and renew the feminist commitments of earlier writers. As Kate Eichhorn writes, "what continues to make feminism relevant to women born during and after the rise of the second wave feminist movement is precisely their preoccupation with an earlier generation's histories of struggles," and many archives of personal narratives document these struggles.[8] Viewing the relationships between generations in this way counters narratives that reinforce "the perception that contemporary feminism is irreparably marked by intergenerational conflict."[9] A feminist rhetoric of personal narrative also serves as a mechanism for addressing homophobia, classism, and racism within existing feminist discourses and movements. Such accounts have formed the foundation of feminist thought in academia, faith communities, consciousness-raising groups, popular cultures, and political coalitions. Even as practitioners trouble the nature of and politics of "the personal," these accounts of lived experiences create new knowledge. Crucially, this shared regard for life narrative facilitates a common ground for contentious but necessary discussions about limitations in feminist theories and practices.

MS. READERS AND THE ICONIC "CLICK!" MOMENT

In "The Housewife's Moment of Truth," published on December 20, 1970, Jane O'Reilly defines "the click! of recognition" as "that parenthesis of truth around a little thing that completes the puzzle of reality in women's minds—the moment that brings a gleam to our eyes and means the revolution has begun."[10] She recounts examples of such "click!" moments in her own life and the lives of women she knows: "In an office, a political columnist, male, was waiting to see the editor-in-chief. Leaning against a doorway, the columnist turned to the first woman he saw and said, 'Listen, call Barry Brown and tell him I'll be late.' Click! It wasn't because she happened to be an editor herself that she refused to make the call." Another anecdote illustrates this dynamic in a working-class family: "Denise works as a waitress from 6 a.m. to 3 p.m. Her husband is a cabdriver, who moonlights on weekends as a doorman. They have four children. When her husband comes home at night, he asks: *'What's for dinner?'*" Through such anecdotes, O'Reilly asks, "What sort of bizarre social arrangement is post-industrial-revolution marriage?" She makes a case for the "blatant absurdity of everyday life" in a society clinging to traditional gender roles.[11]

O'Reilly's article had an influence that extended into the pages of readers' letters in *Ms.* Editors received a remarkable volume of letters, which often followed a pattern that "The Housewife's Moment of Truth" established. The Letters to *Ms.* section—running as long as five pages—created a forum for readers to recount personal experiences and became a key feature of the magazine.[12] Readers shared their "click!" moments, establishing this letters section as a space to sustain a dialogue about changing gender roles and increasingly visible feminist activism. Karlyn Kohrs Campbell describes this type of feminist rhetorical practice: "Faced with constraints on what they could say and where they could say it, women developed theories of rhetoric suited to the kinds of discourse that they were permitted to use. They exploited the crevices, finding spaces in which their voices could be made effective, and they developed nuanced understandings of how to use interpersonal communication as a means to influence and agency."[13] The letter and the woman's magazine genres united to create an inviting and accessible space for stories that were otherwise rarely heard. They also participate in an alternative rhetoric, a practice that engages "the individual's subjectivity rather than attempting to erase it."[14] That engagement with subjectivity manifests in the specificity of experience, the visibility of each writer's individual perspective, and the "click!" of identification and self-recognition.

Like the rhetors Campbell studies, *Ms.* letters include "stylistic elements that [project] femininity, such as inductive structure, which increases audience agency, or the use of personal experience, the single area of expertise acknowledged for women."[15] To understand the characteristics of *Ms.* letters during the second wave feminist movement, I read the twelve issues published in 1973, the magazine's first full year. Readers' letters expressed joy at finding a new kind of women's magazine, appreciation for the topics and voices that the magazine included, and resonance with articles in previous issues. Several writers adopted the "click!" shorthand for moments of realization during reading or during their day-to-day grinds. Others spoke more broadly of the echoes between *Ms.* articles and the concrete realities of their family, work, and school lives. The Letters to *Ms.* section also invited readers to critique the magazine focus, content, and style. Many letter writers grounded their critiques in experiences that differed from the social, political, and economic conditions that seemed to preoccupy the magazine; some writers used the shorthand of a "clunk!" when an article represented women's lives inaccurately or narrowly. In this way, *Ms.* letters gave new relevance to a practice that periodicals at the end of the nineteenth century popularized.

Ms. letters adapted the feminist consciousness-raising practice, developed by Kathie Sarachild in the early 1970s, into a rhetorical strategy. Stacey K. Sowards and Valerie R. Renegar write that consciousness-raising, which involves sharing testimonies in small groups, "allowed women to recognize the connected nature of their personal experiences."[16] Sharing these testimonies in print likewise connects people and also allows readers "to explore diverse feminist perspectives that may not be available to them within their immediate circle of friends and family."[17] Sowards and Renegar show that third wave feminists adapt consciousness-raising for public audiences, but I argue that second wave writers had already adapted these small face-to-face meetings. Consciousness-raising did not "directly seek to generate social activism, protest, sisterhood, confrontation, or movement." Instead, the practice used an invitational rhetoric that offered stories and experiences to cultivate new awareness among participants.[18] Campbell's definition of rhetoric as "self-creation, as discourse through which identities emerge," describes the work of consciousness-raising groups and letter writers.[19] In letters, *Ms.* readers hoped to link self-creation and activism by connecting with other women and supporting social change. In the following decades, *This Bridge* and digital storytelling would likewise circulate writing beyond a small group and would generate personal narratives that confront oppressive ideologies.

THIS BRIDGE CALLED MY BACK

Gloria Anzaldúa and Cherríe Moraga used their status as well-known authors to create a platform for other writers in the 1981 *This Bridge Called My Back*. Anzaldúa's theory of borderlands and crossing, developed in *Borderlands/La Frontera* (1987), has had a wide influence in rhetorical studies, particularly the study of feminist rhetorics.[20] Likewise, rhetoricians have examined Moraga's theories of borders, embodied knowledge, and homelands, often alongside Anzaldúa and usually apart from the other voices in *This Bridge*. I build on these previous studies by locating *This Bridge* in a feminist rhetorical tradition of collecting personal narratives and by examining the ways that it expands and responds to the narratives of American women that *Ms.* had circulated during the previous decade.

Scholars typically describe *This Bridge* as a much-needed counterpoint to white, middle-class, mainstream feminism. However, another important facet of the project is its turn to personal narrative as a rhetorical practice, confirming and expanding the persuasive and coalition-building power of this form. Like *Ms.* readers, *This Bridge* contributors write from "an epistemic stance based on shared experience, participatory interaction in arriving at conclusions, strategic indirection in presenting evidence and argument, and conversation as the predominant mode through which influence occurs."[21] These personal narratives circulate publicly and locate knowledge in personal experiences that readers and editors believe could be of interest beyond the individual. The collection does indeed mount "a thorough challenge to the many faces of privilege" and demand "attention to the intersections of multiple facets of one's identity," but it does so through the practice of composing and circulating personal narratives that had characterized consciousness-raising groups.[22] Studying *This Bridge* reveals radical conceptions of identity and feminist struggle, as well as the crucial ways that personal narrative linked this generation of feminists to the writing and activism of the previous one.

Most strikingly, several contributors describe and reflect on "click!" moments. In her essay "La Güera," Moraga writes, "I have had to confront the fact that much of what I value about being Chicana, about my family, has been subverted by anglo culture and my own cooperation with it."[23] She pinpoints moments of realization, explaining, "it wasn't until long after my graduation from the private college I'd attended in Los Angeles, that I realized the major reason for my total alienation from and fear of my classmates was rooted in class and culture. CLICK."[24] "Three years after that," Moraga writes, "another CLICK." She describes a reading by Ntozake Shange, during which she realized, "in my development as a poet, I have, in many ways, denied the voice of my brown mother—the brown in me. I have acclimated to the sound of a white language."[25] Other contributors narrate similar moments without the explicit "click!" Anita Valerio writes of a flash of self-recognition after using "weird" in a conversation with her mother: "I recoil inside, I don't know the part of me that's said it. My stomach tingles. I feel tight. The word is dry, false—'weird.' Of course, I remember, of course I know. 'Weird' only a non-Indian would say that. Someone who doesn't know, who hasn't been raised to see that life is a continuous whole from flesh to spirit, that we're not as easily separated as some think. I knew that."[26] Narratives like Valerio's intertwine embodied and emotional valences of experience to achieve a particularly vivid quality. All are consciously autobiographical and locate social critique in self-representation.

For the Combahee River Collective, moments of realization unite "Black feminists and many more Black women who do not define themselves as Feminists."[27] *This Bridge* reprints the collective's "A Black Feminist Statement," which explains, "as children we realized that we were different from boys and that we were treated differently. . . . As we grew older we became aware of the threat of physical and sexual abuse by men."[28] However, the collective's statement also shows that the moments of realization and self-recognition central to white feminist writing and activism were more complicated for many black women. The document makes the point that racism and racial politics "still [do] not allow most Black women, to look more deeply into our own experiences, and, from that sharing and growing consciousness, to build a politics that will change our lives and ultimately end our oppression."[29] The consciousness-raising that provided an environment to connect personal experience with systemic oppressions was really only accessible to white women. While *This Bridge* demonstrates that women of color use powerful, effective personal narrative in their rhetoric, the Combahee River Collective statement argues that the conditions allowing or discouraging this rhetorical practice merit attention.

As contributors to *This Bridge* deploy personal narrative to confront racism and sexism, they also explore the limitations of consciousness-raising and "click!" moments. Amy Erdman Farrell describes the "click!" in *Ms.* as "a signifier of a changed identity, a new feminist persona," as well as "a shared vocabulary" and "a shorthand way of documenting the concerns of feminists."[30] In "Across the Kitchen Table: A Sister-to-Sister Dialogue," Barbara Smith and Beverly Smith critique the "click!" moments that *Ms.* cultivated. "There is virtually no Black person in this country who is surprised about oppression," Barbara Smith writes.[31] A portion of the dialogue contrasts race and gender oppression. In answer to the editors' questions of "What do you see as the effects of the pervasiveness of white middle class women in the feminist movement? In your experience how do class and race intersect in the movement?" the two writers raise moments of recognition as a salient difference:

> **Bev:** . . . My sense about the oppression of women is that it's something that people come to often times, but not always, in a more intellectual manner. It's something that's pointed out to them. It's something that they read about and say "Oh, yeah!" I mean, even the concept of the "click," you know, that you can read about in *Ms.* magazine.
>
> **Bar:** They still have "clicks"!
>
> **Bev:** Right. . . . Well, I mean, I guess there are "clicks" among racial lines, but the thing is they're so far back in terms of class that they're almost imperceptible. It just feels to me like it's a different kind of thing.[32]

Noting the ubiquitous, central, yet inadequate "click!" shorthand, Barbara Smith and Beverly Smith highlight a fissure between white mainstream feminism and black feminist thought and activism. Personal narrative offers a medium through which to tell stories of complex identities and intersecting oppressions and—in "Across the Kitchen Table"—exemplifies differences in the ways women of disparate social positions make sense of their lives. Barbara Smith and Beverly Smith tell stories and publicly examine the politics of storytelling, two tactics of rhetorical response that, to quote Paige V. Banaji from this volume, "improve the health of feminist discourse."

By pointing out these continuities in rhetorical uses of personal narrative, I hope that I do not erase differences in the contents and contexts of the narratives themselves. *This Bridge Called My Back* critiqued then-mainstream feminism and continues to call out racism, classism, and homophobia in feminist work. The fact that the collection was widely emulated and continues to be widely read demonstrates two important facets of personal narrative. First, *This Bridge* gained its influence by foregrounding and theorizing subjective experience. Personal narratives make women's lives visible in the public sphere; they also require white feminists to recognize the knowledge of women of color. The "click!" moment created a template for responding to normalized sexism, but writers in *This Bridge* then responded to the latent inequalities and assumptions in a practice that values individual introspection and self-narration. Not all women share the "click!" moment, but personal narrative creates a common vocabulary through which marginalized or overlooked writers successfully confront systems of power within the movement.

Second, we see how personal narrative builds a feminist archive. *This Bridge* collected, circulated, and also preserved writings that today further knowledge, research, and collective memory. Eichhorn argues that the archive is "where a younger generation of feminists have most visibly come to terms with their ressentiment towards second wave feminists" and their feeling that the most important battles took place in earlier generations.[33] Delving into archives like *This Bridge Called My Back* and the Letters to *Ms.* section figures prominently in contemporary feminists' intellectual work. As Eichhorn explains, "for women born during and after the rise of the second wave feminist movement both touching history and being engaged in its making have become part and parcel of what it means to be an engaged feminist activist, cultural worker, or scholar in the present."[34] Far from rejecting or displacing the feminist movements of the 1970s and 1980s, contemporary feminists find increasing value in connecting their activism and study to those earlier periods.

"I DID NOT OFFICIALLY ENTER HELL UNTIL I SPOKE UP": PERSONAL NARRATIVES ONLINE

In contrast to the collections of stories *This Bridge Called My Back* inspired, digital storytelling projects appear to be mobilized not by common (if contested) identities but by defined causes. As feminists increasingly see care and concern as the basis for uniting with other activists, crafting personal narratives and "clicking" links to read the stories of others plays a growing role in forming coalitions. Like *Ms.* and *This Bridge*, *My Duty to Speak* positions writers' subjectivities "within the discourses of power that enfranchise some and marginalize others."[35] The project also invites counternarratives to socially and historically imposed images of the self—here, countering narratives of masculinity, femininity, and sexual violence. This use of counternarratives illustrates two forms of response rhetorics: rhetorics that "arise in response to the conditions of power at a particular historical moment," and rhetorics that engage with audiences' questions and interests.[36] *Ms.* letters and *This Bridge* stories, as I have shown, use personal narrative—at times, counternarratives—to reveal conditions of power that marginalize women, particularly women of color. In this section, I build on those earlier discussions to theorize response rhetorics, which operate explicitly in networked digital storytelling.

My Duty to Speak (https://mydutytospeak.com/) collects stories written by men and women from all branches of the US military who survived sexual assaults during their service. Blog posts bear titles like "Airman afraid to report rape," "Coast Guard Captain calls rape survivor 'liar' and 'nut case,'" or simply "The bystanders." The posts record experiences of violence, retaliation, and indifference from authorities, portraying routine brutality and injustice within the military. At the same time, the specificity of stories—the names of bases where assaults took place and the exact nature of trauma and retaliation—builds credibility and conveys the particular lives that were violated. *My Duty to Speak* began in January 2011, and managing editor Panayiota Bertzikis and her staff continue to screen and publish stories. This archive of testimonies circulates to personalize categories of people whose experiences might previously have been visible only through statistics or third-person accounts. Indeed, Bertzikis envisions the site as a way to undermine victim-blaming perceptions of sexual assault and build support for institutional reform.

My Duty to Speak does not use the label "feminist" to describe itself. However, with its commitment to justice, equality, empowerment, and critiques of systems of oppression, the project clearly aligns with feminist thought and activism.[37] By drawing attention to systemic hierarchies and violence, the project approaches military sexual trauma (MST) in a feminist way. Further, the project aims to create a platform for women to speak, rather than speaking for them; following the precedent of a woman-owned alternative print economy, the site legitimizes "their voices in the public sphere."[38] *My Duty to Speak* highlights violence traditionally regarded as private and instead recognizes its political and public significance. In these ways, the project shows that the feminist rhetorical strategy of personal narrative serves liberatory goals apart from a stated feminist identity. The project does not aim to redefine feminism in postfeminist terms, but, like the Mormon bloggers Tiffany Kinney studies in this volume, the rhetors involved in *My Duty to Speak* chose certain media because "legitimacy is forged through social consensus . . . [and] these texts [were] easily reproduced, circulated, and distributed through material or digital means." Writers and readers meet not in an "avowed relationship" based on identity or affiliation, but rather in what Karma R. Chávez calls "a space of convening that points toward coalitional possibility."[39] The site creates a digital space for geographically dispersed users—who might not agree about other problems or questions—to experience "a coming together, or a juncture, for some sort of change" in individual and shared attitudes toward sexual assault.[40]

My Duty to Speak is one example of a proliferation of self-representation online. Other projects that collect first-person accounts and focus on gender and sexuality include *When I Came Out* (https://whenicameout.com) and *The Everyday Sexism Project* (http://everydaysexism.com). Digital storytelling projects that collect and circulate personal narratives display the influence of predecessors like *Ms.* and *This Bridge Called My Back.* They also invite comparison to personal blogs and to social media, where users increasingly view Twitter, Facebook, and Instagram as platforms for activism (examples include Me Too, the hashtag campaign #BringBackOurGirls, and the conversation surrounding the hashtag #SolidarityIsForWhiteWomen, which Banaji examines in this volume). Digital storytelling websites combine a tradition of feminist self-narration with the affordances of social media that publicize stories quickly and circulate them among wide networks of readers.

Like *This Bridge* contributors and *Ms.* letter writers, *My Duty to Speak* contributors craft personal testimonies that individually and collectively aim to change social attitudes and to counter sexism, injustice, and gendered violence. Public collections of testimonies from multiple voices function differently than do other forms of online self-representation. On the whole, they invite contributions that are longer than 140 (or 280) characters, and they develop over longer periods of time without participation spikes after related events. Not all digital storytelling projects address gender, sexism, or violence, but the many that do reveal developing alliances between online self-representation and feminist activism. *My Duty to Speak* works to set the record straight by going outside the military's judicial and medical systems to report instances of MST that authorities suppressed. A few stories name individual perpetrators and individual commanders who revictimized the survivors. Collectively, the stories portray widespread and systemic failure to carry out justice, and they cultivate responses from readers. The site, along with related advocacy groups, demands broad social change in the way gender and sexual violence are viewed in the United States as a whole and in the military in particular. The project has a more concrete institutional change in view. Bertzikis writes in her greeting to the site, posted on March 8, 2013, "as you can read from the testimonies the military response to rape is often as disturbing and horrifying as the act of rape itself." She invites readers to call their representatives and "demand better treatment for sexual assault survivors in the military."[41] Many posts speak directly to authorities' inadequate responses. Site administration supports this norm by posting news stories of offenders who received light penalties and videos of congressional hearings addressing MST response procedures.

Feminist activism and theory value narratives of lived experience, and digital storytelling projects create avenues for writers who are *discouraged* from telling their stories.[42] The men and women who contribute to *My Duty to Speak* explain that, as survivors of MST, they were initially called on to tell their stories to commanding officers. Afterward, they met retaliation. Mary Gallagher writes in "TSgt Raped at Sather Air Base Iraq," "when I finally left I went to my Commander who told that [*sic*] it is a 'he said she said.' 12yrs of service went down the drain that night. From that point on the Air Force saw me damaged goods and they told me I had PTSD and medically discharged me."[43] In the post "Raped and retaliated against in the U.S. Navy," an unnamed individual describes similar reprisals: "I did not officially enter hell until I spoke up about it and the military commands did everything in their power to distract me, discredit me, demoralize me, and destroy my once promising career as they railroaded me out of the service for political reasons."[44] Other writers report that commanders and colleagues explicitly disputed the truth of their allegations. In many instances, when cases are dismissed because of a lack of evidence, the survivor faces accusations of deceit or mental instability.

Equally often, writers express doubt that their story will be accepted as true. In "Male Recruit Raped at Basic Training," another anonymous poster writes, "Who's going to believe that a male T.I. raped a male anyway. I have never told anyone until now. YOU. this website."[45] Another post, "Coast Guardswoman writes about rape at Coast Guard in Hawaii," expresses the writer's disbelief that the experience was actually rape: "I was thinking. Did he just rape me? No. He did not. It could not have happened. I kept on telling myself that. Of course he did not rape me. I led him on and he took the opportunity to have sex with me. I actually thought that if I left that I would have insulted him."[46] Such statements reveal the degree to which survivors internalize cultural narratives about sexual assault. Many recount accusations and rumors about them that spread, unchecked by leadership. In almost all cases, those rumors constructed narratives that they were liars, culpable, or mentally and medically unfit to serve. A number of survivors recount the testimonies their assailants and commanders gave in judicial hearings or quote the written reports about their cases that were added to their records. The personal stories they submit to *My Duty to Speak* address readers' curiosities by narrating the writers' thoughts, the accusations made in private, and the details of the trauma.

Circulating stories in the public sphere plays an important part in reestablishing contributors' identities after MST. Many write of adjusting to life outside the military, forming a family, and finding a new profession. Others write of coming to realize that they were not at fault for their attacks or for their branches' reactions. These counternarratives aid in forming new identities. The majority of men and women write of undoing the influence of a culture that normalizes misogyny and sexual violence. They act against a cultural imperative to keep silent and "get over" trauma privately by writing their experiences in a forum that anyone with access to the online space may read. By doing so, writers establish themselves as no longer under the explicit or implicit control of the military culture that, many say, betrayed them.

Readers respond to these stories by aiding in the writers' common goal of reestablishing their identities. A reader who identified themself as "V" replied to "Coast Guardswoman writes about rape" in the comments section after the post: "I am so sorry this happened to you. The fact is this: YOU did nothing wrong! . . . I wish you had been able to report this without fear of repercussions, but I know how that goes too. I was raised military, as an AF Brat. I saw too many of my active duty friends suffer the way you have."[47] The writer of "Coast Guardswoman" appears to ask for affirmation that she was not at fault and that her experience is not unusual—and responders declare both. This anonymous writer concludes her post by explaining that she has met with a counselor whose treatment will not show up in her records; she does not want to be labeled as a rape victim; and she is continuing with her service. "Because rape culture is built upon premises of feminine vulnerability," Valerie Wieskamp argues, "it is not enough to indicate the systemic causes of sexual violence; stories must also highlight survivors' strengths."[48] This project empowers survivors in part because it provides opportunities for writers to claim those strengths and opportunities for readers to affirm them.

I read "Coast Guardswoman" as a self-aware narrative, conscious of readers' curiosity, their familiarity with cultural narratives that blame survivors for sexual assault, and their desires to act on the empathic connections the stories evoke. The site's personal narrative archive enacts the response rhetoric that George Yoos theorizes. Personal narratives of MST "furnish audiences with the speaker's beliefs and perspectives" and facilitate readers' access to the writers' thoughts.[49] Whereas appeal "engages an audience in a context of rebuttal and counterargument" and encounters resistance, rhetorics of response "address questions that an audience is wont to ask speakers about."[50] Yoos elaborates: "We explain why we believe something, we explain our motives, purposes, we explain why we think things happened, and we explain why we think things are wrong."[51] These questions propel the acts of testimony and moments of identification in the *Ms.* letters, *This Bridge Called My Back*, and *My Duty to Speak*.

The collection of personal narratives about MST enacts response rhetorics by engaging readers, and also by inviting them to participate as responders. The dialogic nature of this project is distinct from earlier story collections; *My Duty to Speak* circulates not only the composed narratives but also the reactions of readers. Online circulation also creates several affordances: the project is able to publish a large number of stories, can do so more quickly than print forms, and can lower barriers to public writing for writers already reluctant to speak about MST. These collaborative, dynamic narrative spaces forge new identities through the exchanges between writers and readers that become possible online. Whereas publication assured *Ms.* and *This Bridge* writers that they would be heard, readers can tell *My Duty to Speak* contributors "I hear you." In this way, digital storytelling projects build on the response rhetorics that propelled feminist change in earlier decades.

CONCLUSION: SPEAKING OUT

My Duty to Speak deploys the persuasive power of individual stories to address abuses of power and failures of justice. This site, and others like it, appeals to networks outside of the judicial and political systems that fail to defend vulnerable constituents. Publishing testimonies in the online public sphere reports crimes that often go unreported and makes often silenced voices heard. These narratives form "soft weapons" that can intervene in debates and may serve to sustain concern for systems of oppression.[52] They participate in a feminist rhetoric that, as Kinney writes in this volume, avoids "dialogue where aggressive voices dominate," and instead exhorts rhetors to "invent a way to be heard." In these archives of stories, the individuality of each writer matters less than do the similarities, intersections, and points of contact that emerge from reading many stories together. The writers who tell personal stories through *My Duty to Speak* recognize a need to respond to a US culture and a military culture that dismiss their stories, and they are mobilized by the belief that speaking up elicits real effects in the world. These convictions link them to *Ms.* readers and *This Bridge* contributors despite temporal divides and changing conceptions of feminism.

Personal narratives enact rhetorical responses to conditions of power and to the claims and perspectives of others. The strategic self-narration in *Ms.*, *This Bridge Called My Back*, and *My Duty to Speak* exemplifies a personal narrative rhetoric that characterizes feminist movements and increasingly shapes public discourse in the United States.[53] James Berlin describes rhetoric as "grounded in conflict, in dissension, in disorder," and rhetoric, like feminist self-representation, is "a productive process, generating and constructing us and our context."[54] Crucially, personal narratives have been a productive way to bring dissension and conflict to the activist table. Feminist rhetorical practices have necessarily been disorderly as they work to incorporate an array of voices and construct new identities and social realities. Collections of personal narratives labor against the cultural narratives that perpetuate inequalities as well as the scripts of feminist history by which activists "highlight their distinctiveness from—and often superiority to—previous feminist movements."[55] Archives of stories instead shape public perceptions and respond to existing power structures, revealing continuities over the past fifty years of US feminist history. When writers engage in personal narrative as activism, feminist history reaches into the present.

Notes

1. Amy Erdman Farrell, *Yours in Sisterhood: Ms. Magazine and the Promise of Popular Feminism* (Chapel Hill: University of North Carolina Press, 1998), 36.

2. Ruth Rosen, *The World Split Open: How the Modern Women's Movement Changed America* (New York: Penguin Books, 2001), 212.

3. Jessica Enoch and Pamela VanHaitsma, "Archival Literacy: Reading the Rhetoric of Digital Archives in the Undergraduate Classroom," *College Composition and Communication* 67, no. 2 (2015): 219.

4. Terminology can become imprecise in discussions of life writing genres. I use *personal narrative* and *life writing* to refer to first-person narratives grounded in lived experience. Elsewhere, I follow editors and refer to individual texts as *testimonies*, *posts*, or *stories*.

5. For examples, see Barbara Smith, introduction to *Home Girls: A Black Feminist Anthology*, ed. Barbara Smith (New York: Kitchen Table: Women of Color Press, 1983), xxi–lviii; Andrea Lunsford, "Toward a Mestiza Rhetoric: Gloria Anzaldúa on Composition and Postcoloniality," *JAC* 18, no. 1 (1998): 1–27; and Cassius Adair and Lisa Nakamura, "The Digital Afterlives of *This Bridge Called My Back*: Woman of Color Feminism, Digital Labor, and Networked Pedagogy," *American Literature* 89, no. 2 (2017): 255–78.

6. Digital memoir sites share few of the formal features Carolyn R. Miller and Dawn Shepherd use to define blogs, but they do share many of the exigences and social actions that Miller and Shepherd observe. See Miller and Shepherd, "Blogging as Social Action: A Genre Analysis of the Weblog," in *Into the Blogosphere: Rhetoric, Community, and Culture of Weblogs*, ed. Laura J. Gurak et al. (Minneapolis: University of Minnesota, 2004), University of Michigan Digital Conservancy, http://hdl.handle.net/11299/172818.

7. Brenda M. Helmbrecht and Meredith A. Love, "The BUSTin' and Bitchin' Ethe of Third-Wave Zines," *College Composition and Communication* 61, no. 1 (2009): 150–69.

8. Kate Eichhorn, *The Archival Turn in Feminism: Outrage in Order* (Philadelphia: Temple University Press, 2013), 21.

9. Eichhorn, 21.

10. Jane O'Reilly, "The Housewife's Moment of Truth," *New York Magazine*, December 20, 1971.

11. O'Reilly.

12. Amy Erdman Farrell explains, "the preview issue drew in 20,000 letters from readers . . . an amazing number of letters considering that only 300,000 copies of the issue were published. Magazines with four times that publication rate average only 400 letters per issue." *Ms.* emphasized letters more than existing women's magazines did. *Ms.* included five pages in the July 1973 issue. *McCall's* and *Good Housekeeping* each had one page that month, and *Vogue* published none. Farrell, *Yours in Sisterhood*, 45, 156.

13. Karlyn Kohrs Campbell, "Consciousness-Raising: Linking Theory, Criticism, and Practice," *Rhetoric Society Quarterly* 32, no. 1 (2002): 59.

14. David L. Wallace, *Compelled to Write: Alternative Rhetoric in Theory and Practice* (Logan: Utah State University Press, 2011), 5.

15. Campbell, "Consciousness-Raising," 51.

16. Stacey K. Sowards and Valerie R. Renegar, "The Rhetorical Function of Consciousness-Raising in Third Wave Feminism," *Communication Studies* 55, no. 4 (2004): 541.

17. Sowards and Renegar, 542.

18. Sowards and Renegar, 548.

19. Campbell, "Consciousness-Raising," 57.

20. Wallace, *Compelled to Write*, 118–58.

21. Campbell, "Consciousness-Raising," 60.

22. Wallace, *Compelled to Write*, 127.

23. Cherríe Moraga, "La Güera," in *This Bridge Called My Back: Writings by Radical Women of Color*, ed. Cherríe Moraga and Gloria Anzaldúa, 2nd ed. (New York: Kitchen Table/Women of Color Press, 1983), 30.

24. Moraga, 30.

25. Moraga, 31.

26. Anita Valerio, "It's In My Blood, My Face—My Mother's Voice, The Way I Sweat," in Moraga and Anzaldúa, *This Bridge Called My Back*, 42.

27. Combahee River Collective, "A Black Feminist Statement," in Moraga and Anzaldúa, *This Bridge Called My Back*, 211.

28. Combahee River Collective, 211.

29. Combahee River Collective, 212.

30. Farrell, *Yours in Sisterhood*, 162.

31. Barbara Smith and Beverly Smith, "Across the Kitchen Table: A Sister-to-Sister Dialogue," in Moraga and Anzaldúa, *This Bridge Called My Back*, 114.

32. Smith and Smith, 114–15.

33. Eichhorn, *The Archival Turn in Feminism*, 3.

34. Eichhorn, 54.

35. Wallace, *Compelled to Write*, 5.

36. James Berlin, qtd. in Theresa Enos, "Professing the New Rhetorics: Prologue," *Rhetoric Review* 9, no. 1 (1990): 28.

37. Gesa E. Kirsch and Jacqueline J. Royster, "Feminist Rhetorical Practices: In Search of Excellence," *College Composition and Communication* 61, no. 4 (2010): 644.

38. Eichhorn, *The Archival Turn in Feminism*, 15.

39. Karma R. Chavez, *Queer Migration Politics: Activist Rhetoric and Coalitional Possibilities* (Urbana: University of Illinois Press, 2013), 8.

40. Chavez, 8.

41. Panayiota Bertzikis, "Message from Panayiota Bertzikis," *My Duty to Speak*, March 8, 2013, https://mydutytospeak.com.

42. I maintain spelling, grammar, capitalization, and punctuation when I quote posts.

43. Mary Gallagher, "TSgt Raped at Sather Air Base Iraq," *My Duty to Speak*, September 13, 2013, https://mydutytospeak.com.

44. Anonymous, United States Navy, "Raped and retaliated against in the U.S. Navy," *My Duty to Speak*, March 22, 2014, https://mydutytospeak.com.

45. Anonymous, "Male Recruit Raped at Basic Training," *My Duty to Speak*, July 26, 2014, https://mydutytospeak.com.

46. Anonymous, United States Coast Guard, "Coast Guardswoman writes about rape at Coast Guard in Hawaii," *My Duty to Speak*, March 5, 2012, https://mydutytospeak.com.

47. Anonymous, United States Coast Guard.

48. Valerie Wieskamp, "'I'm Going Out There and I'm Telling This Story': Victimhood and Empowerment in Narratives of Military Sexual Violence," *Western Journal of Communi-*

cation 83, no. 2, published ahead of print, August 13, 2018, p. 7, https://doi.org/10.1080 /10570314.2018.1502891.

49. George Yoos, "Rhetoric of Appeal and Rhetoric of Response," *Philosophy & Rhetoric* 20, no. 2 (1987): 113.

50. Yoos, 113.

51. Yoos, 112.

52. Gillian Whitlock, *Soft Weapons: Autobiography in Transit* (Chicago: University of Chicago Press, 2007), 3.

53. See Ben Yagoda, *Memoir: A History* (New York: Riverhead Books, 2008).

54. Qtd. in Enos, "Professing the New Rhetorics," 10.

55. Nancy A. Hewitt, introduction to *No Permanent Waves: Recasting Histories of U.S. Feminism*, ed. Nancy Hewitt and Marisela Châvez (New Brunswick, NJ: Rutgers University Press, 2010), 4–5.

Afterword
(Techno)Feminist Rhetorical Action

Coming Full Circle

KRISTINE L. BLAIR

FEMINIST CONNECTIONS IS UNIQUE IN its efforts to triangulate three diverse modes of inquiry, the historical, the feminist, and the technological, simultaneously deploying concepts of interstitiality and intersectionality to avoid essentializing both women and feminists as universal groups. That such triangulation is necessary is evident on a daily basis as we find ourselves in a kairotic moment in which the rise of feminist rhetorical activism is increasingly digital and inherently multimodal, its roots in the historical exigencies and resulting responses of generations of feminists before us, within and across cultures. Their names are ones we often recognize today as counterpoints to the traditional Western white male canon of orators, politicians, and religious leaders, and their all too privileged rhetorical venues, from the polis to the pulpit. As I finalize this afterword in late 2018, *Feminist Connections'* publication is perfectly timed to coincide with the centennial of the 1920 ratification of the Nineteenth Amendment to the US Constitution, which granted women the right to vote. The full circle of a century represents an important opportunity, as does *Feminist Connections*, to reflect on the power of feminist rhetorics past and present to speak, write, march, and tweet against oppressive power-knowledge dynamics, to privilege voices that have often been silenced or unheard, to speak names we don't recognize but need to know.

The editors' introduction acknowledges the important collective the American suffragists represent in the history of feminism as a global social movement. Yet the collection quickly moves beyond a linear US chronology through its Rhetorical Transversal Methodology (RTM), which foregrounds transnational perspectives to document the ways in which such feminist rhetorical practices transcend context and culture and to better connect feminist historiography and digital feminism. The voices within this collection, despite their diversity of both methods and methodologies and specific feminist rhetorical case studies, question, as do the editors, "what we think we know about rhetorical practices and their emergence and reemergence in different places, spaces, and time periods."

As with the early parlor dialogues of ladies' literary societies and women's clubs in the United States, which shifted rhetorical space from the private to the public sphere, grassroots literacy practices have dominated global feminist action as women navigate and negotiate public discourse, initially conforming to the strict gender norms of the day but over time ultimately subverting and transforming them. Granted, there were often consequences for public protest, as the frequent violence against the suffragists historically attests. But even now, there are risks to speaking out, notably when those actions are undertaken individually, without the solidarity of numbers. Consider two cases: the first involves the Department of Justice (DOJ) prosecution of Code Pink activist Desiree Fairooz, whose crime was to laugh aloud during the confirmation hearing of Attorney General Jeff Sessions at the point when Alabama senator Richard Shelby praised the nominee for his equal treatment of all citizens under the law. In response to her arrest, Fairooz said, "I felt it was my responsibility as a citizen to dissent at the confirmation hearing of Senator Jeff Sessions, a man who professes anti-immigrant, anti-LGBT policies, who has voted against several civil rights measures and who jokes about the white supremacist terrorist group the Ku Klux Klan."[1] On November 7, 2017, the DOJ declined to retry the sixty-one-year-old after a judge dismissed the jury conviction.

The second case involves the example of the Akima LLC government contractor employee Juli Briskman, who was asked to resign from her position in 2017 because the photo of her, on a bicycle, flipping off the presidential motorcade as it passed had gone viral in both traditional and social media, a symbol of many women's response to the policies of the forty-fifth president and his frequent trips to his numerous East Coast golf courses. Briskman consulted an attorney, given that a male employee of Akima was only reprimanded (not fired) for use of more offensive language against liberal politics. In explaining her actions, Briskman concludes that "health care doesn't pass, but you try to dismantle it from the inside. Five-hundred people get shot in Las Vegas; you're doing nothing about it. You know, white supremacists have this big march and hurt a bunch of people down in Charlottesville and you call them good people."[2] In the spirit of digital activism and its crowdsourcing forms of circulation, a GoFundMe campaign in support of Briskman generated over $140,000 from approximately six thousand donors.

Feminist Connections makes visible such activist responses, not as isolated historical moments but as representative rhetorical resistance to networks of power that enable and constrain feminist action. To that end, the collection aligns the historical and the contemporary through the shared purpose of combating oppression, even as those outlets for self-expression span diverse modalities, from the public podium to the modern blogosphere, as Paige V. Banaji documents in her chapter on Ida B. Wells and Mikki Kendall. Yet even as we admire moments of local, national, and global feminist action in multigenre form, I would be remiss to not acknowledge the approximately 53 percent of white women who voted for Donald Trump in the 2016 presidential election, as opposed to the woman candidate for the office, Hillary Rodham Clinton, neither the first woman nor—with hope—the last to seek the American presidency. As Clancy Ratliff asserts in her chapter on the suffragist movement and early blogs, we can and should study the rise of women in the blogosphere and the extent to which early perceptions of women's activities online were diminished in a stereotypical "rearticulation of femininity" that is similar to the original suffragists' struggle to be heard and taken seriously.

These discussions by Ratliff and other contributors could not be more prescient. Consider the 2017 election night upset by Ashley Bennett, a black woman who won her race for freeholder in the District of Atlantic County, New Jersey, against incumbent John Carman. Carman incensed Bennett and others when he posted a meme soon before the Women's March on Washington: "WILL THE WOMEN'S MARCH PROTEST BE OVER IN TIME FOR THEM TO COOK DINNER?"[3] The meme included the image of a woman in the kitchen tending the stove, a form of sexist rhetoric for which Carman refused to apologize, further influencing thirty-two-year-old Bennett's decision to challenge and defeat him, though she had never held public office. The wave of women candidates in the US political system has been significant, including the first transgender statehouse representative, Danica Roem of Virginia, along with the first transgender candidate for governor, Christine Hallquist of Vermont, and the first black woman gubernatorial candidate, Stacey Abrams of Georgia.[4] Bennett's compelling example manifests the ways that misogyny, homo- and transphobia, racism, and the resulting activist responses to such rhetorics of hate circulate through social media in an era in which private thoughts become public protest as diverse women align the realities of their lived experiences against the policies and ideologies that threaten their ability to advance economically and maintain ownership of their bodies and other civil liberties.

Equally important, *Feminist Connections* chronicles the ways that feminist activism has been remixed in the digital age. Technology's ability to span time and space within and across cultures presents opportunities for more global opposition to oppression of and violence against women. Liz Lane's chapter on the Say Her Name movement responds to those moments in ways that align with both a materialist and a technofeminist approach, relying on both the African concept of *nommo*, or naming, and the classical Greek concept of *muthos*, or authoritative speech. For Lane, these hashtag movements represent contemporary forms of circulation that "employ affective discourse and borrow from historical rhetorical tactics to amplify [women's] messages in a crowded digital sphere." Similarly, Lisa Blankenship's chapter builds a theory of rhetorical empathy to the historical plight of women's domestic labor through a juxtaposition of Jane Addams's 1893 speech to the Women's Congress with Joyce Fernandes's use of Facebook to document the generational enslavement of women of color in Brazil. For Blankenship, while both Addams and Fernandes are similar in their advocacy roles, there is a marked distinction between advocacy *on behalf of* and *self-advocacy*, as women today share their stories in ways that have historically been denied them, with the need to address the inherent role of technology in circulating those narratives on a global scale. Ultimately, these and other contributors document the way in which technologies of literacy and communication have become spaces for technofeminist storytelling, responses to master narratives that reinscribe power along the axes of race and ethnicity, class, gender and sexuality, as well as other identity markers.

Given my own technofeminist agenda, I am naturally pleased to see this volume's tacit understanding that all forms of technology have gender implications, particularly in how they enable and constrain agency and embodiment. Notably, Kellie Jean Sharp's chapter analyzes competing rhetorics surrounding the advent of early birth control pill use in the 1960s and the development of HIV prevention drugs in the early 2000s. Sharp deploys queer theory and feminist rhetoric to speak back to pharmacological discourse and marketing that ignores larger material conditions of poverty and racism that result in a lack of sex education. Such work reaffirms the important task of feminism in advocating for women's rights and for a fluid conception of gender identity, as well as establishing a plurality that attends to issues of gender, race, class, and sexuality. In this way, the collection establishes a vital emphasis on multiple feminisms and rhetorics.

Another component of this plurality is the recovery of lost histories, something that occurs in Risa Applegarth, Sarah Hallenbeck, and Chelsea Redeker Milbourne's chapter on women in the workforce. In their case study of both telegraphy and stenography, they reenvision the larger cultural narrative in which feminized industrial workforces become deskilled and devalued, and they seek to recover these often forgotten contributions of women in the early days of information technology innovation. As with other chapters, these authors align the historical with the contemporary to question what has become the essentialized assumptions about women that afford them second-class status in such contexts. And lest we think the contemporary IT industry is a hospitable space for women, we have the 2017 Google diversity memo of software engineer James Damore, who argued that presumed biological differences between men and women, including women's tendency to "neuroticism" and increased stress and anxiety, "may explain why we don't see equal representation of women in tech and leadership."[5] The collection's authors actively and rhetorically combat these instances of ingrained misogyny, responding to the historical and contemporary parallels that impact women's socioeconomic well-being.

Regrettably, space constraints don't allow me to discuss all the chapters in this groundbreaking volume. Nevertheless, what I find most compelling about *Feminist Connections* is that the editors and contributors don't take the easy way out in their organizational pattern for the book, as it would be simpler (but result in a less robust collection) to solicit and frame these powerfully historicized, theorized, and contextualized conversations around chronology. Instead, past and present speak to each other throughout these pages, grounded in an emphasis on revisionist, circulatory, and responsive rhetorics that call readers to action and help us understand that despite how far we have come, current and future feminist generations must realize that it's not as far as we think or want. The news of the day in late 2018 is clear on that front, as sexual harassment in business, entertainment, and political arenas overwhelm our newsfeeds, and the US government makes appointments among those whose personal and political ideologies may soon limit women's control over their own bodies and their ability to gain hard fought equity in so many professional venues. Dr. Christine Blasey Ford's testimony in September 2018 in the confirmation hearings of Supreme Court justice Brett Kavanaugh, not to mention the response to it across the political spectrum, is a harsh reminder, as was the testimony of Professor Anita Hill in the confirmation hearings of Justice Clarence Thomas in 1991, that these struggles are ongoing and include substantial risk. Both Hill and Ford received threats against their personal safety. Ironically, it is the many women who publicly protested Kavanaugh's confirmation who have been labeled as part of a dangerous "liberal mob."[6]

Given our current moment, it's not surprising that *feminism* was Merriam-Webster's 2017 Word of the Year, a testament to the public interest in activism on behalf of women and on gender as an identity marker.[7] These feminist rhetorical practices of the suffragists then and the technofeminist rhetorical actions of digital activists now, and the many less visible and less heralded feminist interventions along the way, represent parallel kairotic moments where we must speak out both academically and politically, individually and collectively, and locally and globally, to find strength and power in our material, epistemological, and ideological plurality against an ever-present patriarchy. Rather than be silent, we must take to the page, the screen, and the streets in multimodal, multivocal, and increasingly multilingual ways. The essays in *Feminist Connections* collectively confirm that feminist rhetorical practices have come full circle as we advocate a more global conscience to better ensure a socially just future.

Notes

1. Code Pink, "CODEPINK Members Stand Trial for Intervening at Jeff Sessions Confirmation Hearing" (press advisory, April 30, 2017), http://www.codepink.org.

2. Eli Watkins and Sophie Tatum, "Woman Who Flipped Off Trump Says She Was Fired for It," *CNN*, November 7, 2017, http://www.cnn.com.

3. Ruth Graham, "This Woman Responded to a Local Legislator's Sexist Facebook Post by Running for His Seat—and Winning," *Slate*, November 8, 2017, http://www.slate.com.

4. Alan Greenblatt, "Transgender Candidate Makes History in a Year of 'Firsts' for Women," *Governing: The States and Localities*, August 15, 2018, http://www.governing.com.

5. James Damore, "Google's Ideological Echo Chamber: How Bias Clouds Our Thinking about Diversity and Inclusion," July 2017.

6. Melanie Zanona and Scot Wong, "Democrats See Hypocrisy in GOP Attacks on 'Liberal Mob,'" *The Hill*, October 10, 2018, https://thehill.com.

7. "2017 Word of the Year: Behind the Scenes," *Merriam-Webster*, January 23, 2018, https://www.merriam-webster.com.

Bibliography

Adair, Cassius, and Lisa Nakamura. "The Digital Afterlives of *This Bridge Called My Back*: Woman of Color Feminism, Digital Labor, and Networked Pedagogy." *American Literature* 89, no. 2 (2017): 255–78.

Adams, John C. "Epideictic and Its Cultured Reception." In *Rhetorics of Display*, edited by Lawrence J. Prelli, 293–310. Columbia: University of South Carolina Press, 2006.

Adburgham, Alison. *Women in Print: Writing Women and Women's Magazines from the Restoration to the Accession of Victoria*. London: Allen and Unwin, 1972.

Addams, Jane. "A Belated Industry." *American Journal of Sociology* 1, no. 5 (1896): 536–50.

———. "Domestic Service and the Family Claim." In *The World's Congress of Representative Women*, vol. 2, edited by Mary Wright Sewell, 626–31. Chicago: Rand, McNally, 1894.

———. *The Long Road of Woman's Memory*. New York: Macmillan, 1916.

———. *Twenty Years at Hull-House*. New York: Signet, 1961.

Adichie, Chimamanda. "The Danger of a Single Story." Filmed July 2009 at TEDGlobal in Oxford, UK. TED video, 18:35. https://www.ted.com.

African American Policy Forum (website). www.aapf.org.

Ahmed, Sara. *Living a Feminist Life*. Durham, NC: Duke University Press, 2017.

Alexander, M. Jacqui. *Pedagogies of Crossing: Meditations on Feminism, Sexual Politics, Memory, and the Sacred*. Durham, NC: Duke University Press, 2005.

American Civil Liberties Union (website). https://www.aclu.org.

Amor, Bani. *Everywhere All the Time* (website). https://baniamor.com.

"Announcement for 1902." *Colored American Magazine* 4, no. 5 (April 1902): 413.

Ansari, Azadeh, and Steve Almasy. "Lochte: 'I Over-Exaggerated' Robbery Story." *CNN*, August 22, 2016. http://www.cnn.com.

Anzaldúa, Gloria, and AnaLouise Keating, eds. *This Bridge We Call Home: Radical Visions for Transformation*. New York: Routledge, 2002.

Aristotle. *On Rhetoric: A Theory of Civic Discourse*. Translated by George A. Kennedy. New York: Oxford University Press, 1991.

Asante, Molefi Kete. *The Afrocentric Idea*. Philadelphia: Temple University Press, 2011.

Associated Press. "Excommunicated Mormon Kate Kelly Loses Appeal, Pledges to Continue Ordain Women Campaign." *Huffington Post*, November 5, 2014. http://www.huffingtonpost.com.

Bailey, Alison. "Locating Traitorous Identities: Toward a View of Privilege-Cognizant White Character." *Hypatia* 13, no. 3 (1998): 27–42.

Bailey, Moya Z. "All the Digital Humanists Are White, All the Nerds Are Men, but Some of Us Are Brave." *Journal of Digital Humanities* 1, no. 1 (2011). http://journalofdigitalhumanities.org.

Ballif, Michelle, ed. *Theorizing Histories of Rhetoric*. Carbondale: Southern Illinois University Press, 2013.

Balsamo, Anne. *Technologies of the Gendered Body: Reading Cyborg Women*. Durham, NC: Duke University Press, 1996.

Barrucho, Luis. "I Am Housemaid, Hear Me Roar." *BBC Trending*, August 1, 2016. http://www.bbc.com.

Bawarshi, Anis, and Mary Jo Reiff, eds. *Genre and the Performance of Publics*. Boulder: University Press of Colorado, 2016.

Beard, Mary. "The Public Voice of Women." *London Review of Books* 36, no. 6 (March 20, 2014): 11–14. https://www.lrb.co.uk.

"Become an Expert Stenographer," *Popular Mechanics*, October 1912, 33.

"Belles Lettres." *Westminster Review* 108, no. 214 (October 1877): 272–78.

Benhabib, Seyla. "Models of Public Space: Hannah Arendt, the Liberal Tradition, and Jürgen Habermas." In *Habermas and the Public Sphere*, edited by Craig Calhoun, 72–98. Cambridge: MIT Press, 1993.

Berger, Peter, and Thomas Luckmann. *The Social Construction of Reality*. New York: Anchor Books, 1966.

Bessette, Jean. "Queer Rhetoric in Situ." *Rhetoric Review* 35, no. 2 (2016): 148–64.

———. *Retroactivism in the Lesbian Archives: Composing Pasts and Futures*. Carbondale: Southern Illinois University Press, 2018.

Bhabha, Homi. *The Location of Culture*. London: Routledge, 1994.

Bierce, Ambrose. "Emancipated Woman." In *The Shadow on the Dial and Other Essays*, edited by S. O. Howes. San Francisco: A. M. Robertson, 1909. Project Gutenberg.

Biesecker, Barbara. "Coming to Terms with Recent Attempts to Write Women into the History of Rhetoric." *Philosophy and Rhetoric* 25, no. 2 (1992): 140–61.

Bizzell, Patricia, and Bruce Herzberg. *The Rhetorical Tradition: Readings from Classical Times to the Present*, 2nd ed. Boston: Bedford/St. Martins, 2000.

Black Girls Code. http://www.blackgirlscode.com.

Black Lives Matter. https://blacklivesmatter.com.

Blair, Kristine. "A Complicated Geometry: Triangulating Feminism, Activism, and Technological Literacy." In *Writing Studies Research in Practice*, edited by Lee Nickoson, Mary P. Sheridan, and Gesa E. Kirsch, 63–72. Carbondale: Southern Illinois University Press, 2012.

Blair, Kristine, and Pamela Takayoshi, eds. *Feminist Cyberscapes: Mapping Gendered Academic Spaces*. Stamford, CT: Ablex, 1999.

———. "Navigating the Image of Woman Online." *Kairos: A Journal of Rhetoric, Technology, and Pedagogy* 2, no. 2 (1997). http://kairos.technorhetoric.net.

Blake, Catriona. *The Charge of the Parasols: Women's Entry into the Medical Profession*. London: Women's Press, 1990.

Blankenship, Lisa. *Changing the Subject: A Theory of Rhetorical Empathy*. Logan: Utah State University Press, 2019.

Boileau, M. L. A. "The Lay Mind." *Magazine of the London School of Medicine for Women* 35 (October 1906): 672–76.

Bordin, Ruth. *Frances Willard: A Biography*. Chapel Hill: University of North Carolina Press, 1986.

Brake, Laurel, Bill Bell, and David Finkelstein. *Nineteenth-Century Media and the Construction of Identities*. New York: Palgrave MacMillan, 2000.

Brim, Matt, and Amin Ghaziani. "Introduction: Queer Methods." *WSQ: Women's Studies Quarterly* 44, no. 3–4 (2016): 14–27.

Brock, André. "From the Blackhand Side: Twitter as a Cultural Conversation." *Journal of Broadcasting & Electronic Media* 56, no. 4 (2012): 529–49.

Brontë, Charlotte. *Charlotte Brontë's Notes of Pseudonyms Used by Herself and Her Sisters, Emily and Anne Brontë*. Champaign, IL: Project Gutenberg, 1999.

Buchanan, Lindal. *Regendering Delivery: The Fifth Canon and Antebellum Women Rhetors*. Carbondale: Southern Illinois University, 2005.

Buchanan, Lindal, and Kathleen J. Ryan. Introduction to *Walking and Talking Feminist Rhetorics: Landmark Essays and Controversies*, edited by Lindal Buchanan and Kathleen J. Ryan, xiii–xx. West Lafayette, IN: Parlor Press, 2010.

Burke, Kenneth. *A Rhetoric of Motives*. Berkeley: University of California Press, 1969.

Campbell, Karlyn Kohrs. "Consciousness-Raising: Linking Theory, Criticism, and Practice." *Rhetoric Society Quarterly* 32, no. 1 (2002): 45–64.

———. *Man Cannot Speak for Her: A Critical Study of Early Feminist Rhetoric*. Vol. 1. Westport, CT: Praeger, 1989.

———. "The Rhetoric of Women's Liberation: An Oxymoron." *Quarterly Journal of Speech* 59, no. 1 (1973): 74–86.

Castells, Manuel. *Networks of Outrage and Hope: Social Movements in the Internet Age*. Hoboken, NJ: John Wiley, 2015.

Chaput, Catherine. "Rhetorical Circulation in Late Capitalism: Neoliberalism and the Overdetermination of Affective Energy." *Philosophy and Rhetoric* 43, no. 1 (2010): 1–25.

Chávez, Karma R. "Counter-Public Enclaves and Understanding the Function of Rhetoric in Social Movement Coalition-Building." *Communication Quarterly* 59, no. 1 (2011): 1–18.

———. *Queer Migration Politics: Activist Rhetoric and Coalitional Possibilities*. Urbana: University of Illinois Press, 2013.

Chávez, Karma R., Cindy L. Griffin, and Marsha Houston, eds. *Standing in the Intersection: Feminist Voices, Feminist Practices in Communication Studies*. Albany: State University of New York Press, 2012.

Chisholm, Shirley. *Unbought and Unbossed*. Washington, DC: Take Root Media, 2009.

Chodorow, Nancy J. *The Reproduction of Mothering: Psychoanalysis and the Sociology of Gender*. Los Angeles: University of California Press, 1978.

Cobb, Jelani. "The Matter of Black Lives." *New Yorker*, March 14, 2016. https://www.newyorker.com.

Code Pink. "CODEPINK Members Stand Trial for Intervening at Jeff Sessions Confirmation Hearing." Press advisory, April 30, 2017. http://www.codepink.org.

Coe, Richard, Lorelei Lingard, and Tatiana Teslenko, eds. *Rhetoric and Ideology of Genre: Strategies for Stability and Change*. New York: Hampton Press, 2002.

Collins, Vicki Tolar. "Walking in Light, Walking in Darkness: The Story of Women's Changing Rhetorical Space in Early Methodism." *Rhetoric Review* 14, no. 2 (1996): 336–54.

Combahee River Collective. "A Black Feminist Statement." In Moraga and Anzaldúa, *This Bridge Called My Back*, 210–18.

Cox, Robert, and Christina R. Foust. "Social Movement Rhetoric." In *The SAGE Handbook of Rhetorical Studies*, edited by Rosa A. Eberly, Kirt H. Wilson, and Andrea A. Lunsford, 605–27. Thousand Oaks, CA: SAGE, 2009.

Crenshaw, Kimberlé. "The Urgency of Intersectionality." Filmed October 2016 at TEDWomen in San Francisco, CA. TED video, 18:49. https://www.ted.com.

Crenshaw, Kimberlé, and Andrew J. Ritchie. *Say Her Name: Resisting Police Brutality against Black Women*. New York: African American Policy Forum, 2015.

Crichton-Browne, James. "The Annual Oration on Sex in Education. Delivered before the Medical Society of London." *British Medical Journal* 1, no. 1636 (May 7, 1892): 949-54.

Damore, James. "Google's Ideological Echo Chamber: How Bias Clouds Our Thinking about Diversity and Inclusion." July 2017.

Davis, Robert, and Mark Shadle. *Teaching Multiwriting: Researching and Composing with Multiple Genres, Media, Disciplines, and Cultures*. Carbondale: Southern Illinois University Press, 2007.

Dean, Tim. "Mediated Intimacies: Raw Sex, Truvada, and the Biopolitics of Chemoprophylaxis." *Sexualities* 18, no. 1/2 (2015): 224–46.

———. *Unlimited Intimacy: Reflections on the Subculture of Barebacking*. Chicago: University of Chicago Press, 2009.

DeGenaro, William. "Politics, Class, and Social Movement People: Continuing the Conversation." In *Active Voices: Composing a Rhetoric for Social Movements*, edited by Sharon McKenzie Stevens and Patricia M. Malesh, 199–211. Albany: State University of New York Press, 2009.

De Szaramowicz, Wanda. "The Woman Doctor." *Pall Mall Magazine* 52, no. 246 (October 1913): 497–506.

DiCenzo, Maria, Lucy Delap, and Leila Ryan. *Feminist Media History: Suffrage, Periodicals, and the Public Sphere*. New York: Palgrave Macmillan, 2010.

Dich, Linh. "Community Enclaves and Public Imaginaries: Formations of Asian American Online Identities." *Computers and Composition* 40 (2016): 87–102.

Dingo, Rebecca A. *Networking Arguments: Rhetoric, Transnational Feminism, and Public Policy Writing*. Pittsburgh, PA: University of Pittsburgh Press, 2012.

Donahue, Patricia, and Gretchen Flesher Moon, eds. *Local Histories: Reading the Archives of Composition*. Pittsburgh, PA: University of Pittsburgh Press, 2007.

Dow, Bonnie J. "The 'Womanhood' Rationale in the Woman Suffrage Rhetoric of Frances E. Willard." *Southern Communication Journal* 56, no. 4 (1991): 298–307.

Dudden, Faye E. *Serving Women: Household Service in Nineteenth-Century America*. Middletown, CT: Wesleyan University Press, 1985.

Durack, Katherine T. "Gender, Technology, and the History of Technical Communication." *Technical Communication Quarterly* 6, no. 3 (1997): 249–60.

Easley, Alexis. *First-Person Anonymous: Women Writers and Victorian Print Media*. New York: Routledge, 2004.

Edbauer, Jenny. "Unframing Models of Public Distribution." *Rhetoric Society Quarterly* 35, no. 4 (2005): 5–24.

Ede, Lisa, Cheryl Glenn, and Andrea Lunsford. "Border Crossings: Intersections of Rhetoric and Feminism." *Rhetorica: A Journal of the History of Rhetoric* 13, no. 4 (1995): 401–41.

Edgar, Amanda Nell. "The Rhetoric of Auscultation: Corporeal Sounds, Mediated Bodies, and Abortion Rights." *Quarterly Journal of Speech* 103, no. 4 (2017): 350–71.

Eichhorn, Kate. *The Archival Turn in Feminism: Outrage in Order*. Philadelphia: Temple University Press, 2013.

Emig, Janet, and Louise Wetherbee Phelps. Introduction to Phelps and Emig, *Feminine Principles and Women's Experience*, xi–xviii.

Enoch, Jessica. "Releasing Hold: Feminist Historiography without the Tradition." In Ballif, *Theorizing Histories of Rhetoric*, 58–73.

———. "There's No Place Like the Childcare Center: A Feminist Analysis of <Home> in the World War II Era." *Rhetoric Review* 31, no. 4 (2012): 422–42.

———. "A Woman's Place Is in the School: Rhetorics of Gendered Space in Nineteenth-Century America." *College English* 70, no. 3 (2008): 275–95.

Enoch, Jessica, Jean Bessette, and Pamela VanHaitsma. "Feminist Invitations to Digital Historiography." *Sweetland Digital Rhetoric Collective*, March 28, 2014. http://www.digitalrhetoriccollaborative.org.

Enoch, Jessica, and Jordynn Jack. "Remembering Sappho: New Perspectives on Teaching (and Writing) Women's Rhetorical History." *College English* 73, no. 5 (2011): 518–37.

Enoch, Jessica, and Pamela VanHaitsma. "Archival Literacy: Reading the Rhetoric of Digital Archives in the Undergraduate Classroom." *College Composition and Communication* 67, no. 2 (2015): 216–42.

Enos, Theresa. "Professing the New Rhetorics: Prologue." *Rhetoric Review* 9, no. 1 (1990): 5–35.

Escobar, Arturo. *Encountering Development: The Making and Unmaking of the Third World*. Princeton, NJ: Princeton University Press, 1995.

Eyman, Douglas. *Digital Rhetoric: Theory, Method, Practice*. Ann Arbor: University of Michigan Press, 2015.

"The Fair Sex and the Faculty." *Punch* 74 (January 26, 1878): 34.

Farrell, Amy Erdman. *Yours in Sisterhood: Ms. Magazine and the Promise of Popular Feminism*. Chapel Hill: University of North Carolina Press, 1998.

Fave, Richard D. "Ritual and the Legitimation of Inequality." *Sociological Perspectives* 34, no. 1 (1991): 21–38.

Filene, Catherine. *Careers for Women*. New York: Houghton Mifflin, 1920.

Fischer, Mia. "#Free_CeCe: The Material Convergence of Social Media Activism." *Feminist Media Studies* 16, no. 5 (2016): 755–71.

Fleckenstein, Kristie S. "Animating Archive and Artifact: An (Anti)Suffrage Caricature in Its Visual Media Ecology." *Peitho* 17, no. 1 (2014): 14–30.

———. *Embodied Literacies: Imageword and a Poetics of Teaching.* Carbondale: Southern Illinois University Press, 2003.

Fletcher, Andrew. *An Account of a Conversation concerning a right regulation of Governments for the common good of Mankind.* Edinburgh, 1704.

Flynn, Elizabeth A. *Feminism beyond Modernism.* Carbondale: Southern Illinois University Press, 2002.

Foss, Karen A., and Sonja K. Foss. "Personal Experience as Evidence in Feminist Scholarship." *Western Journal of Communication* 58, no. 1 (1994): 39–43.

Foss, Karen A., Sonja K. Foss, and Cindy L. Griffin. *Feminist Rhetorical Theories.* Thousand Oaks, CA: SAGE, 1999.

Fraser, Hilary, Stephanie Green, and Judith Johnston. *Gender and the Victorian Periodical.* Cambridge: Cambridge University Press, 2003.

Frederick, John T. "Hawthorne's 'Scribbling Women.'" *New England Quarterly* 48, no. 2 (1975): 231–40.

Fredlund, Katherine. "Forget the Master's Tools, We Will Build Our Own House: The Woman's Era as a Rhetorical Forum for the Invention of African American Womanhood." *Peitho* 18, no. 2 (2016): 67–98.

Friedan, Betty. *The Feminine Mystique.* New York: W. W. Norton, 2001.

Galloway, Alexander R. "'Everything Is Computation': Franco Moretti's Distant Reading: A Symposium." *Los Angeles Review of Books*, June 27, 2013. http://lareviewofbooks.org.

Garcia-Navarro, Lulu. "Photos Reveal Harsh Detail of Brazil's History with Slavery." *NPR*, November 12, 2013. https://www.npr.org.

Gates, Henry Louis, Jr. "Q&A with Professor Henry Louis Gates, Jr." *PBS. Black in Latin America*, November 11, 2015. http://www.pbs.org/wnet/black-in-latin-america.

Gebreyes, Rahel. "Patrisse Cullors Explains How Social Media Images of Black Death Propel Social Change." *Huffington Post*, October 9, 2014. http://www.huffingtonpost.com.

Gilead. "Donald H. Rumsfeld Named Chairman of Gilead Sciences." Press release, January 3, 1997. http://www.gilead.com (removed from website by 2019).

Girl Develop It. https://www.girldevelopit.com.

Glazek, Christopher. "Why Is No One on the First Treatment to Prevent H.I.V.?" *New Yorker*, September 30, 2013. https://www.newyorker.com.

Glenn, Cheryl. *Rhetoric Retold: Regendering the Tradition from Antiquity through the Renaissance.* Carbondale: Southern Illinois University Press, 1997.

———. *Unspoken: A Rhetoric of Silence.* Carbondale: Southern Illinois University Press, 2004.

Gold, David. "Remapping Revisionist Historiography." *College Composition and Communication* 64, no. 1 (2012): 15–34.

Goldberg, Michelle. "Feminism's Toxic Twitter Wars." *Nation*, January 29, 2014. https://www.thenation.com.

Gonzalez, Robbie. "Apple's Heart Study Is the Biggest Ever, but with Catch." *Wired*, November 1, 2018. https://www.wired.com.

Gossel, Patricia Peck. "Packaging the Pill." In *Manifesting Medicine: Bodies and Machines*, edited by Robert Bud, Bernard Finn, and Helmuth Trischler, 105–21. Amsterdam: Hardwood Academic, 1999.

Graban, Tarez Samra. "From Location(s) to Locatability: Mapping Feminist Recovery and Archival Activity through Metadata." *College English* 76, no. 2 (2013): 171–93.

———. "Re/Situating the Digital Archive in John T. McCutcheon's 'Publics,' Then and Now." *Peitho* 17, no. 1 (2014): 73–88.

Graban, Tarez Samra, and Shirley K. Rose, eds., "The Critical Place of the Networked Archive." Special issue, *Peitho* 17, no. 1 (2014).

Graban, Tarez Samra, and Patricia Sullivan. "Digital and Dustfree: A Conversation on the Possibilities of Digital-Only Searching for Third-Wave Historical Recovery." *Peitho* 13, no. 2 (2011): 2–11.

Graff, Richard, and Wendy Winn. "Presencing 'Communion' in Chaim Perelman's New Rhetoric." *Philosophy and Rhetoric* 39, no. 1 (2006): 45–71.

Graham, Ruth. "This Woman Responded to a Local Legislator's Sexist Facebook Post by Running for His Seat—and Winning." *Slate*, November 8, 2017. http://www.slate.com.

Greenblatt, Alan. "Transgender Candidate Makes History in a Year of 'Firsts' for Women." *Governing: The States and Localities*, August 15, 2018. http://www.governing.com.

Gregg, Hilda. *Peace with Honour*. Boston: L. C. Page, 1902.

Gries, Laurie E. Introduction to *Circulation, Writing, and Rhetoric*, edited by Laurie E. Gries and Collin Gifford Brooke, 3–26. Logan: Utah State University Press 2018.

———. *Still Life with Rhetoric: A New Materialist Approach for Visual Rhetorics*. Logan: Utah State University Press, 2015.

Griffin, Cindy L., and Karma R. Chávez. Introduction to Chávez, Griffin, and Houston, *Standing in the Intersection*, 1–31.

Grigsby, Rowan. *CrossKnit* (blog). https://crossknit.wordpress.com.

Grint, Keith, and Rosalind Gill, eds. *The Gender-Technology Relation: Contemporary Theory and Research*. Bristol, PA: Taylor and Francis, 1995.

Gutenson, Leah DiNatale, and Michelle Bachelor Robinson. "Race, Women, Methods, and Access: A Journey through Cyberspace and Back." *Peitho* 19, no. 1 (2016): 71–92.

Hackbright Academy. https://hackbrightacademy.com.

Halbert, Debora. "Poaching and Plagiarizing: Property, Plagiarism, and Feminist Futures." In *Perspectives on Plagiarism and Intellectual Property in the Postmodern World*, edited by Lisa Buranen and Alice Myers Roy, 111–20. New York: State University of New York Press, 1999.

Hallenbeck, Sarah. *Claiming the Bicycle: Women, Rhetoric, and Technology in Nineteenth-Century America*. Carbondale: Southern Illinois University Press, 2015.

——. "Toward a Posthuman Perspective: Feminist Rhetorical Methodologies and Everyday Practices." *Advances in the History of Rhetoric* 15, no. 1 (2012): 9–27.

Hallenbeck, Sarah, and Michelle Smith. "Mapping Topoi in the Rhetorical Gendering of Work." *Peitho* 17, no. 2 (2015): 200–225.

Halloran, Michael S. "Aristotle's Concept of *Ethos*, or if Not His Somebody Else's." *Rhetoric Review* 1, no. 1 (1982): 58–63.

Harper, Frances Ellen Watkins. "We Are All Bound Up Together." In *Proceedings of the Eleventh Women's Rights Convention*. New York: Robert J. Johnston, 1866. Black Past, https://blackpast.org.

Hartelius, E. Johanna. *The Rhetoric of Expertise*. Lanham, MD: Lexington Books, 2011.

Hawhee, Debra, and Christa J. Olson. "Pan-Historiography: the Challenges of Writing History across Time and Space." In Ballif, *Theorizing Histories of Rhetoric*, 90–106.

Hawisher, Gail E., and Patricia A. Sullivan. "Women on the Networks: Searching for E-Spaces of Their Own." In Jarratt and Worsham, *Feminism and Composition Studies*, 172–97.

Helmbrecht, Brenda M., and Meredith A. Love. "The BUSTin' and Bitchin' Ethe of Third-Wave Zines." *College Composition and Communication* 61, no. 1 (2009): 150–69.

Hesford, Wendy. "Global Turns and Cautions in Rhetoric and Composition Studies." *PMLA* 121, no. 3 (2006): 787–801.

Hess, Amanda. "How a Fractious Women's Movement Came to Lead the Left." *New York Times*, February 7, 2017. https://www.nytimes.com.

Hewitt, Nancy A. Introduction to *No Permanent Waves: Recasting Histories of U.S. Feminism*, edited by Nancy Hewitt and Marisela Châvez, 1–12. New Brunswick, NJ: Rutgers University Press, 2010.

Hill, Ian E. J. "Not Quite Bleeding from the Ears: Amplifying Sonic Torture." *Western Journal of Communication* 76, no. 3 (2012): 217–35.

Hill, Symon. *Digital Revolutions: Activism in the Internet Age*. Oxford: New Internationalist, 2013.

Hirsu, Lavinia. "An Overview of Digital Feminist Scholarship (2005–2014): Methods and Methodologies." Part of "From Installation to Remediation: CWSHRC Digital New Work Showcase." *Peitho* 18, no. 1 (2015). http://cwshrc.org/newwork2015.

Hoerle, Helen. *The Girl and Her Future*. New York: Random House, 1935.

hooks, bell. *Feminism Is for Everybody: Passionate Politics*. Cambridge, MA: South End Press, 2000.

——. *Feminist Theory: From Margin to Center*. London: Routledge, 2015.

——. *Talking Back: Thinking Feminist, Thinking Black*. Boston: South End Press, 1989.

Hopkins, Pauline. "Edwin Garrison Walker." Famous Men of the Negro Race. *Colored American Magazine* 2, no. 5 (March 1901): 358–66. Haithi Trust Digital Library.

——. "Phenomenal Vocalists." Famous Women of the Negro Race. *Colored American Magazine* 4, no. 1 (November 1901): 45–54. Haithi Trust Digital Library.

——. "Some Literary Workers." Famous Women of the Negro Race. *Colored American Magazine* 4, no. 4 (March 1902): 276–80. Haithi Trust Digital Library.

Hunt, Elle. "Alicia Garza on the Beauty and Burden of Black Lives Matter." *Guardian*, September 2, 2016. https://www.theguardian.com.

Idaho Semi-Weekly World. "Schools for Women Telegraphers." April 26, 1892. Image 2. Library of Congress: Chronicling America database.

International Labour Office. *Domestic Workers across the World: Global and Regional Statistics and the Extent of Legal Protection*. Geneva: International Labour Office, 2013.

Jack, Jordynn. "Acts of Institution: Embodying Feminist Rhetorical Methodologies in Space and Time." *Rhetoric Review* 28, no. 3 (2009): 285–303.

Jackson, Sarah J., and Sonia Banaszczyk. "Digital Standpoints: Debating Gendered Violence and Racial Exclusion in the Feminist Counterpublic." *Journal of Communication Inquiry* 40, no. 4 (2016): 391–407.

Jacobsen, Margaret. "White Women, You Need to Talk about Racism." *Bitch Media*, November 14, 2013. http://bitchmedia.org.

Jaggar, Alison. "Globalizing Feminist Ethics." In *Decentering the Center*, edited by Uma Narayan and Sandra Harding, 1–26. Bloomington: Indiana University Press, 2000.

Jarratt, Susan C., and Lynn Worsham, eds. *Feminism and Composition Studies: In Other Words*. New York: Modern Language Association, 1998.

Jex-Blake, Sophia. *Medical Women: A Thesis and a History*. New York: Source Book Press, 1970.

———. "Medical Women in Fiction." *Nineteenth Century* 33, no. 192 (1893): 261–72.

Johnson, Sonia. *From Housewife to Heretic: One Woman's Spiritual Awakening and Her Excommunication from the Mormon Church*. New York: Doubleday, 1981.

———. *Going Out of Our Minds: The Metaphysics of Liberation*. New York: Crossing Press, 1987.

———. "Patriarchal Panic: Sexual Politics in the Mormon Church." Presentation at the meeting of the American Psychological Association, New York, September 1, 1979.

———. *Wildfire: Igniting the She/Volution*. Albuquerque, NM: Wildfire Books, 1990.

Jonsson, Terese. "White Feminist Stories: Locating Race in Representations of Feminism in the *Guardian*." *Feminist Media Studies* 14, no. 6 (2014): 1012–27.

Jung, Julie. *Revisionary Rhetoric, Feminist Pedagogy, and Multigenre Texts*. Carbondale: Southern Illinois University Press, 2005.

Junker, Carsten. "Interrogating the Interview as Genre." In *Postcoloniality-Decoloniality-Black Critique: Joints and Fissures*, edited by Sabine Broeck and Carsten Junker, 311–27. Chicago: University of Chicago Press, 2014.

Kanai, Akane. "The Best Friend, the Boyfriend, Other Girls, Hot Guys, and Creeps: The Relational Production of Self on Tumblr." *Feminist Media Studies* 17, no. 6 (2017): 911–25.

Katzman, David M. *Seven Days a Week: Women and Domestic Service in Industrializing America*. New York: Oxford University Press, 1978.

Keating, Cricket. "Building a Coalitional Consciousness." *NWSA Journal* 17, no. 2 (2005): 85–103.

Keller, Evelyn Fox. *A Feeling for the Organism: The Life and Work of Barbara McClintock*. New York: Henry Holt, 2003.

Kelly, Gwyneth. "Travel Writing Doesn't Need Any More Voices Like Paul Theroux's." *New Republic*, September 11, 2015. https://newrepublic.com.

Kendall, Lori. "'White and Nerdy': Computers, Race, and the Nerd Stereotype." *Journal of Popular Culture* 44, no. 3 (2011): 505–24.

Kendall, Mikki. *Mikki Kendall: Proud Descendant of Hex-Throwing Goons* (blog). http://mikkikendall.com.

———. "#SolidarityIsForWhiteWomen: Women of Color's Issue with Digital Feminism." *Guardian*, August 14, 2013. https://www.theguardian.com.

———. "Taylor Swift & Kanye West: White Women, Tears, and Coded Images." *SheKnows Media*, 2010. https://www.sheknows.com (removed from website by 2019).

Kenealy, Arabella. "How Women Doctors Are Made." *Ludgate Monthly* 4 (May 1897): 29–35.

Kinser, Amber E. "Negotiating Spaces for/through Third-Wave Feminism." *NWSA Journal* 16, no. 3 (2004): 124–53.

Kirsch, Gesa E., and Jacqueline J. Royster. "Feminist Rhetorical Practices: In Search of Excellence." *College Composition and Communication* 61, no. 4 (2010): 640–72.

Knight, Louise W. *Citizen: Jane Addams and the Struggle for Democracy*. Chicago: University of Chicago Press, 2005.

Koerber, Amy. "Toward a Feminist Rhetoric of Technology." *Journal of Business and Technical Communication* 14, no. 1 (2000): 58–73.

Konnelly, Alexah. "#Activism: Identity, Affiliation, and Political Discourse-Making on Twitter." *Arbutus Review* 6, no. 1 (2015): 1–16.

Kynard, Carmen. "Writing while Black: The Colour Line, Black Discourses and Assessment in the Institutionalization of Writing Instruction." *English Teaching* 7, no. 2 (2008): 4–34.

"Lady Stenographers!" Reprinted from the *Boston Globe*. *Stenography* 1, no. 12 (December 1887): 145.

Landes, Joan B. "The Public and Private Sphere: A Feminist Reconsideration." In *Feminism: The Public and the Private*, edited by Joan B. Landes, 135–63. New York: Oxford University Press, 1998.

Lanham, Richard. "Digital Rhetoric: Theory, Practice, and Property." In *Literacy Online: The Promise (and Peril) of Reading and Writing with Computers*, ed. Myron Tuman, 221–43. Pittsburgh, PA: University of Pittsburgh Press, 1992.

Lauderdale Graham, Sandra. *House and Street: The Domestic World of Servants and Masters in Nineteenth-Century Rio de Janeiro*. New York: Cambridge University Press, 1988.

LaWare, Margaret. "Encountering Visions of Aztlan: Arguments for Ethnic Pride, Community Activism, and Cultural Revitalization in Chicano Murals." *Argumentation and Advocacy* 34, no. 3 (1998): 140–53.

Lawson, Dominic. "The One Sex Change on the NHS That Nobody Has Been Talking about." *Sunday Times*, January 17, 2016. http://www.thetimes.co.uk.

Lay, Mary M., Laura J. Gurak, Clare Gravon, and Cynthia Myntti, eds. *Body Talk: Rhetoric, Technology, Reproduction*. Madison: University of Wisconsin Press, 2000.

Light, Jennifer. "When Computers Were Women." In *Women, Science, and Technology: A Reader in Feminist Science Studies*, edited by Mary Wyer, Mary Barbercheck, Donna Cookmeyer, Hatice Örün Öztürk, and Marta Wayne, 3rd ed., 60–80. London: Routledge, 2014.

Lillie, Jonathan, and James McCreadie. "Sexuality and Cyberporn: Towards a New Agenda for Research." *Sexuality & Culture* 6, no. 2 (2002): 25–48.

Lipson, Carol S., and Roberta A. Binkley. Introduction to *Rhetoric before and beyond the Greeks*, edited by Carol S. Lipson and Roberta A. Binkley, 1–24. Albany: State University of New York Press, 2004.

Logan, Shirley Wilson. *Liberating Language: Sites of Rhetorical Education in Nineteenth-Century Black America*. Carbondale: Southern Illinois University Press, 2008.

———. *"We Are Coming": The Persuasive Discourse of Nineteenth-Century Black Women*. Carbondale: Southern Illinois University Press, 1999.

Lorde, Audre. *Sister Outsider*. Berkeley, CA: Crossing Press, 1984.

Losh, Elizabeth. *Virtualpolitik: An Electronic History of Government Media-Making in a Time of War, Scandal, Disaster, Miscommunication, and Mistakes*. Cambridge: MIT Press, 2009.

Loveman, Mara, Jeronimo O. Muniz, and Stanley R. Bailey. "Brazil in Black and White? Race Categories, the Census, and the Study of Inequality." *Ethnic and Racial Studies* 35, no. 8. Published ahead of print, September 23, 2011. https://doi.org/10.1080/01419870.2011.607503.

Loza, Susana. "Hashtag Feminism, #SolidarityIsForWhiteWomen, and the Other #FemFuture." *Ada: A Journal of Gender, New Media, and Technology*, no. 5 (2014). https://adanewmedia.org.

Lu, Xing. *Rhetoric in Ancient China, Fifth to Third Century B.C.E.: A Comparison with Classical Greek Rhetoric*. Columbia: University of South Carolina Press, 1998.

Luckerson, Victor. "The Mainstreaming of #BlackLivesMatter." *Ringer*, August 16, 2016. https://www.theringer.com.

Luna, Paul. "Books and Bits: Texts and Technology 1970–2000." In *A Companion to the History of the Book*, edited by Simon Eliot and Jonathan Rose, 381–94. West Sussex, UK: Blackwell, 2009.

Lunsford, Andrea. "Toward a Mestiza Rhetoric: Gloria Anzaldúa on Composition and Postcoloniality." *JAC* 18, no. 1 (1998): 1–27.

Lutes, Jean Marie. "Beyond the Bounds of the Book: Periodical Studies and Women Writers of the Late Nineteenth and Early Twentieth Centuries." *Legacy* 27, no. 2 (2010): 336–56.

Mansbridge, Jane. "Using Power/Fighting Power: The Polity." In *Democracy and Difference: Contesting the Boundaries of the Political*, edited by S. Benhabib, 46–60. Princeton, NJ: Princeton University Press, 1996.

Marantz, Andrew. "Reddit and the Struggle to Detoxify the Internet." *New Yorker*, March 19, 2018. https://www.newyorker.com.

Marble Hill Press (Marbel Hill, MO). "More Women Telegraphers." July 3, 1901. Image 2. Library of Congress: Chronicling America database.

Massanari, Adrienne. "#Gamergate and the Fappening: How Reddit's Algorithm, Governance, and Culture Support Toxic Technocultures." *New Media and Society* 16, no. 8 (2015): 329–49.

Mathieu, Paula, and Diana George. "Not Going It Alone: Public Writing, Independent Media, and the Circulation of Homeless Advocacy." *College Composition and Communication* 61, no. 1 (2009): 130–49.

Mattingly, Carol. "Friendly Dress: A Disciplined Use." *Rhetoric Society Quarterly* 29, no. 2 (1999): 25–45.

———. *Well-Tempered Women: Nineteenth-Century Temperance Rhetoric*. Carbondale: Southern Illinois University Press, 1998.

Maunsell, Jerome Boyd. "The Literary Interview as Autobiography." *European Journal of Life Writing* 5 (2016): 23–42.

May, Elaine Tyler. *America and the Pill: A History of Promise, Peril, and Liberation*. New York: Basic Books, 2010.

McCormack, Rob. "Epideictic Rhetoric: Renewing Vision, Vibe and Values." Presentation at the Australian Association of Teachers of English National Conference, Darwin, Australia, 2006.

"Medical Women as Workhouse Doctors." *British Medical Journal* 1, no. 1729 (February 17, 1894): 371.

Meyerson, Collier. "The Founders of Black Lives Matter: 'We Gave Tongue to Something That We All Knew Was Happening.'" *Glamour*, November 1, 2016. https://www.glamour.com.

Miksche, Mike. "Worried about That PrEP-Resistant Strain of HIV? The Doctor Who Discovered It Has Some Advice." *Slate*, March 3, 2016. http://www.slate.com.

Milkman, Ruth. *Gender at Work: The Dynamics of Job Segregation by Sex during World War II*. Urbana: University of Illinois Press, 1987.

Miller, Carolyn R., and Dawn Shepherd. "Blogging as Social Action: A Genre Analysis of the Weblog." In *Into the Blogosphere: Rhetoric, Community, and Culture of Weblogs*, edited by Laura J. Gurak, Smiljana Antonijevic, Laurie Johnson, Clancy Ratliff, and Jessica Reyman. Minneapolis: University of Minnesota, 2004. University of Michigan Digital Conservancy, http://hdl.handle.net/11299/172818.

———. "Questions for Genre Theory from the Blogosphere." In *Genres in the Internet: Issues in the Theory of Genre*, edited by Janet Giltrow and Dieter Stein, 263–90. Amsterdam: John Benjamins, 2009.

Miller, Jane Eldridge. *Rebel Women: Feminism, Modernism and the Edwardian Novel*. Chicago: University of Chicago Press, 1994.

Miller, Susan. *Trust in Texts: A Different History of Rhetoric*. Carbondale: Southern Illinois University Press, 2007.

Milstein, Cindy. *Taking Sides: Revolutionary Solidarity and the Poverty of Liberalism*. Oakland, CA: AK Press, 2015.

Mohanty, Chandra Talpade. *Feminism without Borders: Decolonizing Theory, Practicing Solidarity*. Durham, NC: Duke University Press, 2003.

Moraga, Cherríe. "La Güera." In Moraga and Anzaldúa, *This Bridge Called My Back*, 27–34.

Moraga, Cherríe, and Gloria Anzaldúa, eds. *This Bridge Called My Back: Writings by*

Radical Women of Color. 2nd ed. New York: Kitchen Table/Women of Color Press, 1983.

Mountford, Roxanne. *The Gendered Pulpit: Preaching in American Protestant Spaces.* Carbondale: Southern Illinois University Press, 2003.

My Duty to Speak (blog). https://mydutytospeak.com.

My PrEP Experience (blog). http://myprepexperience.blogspot.com.

Natsvlishvili, Paata. "For the Genesis of Interview as a Genre." *European Scientific Journal* 2 (2013): 384–87.

Noble, Safiya Umoja. *Algorithms of Oppression: How Search Engines Reinforce Racism.* New York: New York University Press, 2018.

Ordain Women (blog). https://ordainwomen.org.

O'Reilly, Andrea. *From Motherhood to Mothering: The Legacy of Adrienne Rich's "Of Woman Born."* Albany: State University of New York Press, 2004.

O'Reilly, Jane. "The Housewife's Moment of Truth." *New York Magazine,* December 20, 1971.

Ouellette, Jessica. "Blogging Borders: Transnational Feminist Rhetorics and Global Voices." *Harlot: A Revealing Look at the Arts of Persuasion* 11 (2014). http://harlotofthearts.org/index.php/harlot.

Papacharissi, Zizi. *Affective Publics: Sentiment, Technology, and Politics.* New York: Oxford University Press, 2015.

Papillon, Terry. "Isocrates' Techne and Rhetorical Pedagogy." *Rhetoric Society Quarterly* 25, no. 1 (1995): 149–63.

Paré, Anthony. "Genre and Identity: Individuals, Institutions, and Ideology." In Coe, Lingard, and Teslenko, *Rhetoric and Ideology of Genre,* 57–72.

Parker, Meagan. "Desiring Citizenship: A Rhetorical Analysis of the Wells/Willard Controversy." *Women's Studies in Communication* 31, no. 1 (2008): 56–78.

Patterson, Brandon E. "Harrowing Facebook Live Video Shows Black Man Dying after Police Shoot Him during Traffic Stop." *Mother Jones,* November 10, 2017. https://www.motherjones.com.

Prendergast, Catherine. "Before #BlackLivesMatter." In *Rhetorics of Whiteness: Postracial Hauntings in Popular Culture, Social Media, and Education,* edited by Tammie M. Kennedy, Joyce Middleton, and Krista Ratcliffe, 89–91. Carbondale: Southern Illinois University Press, 2017.

Penny, Virginia. *How Women Can Make Money.* Springfield, MA: D. E. Fisk, 1870.

Perelman, Chïam, and Lucie Olbrechts-Tyteca. *The New Rhetoric: A Treatise on Argumentation.* Translated by John Wilkinson and Purcell Weaver. Notre Dame, IN: University of Notre Dame Press, 1969.

Perkins, Frances. *Vocations for the Trained Woman: Opportunities Other Than Teaching.* Boston: Women's Educational and Industrial Union, 1910.

Perry, Ruth, and Lisa Greber. "Women and Computers: An Introduction." *Signs* 16, no. 1 (1990): 74–101.

Phelps, Louise Wetherbee, and Janet Emig, eds. *Feminine Principles and Women's Experience in American Composition and Rhetoric.* Pittsburgh, PA: University of Pittsburgh Press, 1995.

Piepmeier, Alison. *Girl Zines: Making Media, Doing Feminism.* New York: New York University Press, 2009.

Polanyi, Michael. *Personal Knowledge.* London: Taylor and Francis, 2012.

Porter, J. E. "Recovering Delivery for Digital Rhetoric." *Computers and Composition* 26, no. 4 (2009): 207–24.

Pratt, Mary Louise. *Imperial Eyes: Travel Writing and Transculturation.* London: Routledge, 1992.

Preciado, Paul B. *Testo Junkie: Sex, Drugs, and Biopolitics in the Pharmacopornographic Era.* New York: Feminist Press, 2013.

Presley, Katie. "Janelle Monáe Releases Visceral Protest Song, 'Hell You Talmbout.'" *NPR*, August 18, 2015. https://www.npr.org.

Queen, Mary. "Transnational Feminist Rhetorics in a Digital World." *College English* 70, no. 5 (2008): 471–89.

Ramirez, Daniela. "Has #SolidarityIsForWhiteWomen Created Solidarity for Women of Color?" *Mic*, August 27, 2013. http://mic.com.

Ramsay, Stephen, and Geoffrey Rockwell. "Developing Things: Notes toward an Epistemology of Building in the Digital Humanities." In *Debates in the Digital Humanities*, edited by Matthew K. Gold, 75–84. Minneapolis: University of Minnesota Press, 2012.

Ratcliffe, Krista. *Rhetorical Listening: Identification, Gender, Whiteness.* Carbondale: Southern Illinois University Press, 2005.

Rawson, K. J. "Queering Feminist Rhetorical Canonization." In Schell and Rawson, *Rhetorica in Motion*, 39–52.

Ray, Ruth, and Ellen Barton. "Technology and Authority." In *Evolving Perspectives on Computers and Composition Studies: Questions for the 1990s*, edited by Gail E. Hawisher and Cynthia L. Selfe, 279–99. Urbana, IL: National Council of Teachers of English, 1991.

Reed, Thomas Vernon. *The Art of Protest: Culture and Activism from the Civil Rights Movement to the Streets of Seattle.* Minneapolis: University of Minnesota Press, 2005.

Reyes, Antonio. "Strategies of Legitimization in Political Discourse: From Words to Actions." *Discourse & Society* 22, no. 6 (2001): 781–807.

Reynolds, Nedra. *Geographies of Writing: Inhabiting Places and Encountering Difference.* Carbondale: Southern Illinois University Press, 2007.

———. "Interrupting Our Way to Agency: Feminist Cultural Studies and Composition." In Jarratt and Worsham, *Feminism and Composition Studies*, 58–73.

Rhodes, Jacqueline, and Jonathan Alexander. *Techne: Queer Meditations on Writing the Self.* Logan: Computers and Composition Digital Press/Utah State University Press, 2015.

Ridolfo, Jim. "Delivering Textual Diaspora: Building Digital Cultural Repositories as Rhetoric Research." *College English* 76, no. 2 (2013): 136–51.

———. "Rhetorical Delivery as Strategy: Rebuilding the Fifth Canon from Practitioner Stories." *Rhetoric Review* 31, no. 2 (2012): 117–29.

Ridolfo, Jim, and Danielle N. DeVoss. "Composing for Recomposition: Rhetorical

Velocity and Delivery." *Kairos: A Journal of Rhetoric, Technology, and Pedagogy* 13, no. 2 (2009). http://kairos.technorhetoric.net.

Ridolfo, Jim, and William Hart-Davidson. *Rhetoric and the Digital Humanities*. Chicago: University of Chicago Press, 2014.

Risam, Roopika. "Beyond the Margins: Intersectionality and the Digital Humanities." *Digital Humanities Quarterly* 9, no. 2 (2015). http://www.digitalhumanities.org/dhq.

Ritchie, Joy, and Kate Ronald. Introduction to *Available Means: An Anthology of Women's Rhetoric(s)*, edited by Joy Ritchie and Kate Ronald, xv–xxxi. Pittsburgh, PA: University of Pittsburgh Press, 2001.

Roebuck, Harriet. "Court Reporting." *Independent Woman* 5, no. 2 (1922): 11. Gerritsen Index.

Rose, Mark. *Authors and Owners: The Invention of Copyright*. Cambridge, MA: Harvard University Press, 1994.

Rosen, Ruth. *The World Split Open: How the Modern Women's Movement Changed America*. New York: Penguin Books, 2001.

Roth, Bonita. *Separate Roads to Feminism: Black, Chicana, and White Feminist Movements in America's Second Wave*. New York: Cambridge University Press, 2004.

Rowe, Aimee Carrillo. "Be Longing: Toward a Feminist Politics of Relation." *NWSA Journal* 17, no. 2 (2005): 14–46.

———. *Power Lines: On the Subject of Feminist Alliances*. Durham, NC: Duke University Press, 2008.

Royster, Jacqueline Jones. "In Search of Ways In." In Phelps and Emig, *Feminine Principles and Women's Experience*, 385–92.

———. Introduction to Royster, *Southern Horrors and Other Writings*, 1–45.

———, ed. *Southern Horrors and Other Writings: The Anti-Lynching Campaign of Ida B. Wells, 1892–1900*. Boston: Bedford/St.Martin's, 1997.

———. *Traces of a Stream: Literacy and Social Change among African American Women*. Pittsburgh, PA: University of Pittsburgh Press, 2000.

———. "A Wells Chronology (1862–1931)." In Royster, *Southern Horrors and Other Writings*, 209–21.

———. "When the First Voice You Hear Is Not Your Own." *College Composition and Communication* 47, no. 1 (1996): 29–40.

Royster, Jacqueline Jones, and Gesa E. Kirsch. *Feminist Rhetorical Practices: New Horizons for Rhetoric, Composition, and Literacy Studies*. Carbondale: Southern Illinois University Press, 2012.

Ruddick, Sara. *Maternal Thinking: Towards a Politics of Peace*. Boston: Beacon Press, 1989.

Ruddick, Susan. "Constructing Difference in Public Spaces: Race, Class, and Gender as Interlocking Systems." *Urban Geography* 17, no. 2 (1996): 132–51.

Rupiah, Kiri. "The Problem with Lena Dunham, White Feminism, and the Apology Industrial Complex." *Mail and Guardian* (Johannesburg), September 6, 2016. http://mg.co.za.

Ryan, Erin Gloria. "Our Favorite #SolidarityIsForWhiteWomen Tweets [Updated]." *Jezebel*, August 13, 2013. https://jezebel.com.

Saltzstein, Dan. "Travel Blogging Today: It's Complicated." *New York Times*, July 26, 2013. https://www.nytimes.com.

Schell, Eileen E. Introduction to Schell and Rawson, *Rhetorica in Motion*, 1–20.

Schell, Eileen E., and K. J. Rawson, eds. *Rhetorica in Motion*. Pittsburgh, PA: University of Pittsburgh Press, 2010.

Schryer, Catherine. "Genre and Power: A *Chronotopic* Analysis." In Coe, Lingard, and Teslenko, *Rhetoric and Ideology of Genre*, 73–102.

Scribner, Sylvia. "Literacy in Three Metaphors." *American Journal of Education* 93, no. 1 (1984): 6–21.

Segal, Judy Z. *Health and the Rhetoric of Medicine*. Carbondale: Southern Illinois University Press, 2006.

Seneca Falls Dialogues. https://senecafallsdialogues.com.

Sheridan, David M., Jim Ridolfo, and Anthony J. Michel. *The Available Means of Persuasion: Mapping a Theory and Pedagogy of Multimodal Public Rhetoric*. Anderson, SC: Parlor Press, 2012.

Simpson, Pierce Adolphus. "An Address on Post-Graduate Possibilities. Delivered at the Opening of the Medical Classes in the University of Glasgow, October 25th, 1887." *British Medical Journal* 2, no. 1400 (October 29, 1887): 923–28.

Skillcrush. https://skillcrush.com.

Skinner, Carolyn. *Women Physicians and Professional Ethos in Nineteenth-Century America*. Carbondale: Southern Illinois University Press, 2014.

Skripsky, Sarah L. "Rereading McCutcheon's Suffrage Plots: Rising Action in the Digital Archive." *Peitho* 17, no. 1 (2014): 46–59.

Smith, Barbara. Introduction to *Home Girls: A Black Feminist Anthology*, edited by Barbara Smith, xxi–lviii. New York: Kitchen Table: Women of Color Press, 1983.

Smith, Barbara, and Beverly Smith. "Across the Kitchen Table: A Sister-to-Sister Dialogue." In Moraga and Anzaldúa, *This Bridge Called My Back*, 113–27.

So, Richard Jean. "All Models Are Wrong." *PMLA* 132, no. 3 (2017): 668–73.

Sowards, Stacey K., and Valerie R. Renegar. "The Rhetorical Function of Consciousness-Raising in Third Wave Feminism." *Communication Studies* 55, no. 4 (2004): 535–52.

Spinuzzi, Clay. "Who Killed Rex? Tracing a Message through Three Kinds of Networks." In *Communicative Practices in Workplaces and the Professions: Cultural Perspectives on the Regulation of Discourse and Organizations*, edited by Mark Zachry and Charlotte Thralls, 45–66. Amityville, NY: Baywood, 2007.

Squires, Bethy. "The Racist and Sexist History of Keeping Birth Control Side Effects Secret." *Vice*, October 17, 2016. https://www.vice.com.

Srinivasan, Ramesh, Robin Boast, Jonathan Furner, and Katherine M. Becvar. "Digital Museums and Diverse Cultural Knowledges: Moving Past the Traditional Catalog." *Information Society* 25, no. 4 (2009): 265–78.

Srole, Carol. *Transcribing Class and Gender: Masculinity and Femininity in Nineteenth-Century Courts and Offices*. Ann Arbor: University of Michigan Press, 2010.

Stack, Peggy Fletcher. "Gender Gap Widening among Utah Mormons, but Why?" *Salt Lake Tribune*, December 22, 2011.

———. "3 Women Appointed to Previously All-Male Mormon Executive Council." *Salt Lake Tribune*, August 18, 2015.

Stanley, Liz, and Sue Wise. *Breaking Out Again: Feminist Ontology and Epistemology*. New ed. London: Routledge, 1993.

Stanton, Elizabeth Cady. "Declaration of Sentiments." Speech delivered to the Seneca Falls Woman's Rights Convention, Seneca Falls, NY, July 19, 1848.

"The Stenographer's Ten Commandments." *Independent Woman* 4, no. 4 (1922): 8.

Stenography and Typewriting. Boston: Vocation Office for Girls, 1911. Harvard Library Digital Collections, Women Working, 1800–1930.

Stigler, George J. *Domestic Service in the United States: 1900–1940*. New York: National Bureau of Economic Research, 1946.

Stillion Southard, Belinda A. "A Rhetoric of Epistemic Privilege: Elizabeth Cady Stanton, Harriot Stanton Blatch, and the Educated Vote." *Advances in the History of Rhetoric* 17 no. 2 (2014): 157–78.

Sullivan, Patricia, and Tarez Samra Graban. "Digital and Dustfree: A Conversation on the Possibilities of Digital-Only Searching for Third-Wave Historical Recovery." *Peitho* 13, no. 2 (2011): 2–11.

Swenson, Kristine. *Medical Women and Victorian Fiction*. Columbia: University of Missouri Press, 2005.

Tamblyn, Christine. "She Loves It, She Loves It Not: Women and Technology." In *Processed Lives: Gender and Technology in Everyday Life*, edited by Jennifer Terry and Melodie Calvert, 47–50. New York: Routledge, 1997.

Tan, Pelin. "Decolonizing Architectural Education: Towards an Affective Pedagogy." In *The Social (Re)Production of Architecture: Politics, Values and Actions in Contemporary Practice*, edited by Doina Petrescu and Kim Trogal, 77–92. New York: Routledge, 2017.

———. "Transversal Materialism: On Method, Artifact, and Exception." In *2000+: The Urgencies of Architectural Theory*, edited by James Graham, 198–228. New York: Columbia University Graduate School of Architecture, Planning and Preservation, 2015.

"Teaching Girls the Art of Telegraphy." *Journal of the Telegraph* 2, no. 2 (May 1, 1869): 122, Google Books.

"Telegraph School for Women." *Journal of the Telegraph* 2, no. 2 (January 15, 1896): 42. Hathitrust Digital Library.

Tetrault, Lisa. *The Myth of Seneca Falls: Memory and Women's Suffrage Movement*. Chapel Hill: University of North Carolina Press, 2016.

Tillotson, Shirley. "We May All Soon Be 'First-Class Men': Gender and Skill in Canada's Early Twentieth-Century Urban Telegraphy Industry." *Labour/Le Travail* 27, no. 27 (1991): 97–125.

Tindera, Michela. "Gilead Said PrEP Was 'Not a Commercial Opportunity.' Now It's Running Ads for It." *Forbes*, August 7, 2018. https://www.forbes.com.

Todd, Margaret. *Mona Maclean, Medical Student*. Edited by Oliver Lovesy. London: Pickering and Chatto, 2011.

Tong, Rosemarie, and Tina Fernandes Botts. *Feminist Thought: A More Comprehensive Introduction*. 5th ed. New York: Westview Press, 2018.

Towns, Armond R. "Geographies of Pain: #SayHerName and the Fear of Black Women's Mobility." *Women's Studies in Communication* 39, no. 2 (2016): 122–26.

Travae, Marques. *Black Women of Brazil* (website). https://blackwomenofbrazil.co.

Turkle, Sherry. *Life on the Screen: Identity in the Age of the Internet*. London: Phoenix, 1995.

———. *Reclaiming Conversation: The Power of Talk in a Digital Age*. New York: Penguin, 2015.

Valerio, Anita. "It's In My Blood, My Face—My Mother's Voice, The Way I Sweat." In Moraga and Anzaldúa, *This Bridge Called My Back*, 41–45.

Van Leeuwen, Theo. "Legitimation in Discourse and Communication." *Discourse and Communication* 1, no. 1 (2007): 91–112.

Vasquez, Tina. "Why 'Solidarity' Is Bullshit." *Bitch Media*, August 16, 2013. http://bitchmedia.org.

Vaz, Kim Marie, and Gary L. Lemons, eds. *Feminist Solidarity at the Crossroads: Intersectional Women's Studies for Transracial Alliance*. New York: Routledge, 2012.

———. "'If I Call You, Will You Come?' From Public Lectures to Testament for Feminist Solidarity." In Vaz and Lemons, *Feminist Solidarity at the Crossroads*, 1–16.

Wagner, Sally Roesch. "The Iroquois Influence on Women's Rights." In *Indian Roots of American Democracy*, edited by Jose Barreiro, 115–34. Ithaca, NY: Akwe Kon Press, 1992.

Wakabayashi, Daisuke. "Contentious Memo Strikes Nerve inside Google and Out." *New York Times*, August 8, 2017.

Walia, Harsha. "Moving beyond a Politics of Solidarity toward a Politics of Decolonization." *Colours of Resistance Archive*. 2012. http://www.coloursofresistance.org.

Wallace, David L. *Compelled to Write: Alternative Rhetoric in Theory and Practice*. Logan: Utah State University Press, 2011.

Warnick, Barbara, and David Heineman. *Rhetoric Online: The Politics of New Media*. New York: Peter Lang, 2012.

Washington Times. "The Man behind the Telegraph Key." October 13, 1907. Image 5. Library of Congress: Chronicling America database.

Watkins, Eli, and Sophie Tatum. "Woman Who Flipped Off Trump Says She Was Fired for It." *CNN*, November 7, 2017. http://www.cnn.com.

Welch, Kathleen. *Electric Rhetoric: Classical Rhetoric, Oralism, and a New Literacy*. Cambridge: MIT Press, 1999.

Wells, Ida B. *Crusade for Justice: The Autobiography of Ida B. Wells*. Edited by Alfreda M. Duster. Chicago: University of Chicago Press, 1970.

———. *A Red Record: Tabulated Statistics and Alleged Causes of Lynchings in the United States, 1892–1893–1894*. In Royster, *Southern Horrors and Other Writings*, 73–157.

Wells, Susan. *Out of the Dead House: Nineteenth-Century Women Physicians and the Writing of Medicine*. Madison: University of Wisconsin Press, 2001.

Wenger, Étienne. *Communities of Practice: Learning, Meaning and Identity*. Cambridge: Cambridge University Press, 1999.

Whitehurst, Lindsay. "Court Sides with Utah's Planned Parenthood in Defunding Case." Associated Press. *Business Insider*, July 13, 2016. https://www.businessinsider.com.

Whitlock, Gillian. *Soft Weapons: Autobiography in Transit*. Chicago: University of Chicago Press, 2007.

Wieskamp, Valerie. "'I'm Going Out There and I'm Telling This Story': Victimhood and Empowerment in Narratives of Military Sexual Violence." *Western Journal of Communication* 83, no. 2. Published ahead of print, August 13, 2018. https://doi .org/10.1080/10570314.2018.1502891.

Williams, Sherri. "#SayHerName: Using Digital Activism to Document Violence against Black Women." *Feminist Media Studies* 16, no. 5 (2016): 922–25.

Woman's Christian Temperance Union. *Minutes of the Twenty-First Annual Convention of the Woman's Christian Temperance Union*. Chicago: Woman's Temperance, 1894.

Women Who Code. https://www.womenwhocode.com.

Wood, Henrietta Rix. *Praising Girls: The Rhetoric of Young Women, 1895–1930*. Carbondale: Southern Illinois University Press, 2016.

Woodiwiss, Jo. "Challenges for Feminist Research: Contested Stories, Dominant Narratives, and Narrative Frameworks." In *Feminist Narrative Research*, edited by Jo Woodiwiss, Kate Smith, and Kelly Lockwood, 13–34. New York: Palgrave, 2017.

Woods, Carly S. "(Im)Mobile Metaphors: Toward an Intersectional Rhetorical History." In Chávez, Griffin, and Houston, *Standing in the Intersection*, 78–96.

Woolf, Virginia. *A Room of One's Own*. New York: Penguin, 2013.

Workman, Hallie, and Catherine Coleman. "The Front Page of the Internet: Safe Spaces and Hyperpersonal Communication among Females in an Online Community." *Southwestern Mass Communication* 27, no. 3 (2012): 1–21.

Wysocki, Anne Frances. Introduction to *Composing (Media) = Composing (Embodiment): Bodies, Technologies, Writing, the Teaching of Writing*, edited by Kristin L. Arola and Anne Wysocki, 1–24. Logan: Utah State University Press, 2012.

Yagoda, Ben. *Memoir: A History*. New York: Riverhead Books, 2008.

Yeo, Richard. "Lost Encyclopedias: Before and after the Enlightenment." *Book History* 10 (2007): 47–68.

Yergeau, Melanie. "Accessing Digital Rhetoric: Sh*t Academics Say." *Sweetland Digital Rhetoric Collective*, June 17, 2012. http://www.digitalrhetoriccollaborative.org.

Yoos, George. "Rhetoric of Appeal and Rhetoric of Response." *Philosophy & Rhetoric* 20, no. 2 (1987): 106–17.

Zanona, Melanie, and Scot Wong. "Democrats See Hypocrisy in GOP Attacks on 'Liberal Mob.'" *The Hill*, October 10, 2018. https://thehill.com.

Zappavigna, Michele. "Ambient Affiliation: A Linguistic Perspective on Twitter." *New Media & Society* 13, no. 5 (2011): 788–806.

Contributors

RISA APPLEGARTH is an associate professor of English, director of the college writing program, and affiliated faculty with the program in women's and gender studies at the University of North Carolina at Greensboro. Her research on rhetoric, embodiment, and gender has appeared in *Rhetoric Society Quarterly*, *College English*, and *College Composition and Communication*. Her book *Rhetoric in American Anthropology: Gender, Genre, and Science* received the 2016 Outstanding Book Award from the Conference on College Composition and Communication.

PAIGE V. BANAJI is an assistant professor of English and director of first-year writing at Barry University, where she teaches first-year composition, rhetorical theory, and women's literature. Her research interests include feminist rhetorics, history of rhetoric, composition pedagogy, and writing program administration. Her work has been published in *Rhetoric Review* and *Rhetoric, History, and Women's Oratorical Education: American Women Learn to Speak*.

KRISTINE L. BLAIR is professor of English and incoming dean of the McAnulty College and Graduate School of Liberal Arts at Duquesne University. Her 2019 book *Technofeminist Storiographies: Women, Information Technology, and Cultural Representation* challenges larger rhetorics of technological innovation that exclude women's historical and contemporary contributions. In addition to her publications in the areas of gender and technology and graduate student mentoring, Dr. Blair currently serves as editor of the international journal *Computers and Composition*.

LISA BLANKENSHIP is an assistant professor of English and writing director at Baruch College, City University of New York. Her research focuses on rhetorical ethics and engagement across marked social differences, both historically and in contemporary, digital contexts. She has published in *Present Tense: A Journal of Rhetoric in Society* and *Computers and Composition*.

MARIA BRANDT is professor of English and co-coordinator of creative writing at Monroe Community College in Rochester, New York. Maria has published in the *Chronicle of Higher Education, Teaching English in the Two-Year College,* and *American Transcendental Quarterly,* as well as numerous literary magazines. Her novella *All the Words* won the Grassic Short Novel Prize and was published by Evening Street Press, her collection *New York Plays* was produced by Out of Pocket Productions at MuCCC in Rochester and published by Heartland Plays, and her play *Swans* was coproduced by Straw Mat Writers and Method Machine at Geva Theatre Center's Fielding Stage in Rochester. With Jill Swiencicki, she was the 2014 and 2016 co-chair of the Seneca Falls Dialogues, which aim to reinvigorate Seneca Falls, New York, as a feminist space of deliberation and activism.

KATHERINE FREDLUND is an associate professor of English and the director of first-year writing at the University of Memphis. Her historical research focuses on women's literate and rhetorical practices, activist rhetoric, and collaboration, and she has also published on activist pedagogy and teaching with technology. Her work has appeared in *College English, Rhetoric Review, Peitho, Composition Forum,* and *Feminist Teacher,* as well as in edited collections such as *Composing Feminist Interventions: Activism, Engagement, Praxis* and *Engaging 21st Century Writers with Social Media.*

TAREZ SAMRA GRABAN is an associate professor of English at Florida State University, where she also leads an interdisciplinary reading group in the digital humanities, and she serves as codirector of the Demos Project for studies in the data humanities. She is author of *Women's Irony: Rewriting Feminist Rhetorical Histories* and coauthor of *GenAdmin: Theorizing WPA Identities for the Twenty-First Century.* Her historical essays have appeared in *Rhetorica, College English,* and *African Journal of Rhetoric,* as well as in edited collections such as *Networked Humanities: Within and without of the University,* and *Circulation, Writing and Rhetoric.*

SARAH HALLENBECK is associate professor of English at the University of North Carolina Wilmington, where she directs the first-year writing program and teaches in the professional writing undergraduate track. Her work has appeared in *Rhetoric Society Quarterly, Rhetoric Review, Peitho,* and *Technical Communication Quarterly,* and she is the author of the 2016 book *Claiming the Bicycle: Women, Rhetoric, and Technology in Nineteenth-Century America.*

KERRI HAUMAN is an associate professor of writing, rhetoric, and communication and director of first-year seminar at Transylvania University. Her research focuses on feminist rhetorics, pedagogies, and research; digital rhetorics and literacies; and teaching with technology. Her work has appeared in *Pedagogy: Critical Approaches to Teaching Literature, Language, Composition, and Culture* and *Feminist Teacher*. She is the recipient of a 2017–18 Conference on College Composition and Communication Emergent Researcher Award.

TIFFANY KINNEY is an assistant professor of English in the Department of Literatures, Languages, and Mass Communication at Colorado Mesa University. Her research intersects feminist rhetoric, composition, and technical communication as it examines how marginalized social groups construct legitimacy for themselves. Her writing has appeared in *Rhetorica: A Journal of the History of Rhetoric, Peitho, Feminist Spaces*, and *Fat Studies: An Interdisciplinary Journal of Body Weight and Society*.

KRISTIN E. KONDRLIK is an assistant professor of English at West Chester University of Pennsylvania, where she specializes in health communication. Her research, which focuses on the intersections of historical and contemporary medicine with rhetoric, writing, and media, has appeared in *Poiroi: Project on Rhetoric of Inquiry, Victorian Periodicals Review*, and *ELT: English Literature in Transition, 1880–1920*.

LIZ LANE is an assistant professor of English in the writing, rhetoric, and technical communication concentration at the University of Memphis. Her research explores the intersections of activism in digital spaces, feminism, and technical communication. Her work has appeared in *Computers and Composition, Composition Studies, Ada: A Journal of Gender, New Media, and Technology*, and edited collections such as *Thinking Globally, Composing Locally: Applications for International Communication Exchange*. She is also the co-managing editor of *Spark: A 4C4Equality Journal*, an open-access, peer-reviewed journal of activist rhetorics in writing studies, which can be found at https://sparkactivism.com.

BARBARA LESAVOY is chair and associate professor of the Department of Women and Gender Studies at the College at Brockport (SUNY). Her research and publication areas include women's global human rights, identity politics in literature and popular culture, intersectionality and gender equity, and historical to contemporary perspectives on women's rights. She serves as lead faculty for a global classroom linking students at the College at Brockport with students at Velikiy Novgorod State University in Russia. She also has taught several women and gender studies seminars at the NY-St. Petersburg Institute of Linguistics, Cognition, and Culture.

BETHANY MANNON is a visiting assistant professor of English in the rhetoric and composition program at Appalachian State University. Her work analyzes personal narrative as a feminist rhetorical practice in women's movements, religious communities, and the composition classroom. Her recent articles have appeared in *Rhetoric Society Quarterly*, *Peitho*, and *College English*.

JESSICA OUELLETTE is an assistant professor of English and women and gender studies and director of writing programs at the University of Southern Maine. Her research areas include feminist rhetorics, digital rhetorics, affect studies, and transnational feminisms. Her work has appeared in *Computers and Composition*, *Harlot*, and the edited collection *Composing Feminist Interventions: Activism, Engagement, Praxis*.

TARA PROPPER is currently a senior lecturer of English in the Department of Literature and Languages at the University of Texas at Tyler. Her research focuses on the relationship between literacy and identity, specifically the ways in which the production and consumption of newspapers and magazines in the long nineteenth century allowed marginal and minority voices to participate within a public sphere of representation. Her work has appeared in *Dialogue: The Interdisciplinary Journal of Popular Culture and Pedagogy*.

CLANCY RATLIFF is associate professor of English at the University of Louisiana at Lafayette. Her research engages feminist rhetorics, intellectual property, and writing program administration. She has published essays in *Pedagogy*, *Women's Studies Quarterly*, *The Routledge Companion on Media Education*, *Copyright and Fair Use*, *Composition Forum*, *Computers and Composition Online*, and elsewhere. Recently she served as college section chair of the National Council of Teachers of English.

CHELSEA REDEKER MILBOURNE is an assistant professor of English and the director of the technical and professional communication program at California Polytechnic State University, San Luis Obispo. Her research explores how we use spectacular rhetoric—including embodied sensation and feelings of surprise, wonder, or admiration—to publicize and negotiate public engagement with science and technology. Her scholarship has been supported by fellowships from the American Council of Learned Societies, the Huntington Library, and the John Carter Brown Library. She has published in *Rhetoric Society Quarterly*, *Technical Communication Quarterly*, and *Dix-Huitième Siècle*.

SKYE ROBERSON is a PhD candidate in the writing, rhetoric, and technical communication program in the English Department at the University of Memphis. Her dissertation focuses on sustainable writing program design, labor exploitation, and women's work in academia. She is a 2018 Bedford New Scholar and a recent recipient of the International Writing Center Association Future Leaders Scholarship.

KELLIE JEAN SHARP is a clinical assistant professor in the English Department at the University at Buffalo, SUNY, where she recently graduated with her PhD in English. Her dissertation is titled "Experimental Intimacies and Biopolitics: 20th Century Women's Writing and the Politics of Bodily (Ex)Change," and her research is at the intersection of feminist philosophy, queer theory, biopolitics, and experimental writing.

JILL SWIENCICKI is associate professor of English and former director of the women and gender studies program at St. John Fisher College in Rochester, New York. Her research focuses on feminist rhetorical history, activist rhetorics, and the teaching of writing. Her work appears in the journals *Women's Studies in Communication, College English, Peitho,* and *Liberal Education,* along with edited collections such as *Crafting Dissent: Handicraft as Protest from the American Revolution to the Pussyhats; Going Public: What Writing Programs Learn from Engagement; Rhetorical Education in America;* and *Multiple Literacies for the 21st Century.* With Maria Brandt, she was the 2014 and 2016 co-chair of the Seneca Falls Dialogues, which aim to reinvigorate Seneca Falls, New York, as a feminist space of deliberation and activism.

DEBORAH UMAN is professor and chair of English at St. John Fisher College in Rochester, New York, where she specializes in early British literature with a focus on women writers and translators. She has published numerous articles and two books, *Women Translators in Early Modern England* (2012) and the coedited collection *Staging the Blazon in Early Modern Theater* (2013). With Barbara LeSavoy, she serves as coeditor of the biannual *Seneca Falls Dialogues Journal.* Her current project is creating a Clemente Course in the Humanities in Rochester, bringing together several local colleges, universities, and community partners to provide college-level instruction to economically marginalized adult learners.

KRISTIN WINET is an assistant teaching professor in the writing program at Wake Forest University, where she teaches courses in writing and rhetoric. Her scholarship, which examines travel writing as a feminist rhetorical practice, has been published in *Kairos, English Journal,* and a number of edited collections, including *Food, Feminisms, and Rhetorics* and the forthcoming *Widening the View.* She is also an award-winning travel writer and photographer and is at work on her first travel memoir.

Index

Page numbers in italics refer to figures.